COMIC DRUNKS, CRAZY CULTS, AND LOVABLE MONSTERS

Television and Popular Culture
Robert J. Thompson, *Series Editor*

Select Titles in Television and Popular Culture

Becoming: Genre, Queerness, and Transformation in NBC's "Hannibal"
Kavita Mudan Finn and EJ Nielsen, eds.

Bigger than "Ben-Hur": The Book, Its Adaptations, and Their Audiences
Barbara Ryan and Milette Shamir, eds.

Chick TV: Antiheroines and Time Unbound
Yael Levy

Gladiators in Suits: Race, Gender, and the Politics
of Representation in "Scandal"
Simone Adams, Kimberly R. Moffitt, and Ronald L. Jackson, eds.

Perspectives on "Crazy Ex-Girlfriend": Nuanced Postnetwork Television
Amanda Konkle and Charles Burnetts, eds.

Screwball Television: Critical Perspectives on "Gilmore Girls"
David Scott Diffrient and David Lavery, eds.

Television Finales: From "Howdy Doody" to "Girls"
Douglas L. Howard and David Bianculli, eds.

Watching TV with a Linguist
Kristy Beers Fägersten, ed.

For a full list of titles in this series,
visit https://press.syr.edu/supressbook-series
/television-and-popular-culture/.

COMIC DRUNKS, CRAZY CULTS, AND LOVABLE MONSTERS

BAD BEHAVIOR ON AMERICAN TELEVISION

David Scott Diffrient

Syracuse University Press

∞ The paper used in this publication meets the minimum requirements
of the American National Standard for Information Sciences—Permanence
of Paper for Printed Library Materials, ANSI Z39.48-1992.

For a listing of books published and distributed by Syracuse University Press,
visit https://press.syr.edu.

ISBN: 978-0-8156-3775-2 (hardcover)
        978-0-8156-3785-1 (paperback)
        978-0-8156-5569-5 (e-book)

Library of Congress Cataloging-in-Publication Data

Names: Diffrient, David Scott, 1972– author.
Title: Comic drunks, crazy cults, and lovable monsters : bad behavior on American television /
    David Scott Diffrient.
Description: First edition. | Syracuse, New York : Syracuse University Press, 2022. |
    Series: Television and popular culture | Includes bibliographical references and index.
Identifiers: LCCN 2022023072 (print) | LCCN 2022023073 (ebook) | ISBN 9780815637752 (hardcover) |
    ISBN 9780815637851 (paperback) | ISBN 9780815655695 (ebook)
Subjects: LCSH: Television comedies—United States—History and criticism. | Deviant behavior
    on television. | Conduct of life on television. | LCGFT: Television criticism and reviews.
Classification: LCC PN1992.8.C66 D54 2022 (print) | LCC PN1992.8.C66 (ebook) |
    DDC 792.45/6559—dc23/eng/20220811
LC record available at https://lccn.loc.gov/2022023072
LC ebook record available at https://lccn.loc.gov/2022023073

Manufactured in the United States of America

Contents

Illustrations

Acknowledgments

Although I am not, by any stretch of the imagination, in his league comedically speaking, the late Robin Williams once used a metaphor to describe his work as a stand-up comic and joke writer that reminds me of my own writing process. Telling an interviewer that, for him, "comedy starts as a *spew*, a kind of explosion," which he is then forced to "sculpt" into a more refined if still-manic form of humor before delivering it on stage, Williams nails what it is like for most thinkers with a few too many thoughts in their heads to convey the "deeper, darker side" of life in a cogent, hopefully entertaining way. Thankfully, several people have helped me to "shape the spew" leading up to this book's publication—friends and fellow media scholars whose words of encouragement and advice over the years made it possible for me to channel the whirlwind of ideas spinning around in my brain.

First, my colleagues in the Communication Studies department at Colorado State University, including department chair Greg Dickinson, Usama Alshaibi, Karrin Vasby Anderson, Eric Aoki, Martín Carcasson, Thomas R. Dunn, Meara Faw, Katie Gibson, Morgan K. Johnson, Julia Khrebtan-Hörhager, Katherine Knobloch, Ziyu Long, Liz Parks, and Elizabeth Williams, have supported my teaching and research over the years and continue to inspire me with their dedication to higher education and community outreach. My brilliant cohort in the department's Film and Media Studies area, including comedy enthusiasts Evan Elkins, Kit Hughes, and Nick Marx, never fail to impress me with their sharp wits and sharper insights into many of the television shows that I discuss in the pages that follow. I am especially grateful to Carl Burgchardt, my "oldest" friend in the department (I mean that in the *good* way) who at this point in our respective careers is more like a brother than a coworker, someone who never fails to lend a sympathetic ear to some of my weirdest, wildest theories but is not afraid to tell me the truth whenever my ideas are half-baked. My favorite part of teaching at CSU (besides the free candy) is being one door down from his office. Throughout the writing of this book, I have benefitted from the research assistance provided by Ryan Greene, Andy Gilmore, Lisabeth Bylina, Henry Miller, and Andrea Jaques.

Ryan in particular, as someone who has helped me on five different projects, gets a big COVID-era elbow bump.

Besides the people with whom I work, there are many scholars who, wittingly or not, played a part in improving this book, lending their insights during conference and symposia presentations (as fellow panelists), including Christine Becker, Peter Corrigan, Amanda Hickok, Sam Johnson, Emily Kulbacki, Anna Martonfi, Brett Mills, Philip Scepanski, Nicole Seymour, and Mark Stewart. Several critics and theorists of TV comedy have helped me to understand the historical, political, and social significance of this often-maligned cultural form in their own writings: Inger-Lise Kalviknes Bore, Vincent Brook, Jeremy G. Butler, Robin R. Means Coleman, Jonathan Gray, Bambi Haggins, Andrew Horton, Douglas L. Howard, Deborah Jermyn, Jeffrey P. Jones, Amanda Konkle, Alice Leppert, David Marc, Joanne Morreale, Brian Ott, Tison Pugh, Jeffrey Sconce, Janet Staiger, Ethan Thompson, Christina von Hodenberg, and Rosie White. I hope that my meager contribution to the growing list of publications about satires and sitcoms gives them the same pleasure that their books have given me.

A shorter version of Chapter 2, "'Drinking the War Away': Alcoholic Merriment in *M*A*S*H* and Other Military-Themed Sitcoms," appeared in Anna Froula and Stacy Takacs's edited volume *Militarism on the Small Screen* (Routledge, 2018). Anna and Stacy provided exceptionally valuable instructions on how to hone my arguments in that original piece as well as the considerably expanded version that appears in this book. Permission to reprint portions of that chapter has been kindly provided by Taylor and Francis Group LLC. Chapter 4, "Very Crazy Episodes: Cultivating Misconceptions about Cults on American Television" builds upon my previous conceptualization of the "cult imaginary," or how TV comically frames fringe religions—a topic that I wrote about in a 2010 article published by *Historical Journal of Film, Radio, and Television*. David Culbert, the journal's editor before his passing in 2017, championed my work then, and I am so thankful to have worked with him on that earlier version of my chapter. Sue Turnbull and Rhonda Wilcox sagely steered me toward productive readings of *Strangers with Candy* and *Veronica Mars* several years ago, and in 2013, Katherine Larsen, Principal Editor of the *Journal of Fandom Studies*, worked with me to improve an earlier, shorter version of Chapter 5, which concerns those two television programs. Jonathan Cohn and Jennifer Porst, editors of the recently published collection *Very Special Episodes: Televising Industrial and Social Change* (Rutgers, 2021), were likewise generous in providing feedback on my work about the blue-collar sitcom *Roseanne*, helping me to refine my arguments about "Halloween TV." A person could not ask for a better, kinder acquisitions editor than Syracuse University Press's Deborah Manion, who had thrown her encouragement behind my *Gilmore Girls* volume (also published by SUP) years earlier and continues to light the way for researchers in the field.

As always, Hye Seung Chung has been in my corner as both a departmental colleague and a life partner, and her continued support of my work has made it possible for me to reach my goals both as a cultural critic and as a father (to our darling five-year-old Pepper, whose love of television rivals my own). My parents, Donna and Harry Diffrient, have shown me what it means to be a good parent (they even, despite my own tendency toward "bad behavior" as a TV-addicted boy, let me stay up late to watch *Saturday Night Live* when I was perhaps too young to appreciate its "adult" content).

Finally, this book is dedicated to the memory of David Lavery, who, early in my career (and in the middle stage of his own illustrious one), recognized my potential to write about television with the same passion that he brought to his projects. I will never forget the grace, humility, and wisdom that he shared with me on multiple occasions before his passing five years ago (in 2016).

COMIC DRUNKS, CRAZY CULTS, AND LOVABLE MONSTERS

Contemporary TV Comedy

A "Good Place" for "Bad People"

> Do you think I'm a bad person?
>> —hitman Barry Berkman (Bill Hader) inquiring about his own moral character to acting coach and mentor Gene Cousineau (Henry Winkler) in a Season Two episode of HBO's *Barry* (2018–present)

> There's a lot of good people who do bad things.
>> —skateboarder Camille Palomino (Rachelle Vinberg) to fellow teenager Janay (Dede Lovelace) in a Season One episode of HBO's *Betty* (2020–present)

Bad behavior is everywhere on contemporary American television, an increasingly ubiquitous yet curiously overlooked facet of the larger cultural, social, and political landscape that finds its purest, most profane and provocative expression in comedic form. From *Barry* (HBO, 2018–present) to *Brickleberry* (Comedy Central, 2012–15), today's live-action and animated comedies are populated with unconventional protagonists and supporting characters whose words, thoughts, and actions are likely to raise the eyebrows of anyone who has been fed a strict diet of *The Waltons* (CBS, 1971–82), *Touched By an Angel* (CBS, 1994–2003), *7th Heaven* (The WB, 1996–2006; The CW, 2006–7), or any of the other saccharine TV shows that have been singled out by the Parents Television Council as examples of innocuous, family-friendly entertainment.

For instance, in a Season Two episode of Roger Black and Waco O'Guin's animated series *Brickleberry* ("My Way or the Highway" [2.07]), a couple of rangers at a fictional national park in Illinois find themselves on the ballot for the state's upcoming governor election, but resort to a savage, self-targeting form of character assassination upon discovering that the top vote-getter will likely be *literally assassinated* once in office. Specifically, the fifty-five-year-old head ranger Woody Johnson (voiced by Tom Kenny), who has recently admitted to being a war

1

I.1. In one of the many moments of bad behavior that occur in *Brickleberry*, Ethel, a park ranger on the ballot of a governor's race (who is actually trying to lose), tells and shows the public why she is unfit for office. © Comedy Central and DAMN! Show Productions

criminal, and Ethel Anderson (voiced by Natasha Leggero), a female ranger half his age, each take out TV ads in which they tell the viewing audience why they should *not* be elected: She admits to being a "raging unrepentant alcoholic" as well as a Holocaust denier who promises to make her home state "a safe haven for terrorists"; Woody goes even further, saying that he enjoys molesting kids before kneeing a US soldier in the groin and yelling, "Fuck our troops!" Then, grabbing a nursing baby away from her mommy, who is seated on a park bench, he punts the child into the sky like a football before punching another bystander in the face at a women's shelter and proclaiming, "Domestic violence isn't a problem . . . It's a *solution*." Refusing to be bested as the worst of the worst, Ethel ends her TV spot by shoving a Statue of Liberty figurine into her vagina (located just below the frame) and finally performing a blackface minstrelsy routine ("Camptown Races") in front of a large US flag. All of these playfully perverse acts are edited into an outrageous montage of human depravity—a forty-five-second burst of performed "badness"—that is both a put-on (not to be taken too seriously) and a very real, if slightly exaggerated, precursor to the moral vacancy witnessed by millions of Americans during the lead-up to another, more consequential yet equally farcical political election (that of 2016).

By the same token, early in the second season of *Barry*, the title character—a former marine-turned-hitman-turned-actor played by co-creator and *Saturday*

I.2. In a flashback to his days as a U.S. marine in Afghanistan, the title character of *Barry* takes aim at a villager before making his kill, a morally compromised act that informs his subsequent stints as a hitman for hire and a fledgling stage actor. © Alec Berg Productions and Hanarply

Night Live [*SNL*] alum Bill Hader—ponders whether he is "evil" after gunning down a police detective in cold blood ("What?!" [2.04]). The officer, Det. Janice Moss (Paula Newsome), had been doggedly sniffing out clues about the recent murder of another L.A.-based thespian-in-training. That inevitably doomed investigation put Janice on Barry Berkman's corpse-littered trail and culminated with her own death at the end of Season One, paving the way for his apparent moral quandary. In Season Two's "The Power of No" (2.02), he flatly tells the flamboyant criminal kingpin Noho Hank (Anthony Carrigan), who has assumed leadership of the Chechen mafia, "I take no pleasure in killing people." That line, which triggers a disbelieving giggle from the baldheaded mob boss, is spoken robotically by the straight-faced comedian (who for eight seasons honed his abilities as a gifted impressionist and Emmy-nominated featured player on *SNL* [NBC, 1975–present]) with the spiritual emptiness or detachment of someone who has grown accustomed to his grisly line of work. Barry's words also serve as ironic counterpoint to the series' flashbacks to his days as a US soldier in Afghanistan. Nervously smiling from ear-to-ear, the sniper bonds with his fellow grunts on the ground upon making his first kill: a "faceless" civilian whom the laughing Americans call a "sheep-fucker."

The death of the villager in the Taliban stronghold of Sangin is abstracted as a distant, offscreen occurrence in the first episode of Season Two ("The Show Must Go On, Probably?" [2.01]), in much the same way that Muslim wedding guests are referred to as unfortunate casualties of a drone strike issued by President Selina Meyer (Julia Louis-Dreyfus) in an episode of another "pitch-black comedy," HBO's *Veep* (2012–19). Never shown, those invisible victims of the United States' War on Terror and its deeply cynical leader-of-the-free-world's career ambitions are little more than jokey evidence of her dereliction of duty, only slightly more troubling than Selina's willingness to hand Tibet over to China if such a move will help her power-grabbing reelection bid. If the grotesquely caricatured rangers of Brickleberry National Park can trust that the electorate will do the right thing and select someone less "evil" than themselves for high office, no such comfort is to be found in *Veep*, which brazenly suggests that voters might not be all that bothered by the deaths of foreigners and other confirmations of presidential war crimes. As Ben Cafferty (Kevin Dunn), the White House Chief of Staff remarks in Season Seven's "Oslo" (7.06), "Americans don't give a flying fatwa if you drone a bunch of Muslims." That comment, like hundreds more in the f-bomb-littered *Veep* (both during and after creator Armando Iannucci's four-year tenure as the series' showrunner), is withering in its frankness, satirically framing US foreign policy as something to laugh at and cry about. Even though it is difficult to stomach, Ben's statement can be quickly digested as a throwaway line, leaving us little time—before the next bit of bracing dialogue in this fast-paced, puckishly profane comedy series—to ponder the public's continued support for militaristic uses of unmanned aerial vehicles as a counterterrorism measure resulting in civilian casualties.[1]

Judging from the online commentary surrounding them, pleasure—the thing that is absent in Barry's life—is precisely what these critical darlings provide to audiences who can tolerate not just bad but truly abhorrent behavior. In *Barry*, this can be chalked up partially to Bill Hader's deadpan delivery as the soft-spoken assassin who, "blessed with being able to witness the atrocities of war" (to borrow the words of Barry's acting coach Gene Cousineau [Henry Winkler]), appears to be working through his undiagnosed PTSD in pursuit of a better, more peaceful, and honorable (but no-less-deceptive) life and career on the stage. Perhaps some of the enjoyment that comes from soaking up this award-winning HBO series can also be attributed to our own questionable thrill in vicariously witnessing—episode-after-serialized-episode—a number of socially corrosive and physically destructive acts play out at a safe distance, as if seen from the vantage of a trained marksman. Although contained within the parameters of scripted fiction, those moments are unconstrained in their ability to affectively "move" us through whiplash tonal shifts, unexpected dramatic twists, and absurd incongruities or comical juxtapositions (e.g., Barry's friend Monroe Fuches [Stephen Root] using superglue to bind the knife gash in his back; the protagonist ducking bullets in his bedroom while his girlfriend, Sally [Sarah Goldberg], casually Skypes with her mom in the adjoining room). And there is something to be said about the showrunner's apparent lack of interest in giving the audience "what they want," a feature that Dom Nero (a TV critic for *Esquire*) notes in his appreciative take on *Barry*. As the critic states, the titular hero is "emotionally cut off from the world" in much the same way that Zach Galifianakis's character is in *Baskets* (FX, 2016–present), another unconventional comedy that skips "the sentimental stuff" in favor of "some very dark shit."[2]

Although set in very different social milieus, both of these series focus on lonely "saps" who struggle to suppress their feelings of being emotionally wounded from past traumas, something that ironically resonates with audiences despite the absence of any textual signifiers of heroic achievement or personal success that have traditionally been found in commercially lucrative TV shows (especially prior to the emergence of gritty crime dramas such as *The Sopranos* [HBO, 1999–2007] and *Breaking Bad* [AMC, 2008–13]). Finally, my own—and presumably other critics'—semi-delight in watching *Barry*, tempered though it is by the fatigue of consuming yet another redemption narrative about a "difficult man" (i.e., one featuring a loathsome yet compelling antihero in the mold of Tony Soprano [James Gandolfini] or Walter White [Bryan Cranston]),[3] comes from knowing something about the creators of the show. Alec Berg, a former writer on NBC's now-quaintly nihilistic 1990s hit *Seinfeld* (1989–98) as well as an executive producer on HBO's *Curb Your Enthusiasm* (2000–present), shares showrunner duties on *Barry* with Hader and has imported some of the quirkier beats of those earlier cringe-inducing programs into his latest co-creation.

To varying degrees, the above programs, along with countless others, have attracted mainstream audiences as well as smaller circles of devoted fans while "pushing buttons" in ways that would have been inconceivable thirty years ago. Prior to the days when *Seinfeld* and its spiritual meta-sequel *Curb Your Enthusiasm* mined humor from once-verboten topics (including graverobbing, group sex, incest, masturbation, and post-swimming penis shrinkage), network and cable TV writers, producers, and performers generally steered away from material that might offend viewers and advertisers, believing that any such incitements would have had a negative effect on a media organization's or parent company's financial intake. The bottom line was thus the topmost concern among broadcasters, whose decisions throughout the first decades of the medium's commercial history (1940s–1960s) were dictated by the industry's self-regulatory ethical standards (formalized through the 1952 Code of Practices for Television Broadcasters). They were furthermore guided by a principle that executives referred to as "least offensive programming" (or "LOP").

As Michael Curtin and Jane Shattuc observe in their historical overview of the US television industry, the term "LOP" spells out how "artistic or provocative shows might not be the best choice for primetime," that peak viewing period or programming block each night when audiences of various ages (from older adults to presumably impressionable youngsters) can be counted on as reliably pliable consumers.[4] Even those TV producers of the 1950s and 1960s who are remembered as being brave for tackling then-taboo subjects within the talk-show format—for example, drug abuse, gay rights, racial bigotry, and the nuclear arms race—were far more worried about offending their patrons than are today's showrunners when it came to overseeing fictional comedies and dramas. Posthumously inducted into the Television Hall of Fame in recognition of his handsomely mounted adaptations of *The Bridge of San Luis Rey* (1958), *The Moon and Sixpence* (1960), *The Glass Menagerie* (1973), and other literary classics, David Susskind is one such person, a pioneer of intelligent programming who—sensitive to his sponsors' interest in "pre-sold product" (like small-screen remakes of big-screen movies) as a way of garnering mass appeal—freely admitted that he could not in good conscience "roll dice on a quarter of a million dollars of somebody else's money by producing something that might antagonize the public."[5] During that postwar period, when superficially comforting sitcoms such as *The Adventures of Ozzie and Harriet* (ABC, 1952–66), *Father Knows Best* (CBS, 1954–55, 1958–60; NBC, 1958–60), *The Andy Griffith Show* (CBS, 1960–68), and *The Beverly Hillbillies* (CBS, 1962–71) were ratings hits, TV programs were allowed to be "amusing or intriguing," as Curtin and Shattuc point out, but "above all they should be *tolerable*."[6]

What was *intolerable*, at least in the eyes of many sponsors and network chiefs, was any subject that might "provoke passionate responses," including moral indignation or outrage, leading to a disgruntled turning of the dial.[7] Raunchy jokes were unthinkable, although gifted comedians such as Milton Berle, Sid Caesar, Ernie Kovacs, and Red Skelton managed to smuggle off-color humor into their televised standup acts and slapstick skits through innuendo or winking asides to the audience; moments of subterfuge through which they were able to sneak semi-salacious material past the censors.[8] Anatomical nudity of any kind, even of cartoon animals (e.g., the law-enforcing horse Quick Draw McGraw, the unflappable penguin Tennessee Tuxedo, the bowtie-wearing drawling dog Huckleberry Hound, etc.), was a no-no. And the kind of "body humor" that many of us are accustomed to at the present time, such as the sound of a person belching or farting and the sight of someone vomiting or defecating, would have been beyond the pale a mere four decades ago. Such potentially objectionable content is a central feature of recent cultural productions, especially television comedies of the past three decades that trade on spectators' tolerance for repellent or unsavory behavior and forge new definitions of "badness" in the process. That shifting definitional matrix, formed not only by televisual representations but by (mis)perceptions, stereotypes, and the ideological "baggage" that viewers bring to small-screen fictions, constitutes what I refer to as a "social imaginary," an organizing principle through which society comes to grips with itself as a potentially knowable collective made up of ultimately unknowable "others."

Social Imaginaries and "Badness" as a Cultural Construct

> "The idea of an imagined community, which becomes a real one when we all think about it in the same way and act 'as if' it were really there, rests upon this creative capacity for imagining and instituting the social that defines us as humans."
>
> —Graeme Kirkpatrick, *Computer Games and the Social Imaginary* (Cambridge: Polity Press, 2013), 2.

This book draws upon existing theories of social imaginaries (e.g., the work of Cornelius Castoriadis, Charles Taylor, Benedict Anderson, Henri Lefebvre, and others) as well as important studies written by media scholars who focus on gender and genre (including Julie D'Acci, Amanda D. Lotz, Lori Landay, David Marc, and Jason Mittell) to put forth novel approaches to TV comedy. In doing so, I spotlight several recently produced cable and network programs that, despite their popularity or critical acclaim, have yet to generate much scholarly commentary, such as *Strangers With Candy* (Comedy Central, 1999–2000), *It's Always Sunny in Philadelphia* (FX, 2005–12; FXX, 2013–present), *Ugly Americans* (Comedy Central, 2010–12), *The Mindy Project* (Fox, 2012–15; Hulu, 2015–17), *Mom* (CBS, 2013–present), *BoJack Horseman* (Netflix, 2014–20), *Documentary Now!* (IFC, 2015–present), and *Flaked* (Netflix, 2016–17). I also analyze historical precedents of the 1950s, 1960s, 1970s, and 1980s that similarly contributed to an evolving understanding of "badness" as a cultural construct, such as *The Honeymooners* (CBS, 1955–56), *The Munsters* (CBS, 1964–66), *Get Smart* (NBC, 1965–69; CBS, 1969–70), *All in the Family* (CBS, 1971–79), *M*A*S*H* (CBS, 1972–83), and *Roseanne* (ABC, 1988–97). Far from being an inherent or ingrained characteristic of particular offenders (of laws, of social etiquette, or of "good taste"), bad behavior circulates within the culture at large as *a way of seeing*, one that—like Émile Durkheim's concept of "collective consciousness"—is "neither reducible to nor derived from individual consciousness."[9] That is, thanks to conventionalized codes of representation and the ritual enactment of particular "types" in popular culture, we form a picture of society in a way that would be difficult, if not impossible, to achieve outside of symbolic language. But that picture "smudges"—becomes blurry over a surprisingly short period of time—before new images are traced over it; a constellation of signifiers that is likewise temporary or "subject to change," as Manfred B. Steger has noted.[10]

Lest we believe that such epistemological frameworks exist only in the imagination and are thus "not real," Steger reminds us that they materialize through "common practices and deep-seated communal attachments."[11] In his book *The Rise of the Global Imaginary*, Steger states that social imaginaries "should not be dismissed as phantasms or mental fabrications" floating above us in the ether. Seemingly intangible, they are in fact grounded in the material conditions that make actual social practices possible. As I hope to illustrate, television's decades-long contributions to the creation and circulation of these frameworks are tied to its unique features as a communication medium that takes up real (physical) space in our lives while endowing abstract (metaphysical) ideas with the solidity of corporeal performances: those of the comedians and actors who collectively embody what a society—and specifically its most maligned or vilified members (from alcoholics and drug addicts to criminals and prisoners to cult members and other so-called "monsters")—might "look" like.

As of this writing, surprisingly few scholars—either in media studies or in sociology—have turned to the above conceptualization of the social imaginary as a foundation for the critical-historical analysis of US television programming. In his 2012 book *Television and the Moral Imaginary: Society Through the Small Screen*, Tim Dant gives his readers a rare look into just such an approach, productively building upon the theories of Castoriadis, Taylor, Anderson, and Lefebvre while crafting hermeneutic tools that will serve future studies well.[12] One of Dant's most important observations is that, as a "symbolic network of ideas through which a society makes sense of itself," the social imaginary (or what he refers to as the "moral imaginary") is not an "ethical system from which rules of behavior could be derived."[13] We do not necessarily learn how to be "bad" or "good" from watching TV shows, in other words; but we do witness the concretizing of mainstream and alternative worldviews or values through repetitive representations and adherence to genre formulas. One thing that contemporary TV "teaches" us, whether in ostensibly "brainless" reality shows such as *Jersey Shore* (MTV, 2009–12) and *Keeping Up with the Kardashians* (E!, 2007–present) or in high-minded, overtly prestigious forms of "pedagogical television" such as *The Good Place* (NBC, 2016–20), is that network and cable channels' latest offerings—the "new situations and new characters" that Dant alludes to in his book—are "invariably revisions of previous forms."[14] That combination of creativity and tradition, innovation and repetition, makes television especially noteworthy as a purveyor of widespread attitudes, one whose historical continuities and ruptures are neatly replicated in the ceaseless flow yet commercial interruptibility of a medium that, at its industrial roots, is fundamentally contradictory.

TV's paradoxical status as a "consensus medium" prone to eliciting antisocial behavior on the part of impressionable audiences (a contentious claim largely discredited by researchers) as well as kneejerk reactions from its fiercest naysayers is perhaps most nakedly apparent today, in this age of *Family Guy* (Fox, 1999–present), *South Park* (Comedy Central, 1997–present), and other animated sitcoms that might strike some viewers as being simultaneously liberal and conservative, progressive and regressive (as unproductive as those binaries are).[15] Yet American television has long been snagged not only between dueling ideological perspectives but also between the artistic ambitions of talented storytellers (from Norman Lear to Jenji Kohan) and the advertising dollars that make the delivery of those potentially upsetting or offensive stories possible. This is a line of argument that I will pursue through selected case studies over the course of eight interlocking chapters.

Rather than take up the challenge of unpacking one overarching social imaginary from which the current state of US television programming can be generalized, I focus on three subcategories of culturally constructed alterity, looking specifically at what I term the "alcoholic imaginary," the "cult imaginary," and the "monstrous imaginary" (devoting two or three chapters to each). In doing so, I am following in the footsteps of other critics and historians who have explored everything from the "urban imaginary" on view in the British version of *Queer as Folk* (Channel 4, 1999–2000) to the "female mafia imaginary" in contemporary Italian literature.[16] These and other subcategories might alternatively be grouped together under the umbrella term "the mediatized imaginary," which Elizabeth Klaver has coined as a catchall designation of the way that film, television, and other forms of media construct "individual subjectivity in relation to a broad community of others."[17] Inspired by the work of media theorist John Caughie, Klaver's book *Performing Television* makes the case that individuals "find themselves" within a communal identity, situated alongside virtually present but physically distant "others," once they have stepped into the reservoir of delimiting images upon which so much popular culture—past and present—is predicated. Her conceptualization is not unlike German philosopher Jürgen Habermas's notion of an "intersubjectively shared lifeword" that comprises the "massive background" of the public sphere, where "communicatively acting subjects" develop a mutual understanding of one another through official and unofficial channels.[18]

This Habermasian "lifeworld" that, owing to its ubiquity, has receded into the background and all but disappeared from view, is furthermore akin to Steger's description of the global imaginary as a "familiar ocean of circulating symbols" (such as those of a small-town parade, replete with patriotically dressed onlookers, a marching band, waving flags, street vendors, soldiers in uniforms, and "military planes roaring overhead"—all of which are lent an "aura of normality" through the repetition of holiday celebrations).[19] By focusing on humorous depictions of bad behavior on American television, I hope to show how audiences' familiarity with the tropes associated with different types of stereotypically dangerous activities (from drinking oneself into a stupor to engaging in criminal activity to joining a cult) compensates for the disconcerting uncertainty that otherwise attends such potentially life-altering occurrences. However, in making the world safe for cultural consumption, sitcoms conceal as much as they reveal, masking the rationale for socially deviant or deleterious behavior behind figures of ridicule whose motives are rarely disclosed fully over the course of a thirty-minute episode.

Extending Steger's oceanic metaphor, cultural representations, like the proverbial water inside the fish tank (an analogy favored by Marshall McLuhan and subsequent generations of media ecologists), have become "invisible" to the extent that they are *hypervisible*, an ever-present but hardly noticeable part of the artificially natural habitat that we call "home." Here, "home" denotes the actual physical dwelling in which television is as much a member of the family (figuratively) as it is a piece of furniture (literally). But the word also connotes the larger imagined community—namely, the nation—that, ironically, can only be grasped in the abstract, and which is no less a construct than the essentializing images too often mistaken as an accurate reflection of reality. Like a "funhouse of mirrors" (to borrow Klaver's fittingly carnivalesque metaphor), the mediatized imaginary presents a distorted view of the world, pulling it like taffy into grotesque yet recognizable shapes.[20] Because we are encouraged by advertisers, network executives, and writers/showrunners to recognize ourselves in those misshapen images, it is not too much of a stretch to equate the physically embodied act of "watching TV" to that of standing before a funhouse mirror, peering at the person for whom that world was ostensibly created. But this is the illusion that the mediatized imaginary (or social imaginary) foists upon audiences, who mistakenly imagine themselves as subjects rather than objects of ideology, and who take false comfort in the belief that *their* lives—unlike those of fictional TV characters—are self-determined and shaped by free will (rather than, say, market forces and government policies). Nevertheless, *reflection* (in both senses of the word) is possible when audiences cast their collective gaze at individuals whose excessively coded "badness" is designed *not* to be taken too seriously (i.e., it is meant to be laughed at), thereby giving rise to the possibility of negotiated, resistant, or counter-hegemonic readings of ironic, parodic, or satirical televisual texts.

In Klaver's words, "it is primarily the viewer's act of looking, and to a lesser extent listening, that generates entry into an imaginary order." However, "because of the interruptive quality of television programming with its constant insertion of advertisements," the fissures and gaps that are unique to the medium make it possible for audiences to momentarily "break the spell" and to glimpse TV's "fantasy landscape" for what it really is.[21] Hence broadcast and cable networks' need for reliably repetitive representations—for instance, the same kinds of sitcom characters (e.g., the "lovable loser," the "neurotic," the "logical smart one," etc.)[22]— that she and other media scholars conceive of as "suturing" devices; or as means through which television storytellers are able to maintain their hold on audiences who *project themselves* onscreen (not unlike the way that shot/reverse-shots in cinematic texts encourage spectatorial identification with one or more narrative agents across a volley of looks). As I will explain in the forthcoming chapters, the repeated appearance of socially wayward figures on the small screen—from raging alcoholics to brainwashed cult members to actual monsters who are merely exaggerated extrapolations of our own inner demons (like the title characters in *The Munsters* or the undead, flesh-eating real-estate agent played by Drew Barrymore in *Santa Clarita Diet* [Netflix, 2017–19])—has the dual effect of reducing complex individuals to recognizable "types" while neutralizing the presumed threats that they pose. Such representations not only provide strangely comforting reminders that "badness" is a cultural construct, but also prompt us to reflect on our own unspoken proclivities for antisocial behavior, if only in passing.

Without subscribing to monolithic conceptualizations of audiences, which tend to focus on the short-term or long-term effects of television-viewing and posit direct or indirect correlations between media messages and spectatorial behavior, I wish to explore how social imaginaries solidify through the reciprocal interplay between text and context as well as between cultural producers and agentive publics. Though "static" in many ways, the sitcom, like other forms of comedic programming, is a moving target. As soon as a television scholar has an example of the genre in her sights, it flits away and is replaced by an equally instructive but fleeting case study. Of course, context is no less fluid or prone to shift than a televisual text, and what was once disallowed or frowned upon decades ago (such as scenes of sexual foreplay and intercourse) is now the new "normal" thanks to changing social mores and a desire for greater authenticity or realism in small-screen fictions.

Conversely, certain activities that were commonly portrayed in 1950s and 1960s sitcoms, such as cigarette-smoking (on view in *I Love Lucy* [CBS, 1951–57], *The Danny Thomas Show* [ABC, 1953–57; CBS, 1957–64], *The Dick Van Dyke Show* [CBS, 1961–66], and other sitcoms made prior to the 1964 Surgeon General's report on tobacco use), are not likely to appear in contemporary programs, save for *Mad Men* (AMC, 2007–15), *Pan Am* (ABC, 2011–12), and other period dramas that are set during previous decades. To be sure, worse things than cigarette-smoking take place in *Mad Men*, which depicts the womanizing ad executive Don Draper (Jon Hamm)'s addictive tendencies (e.g., alcoholism, serial adultery, etc.) and shows his agency's office manager Joan Holloway (Christina Hendricks) being sexually harassed by her male bosses and company clients, slut-shamed by a few of her female colleagues, and raped by her fiancé Greg (Samuel Page) in episodes that suggest that a more accurate title for the series might be "Bad Men" (to borrow a recurring bit from *Late Night with Seth Meyers* [NBC, 2014–present]).[23] The comparative harmfulness of particular acts—a matter perhaps best left to medical doctors, psychologists, and social scientists—nevertheless continues to attract the interest of communication and media theorists who treat television-viewing as an addiction in its own right; one that, if undertaken with the regularity with which ten-drinks-a-day Draper consumes rye whiskey, could have deleterious effects.[24]

From "Bad Uses" to "Bad Users": Junk TV and TV Addicts

> "No TV and no beer make Homer something something."
> —Homer Simpson (voiced by Dan Castellaneta)
> explaining to his wife Marge (voiced by Julie
> Kavner) why he is in such a murderously bad mood,
> in a Season Six episode of *The Simpsons* (Fox,
> 1989–present)

Public consternation about the dire consequences of excessive television consumption can be traced back to the earliest published works about the medium's "addictiveness," such as the article "I Was Cured of TV," which appeared in the pages of a 1955 issue of *Coronet* (and which was echoed by several subsequent calls to protect innocent children from its "seductiveness" in other magazines).[25] Penned by sportswriter Edward A. Batchelor and subtitled "The Story of a Confirmed Addict and His Long, Hard Fight Back to Life," this facetiously worded yet fearmongering article came out the same year that the *US News and World Report* published a series of interviews with people saying they could no longer "control their television use," including a New Jersey housewife who compared the medium to a monstrous "creature" that had crept into her family's lives and "mesmerized" them.[26] Such discourse amplified an already-growing concern that was sneaking into TV shows around the same time, including domestic sitcoms such as *The Adventures of Ozzie and Harriet* and *The Honeymooners* where the middle-class and working-class breadwinners of their respective families are shown falling under the spell of late-night programming and regressing to a childlike state. "The Pajama Game" (3.22), an episode of the former series that aired on April 1, 1955, reveals that it is the father, Ozzie Nelson, and not his two young sons, who is "unable to use the medium in a responsible, adult way," to quote Lynn Spigel,[27] in much the same manner that Ralph Kramden (Jackie Gleason) is portrayed as an easily triggered viewer of the "boob tube" in an episode of the latter program.

Titled "TV or Not TV" and originally broadcast on October 1, 1955, the pilot episode of *The Honeymooners* introduces audiences to Ralph and his wife Alice (Audrey Meadows), who—in the first of several marital spats that will flare up over the show's thirty-nine-episode run—bicker about the prospect of buying their first television set. Refusing to back down from her cheapskate husband's blustery protests, Alice desperately wants a TV, as she has grown tired of being cooped up inside their tiny, sparsely furnished Bensonhurst apartment where she spends all day at the stove and icebox (while he, a $62.50-a-week bus driver, works outside). "I wanna look at Liberace!" she exclaims, highlighting how housewives might find temporary comfort or respite from domestic duties through cultural performances that are far removed from their prison-like kitchens. In the words of John T. Caldwell, "although Ralph seems content with the dingy working-class tenement that the couple have inhabited unchanged for more than a decade, Alice seems to know that culture exists 'out there,'" and this early peek into their private lives indicates how she is more worldly (relatively speaking) than he is.[28] As will happen repeatedly throughout the series, the female character wins this standoff as a result of her intellectual superiority to the male character (establishing a template for generations of sitcoms revolving around married life). But it is Ralph and his upstairs neighbor Ed (Art Carney)—with whom he splits the cost of this "modern electrical appliance"—who spend the second half of "TV or Not TV" glued to the set, well into the wee hours (so late, in fact, that Alice, blanket in hand, has to tuck them in for the night with "motherly condescension").[29] Watching the DuMont network's kid-friendly sci-fi serial *Captain Video and His Video Rangers* before switching over to a televised prize-fight, the two men are infantilized in the presence of a medium that eventually turns them against one another. Putting up their dukes like boxers, they each claim ownership of the set until Alice finally defuses the situation. Ultimately, once she has seen the effect that such "mindless entertainment" can have on a weak-willed individual like her husband, Alice admits that, for once in his life, Ralph is right: "We *never* should've gotten a television set."

Given this anti-television stance, it might be surprising to learn that, throughout the 1950s, 1960s, and 1970s, a number of other programs featured scenes in which fictional characters criticize the medium on which their existence is predicated, referring to it as a potentially addictive and therefore dangerous substance.

In many cases, it is simply a benign fixture in the lives of characters who, under duress, must learn to amuse themselves through some other means whenever the electricity goes out or the set is on the fritz, as in episodes of *Father Knows Best* ("The Great Anderson Mystery" [5.36]) and *The Lucy Show* (CBS, 1962–68: "Lucy Puts Up a TV Antenna" [1.09]). In these and other series, no one—not even an easily bored horse—is immune to television's magnetic pull, as demonstrated in an episode of the equine-themed situation comedy *Mister Ed* (CBS, 1961–66), "TV or Not TV" (6.07); the telltale title of which was repeated throughout the history of the genre, starting with the aforementioned pilot of *The Honeymooners* and encompassing everything from fantasy sitcoms (or "magicoms") like *My Favorite Martian* (CBS, 1963–66) and *Bewitched* (ABC, 1964–72) to ethnic sitcoms (or "ethnicoms") like *Sanford and Son* (NBC, 1972–77).[30]

Notably, the "TV or Not TV" (1.11) episode of the latter series, a comedy about an elderly African American junk dealer and his grown son who live together in what they both call a "dump," puts the titular dilemma into a cultural context far removed from the proverbial white picket fences of American suburbs. In doing so, that episode reveals how someone's thirst for televisual entertainment might be tied to socioeconomic factors specific to underrepresented communities. To Fred Sanford (Redd Foxx), a big-screen color TV with remote control (which he wants to buy as a replacement for his broken set) is more valuable than the used convertible that Lamont (Desmond Wilson) spends their meager earnings on, and the comfort that he derives from watching television while nursing a beer suggests that the medium has had a positive effect on this low-income denizen of South Central Los Angeles. However, producers Bud Yorkin and Norman Lear's stateside remake of the British comedy *Steptoe and Son* (BBC One, 1962–74) ultimately presents television in an incriminating light, as a habit-forming substance that, like alcohol, promises emancipation or an easing of the mind but which actually enslaves those caught in its grips.

Like its source material from across the pond, *Sanford and Son* revolves around the intergenerational conflict between its two main characters. But the US version features a predominately African American cast, starring former "Chitlin' Circuit" standup comedian Foxx as the rascally protagonist Fred Sanford and Wilson as his long-suffering progeny Lamont. Rarely tackling serious issues such as racial profiling and police brutality head-on (although Fred sometimes cracks jokes about white cops, including LAPD Officer "Hoppy" Hopkins [Howard T. Platt]), Yorkin and Lear's remake nevertheless evokes a social milieu in which Black men face economic hardships and round-the-clock surveillance from law enforcement. Given its setting—the Watts neighborhood of L.A. (where residents participated in a civil uprising during a six-day period in August of 1965)—it should come as no surprise that a deeper sociopolitical commentary percolates below the surface. This is something that Christine Acham emphasizes in her analysis of the show's depiction of an urban underclass for whom television-viewing—and domestic life more generally—functions as an escape from the harsh reality of their heavily policed surroundings.[31] Indeed, TV's centrality within the Sanfords' cluttered home makes its junkiness-by-proxy associations hard to miss, though surprisingly few scholars or critics have bothered to consider the show's seemingly contradictory message that the medium might actually be *bad* for one's health.

To be clear, *Sanford and Son* is "not escapist," although, as Acham points out, many critics "perceived it as such" during its original broadcast. But the frequency with which Fred turns to his TV set as a constant companion—as dependably present in his life as Lamont and his fiancée Donna Harris (Lynn Hamilton) are—hints at his tendency to withdraw from the outside world and hunker down within his own hermetically sealed-off universe (punctured though it frequently is by interlopers). This is how the Season Five episode "The TV Addict" (5.17) begins, with Fred and his friend Grady (Whitman Mayo) sitting down for a marathon-like day of television viewing, or what the cheerful protagonist—holding a can of beer and a bowl of chips—calls "good living." In fact, he and Grady switch on not one but two TV sets (a small one stacked atop a larger one) so that they can watch "the monsters and the soap operas at the same time." Just as the 1943 Bela Lugosi horror film *The Return of the Vampire* begins, Lamont enters their bric-a-brac-filled home and turns off the programs, telling his now-irritated father how important physical exercise is for someone with his medical history. Fred, a recent heart patient who has been dividing his time between sleeping and watching TV (devoting twelve hours to each per day), comes up with excuses not to go to the local YMCA, explaining that he is booked all week with "previous engagements" (i.e., more shows to watch) that prevent him from leaving the house. Tensions flare and voices grow louder as the two characters go back and forth, switching the sets on and off until Lamont accidentally knocks the larger of the two TVs to the ground with a crash. "Oh no!" Fred bellows while peering down at the electronic debris. The scattered remains of the set metaphorically suggest his own emotionally shattered state.

Three days later, the junk dealer is still in a funk and his main source of home entertainment has yet to be repaired. "Why don't you stop acting like a two-year-old!" Lamont says, scolding his father for refusing to leave the house while waiting for the set to be fixed. At this point, Officer Hoppy knocks at the door and enters, then proceeds to tell Fred that he knows how to spot a man with an addiction. Having recently read a pamphlet ("How to Recognize an Alcoholic"), the policeman explains that one sure sign that there is a problem is "if a man

I.3. In *Sanford and Son*, a police officer explains to Lamont that his father, a junk dealer grieving over the recent destruction of his TV set, is a "teleholic." Together, the clutter of the father and son's house and the hollow shell of the TV set suggest a feeling of combined fullness and emptiness that connects allegorically to the experience of television addiction. © Tandem Productions

says he can give up drinking anytime he wants to, but he doesn't." "Pop's not an alcoholic," Lamont chimes in, to which Hoppy replies, "He's a *teleholic*, hooked on television." Informed that he should "stop hitting the tube," Fred (who suffers from depression whenever he is not watching a program) is forced to confront a condition that—if cultural commentators are to be believed—has affected millions of Americans since television's earliest days as a commercial medium (and which is summed up by the title of Bart Andrews's 1978 book *The TV Addict's Handbook*). Ultimately, Fred arrives at the conclusion that he "shouldn't be watching television all the time" (something he admits to Donna, who has been preparing low-cholesterol meals for him) and undergoes hypnotherapy administered by a graduate from the El Segundo Institute of Hypnosis—ironically, another form of mesmerism—as a possible cure. His statement, like the harsh words spoken by Alice in the concluding moments of *The Honeymooners'* pilot episode, echo similar sentiments put forth by journalists from the 1950s to the 1970s; decades when the deleterious effects of television viewing were written about anecdotally, with little to no supporting evidence.

Not until the 1980s, however, would such discourse be mobilized by communication studies researchers in the pages of more reputable, peer-reviewed journals. Since that time, the assumption that media addiction is a "real illness" has been accepted as gospel by many in the field.[32] As Richard Butsch, author of *The Citizen Audience: Crowds, Publics, and Individuals*, explains, numerous scholars from that point forward have glommed onto data provided by medical professionals (in their own studies of addiction) to argue that, like Fred Sanford, individuals who make a "habit" out of watching television—spending considerably more than the average five to six hours a day glued to the tube—might suffer from withdrawal symptoms if made to abstain. They are often said to have little control over their compulsions, exhibiting an inability to stop "using" the medium, as if it were a recreational drug or some other, more dangerous substance that has whittled away their willpower. In their 2002 article for *Scientific American*, Robert Kubey and Mihaly Csikszent-mihalyi allude to the increased levels of aggression, anxiety, boredom, and irritation that frequently result from such abstinence-like efforts, and maintain that "television addiction is no mere metaphor" but rather a "very real phenomenon" experienced by millions of Americans.[33] "The basic allure of the small screen," they suggest, makes the prospect of completely kicking the habit or going "cold turkey" for a lengthy period of time an increasingly unlikely scenario in this age of limitless viewing options. Such discourse, Kubey and Csikszentmihalyi also argue, is "laden with value judgments" about the human subjects who are often treated like objects of pity or derision in both the popular press and academic writing.

Along those lines, Butsch points out that the relatively nascent idea of "media addiction," which nevertheless has its roots in earlier eras' discourses about the presumed dangers of television and other forms of popular culture (for example, the moral panics surrounding the sale of comic books to juvenile readers in the 1950s),[34] bears out a tendency among scholars to infantilize and otherize audiences, especially those who gravitate toward "trashy" rather than "classy" forms of mass entertainment. This trend was especially noticeable during the 1990s, a decade that gave us such syndicated daytime talk shows as *The Jerry Springer Show* (1991–2018), *The Montel Williams Show* (1991–2008), and *Ricki Lake* (1993–2004), in addition to animated hits like *The Simpsons* (Fox, 1989–present) and *Beavis and Butt-Head* (MTV, 1993–97) that offered up their own prescient takes on televisual addiction (not to mention representations of negligent parenting and juvenile delinquency that drew the ire of religious conservatives). Around that time, criticism directed toward certain types of *programming* (e.g., tabloid TV, adult animation, etc.) expanded into a discursive critique of certain types of *audiences* as "bad citizens." Weak-willed and incapable of making smart, informed decisions about their own consumption patterns, such audiences were deemed in need of "guidance or guardianship" lest they completely succumb to the medium's "irresistible power."[35] Unlike the consumers of educational or culturally edifying programs, such as *Masterpiece Theatre* (PBS, 1971–present), the people who take pleasure in "shows that are crap, pure and simple" (or what one critic, writing in 1996, referred to as a "waste of valuable airtime"),[36] have sometimes been analogously "characterized as trash." Summarizing this phenomenon, Butsch states that "the distinction between good and bad *uses* of media is also a distinction between good and bad *users*," and that the latter group—stereotypically made up of individuals behaving in an irrational, self-possessed, and/or destructive manner—is ultimately "the antithesis of a good citizen."

I will return to this divisive, class-based rhetoric in Chapters One, Two, and Three, which explore how "people of subordinate status," including members of the working poor, when identified as struggling alcoholics "engaged in emotionally laundering dirty linen in public" (as seen in TV episodes set partially in AA meetings, for instance), assume a central position within a reductive social imaginary that reinforces existing hierarchies and further deprives addicts of their agency. However, for the sake of clarifying how TV spectatorship, intoxication, and addiction converge in comically disconcerting ways on network and cable television, it will be useful to consider one show's self-conscious, metatextual approach to those topics. That long-running series—*The Simpsons*—is in fact foundational to many of the case studies that I will focus on in the pages that follow, for it has consistently elevated "lowly" pursuits or "trivial" pastimes into subjects worthy of critical analysis and has put forth beloved avatars of bad behavior who remain as relevant today as they were at the time of its premiere over thirty years ago. Specifically, *The Simpsons* has done more to burnish the image of the TV addict into our collective unconscious than nearly any other program produced before and after its debut on December 17, 1989. Ever since the airing of its pilot episode (a Christmas special titled "Simpsons Roasting on an Open Fire" [1.01]), this critically lauded yet controversial satire of suburban life and sitcom tropes (created by American cartoonist Matt Groening) has returned time and again to the image of the titular family and its frequently flummoxed, TV-obsessed patriarch watching the proverbial "boob tube" with the same pathological frequency that characterizes his excessive alcohol consumption. Although any number of episodes of *The Simpsons* might be spotlighted as evidence of its writers' savvy deconstruction of the moral panics that would surround the animated sitcom throughout the 1990s (a key decade in the larger history of bad behavior on the small screen), for the sake of brevity I will highlight just a couple of noteworthy instances in which Homer's two main addictions play into contemporaneous discourses about TV-viewing and other pathologies as "a public safety as well as public health problem."[37]

Widely regarded as a milestone in the history of television animation, "Treehouse of Horror V" (6.06) is arguably the best of *The Simpsons*' thirty (and counting) horror-and-sf-themed episodes to have been aired in the days leading up to or following Halloween every year since the program's sophomore season (1990–91). That it is still considered to be "very special," even when compared to the series' many other "Very Special Episodes," can be attributed to a number of factors, including showrunner David Mirkin's efforts to inject a then-unprecedented amount of "blood and guts" into an animated sitcom that had been threatened with censorship by US congressional representatives (in other words, Mirkin wanted to include as much potentially offensive material as Fox network executives would allow at the time of its original broadcast on October 30, 1994).[38] Additionally, director Jim Reardon's deft handling of graphically violent sight gags and intertextually laced verbal humor across three briskly paced sketches (written by Greg Daniels, Dan McGrath, David X. Cohen, and Bob Kushell) distinguishes this episode from subsequent "Treehouse of Horror" specials, though the creative talent behind more recent entries have gone even further in piling on the viscera and bringing the latent nightmares of small-town America—that of the fictional Springfield—out into the open, where a literally hellraising "bad boy" (Nancy Cartwright's Bart Simpson) and a host of other monsters (including aliens, killer clowns, post-apocalyptic zombies, and Satan himself) lay waste to "traditional family values" in the harsh light of day. Still, this fifth annual Halloween special of *The Simpsons*, which originally aired on October 30, 1994, set a benchmark that has yet to be surpassed in terms of its creators' willingness to break the rules or generic conventions of short-form storytelling and to humorously portray a father's sudden, terrifying descent into familicidal madness when denied access to his two main obsessions in life: TV and beer.

Although the three sketches comprising "Treehouse of Horror V"—"The Shinning," "Time and Punishment," and "Nightmare Cafeteria"—have each generated extensive critical commentary, one of them tends to be singled out as an illustration of what makes the long-running series (with more than 728 episodes under its belt) so distinctive as a meta-commentary on television viewing and other potentially addictive or habit-forming activities. Indeed, the sketch that is most fondly remembered by fans of *The Simpsons* is the episode's first, a parody of Stanley Kubrick's 1980 film *The Shining*, which—as an adaptation of Stephen King's 1977 novel—is itself beholden to a prior text. Taking its title from the words that

Groundskeeper Willie (Dan Castellaneta) uses to describe Bart's telepathic ability, "The Shinning" restages several famous scenes from Kubrick's equally funny yet frightening motion picture, including those revolving around young Danny Torrance (Danny Lloyd)'s supernatural ability to communicate his unspoken feelings to Dick Hallorann (Scatman Crothers), head chef at the Overlook Hotel. Like this latter character, Groundskeeper Willie has serious misgivings about the latest caretakers of Mr. Burns (Harry Shearer)'s haunted lodge, and the Scottish man—transplanted from his janitorial shack at Springfield Elementary—is similarly dealt a lethal axe-blow and left to bleed to death on the floor of this mountain hotel. The person wielding that weapon, of course, is the nominal protagonist, a husband-father who puts his love of TV and beer above the needs of his own family.

Because Mr. Burns has removed all of the Duff Beer from the premises and cut the television cable before leaving his winter lodge in the hands of the Simpsons, Homer lacks the two things that he believes are essential to his wellbeing and which, throughout the series, are normally shown in abundance. Indeed, he can often be found tossing back pints at Moe's Tavern alongside his power plant coworkers or while sitting on his sofa at home, imbibing a constant stream of Channel 6 programming (e.g., news broadcasts such as reporter Kent Brockman's *Eye on Springfield*, talk shows like *Up Late with McBain*, animated segments of *The Itchy & Scratchy Show*, etc.) in the company of his wife and children. Homer's voracious appetite for TV is therefore matched only by his thirst for alcohol, a craving that leads to disastrous consequences in several episodes produced after "Treehouse of Horror V," including "Co-Dependent's Day" (15.15), in which Marge picks up the habit after she and her husband take a drive through Northern California's wine country.

Like the Halloween-themed episode before it, "Co-Dependent's Day" shows Homer, a "chronic alcoholic," endangering the lives of loved ones. In this case it is not the lack but rather the abundance of what Police Sergeant Lou (Hank Azaria) calls "the devil's mouthwash" that clouds Homer's already-addled mind and leads him to do something that some commentators have labeled as borderline "evil." Returning home from their tour of the Lush Valley vineyard, the increasingly frisky couple adds spice to their marriage by downing bottles of merlot and going on movie dates at the local theater (where, fittingly, they watch *The Lost Weekend* [1945], *Days of Wine and Roses* [1962], and *Barfly* [1987]). Then, following a romantic night at Oktoberfest, where Marge nurses a gigantic German stein until she passes out, Homer—inebriated himself—takes to the open highway in their car, which he rolls onto its top (off the side of the road). Before Chief Wiggum (Hank Azaria) and fellow police officers arrive on the scene, Homer (who will lose his driver's license if he gets another DUI) puts his sleeping wife into the upside-down driver's seat, leading to her arrest and her eventual stint in rehab.

Homer's willingness to destroy "his wife's reputation to save his own skin" has been referred to by *ScreenRant*'s Matthew Guida as one of the ten "worst things" that the character has ever done.[39] The horrendousness of Homer's actions is even remarked upon within the episode, when Moe Szyslak (Hank Azaria) calls his bar's most loyal patron (save for town drunk Barney Grumble [Dan Castellaneta]) a "monster." "That is the *worst* thing I've ever heard anybody do to anybody!" yells Moe upon hearing Homer's whispered confession, anticipating the moment when Marge also learns the truth near the end of "Co-Dependent's Day." In the closing scene of the episode, when Homer busts his wife out of rehab and confesses his crime, she angrily rejects his plea for forgiveness but soon comes to the realization that she is "hooked on love." A self-proclaimed "Homerholic," Marge had been drunk on her husband's companionship all along and begrudgingly lets him off the hook with his pledge to never drink clear liquor again. Audiences, too, have been forgiving of Homer's various transgressions, putting aside the many other actions that made Guida's list (e.g., stealing his son's money to cover up a scandal, nudging his neighbor Ned Flanders [Harry Shearer] into bankruptcy, allowing mobster Fat Tony [Joe Mantegna] to shoot an adult film in his house, destroying his father's kidneys and refusing to donate his own, etc.)[40] and continuing to embrace the lovable lush much like Marge does at the conclusion. Just as Bart and his more level-headed sister Lisa (Yeardley Smith) are willing to let Mom and Dad have their drunken night of fun "as long as they're not hurting anybody" (even though the kids will be left home alone with only the TV as their babysitter), *Simpsons* fans seem relatively unperturbed by behavior that, in the real world, would raise flags or sound alarms about a person's mental and physical health.

More so than "Co-Dependent's Day," the first Kubrickian sketch of "Tree-house of Horror V" reveals the monstrous side of someone who undergoes both mental and physical changes as a result of being deprived of two different kinds of intoxicants. When Marge checks in on her beer-and-TV-deprived husband, he responds with a line—one of the most quoted throughout *The Simpsons'* three-decade run—that recalls a similar statement from *The Shining* (uttered by Jack Nicholson's Jack Torrance). Emulating Jack's typewritten message "All work and no play make Jack a dull boy," he tells her, "No TV and no beer make Homer *something something.*" Taking her cue from the dozens of hand-scrawled messages that cover the hotel lobby's walls, Marge fills in that missing information, asking, "Go crazy?" "Don't mind if I do," Homer responds in maniacal singsong style, abruptly leaping toward her in a delirious burst of rubber-faced insanity. Notably,

I.4. In one of the most famous episodes of *The Simpsons'* annual "Treehouse of Horror" Halloween specials, Homer strikes a monstrous pose opposite a mirror as he menacingly approaches his wife. Although distorted, his facial features, stretched as if he were looking into a funhouse mirror, present a truthful, allegorically resonant image of how this character is seen by those who bemoan bad behavior on the small screen. © 20th Television Animation

he not only intimidates his back-peddling wife, who fends off his advances with a baseball bat, but also scares himself when he pauses momentarily on the staircase and sees his reflection in a mirror.

Homer's elastically stretched features, magnified by that reflective surface, recall the "funhouse mirror" metaphor alluded to earlier in this Introduction, when I discussed Elizabeth Klaver's concept of the "mediatized imaginary" as a paradoxically accurate distortion of the real world that is external to television's fictional settings. I am also reminded of a similar moment in a "Very Special Episode" of another sitcom from the 1990s, one that likewise foregrounds the dangers of drinking (albeit with less satirical intent). Specifically, "If You Can't Be with the One You Love . . ." (5.18), from *Boy Meets World* (ABC, 1993–2000), shows young protagonist Cory Matthews (Ben Savage) developing a drinking problem over a single week, beginning with a scene in which he looks at his reflection in a bathroom mirror while tossing back a bottle of whiskey. Split in two—or rather, doubled into the contrasting yet dialectically fused image of "bad" and "good" character traits—Cory confronts himself in a moment of clarity that, while less humorously grotesque than Homer's own run-in with his reflection in "Treehouse of Horror V," is central to the construction of TV's alcoholic imaginary. As Norman K. Denzin, one of the foremost scholars of the alcoholic imaginary, notes, such doubling makes it possible for an individual to "turn back on himself, see himself as subject and object, and distance himself from who he previously was."[41]

Catching a glimpse of himself as a monster on the staircase of the hotel, Homer screams and falls down the steps, enabling his wife to lock him inside the pantry downstairs. Underscoring his ghoulishness, however, a group of more traditional-looking monsters (e.g., Dracula, the Wolf Man, the Mummy) free him from his kitchen prison, thereby unleashing a beast whose savagery can only be soothed by the portable television that Lisa finds near the snow-covered hedge maze. This seven-minute sketch ends with Homer finally dropping his axe and gathering his family together in the "warm glowing warming glow" of the small TV screen. His urge to kill them subsides, though they all appear to be doomed to live out the rest of their short miserable existence in a literally frozen state. For our homicidal (anti)hero, television is not just a companion, but his "teacher, mother, [and] secret lover," something that Homer says in the seconds before he, Marge, Bart, Lisa, and Maggie hunker down in the presence of another kind of "monster"—a metaphor sometimes employed in media-effects research concerning the harmful influence of television.[42]

In the quarter-century that has elapsed since the airing of this episode, few TV series have foregrounded so forcefully the medium's perceived (but hardly proven) power to make viewers "go crazy," even through its absence; a disposition befitting that most tipsy or socially lubricated of all genres: comedy. I include this extended reference to *The Simpsons* because the show, perhaps more than any other animated or live-action sitcom, has mobilized popular opinions about drinking and drunkenness while forging a link between two ostensibly unrelated types of consumption that have been individually scrutinized by social scientists and medical scientists for many years (both prior to and following the original broadcast of "Treehouse of Horror V"). Although I will circle back to these subjects at a later point in this book, it behooves us to begin our trek through the history of bad behavior on the small screen by considering the important role that *The Simpsons* has played in shaping popular discourses of addiction as something that impacts people who are "weak" in some way, or whose dependence on television bespeaks a lack of more "wholesome" or soul-enriching nourishment in their lives. If, like Homer, the medium itself can be thought of as a "monster" (dangerous and destructive to all who fall under its spell), it is only because the often-dismissive critical language surrounding television since its Frankensteinian birth several decades ago has not altered considerably throughout the years; as evidenced in contemporary reviews of satires and sitcoms that either demonize their onscreen talent or bemoan their corrosiveness as cultural productions aimed at the unwashed masses.

"TV or Not TV": Bad for Your Health, But Good for Your Soul

> "Sitting that close to the TV can't be good for you."
> "Talking while the TV's on can't be good for *you*."
> —Marge being casually threatened by her husband
> Homer in a Season Eleven episode of *The Simpsons*

Major changes, both inside and outside the American television industry, occurred between the January 30, 1976, airing of "The TV Addict" (from *Sanford and Son's* fifth season) and the October 30, 1994, airing of the aforementioned Halloween-themed *Simpsons* episode concerning Homer's own irrational attachment to the screen. Those transformations, including industrial deregulation, corporate reorganization and conglomerate buyouts, the introduction of videocassette recorders (VCRs) and other time-shifting devices in the home-viewing market, and the proliferation of premium and basic cable channels such as HBO and Showtime (which offered uncut, commercial-free movies), would fundamentally alter people's perceptions of this consensus medium, leading them to question what its social function or cultural value might be at the very moment when the United States appeared to be fracturing in unprecedented ways along ideological lines. Moreover, as media scholar Evan Elkins maintains, some of those transformations, which date back to the first years of the Reagan administration and which favor free-market principles over those that might best serve the public interest, would affect "discourses of comedy and offense" for years to come,[43] setting the stage for more recent iterations of televised bad behavior as well as less centralized means of policing that behavior within the culture at large (beyond the limited oversight of the Federal Communications Commission [FCC] and in addition to the networks' Standards and Practices [S&P] departments).

In his exploration of stand-up comedy routines on late-night variety and talk shows of the early 1990s, Elkins summarizes some of the developments from the previous decade that made it possible for controversial performers such as Andrew Dice Clay, Martin Lawrence, and Bill Hicks to incorporate offensive material into their profanity-laced stage acts—content that would need to be tamed or contained whenever they made the leap to the small screen (delivering opening monologues as hosts of *Saturday Night Live*, for example). The "bad boy" persona of these and other stand-up comedians—radically different though Clay, Lawrence, and Hicks were from one another in terms of their cultural backgrounds, vocal delivery, and onstage gimmicks or "schtick" (not to mention the actual substance of their acts)— traded on masculinist, sexist, homophobic remarks that might be protected as free speech in the comedy clubs where they got their professional starts, but would face stiff censorship challenges now that television was becoming a key battleground of the nascent "culture wars." The latter expression had gained currency in political debates three years prior to the 1994 broadcast of "Treehouse of Horror V" (the same year that Martin Lawrence famously got himself banned from *SNL* follow- ing a bawdy monologue about feminine hygiene and oral sex). Although intro- duced into the popular lexicon by sociologist James Davison Hunter, whose book *Culture Wars: The Struggle to Define America* was published in 1991,[44] the idea that the United States was splintering into oppositional factions—that its citizens were becoming "polarized into hardened camps"—was certainly not revolutionary, having already rhetorically colored the blue-red divisions of the country, whose two-party system gave rise to fierce displays of partisan politics during the televised presidential campaigns of the 1980s.[45] But it was rightwing presidential candidate Pat Buchanan's "Culture War" speech at the 1992 Republican National Conven- tion, where he railed against environmental causes, taxpayer-funded art, wom- en's reproductive rights, and other hot-button issues, that augured a new period of trumped-up conflict between one side (which promoted itself as standing for a "fundamentalist Christian set of values") and its opposing side (the "purport- edly left-wing, secular pole represented by Democratic presidential candidate Bill Clinton").[46] Battling over the so-called soul of America (or what Buchanan and his cohort called "God's country") but in reality jockeying for position as power brokers, party representatives on both sides claimed to know how to distinguish between the "right" and "wrong" ways not only to govern but also to live according to high-minded moral precepts or religious doctrines that, to this author's way of thinking, have no place in politics.

For many congressional leaders on the "right" side of the political spectrum, the December 17, 1989, debut of *The Simpsons* was retrospectively viewed as a cul- tural flash point requiring stepped-up efforts to combat widespread moral degen- eracy and satirical affronts to traditional family values on the small screen. To do so, however, would be a herculean task in the multichannel era, once televi- sion advertisers, broadcasters, and programmers shifted their strategies away from the "least objectionable" approach mentioned earlier toward "edgier content that would hopefully pry eyes away from cable's laxer decency standards."[47] The oligopolistic structure of the American television industry during and preceding the late 1970s, when the Big Three networks ABC, CBS, and NBC claimed over ninety percent of the primetime audience, had thus given way to a wider array of options for viewers—and for comedy writers and performers—by the time that "Treehouse of Horror V" was broadcast on Fox stations. Those intervening years saw a significant uptick in the number of cable TV subscribers, which climbed to fifty-three million households by the end of the 1980s, as well as an increase in the number of cable TV networks ("from 28 in 1980 to 79 by 1989").[48] All of this means that the playing field was expanding considerably in the leadup to the airing of "Treehouse of Horror V" and subsequent *Simpsons* episodes, and that the various alcohol-fueled "transgressions" for which Homer might be blamed or held accountable could be situated alongside several other instances of bad behavior on competing stations, including those that riled up not only conservative/Republican watchdogs but progressive/Democratic ones as well. It is in that context, Elkins reminds us, that Clay, Lawrence, and other stand-up comedians found their footing even as the ground beneath their feet seemed to shift with each headline-grabbing appearance on late-night TV.

Indeed, the "bad boy" persona that these men nurtured—a kind of adult/R-rated version of young troublemaker Bart Simpson—was paradoxically welcomed and fretted over by network executives who found themselves suddenly "competing with the looser affordances of niche cable programming and the Fox network."[49] Threatened with seven-second delays and cautioned against uttering any of the "seven dirty words" enumerated by George Carlin in his 1970s stand-up acts ("shit," "piss," "fuck," "cunt," "cocksucker," "motherfucker," and "tits"—all of which are now fair game in non-broadcast media operating outside the FCC's obscenity guidelines), straight male comedians of the 1980s and 1990s were instrumental in opening the door to more profane types of political incorrectness. And yet, as Elkins points out, they frequently propped up "traditionally dominant power structures" that either excluded or exploited women and gay men in the process. Hence the reason why spokespeople from *both* sides of the political aisle found something to complain about in that era's most offensive shows, be they syndicated tabloid programs like *The Morton Downey Jr. Show* (1987–89), which incensed liberals with its belligerent, chain-smoking host's in-your-face theatrics, or cartoonish satires of the nuclear family like *Married . . . with Children* (1987–97), which—vilified by conservatives as "the epitome of 'Trash TV'—inspired a national letter-writing campaign led by anti-obscenity activist Terry Rakolta (a homemaker from Michigan who sought to have the Fox show's sponsors boycott it).[50]

Rakolta's and other activists' concerns about the content of television programs capped a decade-long series of battles between audiences and networks that witnessed numerous complaints making their way to formal court proceedings. Perhaps the most famous case from that period was *Zamora v. Columbia Broadcasting System* (1979), in which the plaintiffs—the father and mother of fifteen-year-old Ronny Zamora—sued ABC, CBS, and NBC for damages after their impressionable son shot and killed an eighty-three-year-old neighbor. The plaintiffs' action was brought against the networks on the theory that Ronny had become "involuntarily addicted to" and "completely subliminally intoxicated by" the onscreen violence that he had witnessed as a TV viewer, and that his deadly crime had been stimulated or incited by the atrocities that had aired on primetime shows.[51] Such wording, included in South District of Florida Judge William Hoeveler's final judgment (which decided in favor of the defendants' First Amendment rights), highlights how loaded with meaning the sight of Fred Sanford succumbing to the intoxicating pleasures of television was at the time of its original broadcast.

Of course, what distinguishes Zamora's "addiction" from Sanford's, besides the tragic outcome of the former versus the humorous consequences of the latter, is the age of the person involved. As suggested earlier, of particular concern to media watchdogs and nonprofit lobbying groups such as Action for Children's Television (ACT) was the deleterious effect of TV-viewing on adolescents and kids, exacerbated by court cases involving young boys and girls who inflicted harm on others or themselves after watching everything from *The Mickey Mouse Club* (ABC, 1955–2018) to *The Tonight Show* (NBC, 1954–present).[52] Undergirding many parents' complaints about the content of television was the belief that the federal government's deregulation of the industry had lifted the informal, unenforceable mandate for educational programming (which former FCC Chair Newton N. Minow strongly advocated for in his "Television and the Public Interest" speech, delivered to the National Association of Broadcasters on May 9, 1961) off the shoulders of the networks, who, in the 1980s, found themselves freer to pursue their commercial interests under the less-watchful eye of newly appointed chairman Mark S. Fowler.

Not surprisingly, that decade gave rise to a slew of syndicated children's cartoons based on popular toys, including *Care Bears* (1985), *He-Man and the Masters of the Universe* (1983–85), and *My Little Pony* (1986–87), which took the place of more edifying programs such as *Captain Kangaroo* (1955–84). Ironically, before the Children's Television Act was enacted in 1990 (and enforced by the FCC six years later), the moral panics surrounding these and other animated series (which functioned like promotional tie-ins for plush animals and action figures aimed at parents' pocketbooks) were not unlike Minow's open denunciation of cartoons in his 1961 speech, which equated children's programming of the immediate postwar period to a steady diet of brain-numbing "ice cream" when more nourishing cultural forms—those that might teach and uplift audiences—were needed. Notably, Minow, using a word that is central to the present study, summed up his and many other viewers' dissatisfaction with the medium by noting that "when television is bad, nothing is worse."[53]

Once again, *The Simpsons* is noteworthy for several reasons, not the least of which is its use of animation to put a humorously caricatured—at times monstrous—face on human foibles. Because animation is such a liberating medium, giving artists the opportunity to pursue practically any far-out idea with fewer of the budgetary or physical limitations associated with live-action production, the medium has become a showcase for once-unimaginable subjects and has contributed to a renaissance in bad behavior (on view in everything from Adult Swim's absurdist program *Aqua Teen Hunger Force* [2000–15] to the FX network's espionage meta-comedy *Archer* [2009–16] to Netflix's dysfunctional domestic comedy *F Is for Family* [2015–present]). Moreover, animated satires and sitcoms often find humor in images and ideas that, if rendered in actual flesh and blood, would not likely be tolerated by a majority of television viewers. Consider, for instance, the running gag (in the literal sense) of Homer Simpson putting his son Bart into a stranglehold, angrily choking him whenever American TV's most famous "bad boy" has misbehaved. Now try to imagine that scene—repeated across the thirty-plus seasons of *The Simpsons*—being filmed with real-life actors delivering and receiving a form of corporal punishment that would be outlawed in most states, and one can see how the question of "tolerability" hinges as much on the *medium* or mode of production as it does on the *message*. For this reason, nearly every one of the chapters in this book devotes space to standout animated series that reveal the lengths to which cultural producers will go to test the limits of permissibility in depicting behavior that would be unthinkable in the context of a live-action program.

Although live-action TV shows outnumber their animated brethren (both in this book and within the industry), each of the categories of onscreen representation explored in the following pages encompasses enough examples of those two modes of production to warrant a discussion of both. For instance, in Chapters One, Two, and Three, I explore what I call the alcoholic imaginary, a set of conflicting views on both casual and excessive drinking that—thanks partially to 1950s and 1960s classics such as *The Honeymooners* and *The Dick Van Dyke Show* as well as more recent animated sitcoms like *Family Guy* and *Rick and Morty* (Adult Swim, 2013–present)—has hardened into an ultimately reductive character type:

the comic drunk. In Chapters Four and Five, I turn my focus to the cult imaginary and examine a diverse assortment of cultural productions, from live-action coming-of-age shows such as *Strangers With Candy*, *Veronica Mars* (UPN, 2004–6; The CW, 2006–7; Hulu, 2019), and *Unbreakable Kimmy Schmidt* (Netflix, 2015–20) to contemporary classics of adult animation such as *South Park* and *King of the Hill* (Fox, 1997–2010), which collectively paint a generally dismissive picture of neo-religious community-building and televisual worship while underlining the similarities between TV fandom and fringe religions.

Likewise, a combination of animated and live-action case studies is put under the microscope in Chapters Six, Seven, and Eight, which examine how the most pervasive yet amorphous of my three representational categories—that of the monstrous imaginary—has been cobbled together, Frankenstein-like, from sundry parts and serves as the ultimate nexus between Self and Other. Although the figurative monstrosity of the title character in the working-class comedy *Roseanne*—lent latex flesh during that show's annual Halloween episodes—is the main focus of this book's penultimate chapter, I follow that discussion with a historical overview of sitcoms in which literal monsters drop into the standard familial slots of the genre (as fathers, mothers, and children), albeit within neo-gothic settings that depart significantly from the clean middle-class environs of their more traditional predecessors. From ABC's *The Addams Family* (1964–66) to its short-lived animated spinoff of the same title (produced by rival network NBC in 1973), a number of television shows have unmasked a truly hideous side of US society by comically accentuating people's rush to condemn or pass judgment on that which they do not understand. As "Ugly Americans" (to borrow the title of an adult animated sitcom about demons created by Devin Clark and originally aired on Comedy Central between 2010 and 2012), the many misbehaving men and women in contemporary TV comedies are as prone to vilifying others as they are to being demonized themselves, and that multidirectional spread of disparaging rhetoric has fed into the political divisiveness of recent years, especially in the aftermath of the 2016 presidential election.

In those final chapters and conclusion of this book, I will circle back to the unavoidable shadow that one ugly American, Donald J. Trump, casts over the current media landscape while also gesturing toward recent progressive movements, such as #MeToo, Time's Up, and Black Lives Matter, that enrich our understanding of the social imaginary as a set of "contingent social logics." In the words of Susan M. Ruddick, members of a given collective (including a nation's citizens) are essentially "unknown to each other," yet they "live in the image of communion" through "a range of partial concentrations of power which themselves acquire meaning in relational context."[54] In recent years, as divisions in the country have deepened, US audiences have managed to come together and forge relational bonds around several critically lauded television series that, to varying extents, openly critique institutional abuses of power while posing ethical alternatives to the current status quo. Taking one such show—NBC's *The Good Place*—as a leaping-off point, I thus bring this book to a conclusion by considering some of the possible outcomes of popular culture's collision with political discourse.

Anyone who has been paying attention to the current state of US national politics will know how rife it is with "bad actors" prone to shady, bad-faith dealings or empty promises to various constituencies, many of whom rely on TV as a means of gaining virtual access to otherwise restricted spaces of governance. The discursively articulated "badness" that I highlight in each of the chapters of this book, which problematizes the moralizing tenor that often accompanies public handwringing about some of the culture's most misunderstood, stereotyped individuals, is in fact frequently performed on television and social media sites by politicians whose disregard for ethical standards once revered (if not always upheld) by their forebearers is actually worthy of alarm. As such, it ties into my earlier references to bad behavior as a social imaginary formed from the convergence of both real-world and fictional discourses and subject to flux owing to its historicity—its inherently mutable status as both a mental picture of constructed otherness and a fading snapshot of times gone by.

Like Sophia (Britt Robertson), the twenty-three-year-old anti-heroine in *Girlboss* (Netflix, 2017), who chafes at older generations' tendency to put people into boxes (and does everything in her limited power to break from such constraints), readers might find the arrangement and ordering of the chapters that follow to be too strictly confined to prescriptive categories of bad behavior. Why, you might ask, should comic drunks, comic cultists, and monsters both real and imaginary be singled out to the exclusion of other stereotypical representations of a perceived social danger or "threat" that can be safely dealt with through televisual fictions? In one respect, the oddly selective, segmental approach that I adopt in this book, which explores three distinct classifications of constructed alterity over eight chapters, is indebted to the idea, put forth by philosopher Cornelius Castoriadis, that the social imaginary secures a comforting kind of "world order" for individuals whose autonomy relies on a separation of the human subject from objects within their field of view—subordinated others that find their "natural" resting spot amongst other nonhuman (or dehumanized) things kept at an observable distance.[55] That world order, simulated by the rigid narrative structures and familiar character types that hold sitcoms and other ritualistically enacted comedic forms together (as genres), ultimately rests upon a false premise. For, in reality, we find ourselves knee-deep in a vaporous terrain of potentially unresolvable problems: thorny ethical dilemmas and moral quandaries that simply cannot be completely untangled in the space of a thirty-minute or sixty-minute TV episode (not even in the so-called "Very Special Episode," which I touch upon at various junctures). Putting a twenty-first-century spin on Castoriadis's theory, we might say that the social imaginary, like the "supposedly ordered universe" that gives *The Good Place* its name, is "actually a rickety bureaucratic nightmare of mundane cruelty and lazy problem-solving,"[56] a fundamentally flawed system of organization in which people are trapped inside prisons of their own making and whose outward appearance of rational design masks an unsettling, potentially emancipatory unknowability.

If, by the end of this book, it seems that I have been discriminatory in selecting certain topics over others, it is only because onscreen embodiments of drunkenness, neo-religious practice, and outright monstrosity have themselves been subjected to prejudicial thinking within US popular culture, and one way to address or redress that irrational, reductive sort of reasoning is to probe the deterministic tropes of rational discourse *from within*. In this way, I find myself mimicking the posthumous actions of Eleanor Shellstrop (Kristen Bell), the female protagonist in *The Good Place*, who divines a way *out* of the weirdly hellish "heaven" to which her earlier bad behavior had doomed her by learning the ropes of the afterlife and turning the literally tortuous institutional limitations of that titular place—its structures of inclusion and exclusion (based on an apparently arbitrary point system)—*against itself*. The fact that she does all of this while heeding the teachings of a professor of ethics and moral philosophy (William Jackson Harper's Chidi Anagonye) and keeping her scabrous sense of humor intact makes Eleanor the *best* kind of "bad person": an ostensibly unlikable, selfish, rude, and manipulative woman whose power to positively change—herself and others—is worthy of imitation.

PART ONE: TV's Alcoholic Imaginary

Comic Drunks, Militaristic Drinking,
and the Rhetoric of Recovery

1

Very Drunken Episodes

Comedy TV's Discourses of Insobriety

> Laughter is a harlequin that shows two faces—one smiling and friendly, the
> other dark and ominous. Mardi Gras floats and sinister mechanical jokesters
> of old carnival fun houses mirror this duality—a volatile mix of gay and maca-
> bre that speaks directly to the emotional centers of our brain.
> > —Robert R. Provine, *Laughter: A Scientific Investigation*
> > (New York: Penguin Putnam, Inc., 2000), 2.

> Let me have what you're drinking. I wanna get loaded, too!
> > —Ralph Kramden to his wife Alice in the pilot episode
> > of *The Honeymooners* (CBS, 1955–56)

Before venturing any further into the topic of bad behavior on American television, it might be helpful to ask a fundamental question: Why *comedy*? Why should
one limit oneself to a single genre when social imaginaries are enacted across a
broad spectrum of TV offerings, including daytime and primetime dramas, not
to mention reality programming where all manner of human degradation is on
ample display? One way to begin answering this question is to think about what
distinguishes comedy in all of its sundry forms—farce, parody, satire, slapstick,
etc.—from other types of cultural production; and how humorous discourse in
general has been put to use within the public sphere as either a palliative means
of caring for one another or a weaponized means of mocking and humiliating (if
not literally injuring) the most powerful among us. Of course, these and other
motives might coexist within a given work, just as we can discern contradictory
tendencies within a genre that has been said to "help" and "hurt" society in equal
measure. Still, as slippery as comedy is, getting a grasp on its unique characteristics in the context of network and cable programming will help to materialize
or solidify a largely neglected social imaginary that, ironically, has been present
since television's earliest years as an advertisement-driven entertainment medium
(during the late 1940s and early 1950s). Namely, the *alcoholic imaginary*, which

is paradoxically predicated on humorous displays of insobriety as well as rehabilitative claims of sobriety, lends itself to the simultaneously transgressive and
conservative genre of TV comedy, which is itself tethered to much earlier cultural
traditions (e.g., Dionysiac celebrations or "phallic processions," the ancient Roman
festival of Saturnalia, carnivals, lampoons, "drinking songs") in which rule-breaking was ironically ritualized, or made to conform to accepted standards of performance through repetitive acts of naughtiness.

Since the time of the ancient Greeks, countless philosophical treatises have
been written about the nature of humor and the socially productive function of
laughter, which can relieve stress, level differences, and forge a stronger sense of
(imagined) community than other sorts of bodily response can. Indeed, entire
books have been devoted to the basic idea that comedy is a distinct artistic form
capable of "doing" things for which drama (or tragedy) is ill-suited. Going back to
Aristotle's *Poetics* (335 BCE), a foundational text primarily concerned with tragedy, and articulated in recent publications concerning comedy (e.g., John Morreall's *Comic Relief* [2009], Paul McDonald's *The Philosophy of Humour* [2012],
Steven Gimbel's *Isn't that Clever* [2018]) is the notion that joke-telling often ele-
vates lowly subjects and lowers elevated subjects through deliberate violation (for
instance, by foiling expectations and revealing an unforeseen actuality, or by
contravening established codes of conduct or "good behavior").[1] Base desires and
ugly or painful truths lie just below the surface of many jokes, especially those
that are designed to challenge authority, prompt critical reflection or action on
the part of an audience, and proffer an alternative view on the (often unfunny)
state of the world.

Of course, laughter is only one of "innumerable intended, potential, and actual
responses to humor," as Gimbel notes, and a joke's recipient might take offense
and frown when certain subjects are broached indelicately, or without the requi-
site cleverness that he and other theorists believe to be central to comedy.[2] This is
almost certainly true whenever taboo topics—running the gamut from death, sickness, and other sad facts of life to more controversial matters such as cannibalism,
incest, and sexual abuse—are exploited for their shock value or presented in such
a way that the potential for a positively imbued experience (amusement, enjoyment, pleasure, uplift, etc.) is clouded by the "negative ethics" of humor. The latter
idea, according to Morreall, encompasses a range of dismissive attitudes toward
comedy as a socially *destructive* rather than productive form; one that is accused
of fostering hostility toward others, diminishing one's self-control, and promoting
hedonism and idleness (among other bad habits).[3]

People on the receiving end of such jesting, or who fail to see the point of a "dick
joke," for example (a running gag on *3rd Rock from the Sun* [NBC, 1996–2001]

and other sitcoms from the past three decades), might consider that type of humor to be base, mean-spirited, or in bad taste. They might furthermore judge it to be an aesthetic failure since it has not risen above clichés or the structural parameters of a given medium to stimulate the mind's higher faculties. However, if something appears obscene to some audiences—if it has managed to stir up controversy as a morally objectionable response to a serious problem—then it has successfully exposed the gap between expectation and actuality. Perhaps it has even drawn attention to "pernicious attitudes and beliefs" within a society that would prefer to keep its dirty laundry hidden from view.[4] Still, the longstanding notion (traceable to Plato's *Philebus*, a Socratic dialogue composed in the fourth century BCE) that laughter is an expression of malice or scorn rather than an enlightened worldview, continues to color the critical literature around comedy, which has been conceived of as a kind of "foul discourse"—a morally suspect way for people to take derisive pleasure in others' misfortunes.

Though he does not subscribe to this belief, Morreall explains the logic behind it, noting that many of the stock characters of ancient Greek comedy—"the liar, the lecher, the adulterer, the glutton, and the drunk"—are figures of excess whose wrongdoings elicit a similarly inappropriate response from their audiences, whose audible enjoyment in seeing those comic fools fall on their asses, get caught red-handed, receive their comeuppance, or suffer other fateful consequences of their bad behavior is just as dubious. This problem of suspending moral concern for another person defined by their own questionable morality is magnified once the line between theatrical artifice and real life blurs. As he states, "Laughing at a friend who is too drunk to stand up . . . we're not trying to help that person. And when we laugh at drunks in movies, this critique says, we are inuring ourselves to the problem of alcoholism in our culture. A morally responsible attitude toward people with vices includes the desire to reform them and rules out enjoyment of their vices."[5] Morreall's use of the drunkard as an example of someone deserving of sympathy but often reduced to being a target of ridicule is significant, for it points toward one of the most archetypal figures in comedy. Indeed, the comic drunk has been a perennial fixture of humorous discourse since the time of Aristophanes, Cratinus, and Eupolis.[6]

Centuries after these practitioners of ancient Greek comedy took inspiration from the drunken processions known as the *kōmos*, William Shakespeare and other writers of the English Renaissance continued the tradition of showing the comic fool in the grips of intoxication. But they did so in a way that balanced scorn with sympathy, allowing audiences to hold these contrasting perspectives at the same time. Several of Shakespeare's plays feature such scenes, although one need only to consider his "most popular comic creation," the charismatic yet deceitful and disgusting character Falstaff (from *Henry IV*, Parts 1 and 2, *Henry V*, and *The Merry Wives of Windsor*), to see how such a figure came to embody the "vices and virtues" of an era when ale and wine were dietary staples (owing to the lack of clean water) but also devilish concoctions responsible for men's physical and spiritual ruin (according to religious adherents). As Iain Gately notes in *Drink: A Cultural History of Alcohol*, despite his outward appearance as an old, overweight, and ugly swindler, Falstaff was an endearing character for Elizabethan audiences. Like fellow tippler Sir Toby Belch from *Twelfth Night*, he has an enviable zest for life that is ignited, not snuffed out, by alcoholic intake (an activity typically carried out in the company of other "lowlifes" at the Boar's Head Tavern, located on London's Eastcheap Street).[7] Still, Falstaff is, in the words of one contemporary commentator, "just about the *worst* of men," someone whose career as a "small-time criminal" would not normally be thought of as laudable or worthy of emulation. In creating this most contradictory of characters, though, Shakespeare set the stage for other Falstaffian fools in the years that followed, including those who "lubricate the plays in which they move as effectively as they do their own throats."[8]

That statement, written by Albert H. Tolman in 1919 (on the eve of Prohibition in the United States), acknowledges how cultural productions themselves—like the comic drunks who populate them—can be thought of as being "intoxicated," or momentarily suspended in a state of drunken revelry. Perhaps more so than the Greek classics of the genre, contemporary comedy is juiced up and lubricated insofar as it indulges in a relatively fluid, border-crossing form of social interaction in which rules are bent, roles are reversed, and masks are dropped to reveal the true face of a hero or villain otherwise treated in the abstract (i.e., as a "type"). Moreover, comedy's sometimes anarchic staging of life's many absurdities as humorous incongruities can sometimes seem sloppy; a deliriously muddled mishmash of signifiers that threatens to spill over the rim of its "container" (i.e., the medium through which a humorous story or anecdote is delivered).

I am reminded of this every time I watch Mel Brooks's *Blazing Saddles* (1974), a satirical commentary on US race relations as well as a parodic reworking of Western film conventions that culminates with a chaotic sequence in which boundaries are literally breached (when the brawling actors/characters from one movie break through a Warner Bros. soundstage wall into another movie's production). Written by no fewer than five people (Brooks along with Norman Steinberg, Andrew Bergman, Richard Pryor, and Al Uger), and topped off with a minute-long pie fight (one of its many nods to the history of anarchic humor on the silver screen), Brooks's film might seem like a slapdash affair. However, its messiness is intentional, and the manner in which this narrative disorder plays out during its final scenes evokes not only the liberating drunkenness of comedy but also the lawlessness of the Old West. Given the fact that "liberation"—an idea larded with political connotations at the time of its theatrical release (on the tail-end of the Civil Rights era)—is one of *Blazing Saddles*' main themes, it makes sense that the filmmaker would use comedy as a vehicle for imagining alternatives to the social status quo and for unchaining the Western from its ideological conservatism. Funnily enough, when asked to describe the equally chaotic process of making this motion picture, Brooks used a metaphor long associated with comedy—that of intoxication—and told his interviewer that "*Blazing Saddles* was more or less written in the middle of a drunken fistfight. There were five of us all yelling loudly for our ideas to be put into the movie."[9] Besides bringing to mind the comical scene of collective fisticuffs that caps his film, Brooks's analogy draws attention to the volatile underpinnings of the alcoholic imaginary, which leverages the innocent fun of inebriation against the dangers of engaging too heartily in an activity that— to paraphrase Cleavon Little's character in *Blazing Saddles* (a sheriff who cautions Gene Wilder's "Waco Kid" about drinking whiskey on an empty stomach)—could result in serious harm.

Turning our focus away from theater and film back to television, I am tempted to say that, taken together, the genre (comedy) and the medium (TV) evince a capacity for drunken misbehavior, even though such liberatory potential is ultimately kept in check or policed by regulatory and moral forces inside and outside the industry. As I seek to explain in this and the next two chapters, American television's tendency to highlight the humorous yet harmful effects of alcohol consumption corresponds to broader discourses in which equally contradictory messages are communicated to a public increasingly inured to the sight of characters behaving badly as a result of one too many drinks. But there is still something unique about TV's depiction of comic drunks, necessitating a thorough investigation into how they draw upon yet depart from earlier representations (in theater and film) and why they might be symptomatic of the medium's own intoxicating mix of stifling regulation and transgressive rule-breaking.

Here I am following in the footsteps of several other scholars who have argued that the medium "readily lends itself to comedy."[10] In his essay "Why Comedy Is at Home on Television," Alex Clayton makes the case that TV is unique not despite but *because of* its "mixed inheritance from a range of other media," pointing toward its "tendency towards segmentation and partiality" (borrowed from variety theater), its "privileging of the sound of the spoken voice" (borrowed from radio), and its "preference for 'individualities'" (borrowed from film). Moreover, TV's candor about "contrivance and stripped-down composition" (which, he believes, is reminiscent of puppet theater) "works positively to comedy's advantage. Rather than making efforts to camouflage the signs of constructedness, comedy is so often disposed to declare its own artifice, relieving viewers from an absorption in fiction to following the workings of comic operation as such."[11] Ultimately, Clayton sees the various "conditions" of television—including its hybridized heritage as the bastard offspring of film, radio, and theater—as "opportunities" to rethink how comedy functions not only as a paradoxically circumscribed (or rule-bound) yet liberatory form, but also as a very truthful reflection of the lies we persist in telling ourselves.

It does not take a genre theorist to know that, even in its subtlest forms, comedy has a knack for overplaying tropes and exaggerating stereotypes for humorous effect. This means that the social imaginaries under consideration in this book, which might otherwise be veiled behind an aesthetic of representational "realness" or verisimilitude in a drama (making them harder to pinpoint), are laid bare in all their grotesqueness or obviousness when filtered through a comedic lens. However, I maintain that *hypervisibility*, if not exactly the metatextual transparency to which Clayton alludes, can render a particular onscreen representation or ideological orientation *invisible*, such that the comic drunk—a morally circumscribed fixture of US television since the late 1940s—has gone relatively unnoticed in critical accounts of what Clayton refers to as the genre's "laminate tendencies." As he explains, part of comedy's appeal lies in its "obsessive attention to the surface of social life, with its varied forms of more or less harmless pretense."[12] It is precisely *because* it presents us with a seemingly superficial gloss on human foibles and the societal limitations placed on individuals who simply yearn to be free—free to do "bad" or harmful things—that comedy TV deserves an in-depth consideration for its role in solidifying social imaginaries, or particular ways of "seeing" and thereby "knowing" others from a safe distance.

Having Fun, Throwing Up: Two Ways of Seeing the Comic Drunk

> To alcohol! The cause of—and solution to—all of life's problems!
> —Homer Simpson (voiced by Dan Castellaneta)
> in a Season Eight episode of *The Simpsons* (Fox,
> 1989–present)

In order to understand the alcoholic imaginary as a kind of binocular "way of seeing," it is necessary to sketch in the actual look of the disheveled dipsomaniac—the bumbling, stumbling figure of combined sympathy and ridicule whose distinctive physical tics likely spring to the mind's eye as a result of our periodic exposure to such performances. As I will explain a bit later, the culturally engrained mannerisms performed by Red Skelton, Foster Brooks, Larry Storch, and other TV comedians during the 1950s and 1960s would be "quoted" or rehashed through-out the decades that followed, in everything from African American series of the 1970s such as *Good Times* (CBS, 1974–79) and *The Richard Pryor Show* (NBC, 1977) to the earliest seasons of *The Simpsons* in the 1990s to more recent sketch comedies such as *Tim and Eric Awesome Show, Great Job!* (Adult Swim, 2007–10). To watch the Oscar-nominated actor John C. Reilly slurping down a glass of Sweet Berry Wine, slurring his words through red-stained lips as the dopey food expert Dr. Steve Brule in an episode of the latter program, is to witness only the latest in a long string of physically adept jokesters playing on audiences' famil-iarity with conventions that predate the television medium. Indeed, one would have to go back much earlier than *I Love Lucy* (CBS, 1951–57) and *The Honey-mooners* (CBS, 1955–56)—two of the first sitcoms to feature scenes of inebriated clowning—to locate the sources of more recent iterations of comic drunkenness in popular culture.

What sets a contemporary program like *Tim and Eric Awesome Show, Great Job!* apart from its classic predecessors of the postwar era is its fixation on what Jeffrey Sconce refers to as "bathroom humor" (or its reliance on "fart, shit, piss, cum, menstruation, snot, and vomit jokes, frequently made in conjunction with the various 'naughty' body parts that produce these substances").[13] Though Jackie Gleason, Jack Tyler, Frank Fontaine, and other comedians had performed drunk routines on TV as early as the late 1940s (in variety programs such as *The Arrow Show* [NBC, 1948–49], *For Your Pleasure* [NBC, 1948–49], and *The Lambs Gam-bol* [NBC, 1949]), at no point would they have been allowed to descend to the depths of vomitous squalor on view in more recent shows, including those that regurgitate comic traditions dating back to ancient Greek comedy (literally nause-ating ballads and plays such as Ameipsias's *Cottabus Players* [420s BCE] and Aris-tophanes's *The Frogs* [405 BCE] that demonstrate a "wide tolerance for jokes about excretion, belching, vomiting, and other indelicacies").[14] Indeed, one of the most deeply engrained images that we have of the comic drunk, and which cultural producers have milked for its schadenfreude-like humor over the past twenty years, is that of a person cradling a toilet bowl or hunched over a wastebasket, coughing up the contents of his or her stomach and putting a different spin on the notion of comedy's narrative "messiness." As seen in everything from FX's outrageously vulgar *It's Always Sunny in Philadelphia* (2005–present), in which Dee (Kaitlin Olson) dry-heaves on multiple occasions and finally vomits inside an airplane's water closet (owing to her combined drunkenness and nervousness leading up to a standup comedy performance), to the same network's animated series *Archer* (2009–16), in which the title character (voiced by H. Jon Benjamin) lives up to his own mother's description of him as a "vain, selfish, lying and quite possibly

1.1. An increasingly common occurrence in contemporary animated and live-action TV comedies is the act of throwing up into a toilet, often after a drunken night of debauchery. This occurs so frequently in the cult TV show *Archer* that it has become a running gag over its twelve seasons. © Floyd County Productions

alcoholic man-whore" on multiple occasions (including those showing him barfing into toilets and trash cans, even as a child), retching excess is a core element in a social imaginary that, ironically, promotes *restraint*, or a refraining from the very indulgences that we are meant to laugh at.

Of course, anyone who has ever found himself or herself "praying to the porcelain gods" while nursing a hangover might find little to laugh at when confronted with such stomach-churning scenes. However, as Noël Carroll emphasizes in his theoretical assessment of humor, laughter is "expulsive," a vomitous way to "cognitively cleanse" ourselves by casting out toxic or disgusting things that we share in common with other people, but which (until recently) were generally not depicted in popular culture.[15] Now that the sight of people throwing up is practically ubiquitous on American television, the shock value of such moments has faded and we are left to ponder their deeper meaning within humorous scenarios or embarrassing situations that treat public drunkenness as both a laughing matter and a way to expose an otherwise hidden side of characters' private lives. For their part, several TV critics have already noted this trend, this preponderance of puke on the small screen, which the *New York Times* contributor Neil Genzlinger calls a "cliché."[16] Bemoaning the fact that "vomit is all over television these days, graphic and gooey" and disrespectful of the viewer's imagination, Genzlinger longs for the comparatively tasteful way that inebriation and its offscreen splashy aftermath were handled before the turn of the twenty-first century; prior to the industry-wide decision to depict, in meticulous detail, something resembling oatmeal or beef stew streaming out of a person's mouth.[17]

In her own exploration of the subject (which she christens "Peak Puke TV"), *Vulture* contributor Jen Chaney summarizes Genzlinger's and other critics' complaint that "throwing up is not particularly illuminating and, in comedies, tends to be more juvenile than funny," but she also acknowledges that "vomit speaks to a common denominator in so much of TV right now . . . which is: a commitment to showing humans in all their ragged, jarring reality."[18] Her examples include *Girls* (HBO, 2012–17), *Review* (Comedy Central, 2014–17), *Love* (Netflix, 2016–18), *Baskets* (FX, 2016–present), *Santa Clarita Diet* (Netflix, 2017–19), and other "no-holds-barred" cable and online series that, to varying degrees, hinge on the dilemmas of "self-loathing, neurotic, or conflicted people" whose loss of control over their lives is physically externalized after they become panicked, witness something shocking, or simply imbibe too much alcohol. But another, more basic reason "why writers and directors keep going back to [that] nasty well" is because, in the words of Tim Heidecker (the co-creator and co-star of *Tim and Eric Awesome Show, Great Job!*, reminding us once again of comedy's lowly origins), "pee and poop and farts and vomit—those are the essentials, *the first jokes*."[19]

Immoderation has long been part of the alcoholic imaginary, or the cultural construction of public drunkenness as a performance predicated on rule-breaking and the violation of social etiquette. In this it shares much in common with comedy, one of the primary appeals of which is "the unconscious desire to break society's rules" (as Erich Segal, channeling the spirits of Plato and Freud, points out).[20] In his book *The Death of Comedy*, Segal makes passing remarks about *aischrologia*, or "gross humor involving such primitive bodily functions as defecating and vomiting," which he refers to as "favorite Greek topics."[21] If, as he states, the chamber pot was so omnipresent in Old Comedy that it was "almost a stock character," then the toilet bowl occupies a similarly central position in contemporary TV comedy (going back to "One for the Road" (2.14), a "Very Special Episode" of *Roseanne* [ABC, 1988–97] that shows fourteen-year-old Becky [Alicia Goranson]—feeling the effects of drinking "torpedoes" the previous night—in the now-familiar position on the bathroom floor). Of course, the road from *kōmos* to commode is not a direct line, but rather a set of forking paths snaking past moral watchdogs for whom the "smelly and ugly" act of barfing is not only a "social nonstarter" but also an inappropriate subject for artistic works that should be figuratively fragrant and pleasing to the eye. But, as Rupert D. V. Glasgow states in his book *Madness, Masks, and Laughter*, vomit, which is often linked with the theme of inebriation, "possesses a comic potential analogous to that of the turd . . . It is as if our antisocial bodily innards are explosively heaving their way past the cosmetic social mask that normally keeps such nastiness concealed."[22] And this, I feel compelled to emphasize, can *only* be a good thing, or at the very least a productive way to unveil a social imaginary that otherwise tends to hide behind its most wretched and retching stock character.

Besides ancient Greek and Elizabethan comedies, a number of literary texts, stage plays, and operatic works of the Victorian era, including Washington Irving's 1819 short story "Rip Van Winkle," Douglas William Jerrold's 1828 theatrical drama *Fifteen Years of a Drunkard's Life*, and Gilbert and Sullivan's 1878 comic opera *H.M.S. Pinafore*, brought forth scenes of comic drunkenness well before TV writers landed on the subject, laying the foundation for twentieth-century cultural productions. This includes a number of motion pictures from the silent and early sound periods (1900s–1930s) that wedded temperance and tipsiness, giving physically skilled comedians the opportunity to break the conventions of public decorum and do "inappropriate" things on the silver screen, even as producers within the nascent film industry were being pressured by teetotalers to cut down on representations of alcoholic consumption both prior to and after Prohibition.

Though several lesser-known figures, such as Arthur Housman and Jack Norton, made careers in Hollywood playing boozers and binge-drinkers, the screen icon most closely associated with the comic drunk is Charlie Chaplin, the internationally recognized star of several silent shorts and feature-length talkies dealing with inebriation (e.g., *Mabel's Married Life* [1914], *Rounders* [1914], *His Favorite Pastime* [1914], *A Night Out* [1915], *One A.M.* [1916], *The Cure* [1916], *City Lights* [1931], etc.). As film historians have noted, Chaplin's training in British music halls provided him with a repertoire of vaudevillian "moves" (e.g., head-bobbing hiccups, tipsy sidesteps, wobbly-kneed teeters, etc.) that he would harness well into the twilight of his fifty-year career.[23] One of his last productions is the pathos-filled *Limelight* (1952), a semi-autobiographical work that he also wrote and directed in which he plays a washed-up stage comedian named Calvero, who overcomes his addiction long enough to help a suicidal woman named Terry (Clair Bloom) regain her footing as a dancer. Calvero's personal battle with the bottle is less a reflection of Chaplin's own life experiences than a look into the reasons for his hard-drinking father's demise a half-century earlier (at the age of thirty-eight, from cirrhosis of the liver).

Coincidentally, this film—Chaplin's final effort to revive his frequently intoxicated Tramp persona—was theatrically released the same year that the *Washington Post* published a controversial article titled "Alcoholism Can Be Cured." Written by Glen R. Shephard, M.D., this short piece enumerates several of the early, middle, and late symptoms of a disorder that was increasingly being defined as a disease, including physical signs such as nausea and fatigue as well as mental conditions such as depression and self-deception.[24] The alcoholic, Shepherd flatly states, is a "sick man—sick in body function as well as in personality," though the doctor's description of that "deficiency" in a person's character is limited to remarks about one's tendency to lie in order to maintain an illusion of soundness (in mind and body). Like other medical specialists at the time, Shepherd makes a distinction between alcoholics and heavy drinkers, stating that the latter can be said to have their compulsions under control; whereas, for the former, "one drink is always too many because it is never enough." Echoing the sentiments of a growing minority in his field, he concludes that, "without psychotherapy, such as AA offers, reflex or chemical conditioning against alcohol will not be permanently successful."[25] As we shall see (in Chapter Three), Shephard's article was one of several attempts to make Alcoholics Anonymous a central component of recovery during the postwar years. That is, AA was made out to be a valuable supplement to medical treatment (the latter, in his words, offers only a "stop-gap"), one that might furthermore dispel some of the myths being propagated in American popular culture and counterbalance the stereotype of the disorderly/unruly comic drunk with images of men and women gaining control of their lives (something that Chaplin's Calvero is only partially able to do in *Limelight*). Notably, that same year (1952) also brought forth one of the most hilarious scenes in television history, one in which another comic legend—Lucille Ball—loses her inhibitions under the influence of alcohol and practically falls over herself to the amusement of millions.

Like many other episodes of *I Love Lucy*, the meta-reflexive "Lucy Does a TV Commercial" (1.30) concerns the title character's attempt to scheme her way into a musical variety show that her husband—bandleader Ricky Ricardo (Desi Arnez)—is hosting. One of the products that will be advertised during his televised show is Vitameatavegamin, a concoction that promises to combat listlessness in those who consume it. Determined to be the "Vitameatavegamin Girl," Lucy—presenting herself as Lucille McGillicuddy "because Ricky, as usual, does not know what she is up to and has not sanctioned her application"—rehearses her lines repeatedly while doing a mock commercial in the studio, each time sipping a spoonful of the tonic, which is twenty-three percent alcohol.[26] She initially shudders at its medicine-like taste, but soon warms up to the drink, putting the spoon aside in order to ingest mouthfuls straight from the bottle. By the end of Lucy's failed audition, she is unable to say the name of the product, slurring the words "Veeda-vida-vigee-vat" between hiccups and simply encouraging the audience to "get a bottle of . . . this stuff." As the most fondly remembered moment of intoxication from the early

1.2. "Lucy Does a TV Commercial," from the first season of *I Love Lucy*, gave audiences one of the most indelible images of comedic drinking in the history of American television, one that shows the title character tossing back a bottle of tonic and getting progressively plastered while running lines for a TV commercial. © Desilu Productions

period of American network television, "Lucy Does a TV Commercial" (broadcast on CBS stations on May 5, 1952) showcases how thoroughly entertaining, rather than depressing, a person succumbing to insobriety could be.

As Rosie White explains, the episode "offers a reflexive commentary on television, consumer culture and femininity," the latter topic brought to light by the main character's inebriated descent into "'unfeminine' behavior."[27] Lucy departs, then, from *two* scripts: one being the actual set of words that she successfully memorizes but begins to drunkenly disarticulate with each sip of the powerful medication ("Do you pop out at parties? Are you unpoopular?"); the other referring to a *social* script that, during the 1950s, demarcated acceptable behavior for women (both inside and outside the domestic sphere) and, abetted by the advertising industry, encouraged housewives "to subsume their desires to those of their family."[28] Popular opinion held that alcohol might either release women's inhibitions "to the extent that they would violate approved sexual standards" or interfere with their "responsibilities of childcare and provision of family emotional support."[29] This morally tinged "disapproval of women's drunkenness," according to Barbara C. Leigh, reflects a double standard that essentially lets men off the hook for giving in to temptation (be it liquid or libidinal) while maintaining a strict "division of labor within a household" where wives are expected to put the needs of others before their own.

There is, of course, a *third* script: that of the episode itself, cowritten by producer/showrunner Jess Oppenheimer and frequent collaborators Madelyn Pugh and Bob Carroll Jr., who give star Lucille Ball numerous opportunities to show off her verbal dexterity and physical clowning skills during a scene in which her stardom-seeking redhead, now thoroughly sloshed, wanders into frame as Ricky is performing his first number. Significantly, she "disrupts the live television show, following him around the stage as he tries to escape and drowning out his singing with her raucous imitation."[30] All of this chaos and disorder, then, has been "carefully choreographed" for the cameras and is performed with unparalleled proficiency by a woman who was intimately familiar with alcohol's more pernicious effects. Having met her hard-drinking husband Desi Arnez on the set of RKO's *Too Many Girls* (1940) when they were both plastered, Ball would eventually divorce him twenty years later, after his own much-publicized addictions—to "booze and broads"—had interfered not only with their home life and private affairs but also with their professional endeavors as studio executives. With their 1960 divorce still eight years away when "Lucy Does a TV Commercial" originally aired, and with most audiences unaware of the couple's marital problems, there was little to interfere with the screenwriters' efforts to make temporary drunkenness seem funny.[31]

As a sign of its enduring appeal, this episode—and the queen of comedy's performance within it—would inspire several subsequent attempts to mine humor from a subject that continues to be a matter of public concern; as seen, for instance, in "The TV Commercial" (1.11) from *Good Times*, "Candy is Dandy" (6.05) from *Laverne & Shirley* (ABC, 1976–83), and "The Fifties Show" (8.06) from *Roseanne*. Also known as "That's Our Rosey," the latter episode—a forerunner to the more recent "We Love Lucy" (11.16) episode of *Will & Grace* (NBC, 1998–2006, 2017–20)—is significant as another instance of industrial reflexivity. In this black-and-white spoof of sitcom conventions, the cast of the working-class comedy appears to have been teleported to the Eisenhower era. It begins with Roseanne Barr's title character (who, decked out in an apron and pearls, is made to look like a 1950s suburban homemaker) serving her fedora-wearing husband—her Dan in the Grey Flannel Suit (John Goodman)—a double martini. Twenty minutes later it concludes with her getting "sloshed in a socially prescribed fashion," downing gulps of a prescription-bottle magic potion in a clear nod to "Lucy Does a TV Commercial."[32]

We should bear in mind that the "stuff" Lucille Ball's tipsy redhead promotes in the episode—the bottle of vitamin-laced alcohol that tastes "just like candy"—could not have appeared in an actual TV commercial at the time of its broadcast. Although American brewers faced no such advertising limitations in the 1950s (as evidenced by the fact that Budweiser became the first beer company to sponsor a network series, CBS's *The Ken Murray Show*, beginning in 1951), hard-liquor ads were prohibited. This occurred because the Distilled Spirits Institute (DSI), the main trade association of American distillers, had issued a self-regulatory advertising code. As Iain Gately mentions in *Drink: A Cultural History of Alcohol*, the DSI's "decision not to advertise on TV was subsequently confirmed by a ban from the National Association of Broadcasters."[33] Fearing that increased alcohol consumption among the nation's youth (impressionable juveniles presumably seduced by images of adults actually enjoying spirits) might antagonize temperance advocates and lead to a revival of Prohibition (a constitutional disaster by all accounts), US legislators likewise threw their support behind the trade association's efforts to police itself. Although, as Gately states, television "offered wonderful opportunities" for drink manufacturers "to place an image of their products in the front rooms of American households," for the most part these images found their way into *fictional* programming rather than in the commercial advertisements that were such an integral part of the medium's economic-industrial function.[34] Ultimately, the sight of Lucy Ricardo getting progressively plastered while sipping spoonfuls of "Vitameatavegamin" health tonic lends credence to a comment uttered by Chaplin's character in *Limelight*. In a key scene of the film, when Terry finds Calvero three sheets to the wind, he defends his behavior by arguing for alcohol's handiness to his profession and informing her that "a man's *true* character comes out when he's drunk. Me, I'm *funnier.*"

This idea that laughter flows more freely in the company of a drunk, whose presence alone ensures entertainment in the form of pratfalls, slurred speech, and other signs of one's loss of bodily control, has been part of comedy TV's alcoholic imaginary for decades, dating back to that widely adored episode of *I Love Lucy* and running through such 1960s and 1970s programs as *Bewitched* (ABC, 1964–72) and *The Dean Martin Show* (NBC, 1965–74), the latter a musical variety show that, according to Mary Ann Watson, "bolstered the notion of drunkenness as a lark." That show's tuxedoed star, a member of the colorful Rat Pack, projected the aura of "a relaxed crooner, always a little looped and often downright sloshed" (so much so that he frequently flubbed his lines), and both his offscreen and onscreen personas communicated the "unfortunate message . . . that liquor enhances life."[35] More recent productions, ranging from the intentionally "shocking" reality sketch comedy *The Tom Green Show* (The Comedy Network, 1994–99;

MTV, 1999–2000), which has the host downing rum & Coke and cradling a toilet bowl, to the more conventionally comforting sitcom *Friends* (NBC, 1994–2004), have generated episodes in which a character is believed to be amusing only when he is drunk. In fact, one of Monica (Courtney Cox)'s boyfriends during the first and second seasons of NBC's ratings hit is "Fun Bobby" (Vincent Ventresca), a young man whose nickname hints at his hard-partying past but which no longer fits once she helps him to sober up. Having become boring in the process of giving up drinking, the character is soon rechristened "Ridiculously Dull Bobby" by Chandler (Matthew Perry), who will eventually reveal himself to be a better (i.e., funnier, less alcohol-averse) romantic partner to Monica, years after she has tried and failed to reconnect her former beau Bobby to the pleasures and, yes, *fun* of drinking.

In the years since the January 4, 1996, airing of "The One With Russ" (2.10), which shows Monica ironically trying to steer Bobby back to the bottle after initially drying him out, episodes from other television series have brought forth dialogue affirming the deep-seated belief that alcohol functions as a social lubricant, improving one's chances of having a "good" time while increasing the likelihood of "bad," socially deviant and/or physically destructive behavior. "Drink me! I make life more fun," says the lovable lush Karen (Megan Mullally) to her former friend Val (Molly Shannon) in an episode of *Will & Grace*, holding up a martini glass and taunting the recovering alcoholic in the "voice" of the cocktail. "Everybody from a high school kid to a bum on the street knows *that*," Karen concludes, projecting an all-inclusive image of individuals (e.g., underage drinkers, homeless people, etc.) who might suffer harmful consequences as a result of consuming the stuff. Such dialogue gives us a clue to the inherently contradictory nature of a social imaginary that sees mirth and misery as two sides of the same coin. Audiences encounter a similarly Janus-faced presentation of alcohol as a life-enhancing yet potentially career-ending substance in the pilot episode of *Terriers* (FX, 2010), a comedy-drama in which one of the two main characters, Britt (Michael Raymond-James), a former prisoner-turned-private investigator, says to his partner Hank (Donal Logue), "I wish I knew you when you were drunk. I bet you were so much more fun then." As an ex-cop who lost his job as a result of letting the bottle get the best of him, Hank responds, "Yeah, fun like prison." Similar to the aforementioned *Will & Grace* episode ("One Gay at a Time" [7.03]), *Terriers* features scenes set in Alcoholics Anonymous meetings, where recovering addicts are able to perform their *sobriety* with the same regulated consistency and reliance on well-known tropes that comic drunks of yesteryear brought to their performances of *insobriety*. It is to the latter type of performance that I now turn before interrogating the comedic-cathartic function of AA in a later chapter.

"How to Imitate a Drunk": Performing Insobriety

> [I]t was important that we were clear that we weren't making fun of alcoholics. What the audience and the world didn't know was that I had a drinking problem of my own at the time.
>
> —comedian Sid Caesar, discussing the making of "A Drunk There Was" (a sketch from *Caesar's Hour* [NBC, 1954–57]), in his autobiography *Caesar's Hours: My Life in Comedy, With Love and Laughter*[36]

As alluded to earlier, some of the first televised representations of drunken behavior can be found in programs that originally aired during the early 1950s, a time when the annual per capita consumption of pure alcohol in the United States was two gallons (double what it had been during the post-Prohibition low set in 1934).[37] This was only a few years after the "Big Three" networks (CBS, NBC, and ABC) expanded their commercial operations beyond radio and initiated TV broadcasts in the mid-to-late 1940s. Many of the most popular series of that period, such as *The George Burns and Gracie Allen Show* (CBS, 1950–58) and *The Red Skelton Show* (NBC, 1951–53; CBS, 1953–70), were based on popular radio programs, but the added element of visual imagery brought these performers' background in vaudeville (where they had honed their talent for slapstick and sight gags) to the fore.[38] Red Skelton is a good case in point, for this former vaudevillian—someone trained in pantomime from an early age and capable of playing believable drunk routines on stage—was not able to fully flesh out his perpetually inebriated character Willie Lump-Lump until he transitioned from radio (*The Raleigh Cigarette Program* [1941–44]) to television (*The Red Skelton Show*). As an audiovisual medium, TV allowed the boisterous comedian to play up the vocal and bodily characteristics of dipsomania, as demonstrated in a famous monologue from the latter program titled "How to Imitate a Drunk." Brief though that sketch is, it highlights how a combination of visual signifiers—disheveled appearance, stupefied expression, halting gait—comprise the perennial image of drunkenness that, with only slight exaggeration, can generate laughter or derision.

Historical hindsight makes it possible to see how the performative eccentricities of Red Skelton's drunken impersonation fed into subsequent efforts to make dipsomania seem funny. For instance, Dick Van Dyke, a gifted entertainer on stage and screen whose penchant for comic pratfalls has earned him numerous accolades and honors throughout his career,[39] demonstrates a knack for alcoholic impressions in the 1960s sitcom that bears his name. Not insignificantly, the first episode of *The Dick Van Dyke Show* (CBS, 1961–66), which originally aired one year after a failed pilot episode (starring series creator Carl Reiner) introduced audiences to the fictional television comedy writer Rob Petrie, gives the actor an opportunity to demonstrate

1.3. Like Red Skelton before him, comedy legend Dick Van Dyke had a knack for imitating drunks that was sadly informed by personal experience (his own battle with the bottle). He shows off this talent in more than one episode of his eponymous series from the 1960s, using an arsenal of physical moves and verbal tics that had been developed by vaudeville comedians decades earlier. © Calvada Productions

his loose-limbed physicality in a skit about his wife Laura (Mary Tyler Moore)'s "Drunk Uncle," whom he imitates during a dinner party. Before launching into his performance, Rob sets up the premise for fellow workers and friends who have gathered at the home of Alan Brady (the character that Reiner played after handing over the show's principal role to Van Dyke). Rob explains that Uncle Henry always "becomes fearless" after having "one short beer" at his own annual office party. The alcohol, therefore, is said to make Henry "afraid of nothing, except maybe his wife," and Rob proceeds to play up the inebriated man's tipsy movements in front of a rapt, laughing audience. In fact, he veers wildly between two states—being drunk and appearing to be sober whenever his wife (played by Rose Marie's character Sally Rogers) suddenly drops in on him—in a manner that suggests that each state is a kind of "mask" that can be donned at will. This "yo-yo effect," swinging from one physically exaggerated display to its diametrical opposite, produces laughter by virtue of the incongruity of witnessing a potentially distressing, personally destructive form of antisocial behavior within a warm and welcoming social setting.

Van Dyke plays another comically intoxicated figure in the Season Two episode "My Husband is Not a Drunk" (2.06), and once again without the taint of showing his character consuming any actual alcohol. The episode, which first aired on October 31, 1962, begins inside Rob and Laura's house in New Rochelle, where four of their friends—Sally, her writing partner Buddy Sorrell (Morey Amsterdam), and next-door neighbors Jerry and Millie Helper (Jerry Paris and Ann Morgan Guilbert)—await the arrival of another guest. Sitting in the Petries' spacious living room, they chat about Rob's old Army pal, a professionally qualified hypnotist named Glen Jameson (Charles Aidman) whose imminent arrival makes them eager to witness a demonstration of his abilities. Eventually, after Glen enters their home and settles into after-dinner pleasantries, he puts each of them into a trance, one after the other; culminating with a posthypnotic suggestion to Buddy (who, though initially skeptical about this "hypnotism game," appears to be sleeping soundly on the sofa), that he will become a "roaring drunk" whenever he hears a bell ring. A second ringing sound, Glen tells his barely conscious subject, will restore him to a sober state. Throughout this portion of the scene, Rob, who had gone to the kitchen for a glass of water, has been listening to the sound of his friend's literally hypnotic voice and—as an innocent bystander—is himself put into a trance, mistaking the cup of clear liquid in his hand for gin. The spell is broken with a snap of Glen's fingers. But a sudden ringing of the telephone makes both Buddy (in the living room) and Rob (still in the kitchen) wobbly kneed, woozily leaning to-and-fro to the audible amusement of the in-studio audience. A second telephone ring brings them out of their drunken stupor, but Buddy, who had accurately predicted that he is "unhypnotizable," explains that he has just given a "magnificent performance" and has merely faked his tipsiness. This foregrounding of the performative aspects of televisual drunkenness, accentuated through the main character's unwitting enactment of the very thing that Buddy has only *pretended* to be (i.e., a comic drunk), is further magnified in a subsequent scene set inside Rob's place of work.[40]

In fact, being a TV comedy writer makes it possible for Rob to distance himself from the socially detrimental aspects of heavy drinking, even that which is only imagined and not actually performed through the ingestion of liquid intoxicants. We next see him in his office the following day, expecting a phone call from Mel Cooley (Richard Deacon), the producer of *The Alan Brady Show*, the fictional variety series for which Rob is the head writer. Notably, Rob needs to talk to Mel before a sponsors' conference that had been scheduled later in the afternoon, a reminder that advertisers' concerns weighed heavily on the creative decisions of network television personnel during the 1960s. Soon enough, the phone call comes through. The sound of the receiver makes Rob go rubbery again, drunkenly slurring his words over the line and struggling to put on his sports jacket at the same time. A few comic beats later, Mr. Boland (Roy Roberts), one of the sponsors' representatives, accompanies Mel into the office, where they find Rob, three sheets to the wind, talking into his coat as if it were a phone. Shocked by this display of on-the-job boozing, Boland harrumphs that "it's a little early in the morning for a man to be in that condition, isn't it?" But he soon interprets this showy display of inebriation as a "comedy routine" that Rob is working out. "That's very amusing," the ad man laughs, delighted to see such a practiced ham "playing drunk." At the metatextual level, this (mis)interpretation is correct, as Van Dyke (who first trotted out his comic drunk persona in the 1959 Broadway musical *The Girls Against the Boys*) had honed that routine for years, but worried that showing his character in *The Dick Van Dyke Show* in such a state might betray the "integrity" of someone who was "firmly established as an upstanding husband, father, and all-around pillar of the community."[41] Allowing Rob to "slip into a posthypnotic trance at the top of the show," as the cultural historian Vince Waldron states, was an ideal way for the sitcom's writers to put their "straitlaced star into a drunken stupor without having him touch so much as a drop of booze."[42]

In her monograph about *The Dick Van Dyke Show*, TV scholar Joanne Morreale discusses this episode, noting that creator-writer Carl Reiner was able to deflect any criticism that network censors or pressure groups might have leveled against his series by having the protagonist's inebriation be triggered *not* by liquor but by hypnosis.[43] As Morreale states, the ire of temperance advocates and other viewers who "might feel that inebriation was inappropriate on a family sitcom" could be quelled through this admittedly farfetched textual maneuver. Moreover, as Reiner himself has noted, "No one's sense of propriety was shaken because the 'sin' was taken out of it."[44] Reiner's use of the word "sin" brings to mind alcoholism's longstanding association with wickedness and corruptibility, the kind of attributes that religious leaders and other moral watchdogs have sought to address through the adoption of what Kenneth J. Meier refers to as "morality policies."[45] Such discourses, embedded in doctrinaire teachings and theological codes-of-conduct for those wishing to walk the "righteous" path toward spiritual salvation, rhetorically link drunk driving, drug abuse, and other sinful failings on the part of weak-willed individuals to more egregious actions (putting them on nearly equal footing with serious criminal offenses such as murder or manslaughter). The "disease or sin" dilemma that has long haunted the discursive framing of heavy drinking as "a failure of the will" and a sign of someone's "weak moral character,"[46] though rarely ever tackled in sitcoms of the 1950s and 1960s, was at the very least an unspoken part of the alcoholic imaginary being perpetuated through popular culture texts at that time. The title of *The Dick Van Dyke Show*'s first episode, "The Sick Boy and the Sitter," references the faltering health of Rob and Laura's young son Ritchie

(Larry Mathews), who, despite his sickness, is left behind with a babysitter while they attend a social gathering. But it also hints at the "illness model" of alcoholism that was gaining currency within the scientific community and beyond at the time of his program's broadcast. As Stephen P. Apthorp points out, that important shift can be partly attributed to the American Medical Association's efforts, beginning in 1956 (a full decade after the United Presbyterian Church had accepted the illness model), to spread information that intemperance was a *disease* best dealt with through psychiatric evaluation and therapeutic treatment.[47]

The Red Skelton Show and *The Dick Van Dyke Show* gave their main performers multiple opportunities for virtuosic "star turns," demonstrating in the process those actors' knack for putting on a drunken show without actually downing any drinks. Similarly, the CBS variety program *The Jackie Gleason Show* (1952–57), besides introducing audiences to the character of Ralph Kramden (who would eventually take center stage in the classic sitcom *The Honeymooners*), provided space for the title host to try out several of his comic roles, including Reginald Van Gleason III. This playboy millionaire, prone to pomposity and known to toss back the bottle at inopportune times (for example, just minutes before appearing in court on a drunk-and-disorderly charge), was actually introduced in *Cavalcade of Stars* (1950–52), the Dumont Television Network's forerunner to the aforementioned show featuring many of the same technical crew and on-camera talent in addition to the same live-broadcast sketch-comedy format. By the time that Gleason—both the character and the actor playing him—jumped to CBS in 1952, the viewing public had become familiar with the exploits of Reginald, an object of ridicule as well as a reflexive jab at the star's own larger-than-life persona, exaggerated though it was in the guise of a tuxedoed snob to whom both boozing and womanizing seemed to come naturally. It is telling that Van Gleason was the only character in the comedian's repertoire who shared his name, something that David Sterritt points out in his study of *The Honeymooners*.[48] Quoting Gleason's biographer William A. Henry III, Sterritt suggests that this much-loved character—one of TV's earliest representations of potentially self-destructive drunken behavior—provided postwar audiences with "a personally resonant truth about the horrors that boozing could visit on family life." Indeed, it was a topic that the star understood "as both sorrowing child and sodden parent,"[49] similar to the way in which Dick Van Dyke battled alcoholism during the 1960s and admits to having frequently shown up to work with "terrible hangovers."[50]

For all the underlying sadness that biographers and historians detect in the real-life circumstances surrounding Gleason, Van Dyke, and other Golden Age stars' off-screen bouts with alcoholism, laughter and happiness were the favored responses in terms of how spectators were to perceive those stars' onscreen drinking.

Taking their cue from the in-studio audience, viewers watching *The Honeymooners* at home likely chuckled when Ralph Kramden and Ed Norton (Art Carney) get plastered on a bottle of grape juice in the episode "Head of the House" (1.27). Mistaking the juice for wine, the two men toast their "emancipation," having recently declared to their wives Alice (Audrey Meadows) and Trixie (Joyce Randolph) that they are the "bosses" of their households. Hilarity results not only from Ralph and Ed's loose-limbed physical antics, but also from the gap that opens up between the women's (and audience's) superior knowledge of the beverage's actual ingredients and the obliviousness of their husbands, who get progressively smashed with each swig of the juice bottle's contents.[51]

Widely believed to be a "releaser of inhibitions," alcohol is shown to be merely a vehicle through which the men are able to *perform drunkenness*; that is, to convince themselves that alcohol's somewhat paradoxical effects—as a depressant of the central nervous system that can elevate a drinker's mood—are *biochemical* rather than *social* in nature.[52] Rather than actually *being* drunk, Ralph and Ed *act* drunk according to socially established protocols, in the process revealing the constructed nature of cultural representations more generally. Indeed, *The Honeymooners*' foregrounding of drinking behavior as a sociocultural phenomenon in this episode corresponds to Craig MacAndrew and Robert B. Edgerton's argument that "the way people comport themselves when they are drunk is determined not by alcohol's toxic assault upon the seat of moral judgment, conscience, or the like, but by what their society makes of and imparts to them concerning the state of drunkenness."[53] In this light, it is telling that Alice, gazing down at her passed-out husband, should remark to Trixie, "100-proof male ego," indicating a linkage between the strength of a stiff drink and the power of suggestion on men who exert questionable authority in the domestic sphere.

Good Times, Bad Times: Reframing and Reforming Comic Drunks

> Yes, alright, everything *bad* in my life happened because of my drinking. Also, everything *good* in my life.
> > —former Major League baseball announcer Jim Brockmire telling his friend Charles (Tyrel Jackson Williams) that people only like him when he is drunk and that "nobody would give a shit" about him if he were sober, in a Season Two episode of *Brockmire* (IFC, 2017–20)

Fans of *The Honeymooners*—myself included—are sometimes asked to reconcile their love of the show with their distaste for Ralph Kramden's belligerent attitude toward his wife. Time and again, we see him balling his hand into a fist and making (thankfully empty) threats of domestic violence during emotional out-bursts that are eventually soothed once he is shown the error of his ways and the two characters slide "into fits of uncontrollable laughter."[54] "One of these days, Alice, POW! Right in the kisser!" became the show's catchphrase, and Ralph's finger-pointing itch to send his wife "to the moon" has been seen as a reflection of the public insensitivity to the problem of spousal abuse that affected millions of US households at the time of its original airing.[55] Undoubtedly exacerbated by economic hardships and the conditions of living in a cramped, sparsely furnished apartment (one that seems more like a prison than a home), familial flare-ups serve as questionable comedy fodder, and the humor of seeing the 250-pound man of the house finally being put in his place by a much smaller woman is offset by the harsh reality that lies just below the surface of this scripted fiction. However, Ralph's bellicose exterior and penchant for petulance mask a fundamental lack, meaning that he is simply putting on a "show"—playing up the excesses of a fierce but ultimately failed patriarchy—as a way to compensate for his incompetence. In this way, the nonalcoholic drinking that he does in the tellingly titled episode cited above, which leads him to pretend to be something that he is *not*, offers a handy metaphor for thinking about his gendered performances more generally. Indeed, Ralph's blustery machismo in "Head of the House" and nearly every other episode of *The Honeymooners* is no less a performance than his drunk act, though both displays of bad behavior reveal something truthful about the institution of marriage as a kind of mask in its own right; an outward projection of domestic con-tentment behind which are barely disguised problems that might be aggravated by alcohol and other depressants/stimulants.

A decade after *The Honeymooners* ended its thirty-nine-episode run, the show's real-world context was unpacked by sociologist Mirra Komarovsky. In her 1964 study *Blue-Collar Marriage*, Komarovsky notes that the "economic fail-ure" experienced by working-class husbands during the postwar years magnified shortcomings and fed into their growing frustrations of not being able to provide for their families. As she states, "Not many men can handle these destructive emotions without further consequences, such as drinking, violence, irritability, increased sensitivity to criticism, and withdrawal."[56] As performed by Jackie Glea-son (a comedian who, to borrow the words of one critic, "threw together one of the greatest feats of television history while fully in the bag"), Ralph brings forth the contradictory elements of the alcoholic imaginary and, though he never hits Alice, embodies some fairly deplorable aspects of domestic abuse, which, according to Chris Murphy, was "beginning to feel a bit taboo" once the show was aired as reruns in the years following its original broadcast. As he states, during the 1960s and 1970s greater numbers of Americans "viewed male violence against a spouse or partner to be a *private*, not public matter,"[57] and certainly not something that should intrude into TV viewers' lives through situation comedies filmed in front of studio audiences. Nevertheless, as television comedy entered a period of what critics have referred to as "relevancy" (marked by producers' willingness to broach mature subject matter, including abortion, impotence, racism, and rape), fists were clenched and faces were slapped in domestic settings where men took out their anger on women (often after having one too many drinks).

A quarter-century after *The Honeymooners*' debut, a final-season episode of the Norman Lear–produced comedy *Good Times* (CBS, 1974–79) took up the issues of alcohol abuse and domestic abuse, showing how the two can sometimes become intertwined within contexts marked by substandard housing, unemployment, and other markers of economic precarity. Created by Eric Monte and Mike Evans, this sitcom set in a Chicago inner-city housing project focuses on the members of the Evans family—Florida (Esther Rolle), James (John Amos), J.J. (Jimmie Walker), Michael (Ralph Carter), and Thelma (Bern Nadette Stanis)—who have each seen their fair share of "trouble" in the form of criminal activity outside their South Side tenement building, financial hardships and lost jobs, death and illness, and other generally "depressing aspects of ghetto life."[58] Nevertheless, a positive vibe permeates the series, emanating from the frequently bickering but loving and supportive family members and directed toward the show's viewers, including the in-studio audience whose laughter is often as disarming as *Good Times*' provocative storylines, not to mention its characters' sarcastic punchlines. Near the end of this series' six-year run, its writers decided to show how low the recently introduced character Keith (Ben Powers)—a former college football star looking to sign a million-dollar NFL contract—has sunk in the weeks following his and Thelma's wedding. When his plan to play for the Chicago Bears falls through due to a knee injury, Keith gets a job as a taxi driver, but that too goes down the drain and he is forced to look elsewhere for employment opportunities. By the time audiences get to "The Evans' Dilemma" (6.23), the 24-year-old man, still desperate for a job, has turned to alcohol as way to get through each day, though he stashes his "joy juice" (a bottle of ninety-proof vodka) in the toilet in order to hide his predicament from his wife.

Eventually, Thelma and her brothers begin to sense that something is wrong with Keith, whose wild mood swings—from depression to elation—are brought to a head during a scene at the dinner table, where he shares a bottle of Scotch with his friend and fellow footballer Joe (Daryl Roach). Sipping the beverage, Keith invokes the spirits of past comic drunks, remarking, "As Jackie Gleason would say . . . 'Smooooooth,'" and then doing his best W.C. Fields impression for his

1.4. By the time this episode of *Good Times* aired near the end of the 1970s, the topic of alcohol addiction had been broached in several of that decade's most "relevant" situation comedies, from *The Mary Tyler Moore Show* to *Maude*. Here, though, it is grafted onto the issue of domestic violence, one of many social problems explored in this program (created by the African American writer-producers Eric Monte and Mike Evans). © Tandem Productions

unimpressed guest: "I only drink this in case of a snakebite. And I always carry a snake with me." Tellingly, the two actors that he mentions by name, noted for their proficiency in playing intoxicated versions of their larger-than-life personas, drew upon their actual experiences as the basis for fictionalized drunkenness, making Keith's inebriated performance—and Ben Powers's *performance of that performance*—doubly (or triply) significant. Like the star of *The Richard Pryor Show*, who (in a sketch aired two years earlier, in 1977) seemed to channel Red Skelton's "Willie Lump-Lump" character in the guise of the rambling, shambling tramp "Willy the Drunk," Keith and the actor who plays him can be thought of as a medium through which audiences of the day are brought into virtual contact with past performances. In being reframed from the vantage of an African American man during the 1970s, the comic drunks played by Fields, Gleason, and Skelton in the 1930s, 1940s, and 1950s are brought into clearer view as the cultural constructs they always were. Unlike those earlier tipplers, however, Keith loses control and takes out his anger on his wife, whose face he slaps in the lead-up to their eventual reconciliation.

As numerous researchers have pointed out, partner aggression can take different forms, from verbal insults to physical violence. The latter, of course, is much less likely to occur in situation comedies than the former; especially in shows like *Good Times* where so much of the humor derives from the spoken mockery between siblings and spouses. Though Keith's mounting frustration is sufficiently contextualized within the series, that slap still comes as a surprise, and the in-studio audience's own audible shock in that moment lets us know that we are right to be horrified at what he has done. Like Ralph Kramden before him, this man is no batterer, but the swiftness with which the couple's domestic spat descends into masculine aggression hints at the way that alcohol, especially hard liquor, was being reframed as a destructive force in 1970s and 1980s television programs.

While heavy or habitual drinking would have been "an unattractive source for sitcom humor" in the 1950s,[59] cropping up only occasionally in one-off dramas and live teleplays such as *Playhouse 90*'s October 2, 1958, presentation of J.P. Miller's *Days of Wine and Roses*, television increasingly accommodated such representations in the 1960s and 1970s, with examples ranging from "Granny" Daisy Moses (Irene Ryan), the moonshine-swilling matriarch in *The Beverly Hillbillies* (CBS, 1962–71), to Archie Bunker (Carroll O'Connor), the blue-collar beer drinker in *All in the Family* (CBS, 1971–79), and Fred Sanford (Redd Foxx), the Ripple-loving junk dealer in *Sanford and Son* (NBC, 1972–77). Pop culture commentator Scott Meslow, writing for the *Atlantic*, has argued that TV's "greatest early example" of the town drunk archetype (which can trace its literary roots back to Shakespeare's Falstaff and Mark Twain's Pap Finn) is Otis Campbell, the perpetually plastered character played by Hal Smith in *The Andy Griffith Show* (CBS, 1960–68).[60] It is not surprising that Meslow and other critics should reference Smith's loveable lush as the basis for subsequent representations, given how frequently Otis was deployed by that series' writers as a dependable laugh-getter, whose home-away-from-home became the jailhouse that Mayberry Sherriff Andy Taylor (Andy Griffith) policed with laid-back, yet paternalistically protective, authority. Deputy Barney Fife (Don Knotts), on the other hand, viewed the town drunk as a societal problem, something that needed to be taken off the streets and which might be remedied through applied "scientific" methods or, in the words of Richard Michael Kelly, "pseudo-psychological techniques."[61]

While jailhouse regular Otis became a running gag on *The Andy Griffith Show*, staggering into his jail cell in 32 of its 249 total episodes, another sitcom from that decade, *Car 54, Where are You?* (NBC, 1961–63), devotes only one of its episodes to this subject. And yet, "Here Comes Charlie" (2.23), from the show's second season, went even further than its small-town predecessor in suggesting that drunks can be public nuisances in need of institutional assistance if they are to enjoy socially productive and self-sufficient lives. Unlike creator Sheldon Leonard's program, which is set in a rural North Carolina community (home to moonshiners and few other criminals besides out-of-towners simply passing through), Nat Hiken's series concerns a dedicated yet bumbling team of big-city cops—specifically, officers at the fictional 53rd precinct in the Bronx—who deal with lawbreakers of every stripe, including a repeat offender affectionately known as "Charlie the Drunk." Played by guest star Larry Storch,[62] Charlie has become something of a mascot at the police station, a fact that Captain Block (Paul Reed) bemoans in this episode's opening scene. Although he recently "disturbed the peace" by tearing up a bar and grill, according to the precinct chief, Charlie has yet to be booked. Instead, he arrives at the station each night as if looking for room and board. Indeed, similar to Mayberry's Otis, he is allowed to sleep off his hangover in an empty cell before resuming his life as a lay-about bum the following day. "He's got the greatest job in the world," Block sarcastically tells his men, declaring that he is done giving Charlie any more chances. Officers Toody (Joe E. Ross) and Muldoon (Fred Gwynne) implore their captain to let them try a kind of social experiment, which they hope will ultimately reform (or, in their words, "straighten out") the alcoholic and reduce future costs of prison upkeep. Their philanthropic gesture is eventually deemed a success, but only after several attempts to help Charlie land a job that will distract him from his nagging thirst.

First, Toody and Muldoon take him to a local bakery, but he ends up drinking all the distilled beverages set aside for rum cakes and is brought back to the precinct. Next, they get him a job as a mechanic's assistant at a garage, but he gets "tanked-up" while refilling the antifreeze in a car and has to be taken back to the station once again. The officers persist in their efforts to get him back on his feet, eventually escorting him to a diamond cutting lab, where steady hands and a laser-focused vision are essential. Surely here, Toody and Muldoon surmise, he will have to stay sober, or at least will aspire toward a mental and physical state to which the many signs on the office walls (which read: "Beware the Demon Rum," "Drink is the Road to Ruin," and "Whiskey and Work Don't Mix") serve as inspirational reminders. Tellingly, Charlie's new boss at the diamond cutters verbally links his company's business ethics and hiring practices to the kind of sanctified rectitude being sought in potential employees, informing Toody and Muldoon, "What we're looking for is a young man with strong moral fiber. Bright, alert, with steadiness of hand and brightness of eye, who's never been dissipated by liquor." As in other episodes of *Car 54, Where Are You?*, a comical inversion occurs near the

1.5. Rubber-faced actor Larry Storch, who plays the titular neighborhood drunk in "Here Comes Charlie" (an episode from the second
season of *Car 54, Where Are You?*) makes himself "inebriated" simply
by describing his recent barroom experiences. Adopting excessive facial
tics and bodily gesticulations, the performer illustrates the often-exag-
gerated manner in which alcoholics were portrayed in U.S. television
programs during the 1950s and 1960s. © Eupolis Productions

conclusion of "Here Comes Charlie," one that ironically redirects the employer's
comment concerning the questionable morality of alcoholics back toward himself
and the other members of his team—nerve-jangled men and women who grow so
jumpy at the sight of law enforcement figures (who keep checking in on Charlie)
that they take to the bottle themselves. These teetotalers are presented as hyp-
ocrites, susceptible to the same temptations or "sins" that Charlie is not able to
fully shake. As might be expected (owing to the cyclical structure of most sitcoms,
which return to a state of equilibrium by episode's end), Charlie reverts back to
an inebriated condition and finds himself, once again, inside his own comfortably
furnished cell at the police station.

It is worth mentioning that Larry Storch's performance as the neighborhood
drunk draws upon the exaggerated mannerisms that Red Skelton and Dick Van
Dyke displayed in their earlier onscreen enactments of dipsomania—meticulously
controlled distillations of, ironically, an uncontrolled state. His Charlie, like their
characters, manifests some of the stereotypes associated with alcoholism through
bodily display, and without recourse to actually imbibing any drinks onscreen. As

one of the officers at the 53rd precinct says, Charlie's "system is so full of booze just the smell of the stuff gets him started." In fact, as another patrolman informs Captain Block, "All he has to do is think about it [liquor]" to exhibit some of those physical characteristics. And, indeed, this episode's most significant scene shows Charlie incrementally disintegrating "from stone-cold sobriety to reeling, cross-eyed inebriation just by reminiscing about the gin mills he used to frequent."[63]

Besides the aforementioned comic actors, another fixture of primetime programming came to embody both sides—the "good" and the "bad"—of the alcoholic imaginary throughout the 1960s and 1970s, becoming so synonymous with onscreen drunkenness that he would continue serving as the "model" for immoderation in the decades that ensued. However, partially because he was associated with a once-acceptable but no-longer-kosher mode of politically incorrect humor, this aging figure fell out of fashion with contemporary audiences of the 1980s and beyond, a trajectory that parallels society's shifting attitudes toward alcohol consumption more generally (summed up by one TV critic's statement that "drunks just seem like alcoholics now").[64] Foster Brooks, an occasional guest on *The Dean Martin Show*, turned his Las Vegas nightclub act into comedy gold on the small screen, frequently outshining that variety program's host (himself an icon of pretend inebriation) as second banana. While Martin, like his forerunner Joe E. Lewis, specialized in a more suave and subdued type of tipsiness (one in which his playboy image was completed by an ever-present cocktail in hand), Brooks tended to ham it up, adopting halting, hiccupping, indigestion-filled speech patterns that were the locutionary equivalent of his lurching physical movements.

To quote one critic's description of the silver-bearded comedian, Brooks "managed to interlace his rumbling baritone with various micro-belches, sideways mispronunciations, and nano-repetitions, resulting in a polyphonic symphony of besottedness."[65] By the time he began popping up in episodes of *The Dean Martin Celebrity Roast* (NBC, 1974–84), gently ribbing fellow comedians Lucille Ball, Jackie Gleason, Bob Hope, Don Rickles, and Redd Foxx at the New York Friars' Club, Brooks had perfected his craft and become a highly sought-after character actor in the process. He played lovable lushes in everything from the Western adventure series *The High Chaparral* (NBC, 1967–71) to the urban crime drama *Starsky & Hutch* (ABC, 1975–79). But he was most at home in absurdist sitcoms, whether sidling up alongside a pig at an airport bar and drunkenly mistaking the animal for a pilot in *Green Acres* (CBS, 1965–71) or trying to oversee a rabbit-breeders convention while getting progressively plastered in *The Monkees* (NBC, 1966–68).

The character that this former disc jockey and radio newscaster played most often, however, was *himself*; or, rather, a bobble-headed version of his offscreen

1.6. The oversized glass of spirits in this shot's foreground hints at the excessiveness of comic legend Foster Brooks's appetite for strong drink, something that he demonstrated more than once as a special guest on *The Dean Martin Show*. © Claude Productions and Greg Garrison Productions

persona in dozens of variety programs, late-night talk shows, and celebrity game shows (e.g., *The New Bill Cosby Show* [NBC, 1972–73], *Dinah!* [1974–81], *The Bobby Vinton Show* [CTV, 1975–78], etc.). Appearing onscreen as "Foster Brooks," he consistently blurred the line between representation and reality, forcing audiences to sort out how much of his act was pure fiction and how much was based on the facts of his earlier battles with the bottle.[66] Whenever he was asked about the correlation between the two, Brooks admitted to interviewers that he "used to drink . . . anything and everything," but that he "wasn't an alcoholic."[67] "I was a weekend drunk. Never drew a sober breath from Friday night to Monday," he told Cecil Smith, before going on to explain that he quit the habit eight years prior to their 1972 interview.[68] Nevertheless, Brooks was so adept at playing "the guy who knows he's drunk but is trying not to let anybody else know it" that, in the words of Martin Kich, "it was almost impossible to tell when [he] may have actually been at least somewhat inebriated while performing."[69] For example, near the end of his drunken monologue at the October 31, 1974, celebrity roast of Bob Hope, Brooks turns to his friend Dean Martin (seated to his right) and whispers "I think I'm going to throw up"—a seemingly off-the-cuff comment that hints at the deleterious effects of immoderation and intensifies the spectatorial confusion that might arise whenever someone is *too believable* in their embodiment of clichés.

According to one contemporaneous TV reviewer, Brooks also blurred the line between comedy and tragedy. As someone who, "in his tattered dignity, has the elements of the bum trying to maintain elegance," he was able to combine "high" and "low" while gesturing toward "the human costs of alcoholism."[70] Eventually, the latter would begin to crowd out the humorous effects of dipsomania in onscreen representations from the 1980s going forward, when "some subjects that were once staples of both standup routines and situation comedies [went] out of fashion."[71] Representational changes thus followed attitudinal shifts and legislative efforts to help those who had fallen off the wagon, beginning with the US Congress's passing of the Comprehensive Alcohol Abuse and Alcoholism Prevention Treatment and Rehabilitation Act of 1970 (amended in 1979, when "the era of the comic drunk began to draw to a close" and "making fun of an illness was society's red line," according to Wayne Curtis).[72] Reflecting that change in attitude, in 1986 Alan Wurtzel (then–vice president of broadcast standards at ABC) declared that "drunkenness is not considered amusing anymore."[73] Four years later, Brooks—still remembered by younger comedians for playing drunks better than "real drunks" could—was being referenced by commentators as a point of contrast; to remind readers how he and other standup comics from the 1950s, 1960s, and 1970s "would have to look elsewhere (beyond the bottle) for laughs" now that jokes about heavy drinking were no longer funny. "Woe be unto the comedian who thinks people still laugh with that lovable drunk," states Doug Grow, whose 1990 article "Drunks Who Once Got Laughs Get Convictions" echoes the sentiments of several critics claiming that the "friendly drunk" (whom everyone liked decades ago) is "a thing of the past."[74]

Laughter and Tears (and *Cheers*)

> It is simplistic to expect, or even to desire, the eradication of alcohol from TV stories; these stories are no place for textbooks on alcohol education.
>
> —Warren Breed and James R. De Foe, "Drinking and Smoking on Television, 1950–1982," *Journal of Public Health Policy*, Vol. 5, No. 2 (June 1984): 269.

In their application of quantitative techniques and social-learning/modeling theories to the parallel histories of drinking and smoking on American TV, Warren Breed and James R. De Foe enumerate some of the reasons why the former pastime—on view in dramas and situation comedies in which characters not only ingested from but also held glasses, cups, cans or bottles with alcoholic contents—occurred more frequently than the latter activity over a period of roughly three decades.[75] Between 1950 and 1982, the frequency of cigarette consumption decreased considerably compared to that of alcohol consumption, especially after the first Surgeon General's report of January 1964 fed into an anti-smoking campaign that, though launched a decade earlier (by the American Cancer Society and the American Lung Association), would not achieve its first major victory until January 1971 (when congressional leaders imposed a ban on cigarette commercials).[76] During that period, as the cultural climate surrounding nicotine—an addictive, unhealthy chemical—shifted away from earlier representations of cigarettes as a symbol of glamour or cool sophistication, the "rates of actual ingestion of alcohol beverages moved generally upward." Accordingly, onscreen portrayals of that activity increased as well, becoming a "growing phenomenon in TV primetime shows" where "some form of alcohol was present . . . in from 6 to 16 percent of all scenes."[77] In her own study of that phenomenon, Mary Ann Watson says much the same, noting that the "pervasive presence of alcohol" in 1960s programs "did not wane as the 1970s began."[78] Indeed, as suggested in my brief discussion of Foster Brooks's career (and as I will flesh out in the next chapter, partially devoted to the military comedy M*A*S*H [CBS, 1972–83]), "jokes about heavy drinking remained a staple of television entertainment" until the early 1980s (when the number of onscreen depictions of alcohol consumption dropped off significantly).

As for the reasons for that increase, Breed and De Foe single out some of the unique "properties" of alcohol that might lend "appeal" to a scripted TV series, including: "creating tension in the story; changing a character from benign to threatening; aiding the plot when believable complications arise as a character becomes intoxicated; revealing hidden truths about a character; and permitting a drinker to go 'out of character,' often resulting in humorous behavior."[79] The last of these creative opportunities is especially important to comedy's reliance on incongruity and the foiling of audiences' expectations as dependable means of generating laughter. Although the Hollywood-based Caucus of Producers, Writers and Directors advised industry personnel to avoid glamorizing alcohol consumption and showing gratuitous amounts of inebriation "without consequences," a number of the patterns established as early as the 1940s and 1950s (and even earlier, if one goes beyond the television medium) remained in place as Brooks and other performers staggered into frame during the 1960s and 1970s. In the years that followed, however, audiences were more likely to share the feeling "that those who drink must be held accountable for their actions," and thus tended to cast a generally disapproving gaze upon characters who might have turned to alcohol as a way to "escape the constraints and responsibilities of adult life."[80]

Running parallel to the cultural infantilization of drunks was the tendency in 1980s and 1990s sitcoms to show teenagers and adolescents being tempted by alcohol, which—initially perceived of as an enticing way to quickly "grow up" and get a literal taste of illicit danger—inevitably brings physical pain, emotional suffering, and/or parental reproach in the form of scolding and grounding. Melodramatic depictions of the sometimes fatal consequences of underage drinking are on view in "Very Special Episodes" such as "Cheers to Arnold" (7.19), from the seventh season of Diff'rent Strokes (NBC, 1978–85; ABC, 1985–86), "Life of the Party" (2.18), from the second season of Family Matters (ABC, 1989–98), "Intervention" (2.07), from the second season of Blossom (NBC, 1990–95), and "Under the Influence" (8.10), from the eighth season of Full House (ABC, 1987–95). Though that industrial trend in television programming was most pronounced during the 1980s and 1990s, when problems like alcohol addiction and drunk driving were treated by those programs' writers as isolated events in the lives of teens (rather than as systemic issues plaguing society), the idea that inebriation brings out the worst in people has continued to suffuse TV shows ever since. For instance, in "Mixology Certification" (2.10), an episode of the ensemble comedy Community (NBC, 2009–14; Yahoo! Screen, 2015), Troy (Donald Glover) looks forward to celebrating his 21st birthday by joining his older college study buddies at a bar, where he plans to legally order a highball cocktail for the first time in his life. However, upon seeing his friends succumb to the "dark side" of drunkenness (which turns them into angry or depressed versions of their normally upbeat selves), Troy leaves the establishment completely sober and utterly disillusioned. Stepping into the role of designated driver and seeing for the first time that adults are just as clueless and prone to juvenile behavior as kids are, he concludes that "alcohol makes people sad"—a sentiment that neatly sums up the general attitude toward libations on the small screen since the 1980s.

Significantly, the sitcom from that decade that most consistently put alcohol front and center was one that also signaled a retreat from—if not a complete abandonment of—the comic drunk archetype that has been an indelible part of the genre since its earliest days. Created by Glen and Les Charles and James Burrows, and recently declared by Alan Sepinwall and Matt Zoller Seitz as the greatest live-action TV comedy of all time,[81] Cheers (NBC, 1982–93) has received its fair share of commentary over the years, and thus will not be discussed at length here. However, it bears mentioning that its eleven-season run coincides not only with the roughly decade-long heyday of the "Very Special Episode" as a staple of the TV industry, but also with the concerted efforts of government officials and nonprofit organizations such as Mothers Against Drunk Driving (MADD) to regulate the marketing of liquor, set a national standard for the minimum legal drinking age, educate the public about the dangers of underage drinking, and create a new temperance movement in the process. Tellingly, the pilot episode of this critically lauded series, which debuted on September 30, 1982, begins with a scene in which the main character—former Boston Red Sox relief pitcher-turned-bartender Sam Malone (Ted Danson)—is forced to turn away a boy who has walked into the bar in pursuit of a beer.

The opening exchange between the protagonist—a recovering alcoholic whose big-league career ended because of his heavy drinking—and a teenager trying to fake his age "sets the tone for the show" as a whole, in terms of highlighting how an increasingly touchy subject would be handled in the ensuing episodes. As Joseph J. Darowski and Kate Darowski argue in their cultural history of *Cheers*, Sam's first spoken line ("How 'bout an ID?") indicates that the show's producers and writers would not take "the implications of serving alcohol" lightly.[82] Nor would Burrows and the Charles brothers forget that it was the *people* who patronize the bar, rather than the *bar* itself, that makes *Cheers* such an ideal place in which to hang out; a virtual community where audiences are made to feel welcome each week and where—to quote the show's theme-song—"everybody knows your name."[83]

Nevertheless, as the series entered its final seasons (in the early 1990s), the moral panic surrounding young people's exposure to alcohol (in the form of television programming and advertisements) was beginning to die down a bit, and its producers and writers stepped up their efforts to reclaim the humorous side of intoxication through storylines that made light of characters' inebriated condition. Though episodes from earlier seasons, including "Endless Slumper" (1.10) and "Rebound, Part 1" (3.01), had revealed the extent to which Sam's alcoholic past had gotten the best of him (and even showed him relapsing following a breakup with Diane [Shelley Long] and then seeking help from psychiatrist Frasier Crane [Kelsey Grammer]), a few installments toward the end of *Cheers*' run gave him and the audience front-row seats in the spectacle of his friends' booze-loosening shenanigans. For example, Season Eleven's "The King of Beers" (11.03) revolves around barfly Norm Peterson (George Wendt)'s new dream job as a taste-tester at a Boston brewery, earning money for work that he would gladly do for free. Ultimately, he is not hired after the probationary trial period ends (since he does poorly during his interview with the brewing company's president) and thereafter resigns himself to the life of an unemployed "loser." Norm ends the series just as he began it: content to keep running up his tab as a heavy drinker whose name—shouted by other patrons whenever he enters the bar—is a running gag. Notably, it is the bar's manager Rebecca Howe (Kirstie Alley) who calls Norm a "loser," after having recently declared (in the episode "The Little Match Girl" [11.01]) that she would no longer be a victim to her own addiction: nicotine. The fact that *Cheers* steered toward the topic of cigarette smoking during its final season and showed Rebecca committing herself to being, in her words, a "better person" by abstaining from the habit is significant, for it suggests a return to older concerns about other addictive substances and a willingness to let comic scenes of drunkenness come to the fore after years of abstaining from that subject.

Later that same season, "It's Lonely on the Top" (11.22) shows Norm and other fixtures at Cheers (including Cliff Clavin [John Ratzenberger] and Frasier Crane) coping with hangovers and coming to terms with their newly inked tattoos after a night of drunken revelry. Besides anticipating a slew of sitcoms that similarly featured "Very Drunken Episodes" about hangovers, from *The Nanny* (CBS, 1993–99) to *Just Shoot Me!* (NBC, 1997–2003), this lead-up to the series finale generates laughter from the sight of the supporting characters readying themselves for the taste of hard liquor, specifically the nearly lethal concoction poured into a blender by feisty barmaid Carla (Rhea Perlman), who becomes so drunk herself that she ends up sleeping with someone whose face and name she cannot remember the next morning. Moreover, "It's Lonely on the Top" paved the way for *Cheers'* final episode "One for the Road" (11.26); or, rather, the live *Tonight Show with Jay Leno* interview that aired immediately after that hour-and-a-half-long broadcast on May 20, 1993.

Retroactively referred to by the host of the *Tonight Show* as a "mistake," that interview (conducted at Boston's Bull and Finch pub the night *Cheers* went off the air) is notorious for showing the cast members behaving as people typically do in an actual bar: drinking alcohol and letting loose to such an excessive degree that Leno found it difficult to "hold things together."[84] Apparently, the actors had arrived hours prior to the telecast and had become more than a little tipsy by the time Leno sat down for the chat, leading the editors of *Entertainment Weekly* to wonder "who had the biggest hangover the next day" while admitting that they "sure looked like they were having a good time."[85] The cast members' boisterous farewell party, attended by several famous Beantown celebrities and politicians (including standup comedian Steven Wright, Celtic hall-of-famer Kevin McHale, third baseman Wade Boggs, sportscaster Bob Costas, and Senator John Kerry) and televised for nearly all the world to see, is like the cork in a bottle of champagne that finally pops. It provides a cathartic, chaotic release for those of us who might have found earlier seasons of *Cheers* somewhat lacking or disingenuous in terms of suppressing the drunken antics of its characters for the sake of placating temperance groups.

To the 84.4 million viewers who tuned in to watch the finale (the second most-watched ending in TV history, behind that of *M*A*S*H*) and who stuck around for that live fiasco in which "people were . . . vomiting" off camera (according to Leno), *Cheers'* contradictory status as a comedy torn not only between laughter and tears but also between rule-abiding and rule-breaking was foregrounded. Beginning with a shot of the late-night host warning audiences that "you must be 21" in order to enter the dark, cellar-like Bull and Finch, and sprinkled with raunchy sex jokes and four-letter words (prefaced by cast member George Wendt warning Leno that "anything can happen"), this "last call" was the first of many moments of uncouth truthfulness on American television during the 1990s, paving the way for recent comedies of bad manners on network and cable TV (including those largely set within bars, such as *It's Always Sunny in Philadelphia*). For better or worse, it opened the door to more excessive displays of *actual*, rather than faked, drunkenness, on view in pub-crawling travel shows such as *Insomniac with Dave Attell* (Comedy Central, 2001–4), late-night talk shows such as *Too Late with Adam Carolla* (Comedy Central, 2005), and the unclassifiable series *Drunk History* (Comedy Central, 2013–19). The latter program in particular—a collection of dramatic reenactments of historical events, recounted by inebriated raconteurs from the comfort of their homes and lip-synced by a rotating cast of talented actors dressed in period-appropriate costumes—stands out for its combination of old and new, past and present.

Created by Derek Waters, who appears in each episode as the onscreen recipient of a drunken storyteller's tale, this surprisingly well-researched and educational farce generates laughter from the incongruity of seeing important figures from decades or centuries ago being "brought to life" by some of today's most gifted comedians, who stumble over their words and struggle to remember key dates and other facts while sipping everything from vodka cranberries and whiskey sours to absinthe shots and Jägerbombs. Slipping between first-person and third-person narration verging on stream-of-consciousness, and peppered with the sound of burps, farts, hiccups, and—in the case of Chris Romano (who is partially pixelated during a bathroom scene)—urination, *Drunk History* is at once sophisticated in its narratively complex questioning of our tendency to mythologize previous eras' pioneers yet rude in its foregrounding of scatological humor as the basis for comedic truth-telling. As the historian Bob Beach concludes in his reading of the show, "Booze helps bring out the truth," though he admits that "sometimes the truth is a little incoherent" and that we should be somewhat circumspect about the "unpleasant consequences" of problematic drinking behaviors depicted on *Drunk History*.[86]

As a genre long associated with both social leveling and truth-telling, comedy might be best when it is "liquored up" and a little dangerous (or, at the very least, unpredictable). *Drunk History*, a very funny, very intoxicated series sensitive to the marginalizing of women and people of color in official narratives of yore celebrating "Great White Men," is singular in the way that it brings the sad facts of the comic drunk's much-ridiculed existence to the fore even as it forces "passive viewers to question the accuracy of what they are seeing."[87] In doing so, it not only reminds us of comedy's effectiveness as a platform through which to complicate traditional accounts of the past and open our eyes to alternative ways of dealing with present-day concerns, but also gives us a better view of an archetypal character's place in a deeply engrained social imaginary that is itself subject to historical revisionism.

2

"Drinking the War Away"

Alcoholic Merriment in M*A*S*H and Other Military-Themed Sitcoms

> We do not assume . . . that when the viewer sees Hawkeye and Col. Potter in
> *M*A*S*H* sip a martini, the viewer rushes to get a drink. We do assume that
> as a daily part of the environment the media play a role in how people form
> notions about approved and disapproved behavior.
>
> > —Warren Breed and James R. De Foe, "Drinking
> > and Smoking on Television, 1950–1982," *Journal of
> > Public Health Policy,* Vol. 5, No. 2 (June 1984): 258.

> Around here, we brush our teeth with scotch.
>
> > —US Marine Corps aviator Major Greg "Pappy"
> > Boyington Gregory (Robert Conrad) to Lieutenant
> > Douglas Rafferty (Donald Petrie), a new member
> > of Attack Squadron 214, in a Season One episode of
> > *Baa Baa Black Sheep* (a.k.a., *Black Sheep Squadron;*
> > NBC, 1976–78).

The television programs mentioned in the preceding chapter collectively evince
two contrasting sets of attitudes vis-à-vis the comic drunk, a frequently stereotyped
figure of combined anxiety and humor. They also register the ways in which discourses
surrounding public drunkenness had begun to diverge in popular culture
texts during the 1960s, with greater emphasis being placed on the "reform" of
alcoholics who, if simply put to work and given sufficient care, can overcome their
afflictions and thereby slough off the very things that made them such laughable
figures in sitcoms seeking to have it "both ways." One example of that rehabilitative
trajectory discussed in Chapter One is "Here Comes Charlie" (2.23), an episode
from the cop comedy *Car 54, Where are You?* (NBC, 1961–63) that pivots on
the question of whether the titular drunk—a repeat offender and frequenter of the
53rd precinct played by Larry Storch—can overcome his addiction and become a
productive member of society under the supervision of potential employers and

71

the surveillance of police officers who have his well-being in mind. Although NYPD officers Toody (Joe E. Ross) and Muldoon (Fred Gwynne) are ultimately unable to break Charlie's self-destructive cycle, and while they are saddened to see him once again inside his holding cell at the police station by episode's end, their tireless efforts to clean him up and find him a steady job highlight the tremendous amount of institutional support and taxpayers' dollars needed to undertake such a commendable, costly program.

Notably, the same year that "Here Comes Charlie" aired on NBC stations, another program on the same network, *Don't Call Me Charlie!* (1962–63), brought forth the theme of alcoholic reform in an episode that highlights the struggles faced by a former Army veterinarian (played by guest star Leo Penn). Named after that vet, the episode "Lorenzo Johnson, D.V.M., Retired" focuses on a man who has "hit the skids since leaving the service," as well as the determination of two officers, Colonel Barker (John Hubbard) and Sergeant Wozniak (Cully Richards), to "rescue" him. At the time of this episode's airing, the US military had begun implementing addiction treatment programs, moving alcoholism and other drug problems "from the status of personal misconduct to that of a treatable illness."[1] As will become apparent throughout this chapter, cultural productions have kept pace with social transformations and health policy changes affecting every branch of the armed services, from the Army (which initiated an Alcohol and Drug Abuse Prevention and Control Program in 1971) to the Navy (which established an informal version of the Alcohol Rehabilitation Service in 1967 before expanding its treatment capabilities to include detoxification, group counseling, and participation in AA meetings in the early 1970s).[2] To a certain degree, *Don't Call Me Charlie!* reflects some of the tentative shifts in military thinking precipitating those major developments. Sadly, though, this short-lived, critically disparaged footnote to history is not known to most readers today, and thus is of relatively little value for anyone looking to better understand the sometimes-contradictory representations of drinking and drunkenness on American television during the 1960s.

For a more widely available, fondly remembered classic from that period, one need only to turn to "Beaver and Andy" (3.20), a representative episode of the suburban sitcom *Leave It to Beaver* (ABC, 1957–63), to sense how entrenched this "rescue and reform" aspect of the alcoholic imaginary was becoming at the start of that decade. Originally broadcast in February of 1960, this third-season episode revolves around a former sailor, Andy Hadlock (Wendell Holmes), whose wartime experiences are an important, if unspoken, reason why he has battled addiction as a civilian for so long. When he shows up outside the white picket fence of June and Ward Cleaver (Barbara Billingsley and Hugh Beaumont)'s Mapleton Drive address, Andy approaches their youngest son, "the Beav" (Jerry Mathers), inquiring if he can speak to the male head of the family. Andy and Ward, it turns out, are old friends, and the former is now seeking temporary employment from the latter, asking him if he might need a fence painter. The Cleavers hesitantly agree to hire him in that capacity, a token of friendship in the face of what June fears *might* happen should Andy revert back to his alcoholic ways. Speaking in euphemisms so as to shield their sons from the truth of their old acquaintance's drinking problem, June asks Ward if he has asked Andy about "you know what," to which her husband responds, "He hadn't 'you-know-whated' in the last six months." To the confusion of the Beav and his older brother Wally (Tony Dow), Ward explains that Andy has been "trying very hard to overcome his, uh . . . 'trouble,'" adopting a form of rhetorical obfuscation that is in keeping with earlier televisual texts' refusal to directly address or even show the manner in which drinking becomes a source of combined pleasure and pain for many addicts.

What is particularly illuminating about this episode of *Leave It to Beaver* is its indirect reference to Andy's wartime experiences as a sailor during the Korean War—an international "police action" of the early 1950s that is not mentioned by name, but subtly alluded to in a passage of dialogue between the two brothers. Beaver has just learned that his new friend, who has been sharing stories of his life as a sailor, was on a ship "that got hit by bullets and sunk and other guys rescued him." When Wally asks, "What war was that?" his brother answers, "I don't know." Those words not only indicate the young boy's innocence, which his parents are trying to keep intact, but also suggest that the Korean War (which, given Andy's age, is likely the conflict in which he was involved ten years earlier) had already become a "forgotten war" by the time this episode was broadcast. Additionally, the idea that this veteran needs "saving" as he descends deeper into a posttraumatic stupor—verbalized in Beaver's unintentionally hurtful comment, "My brother says that people drink to be happy, but you sure don't look happy"—had been anticipated by that instance in his past when fellow sailors prevented him from "going under." Ultimately, after this initially welcoming middle-class family discovers that their guest has sipped some of Uncle Billy's rum (which Beaver had given to him, not knowing that it would send him "off the wagon" once again), Andy learns his lesson. A self-described "bum," he sums up his wasted days, saying "An empty life and an empty bottle go pretty much together." He finishes up his painting job and then leaves this suburban neighborhood, never to be seen again. It is a sobering reflection of the way that postwar sitcoms framed insobriety as a topic demanding serious attention, even as they continued exploiting it for its humorous potential.

In his brief historical overview of US television's various depictions of alcohol consumption and addiction, David C. Pratt casts his net over a wide range of programming from the 1950s onward—from daytime talk shows to primetime dramas—in order to show how contradictory such representations often were.[3] Of the many genres that have been mobilized by TV producers, writers, and showrunners as a formulaic vehicle through which to attract advertisers and viewers while building consensus around these and other socially relevant topics, the situation comedy is especially significant, given the many challenges involved in finding and mining humor from such difficult subjects. Those challenges are compounded by the fact that, in the US national context—and especially during the first decades of the medium's history as an increasingly prevalent fixture in middle-class American homes—controversial issues were stringently avoided by network executives in order to appease their true patrons (sponsors) as well as the spectators who sought comfort rather than conflict in the warm glow of the cathode-ray tube. Additional pressure was applied by temperance advocates, who sought to ban advertisements featuring liquor, keeping the airwaves relatively clean and family-friendly throughout the 1950s and 1960s. It might be surprising, then, to learn that sitcoms "have provided TV audiences with more memorable representations of alcohol" than any other type of programming, something that Pratt comments on before concluding that the genre ultimately has served to concretize "broadly accepted ideas about sensitive issues like alcohol abuse."[4]

And what might those broadly accepted ideas be? The previous chapter set about answering that question, but the present chapter delves deeper into the subject by considering a number of small-screen representations of drinking and drunkenness that Pratt and other cultural historians have, for various reasons, left out of their discussions. Focusing on military-themed programs, including the long-running Korean War medical comedy *M*A*S*H* (CBS, 1972–83), which Pratt says is "singular among Vietnam-era sitcoms for the central role that convivial heavy drinking plays in the series,"[5] I wish to substantiate the claim that cultural productions make it possible for Americans to see and perhaps question their own complicity in the creation of a reductive, potentially damaging social imaginary. As promulgated in *M*A*S*H* but apparent in many other US sitcoms as well, the "alcoholic imaginary" reflects the often-contradictory values that mainstream society attributes to drinking as both a recreational/relaxing pastime and a potentially addictive behavior to be stamped out. A deeper consideration of American television programming during the post-WWII era (1950s–60s) bears out the dueling imperatives to conform to standardized representational practices and to bring potentially provocative topics into the national conversation; a sometimes-frivolous flirtation with serious social matters that morphed into a more committed form of consciousness-raising as the genre transitioned into an age of "relevance" in the early 1970s.[6] This chapter therefore builds on an existing framework through which to adduce the meaning and function of liquid intoxicants on television, a form of mass communication that has been said to engender addictive behaviors on the part of audiences who consume individual episodes and entire series with ritualistic regularity (especially so in this age of "binge-watching").

As discussed briefly in the Introduction, during the 1980s and 1990s a considerable amount of quantitative research was conducted by scholars with a vested interest in mitigating the harmful effects and enhancing the positive effects of media exposure, particularly with regard to television programming containing images of, or messages about, alcohol consumption. Examples of that scholarly output, in the form of published journal articles, are too numerous to cite in their entirety, although representative studies share depressingly generic titles (e.g., "Alcohol Use in Television Programming: Effects on Children's Behavior" [1983], "Portrayals of Alcohol on Prime-Time Television" [1990], "Alcohol Portrayals and Alcohol Advertising on Television" [1993], "Television Alcohol Portrayals, Alcohol Advertising, and Alcohol Expectancies Among Children and Adolescents" [1995], etc.) that hint at the field's narrow view of a subject that would not be conceptually framed from a critical-cultural perspective until the 1990s and 2000s.[7] Following the publication of important contributions by Norman K. Denzin, author of a historical overview of alcoholism in American cinema (*Hollywood Shot by Shot* [1991]) in addition to autoethnographic and qualitative studies of "addiction culture" that find him drawing upon semiotics, psychoanalysis, and feminist theory, a few historians and anthropologists, including Mary Ann Watson and Janet Chrzan, began to focus on drinking as a "deeply cultural act," one that is embedded in social practices that continue to be reimagined through fictional and nonfictional representations. Still, by and large, the voluminous amount of academic literature concerning TV and alcohol remains rooted to older media effects models and data sets demonstrating a connection between televisual content and audiences' malleable attitudes toward excessive drinking.[8] Not coincidentally, many of the most frequently cited studies from that era, including the one by Warren Breed and James R. De Foe quoted as an epigraph earlier, make passing references to the military-themed sitcom *M*A*S*H*, a singular yet representative example of sobering insobriety on network television that I will return to soon.

Rather than limit myself to a single case study from the 1970s and early 1980s whose many scenes of liquor consumption and inebriated behavior are worthy of in-depth study, I wish to begin this chapter by examining a broader array of texts within a larger contextual field, laying out a historical continuum in which other TV series are cited as examples of the medium's longstanding engagement with the topic of alcoholism. Having already alluded to such pioneering episodes as "Lucy Does a TV Commercial" (from *I Love Lucy* [CBS, 1951–57]) and "Head of the House" (from *The Honeymooners* [CBS, 1955–56]) in the previous chapter,

I point toward a few overlooked instances of the subject being broached in military-themed television shows, ranging from popular hits like *McHale's Navy* (ABC, 1962–66) and *Hogan's Heroes* (CBS, 1965–71) to little-known footnotes to history such as the "women in war"–themed sitcom *Broadside* (ABC, 1964–65) and the short-lived, decidedly male-focalized action-adventure series *Baa Baa Black Sheep* (a.k.a., *Black Sheep Squadron*; NBC, 1976–78). The latter program in particular, though generically codified as a "drama" by industry personnel and TV critics at the time of its broadcast, mobilizes humorous discourses around scenes of public drunkenness and liquor-fueled hypermasculinity in several episodes; and the frequency with which it depicts men—specifically, a tightly knit group of fighter pilots based in the Solomon Islands during the Second World War—hitting the bottle (which they do as often as they attack the enemy) deserves at least passing consideration in light of the general lack of critical commentary surrounding this program.[9] Indeed, like the more widely praised and critically analyzed *M*A*S*H*, creator-producer Stephen J. Cannell's *Baa Baa Black Sheep* foregrounds alcoholism as a response to, and result of, *war*; something that relatively few of the sitcoms made prior to its broadcast fully addressed.

No Time for Drunken Sergeants: Masculinity and Militaristic Drinking

> Us infantry guys, we were a bunch of alcoholics.
> —Gonzalo Baltazar, a private serving with 2/17th
> Cavalry (Airborne Division) in Vietnam.[10]

Although it is not a sitcom but instead a stand-alone episode of the genre-hopping anthology series *The United States Steel Hour* (ABC, 1953–55; NBC, 1955–63), "No Time for Sergeants" gave many audiences their first sustained look at the humorous effects of alcohol on US servicemen. Adapted by Ira Levin from Mac Hyman's fictionalized memoir of the same title (noted for its "profane disrespect" for military brass),[11] and broadcast live to a nation of thirty million TV households on March 15, 1955, this historical artifact from the Golden Age of Television is perhaps best known for introducing viewers to Andy Griffith. A North Carolina–born monologist with no prior acting experience, Griffith had gained notoriety for his folksy standup act, specifically a comic routine about football that he performed with a syrupy Southern drawl on *The Ed Sullivan Show* (CBS, 1948–71) one year earlier. In that routine, he played up the stereotype of the ever-grinning country bumpkin. This made him a natural choice for the role of Will Stockdale, a clueless rube who is drafted into the US Army at the beginning of "No Time for Sergeants" and who manages to coast through his service in the military thanks to his natural charm and blind luck, not to mention his inhuman ability to toss back the bottle with no discernible change to his demeanor.

Midway through this hour-long teleplay, after being assigned to the Air Force, the dimwitted hayseed is taken by his commanding officer, Sergeant King (Harry Clark), to the Purple Grotto, a watering hole for soldiers and airmen where a round of drinks is ordered. The CO's secret mission is to get this rookie private drunk as payback for the many headaches that he has unwittingly caused since arriving at the barracks. However, because Stockdale—a former plowboy from the moonshine state of Georgia—is accustomed to the taste of corn liquor laced with kerosene, he is unfazed by the tall glasses of whiskey and lighter fluid that he knocks back, one after the other, to King's dismay. Though he remains sober (and thus will *not* fail the next day's inspection as the sergeant had intended), Stockdale's drinking companions get progressively plastered. What begins as a scene of affable camaraderie builds into a barroom brawl between the main group of characters and a bunch of infantrymen who claim to be stronger and better representatives of the US armed forces. In this way, the teleplay points toward a key aspect of drinking when performed by members of the military, especially men for whom beer, whiskey, and wine are the means through which they can access and perform a side of their masculinity that would otherwise be kept in check by the disciplinary protocols of their profession. Besides serving as the inspiration for *Gomer Pyle, U.S.M.C.* (CBS, 1964–69), a sitcom that will reemerge at a later point in this discussion, "No Time for Sergeants" established many of the genre conventions that would be mobilized in other military-themed comedies of the 1960s and 1970s. These include the unintentional breaking of the military's hierarchical chain of command by innocent draftees and the scheming of more seasoned airmen, sailors, and soldiers who, prone to childish horseplay and drunken shenanigans, sneak behind their frequently flummoxed commanding officer to partake in things that, strictly speaking, are off-limits.

Along those lines, a Season Four episode of *McHale's Navy* titled "Fire in the Liquor Locker" (4.17) revolves around a group of American sailors—the crew of PT-73, led by Lieutenant Commander Quinton McHale (Ernest Borgnine)—who, disguised as Italian peasants, earn a few extra lira while stationed in the fictional town of Volta Fiore by peddling "homemade hooch" to US soldiers. When their commanding officer, Captain Binghamton (Joe Flynn), confiscates their bootleg liquor, the five men scheme to find a new way to make and deliver booze. Ultimately, they repurpose an abandoned fire engine in the neighboring town of San Marcello, turning it into a "four-wheel speakeasy." In order to keep a tight lid on their operation, the men misinform Binghamton of the vehicle's purpose, telling him that they plan to put out fires in the surrounding villages and thus fulfill his goal of positively impacting the local populace. In fact, their Captain had been tasked with putting aside his "junior G-Man" tendencies by his own supervisor, General Bronson (Simon Scott), who informed him that his job as a military governor was "to look after the civic betterment of [his] people." When Binghamton explains, in that earlier scene, that by "running the rum-runners right out of town" he was "keeping the town of Volta Fiore sober," Bronson warns his subordinate officer that he will look for a "more civic-minded replacement" if he does not come up with something "that *really* benefits [his] people." This threat, combined with Bronson's complaint that his own officers' club "can't keep the bar stocked" because Binghamton appears to have stockpiled "all the liquor in the area," suggests that what the Pentagon has in mind as a socially productive way to improve the lives of civilians and soldiers does not accord with this teetotaler's attempts to bring sobriety to the masses.

Ultimately, the alcohol that has been secretly distilled inside the "100-proof fire wagon" brings civic destruction to the town of Volta Fiore when the repurposed engine is called upon to put out an actual fire. When Binghamton, who remains oblivious to the contents of the engine, takes command of the hose and sprays an engulfed building, the flammable liquid is misdirected and douses the General's jeep, setting it ablaze and sending the volunteer fire department scurrying for safety. While not quite "the biggest eruption since Vesuvius," as Lt. Commander McHale warned it might be, the blast infuriates Bronson and literalizes the "combustible" nature of a topic—specifically, alcohol use and abuse within the military—that was sure to draw as many disapproving looks as it would guffaws among TV audiences of the 1960s. Still, this episode, like so many other sitcom narratives, returns to a state of equilibrium at the end by showing the sailors (who appear to have learned their lesson) "making a little after-dinner brandy" on a phonograph machine-turned-homemade still. Not surprisingly, this inventive use of a record player pleases McHale, who in earlier seasons had been shown making his own moonshine, flaunting Naval regulations while stationed on the heavily bombed Pacific Island of Taratupa.

An earlier *McHale's Navy* episode, "Ensign Parker, ESP" (2.31), features a scene in which the bumbling Lieutenant Carpenter (Bob Hastings) defends his presence at the local canteen on Taratupa (a fictional US naval operations base in the Solomon Islands). Carpenter tells his furious commanding officer, Captain Binghamton (who claims to "never touch a drop" of liquor and has, by his own estimation, "a very clean liver"), that he is "never under the influence [while] on duty." Although he appears to be "lushing it up again," according to the CO, he is in fact drinking harmless Shirley Temples. The humor of this scene (cued through the audible canned laughter) hinges on Binghamton's misinterpretation of the situation as well as his adherence to traditional notions of military masculinity; for

2.1. "One of these days I'd like to bend your straw!" These words, barked by Captain Wallace Binghamton to Lieutenant Elroy Carpenter upon learning that his cocktail is really just a Shirley Temple, suggest that the latter's drink does not accord with traditional notions of military masculinity, a theme that emerges not only in *McHale's Navy* but in other TV series throughout the 1960s and 1970s. © Sto-Rev-Co Productions

he initially complains that he cannot "step off the base for one minute" without his aide getting "bagged" (to borrow his euphemism) only to fly into a rage upon learning that Carpenter's nightcap is not really alcoholic (meaning that it is a "sissy" drink rather than a manly concoction).

Referred to by some critics as "the female version of *McHale's Navy*,"[12] creator Edward J. Montagne's *Broadside* is just as saturated with references to liquid intoxicants as its forerunner was. The show's emphasis on bottled spirits is apparent from the opening minutes of the first episode. The title of that episode, "Don't Make Waves" (1.01), references the acronymic name given to the Women's Reserve, better known as the WAVES (Women Accepted for Volunteer Emergency Service), a branch of the United States Naval Reserve that was established in July of 1942. Set two years after that date, *Broadside* begins with an establishing shot of its main setting, Ranakai Island, where sailors attend to their duties outside the US Naval Supply Depot and the headquarters of their commanding officer, Roger P. Adrian (Edward Andrews). A male voiceover provides further expositional orientation, indicating that "invasion forces have moved on, but conditions are still rugged, and the keynote now is *logistics and planning*." An interior shot of the commander's office fades in, and the episode's first visual joke results from seeing what is *really* meant by "logistics and planning." Commander Adrian holds up a glass of wine, admiring it in the light, and then puffs on a pipe before taking a long sniff of the beverage. Within a few seconds, this exaggerated display sketches in this character's social status and background as a pompous connoisseur of the finer things in life. He instructs his chef, standing at the ready with notepad and pencil, that Thursday he will have the pressed duck and Friday he will dine on Lobster Thermidor and Oysters Rockefeller. Clearly, organizing his weekly schedule of French gourmet dishes takes precedence over military preparations, which is further evidenced by the collection of vintage wines that he proudly shows off once Lieutenant Trotter (Dick Sargent) rushes into his office. Although Trotter brings important news about the incoming motor pool personnel, which will be made up of a small group of WAVES led by Lieutenant Anne Morgan (Kathleen Nolan), his CO is less concerned with matters of war than he is with his own wall of wine, which is revealed with exaggerated flourish by the pull of a curtain cord.

By the end of this episode, Commander Adrian's attention has shifted fully to the newly arrived women, whose presence, he fears, augers potentially drastic changes for him and the other men at the naval base. As he muses later in the episode, "First we get a women's motor pool, then we get women cooks, the next thing you know we'll be walking into the officer's club and calling the bartender Za-Za." His misogynistic attitudes are enflamed when one of the so-called "female grease monkeys," swinging her hips in a suggestive manner outside headquarters, distracts the driver of a jeep, forcing him to veer dangerously close to the building. The rumble of the swerving vehicle sends all of Adrian's wine bottles crashing to the floor—an apt metaphor for his loss of control over this so-called "island paradise" and from which chaos will likely ensue. "This is going to be a lousy war," he surmises, not only because he anticipates several future run-ins with the WAVES, but also because "there isn't a decent bottle of wine left on this entire island" and he will now "have to drink cooking sherry with [his] oysters."

In many respects, *Broadside* sits squarely within a formulaic "battle-of-the-sexes" framework that might seem retrograde to contemporary audiences.[13] However, the fact that it at least partially inverts normative gender roles and shows an effeminate male commander (who is drawn to wine rather than whiskey) antagonistically pitted against a group of female mechanics suggests that this military-themed comedy is distinct from other 1960s sitcoms, especially those that are set during times of war. Yes, the women in the program sometimes resort to repairing damaged engines with garter belts and hair pins, and occasionally fight over pairs of nylons—a valuable commodity at that time. And they are even shown making lipstick rather than sour mash or white lightning with a moonshine still. But their often-defiant attitude toward military brass anticipates the approach taken by producers Larry Gelbart and Gene Reynolds in their liquor-filled antiwar comedy *M*A*S*H* and was matched only by Bernard Fein and Albert S. Ruddy's *Hogan's Heroes* during *Broadside's* original broadcast run.

Stiff drinks rather than weak concoctions feature more frequently in military-themed programs of the mid-to-late 1960s and early 1970s, some of which incorporate alcohol into plots as part of the protagonists' conspiratorial scheming against higher-ranked officials. For example, the second half of "Happiness is a Warm Sergeant" (1.11), a Season One episode of *Hogan's Heroes*, pivots on the efforts of a group of Allied POWs—the titular protagonists imprisoned at Stalag 13—to have the inept German officer Han Schultz (John Banner) reinstated as Sergeant of the Guard after he has angered "Big Shot" Colonel Klink (Werner Klemperer). What has upset Klink is the fact that Schultz had to be brought back to the camp by wheelbarrow after getting drunk at a nearby bar, something that the bumbling officer's replacement, Sergeant Krebs, would never do. Unbeknownst to Schultz, Corporal Newkirk (Richard Dawson) surreptitiously dropped

2.2. British troublemaker Corporal Newkirk has to wheel the drunken German officer Hans Schultz back to the POW camp where his already questionable "authority" is cast in comic relief opposite the savvy Allied prisoners in *Hogan's Heroes*. © Bing Crosby Productions

a shot of whiskey into the sergeant's beer, making it a potent boilermaker. Because he is to blame, the British conman and his fellow Allied prisoners undertake a phony escape attempt that will lead to Schultz's reinstatement into the normal chain of command, thus bringing narrative equilibrium back to this show about military tomfoolery.

Similar scheming takes place in the episode "Some of Their Planes are Missing" (3.02), from the third season of *Hogan's Heroes*. Liquors of several varieties are served to German officers during a Commandant party, one that the roguish American Colonel Robert Hogan (Bob Crane) has been granted permission to attend thanks to his ability to charm Colonel Richard Leman (John Doucette), a veteran of the Norwegian Campaign for which he flew bomber missions. Leman's superior, General Burkhalter (Leon Askin), agrees to let the American take part in the festivities, thinking that if he is "oiled up" he might "loosen his tongue" and divulge secrets to the Germans. However, Hogan feigns swallowing the spirits, covertly pouring his drinks into Leman's and other officers' cups. So convincing is Hogan's drunk act that Burkhalter allows him to "pass out" in an adjoining bedroom. But this is merely a ruse, part of an elaborately orchestrated means of sabotaging German efforts to infiltrate Royal Air Force (RAF) squadrons and shoot British planes down. Nicknamed "Operation Albatross," that plan on the part of Leman, Burkhalter, and Klink is ultimately foiled, in part due to their ability to be fooled by the kind of fake inebriation alluded to in the previous chapter (as part of my discussion of *The Red Skelton Show* [NBC, 1951–53; CBS, 1953–70] and *The Honeymooners*).

Historically sandwiched between the two above-mentioned episodes of *Hogan's Heroes*, "Show Me the Way to Go Home" (3.05), a 1966 episode of *Gomer Pyle, U.S.M.C.*, is worthy of mention. By the time this episode was televised by CBS stations on October 12 of that year (during the show's third season), audiences had learned to associate the titular character—a Carolina-born gas station attendant (Jim Nabors) who joins the Marine Corps during peacetime—with qualities that were beginning to disappear from cultural productions of the Vietnam War era, specifically his gee-whiz optimism, generosity, and innocence. Gomer is someone who, according to his drill instructor, gunnery sergeant Vince Carter (Frank Sutton), "doesn't drink." Or, more accurately, he rarely indulges in anything "stronger than a vanilla malt." Those words are spoken in "Show Me the Way to Go Home," an episode whose title is borrowed from that of a popular song written in 1925, one whose lyrics reference alcoholic intake and the perils of journeying that result from having one too many drinks.[14] The lyrics might just as well describe the challenges facing Harry Purcell (Keenan Wynn), a man so inebriated that he is unable to return home without the assistance of Private Pyle (who has

2.3. "Typical American weakness. Can't drink. Can't finish the wars they start." These words, spoken by a German officer in the World War II–set TV comedy *Hogan's Heroes*, hint at a linkage between military prowess and the masculine pastime of partaking in stiff drinks—an idea that is lent additional meaning given the fact that the program aired during the Vietnam War. © Bing Crosby Productions

just left a movie theater near the base and spotted the drunkard leaning on a lamp post). Warned by his friend Private "Duke" Slater (Ronnie Schell) that he should not get involved in the problems of strangers, Gomer believes that it is his duty to intervene, to ensure the safety of someone who might get into an automobile accident without his assistance. Complications ensue once Harry's wife catches him returning home in a drunken state and wrongly blames Gomer for allowing such a thing to happen.

The following day, a now-sober, thoroughly embarrassed Purcell wants to show his gratitude to Gomer, asking the private to join him for a steak dinner that evening. When we next see them together, Harry supplements his sirloin with stiff drinks, which once again rob him of his faculties and force Gomer to drive him home. This results in another run-in with Mrs. Purcell, who, in a huff, goes to the military base to tell Sergeant Carter that Gomer is corrupting her husband. "He's been using poor Harry for a drinking buddy and Harry doesn't drink!" she yells, provoking confusion and disbelief. "He's grown up! My boy has grown up," the sergeant enthuses, suggesting that "children" become "men" in the military once they embrace its deeply embedded drinking culture. Eventually, Carter chances upon the sight of Gomer and Harry together inside a diner, where the latter dances drunkenly to the amusement of the patrons. The sergeant soon discovers the truth of the situation, and forces Harry out of the diner, where he has made a spectacle of his own inebriated state. Harry responds by telling Carter that Pyle is a "goodie-goodie" who would "be better off" if he tossed back the bottle on occasion, an idea that is amplified in the penultimate scene, which shows the sergeant and another officer in the diner sipping beers as a way of blowing off steam. Besides introducing the notion that drinking culture within the military functions as a means to achieve maturity or manhood, this episode concludes with the suggestion that alcohol can "save" a person—can rescue someone from his innocence and incorruptibility and serve as a release valve. This is an idea that would subsequently infuse the first few seasons of another CBS military series, *M*A*S*H*.

Popular discourses concerning alcoholism took a critical turn during the postwar era, but that divergence also parallels the manner in which the US armed forces had become a "divisive symbol" in the eyes of many people throughout the Vietnam War years, particularly once military operations (including secret bombing campaigns) expanded into Laos and Cambodia in 1968. Significantly, that was the year when television's foremost signifier of nostalgia and down-home innocence, *The Andy Griffith Show* (CBS, 1960–68), ended its broadcast run, permanently closing the cell door on friendly town drunk Otis Campbell (Hal Smith).[15] As the media historian Gordon Arnold states, America's once-untarnished image of the armed forces, which embodied "the ideals of patriotism for many of those who supported the war and its aims," had become "a symbol of what was wrong with America in the eyes of many war opponents."[16] Moreover, as Robert Bray, Mary Ellen Marsden, John F. Mazzuchi, and Roger W. Hartman explain, illicit drug use among American servicemen stationed in Vietnam was partly responsible for the development of early Department of Defense (DoD) policy directives designed "to monitor, regulate, and eliminate substance abuse among military personnel."[17] Having assembled a task force in 1967 whose primary goal was to investigate the use of heroin, opium, and other drugs, the DoD was primed to set forth a robust directive three years later, one that would roughly coincide with the launch of CBS's Korean War dramedy *M*A*S*H* and would guide "military efforts to confront drug and alcohol abuse" within its ranks over the next decade.

One of the few television series of its generation to consistently tackle the issue of alcoholism, *M*A*S*H* showcases the humorous as well as harmful effects of intemperance in spaces where sobriety and more than a small measure of good judgment are called for. Although the men and women of the 4077th Mobile Army Surgical Hospital refrain from such activities in the makeshift operating room where incoming wounded arrive around the clock, they sip martinis and down shots of whiskey nearly everywhere else, including inside "the Swamp." As one of the main settings in the series, this temporary home away from home for Benjamin "Hawkeye" Pierce (Alan Alda), "Trapper John" McIntyre (Wayne Rogers), and the other spiritually drained surgeons is little more than a small tent outfitted with standard military-issue cots. However, the Swamp's centerpiece is a homemade distillery, which on more than one occasion is used as a plot device driving the medical staff toward insobriety, a state of mind and body that gives the doctors and nurses temporary respite from the war.

As indicated in a line of dialogue spoken by B.J. Hunnicutt (Mike Farrell) in the episode "End Run" (5.18), alcohol is "supposed to make you feel nothing." Many devoted fans of M*A*S*H will be accustomed to hearing this sentiment, which is expressed repeatedly throughout the eleven-season run of the series. For example, the Emmy-nominated episode "Alcoholics Unanimous" (3.09) shows the lengths that Major Frank Burns (Larry Linville) will go to bring prohibition to the camp, in his role as temporary Commanding Officer. Ultimately, by the end of that episode, the teetotaling party-pooper discovers what everyone—even Father Mulcahy (William Christopher), who "takes a few snorts to get his nerve up" before a temperance sermon—already knows: that hard drink softens the senses and thus dulls the pain of war.[18]

Throughout the remainder of this chapter, I explore the multiple functions and meanings of alcohol in M*A*S*H, looking at specific episodes that deploy drinks and drunkenness in thematically significant ways. Key case studies include "Fallen Idol" (6.03), "Bottle Fatigue" (8.16), and "Bottoms Up" (9.15), which together highlight the fact that almost everyone in the camp turns to beers, wine, cocktails, and other spirits as a means of much-needed relief. More importantly, these episodes also contain scenes in which the main characters confront the reasons for, and effects of, periodic drinking. In examining the interrelatedness of alcohol and war, I draw upon published studies about the psychological effects of military conflicts in the lives of US soldiers and medical personnel in order to consider the reasons why Hawkeye and other characters might turn to the bottle from time to time. I also reiterate what James Wittebols and other media scholars have argued about M*A*S*H: that it is a cultural production of social and political relevance which not only entertains but also enlightens; serving an edifying role even as its controversial content and tonally schizophrenic form (shifting from comedy to drama and vice-versa) disturb some audiences.

But I seek to go one step further in pinpointing the series' slippery, sometimes contradictory messages about drinking, which is alternately scrutinized as a negative practice and celebrated as a social activity conducive to community-building and stress-reduction. Such paradoxes contribute to US popular culture's "alcoholic imaginary," an expression that I have coined by modifying the language used by Charles Taylor, Bill Nichols, and other theorists who have presented different ways of thinking about social imaginaries. Positive outcomes of drinking are frequently depicted in *M*A*S*H*. Near the end of the episode "Local Indigenous Personnel" (2.07), a racist investigator from I-Corps finally approves the marriage of an American GI and his Korean girlfriend after the Swamp-mates have gotten him drunk, as if alcohol not only can whittle away at one's social inhibitions but also can bring moral clarity to matters of intercultural and cross-generational bonding. As I will later explain, such moments, along with the show's many toast scenes (depicting medical personnel raising their glasses after a long stint in the OR), highlight the constructive, cathartic, and ritualistic dimensions of drinking, which serves an important role in the military. But less positive aspects are also on view in this series, indicating that its messages about alcohol-consumption shifted alongside changing societal attitudes and political campaigns during the late 1970s and early 1980s.

Compulsively Consumptive: *M*A*S*H*, Korea, and the Alcoholic Imaginary

> Korea was the easiest place in the world to become an alcoholic.
> —a US commanding officer to a junior pilot, quoted in
> · John Darrell Sherwood's *Officers in Flight Suits*[19]

In his overview of drinking on American television, David Pratt explains that, "from the late 1960s through the early 1970s, producers like Norman Lear created sitcoms that reflected the tense social and political debates of the Vietnam era." Because alcoholism "did not rank among the major controversies of the era," writers and producers "exercised freer rein in showing alcohol use on sitcoms primarily concerned with more volatile topics like race, poverty, and the Vietnam War itself."[20] A bevy of TV comedies from that time period, including *The Mary Tyler Moore Show* (CBS, 1970–77), *Maude* (CBS, 1972–78), *Barney Miller* (ABC, 1975–82), and *WKRP in Cincinnati* (CBS, 1978–82), occasionally broached the subject of drinking (and drunkenness) in the workplace, turning a harsh light on characters who, despite their foibles, nevertheless remain "lovable" in the eyes of audiences. For Pratt, however, cocreators Larry Gelbart and Gene Reynolds's *M*A*S*H* is second-to-none in terms of its foregrounding of convivial heavy drinking, which plays a central role in helping the audience to understand the predicaments faced by its characters.[21]

It is significant that *M*A*S*H* debuted around the same time that the Department of Defense commenced a series of policy directives to reduce or eliminate substance abuse among members of the US military (a campaign that the Armed Forces Vietnam Network threw their support behind, with talk-show episodes devoted to the subject).[22] Initially, emphasis was placed on rehabilitation and preventative measures that could be integrated with existing education and law enforcement procedures, so that "detection and early intervention" were parts of a two-pronged approach. In 1971, at the behest of President Richard Nixon, the plan accommodated a urinalysis testing program, which was random and mandatory for service members returning to the United States from the Southeast Asian theater of war. Controversial from its inception, the testing program was soon challenged in the courts (US v. Ruiz, 1974) and eventually discouraged by members of Congress, who argued that it was not a cost-effective means of addressing the problem of substance abuse in the military. The rhetoric of alcohol- and drug-prevention in the military died down for a period during the 1970s, only to reemerge at the beginning of the next decade, coinciding with the broadcast run of *M*A*S*H*'s final seasons.

Although launched on September 17, 1972, during the final stages of the Vietnam War, the series is set during the Korean War, an international conflict (or "police action") that took place between June 25, 1950, and July 27, 1953. Because "officers in the 1950s were less well informed about the dangers of drinking and operating aircraft" than today's soldiers and they would sometimes fly drunk (according to combat specialist and historian John Darrell Sherwood), the Korean War turned several pilots and other military personnel into "lost souls." That is, they left the theater of war as alcoholics due to their frequent exposure to liquor during the lulls between fighting.[23] In her recently published study of Americans who fought in the Korean War, *In the Shadow of the Greatest Generation*, Melinda Pash cites veterans of that conflict who resorted to substance abuse during and after the fighting, using alcohol to "numb the pain, and keep the nightmares away." Alcoholism, Pash states, "particularly plagued Korean War veterans who participated in combat, at rates somewhat elevated above those of their contemporaries."[24] While this and other studies have brought attention to previously overlooked aspects of the "Forgotten War," the social and psychological role of drinking in the lives of medical personnel has yet to receive the same critical and historical treatment, a surprising fact given that *M*A*S*H*—a mainstream television program adored by millions of fans—brought the issue to the forefront of popular discourse during the 1970s and early 1980s.

Much has been made of *M*A*S*H*'s long broadcast run (1972–83), which surpassed the duration of that mid-century war by eight years and attests to the syndicated television show's perennial status. In each of its eleven seasons, *M*A*S*H* adopted an irreverent yet impassioned mode of satirical anti-war discourse that distinguished it from earlier military-themed sitcoms, including *Gomer Pyle* and *Hogan's Heroes*. Tackling touchy subjects such as xenophobia, racial discrimination, sexism, and the often-dehumanizing bureaucracy of the US military, the TV program—like the Robert Altman–directed feature film of the same title theatrically released in 1970—lent a realistic air to a genre that was normally devoid of progressive political commentary. Gelbart and Reynolds also appear to have been inspired by Altman's iconoclastic interest in rebellious personalities, who take the form of martini-sipping draftee surgeons making the best of a bad situation by engaging in libation, foreplay, and other forms of hedonistic activity. In particular, Alan Alda's Captain Benjamin "Hawkeye" Pierce, a role the actor inherited from Donald Sutherland (in Altman's film), stands out for his anti-authoritarianism and low tolerance for "regular army clowns." In the words of Michael B. Kassell, Hawkeye "fought the insanity of war with not only his surgical skills but also his humor, alcohol abuse, and women chasing"—attributes and activities that were first brought together in the show's pilot episode.[25]

Originally broadcast on September 17, 1972, the pilot (written by Gelbart and directed by Reynolds) establishes not only the show's principal setting but also the main character's reliance on recreational spirits to lift his morale. Returning to his tent after putting in a grueling shift at the OR (where he casually dropped sexist one-liners into his speech while operating on patients), Hawkeye relaxes in his cot while nursing a martini prepared for him by the Korean "houseboy" Ho-Jon (Patrick Adiarte). He takes a sip and says to Swamp-mate "Trapper John" McIntyre, "You know, we gotta do it someday: Throw away all the guns and invite the jokers from the North and the South in here for a cocktail party. Last man standing wins the war." Although Ho-Jon is a minor character slavishly assisting his "masters" in their makeshift home-away-from-home, he serves as a visible sign of the show's cultural-historical context, reminding audiences that the war-torn country of South Korea is its principal setting, despite the young actor's Filipino ethnicity. He also provides demonstrable evidence of Hawkeye and Trapper's benevolent ability to look beyond their own libidinal interests and lend a helping hand. For they ultimately raise $2,000 to send the young Asian man to the United States where he will attend Hawkeye's alma mater, Androscoggin College, and presumably gain access to a "better life."

Hawkeye and Trapper are able to come up with that money thanks to the "generosity and thirst" of the camp; that is, by charging "ten bucks a head" in

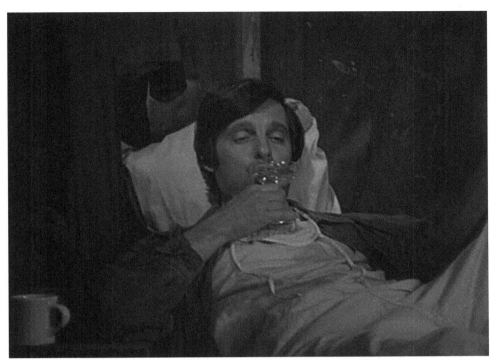

2.4. The pilot episode of *M*A*S*H* establishes Hawkeye and Trapper's proclivity to drink between surgical shifts, as illustrated in this early scene, which shows the Korean houseboy Ho-jon bringing the American doctors a drink. © 20th Television

an all-you-can-drink raffle, the winner of which will be given a weekend pass to Tokyo in the company of an attractive nurse, Lieutenant Dish (Karen Phillip). Ironically, the raffle winner is Father Mulcahy, a man of the cloth who abstains from both sex and alcohol for much of the series (with the notable exception of the later episode "Alcoholics Unanimous"). The festivities come to an abrupt end once helicopters filled with Canadian soldiers land, bringing a fresh supply of injured bodies to the receiving ward in the episode's penultimate scene. One might pause to consider the ethical implications of medical personnel undertaking surgical practices only minutes after imbibing mixed drinks. Regardless, the pilot's foregrounding of drinking culture lays the foundation for ensuing moments in the series when two seemingly unholy alliances—that between [1] war and comedy and that between [2] exploitation and charity—are shown to be ripe for narrative and thematic development. Alcohol is thus central to the show's representational polarities—*M*A*S*H*'s tendency to "have it both ways" generically and ideologically (with regard to the contradictory messages that it communicates about gender, religion, and other topics).

For instance, in the episode "Rainbow Bridge" (3.02), the doctors and nurses of the 4077th are invited by Lieutenant Colonel Henry Blake (McLean Stevenson) to have a drink, "Dutch treat," after they have put in thirty-six straight hours of surgical work (handling 473 cases, including eighteen laparotomies, twenty-one busted femurs, and sixteen bowel resections). "I think that's an all-timer," Trapper remarks as he pops open a bottle of alcohol, pouring it into a coffee cup. The incongruity of that beverage container and its liquid contents is metaphorically aligned with what transpires later in the episode, when the American doctors—having been sent a communique from the Chinese, who have nine shot-up US soldiers on their side requiring medical attention—cross the front line and meet with the Communists at the titular pickup point, Rainbow Bridge (some fifty miles inside the enemy's territory). "You're doing something decent in the middle of a giant indecency," Hawkeye tells one of the English-speaking Chinese officers (Mako), a comment about heretofore unthinkable cultural mixing and international cooperation that had been anticipated by the doctors' earlier combining of liquor and coffee.[26] Not insignificantly, this episode ends with Trapper and Hawkeye sleeping in their cots, exhausted after performing another sixteen hours of surgery (and thus unable to make their planned R&R trip to Tokyo). The final image is both humorous and solemn, in keeping with the show's contradictory discourses concerning drinking: A half-filled martini glass is propped up in Hawkeye's hand, as if to remind audiences that alcohol is central to M*A*S*H's tonally and generically hybrid combination of pathos and comedy, sentimentality and satire.[27]

Unlike Hawkeye and Trapper in the above episode, Colonel Sherman Potter (Harry Morgan), Blake's replacement, takes off for that most privileged of travel destinations, Tokyo, following a late-night call in "Old Soldiers" (8.18). The reason for his trip is not, however, rest and recuperation. Instead, he is visiting a sick friend, whose passing makes Potter the last surviving member of a group of once-tightly knit World War I veterans. When the heartbroken commanding officer returns from Japan to the 4077th, which has become overrun by Korean orphans (war refugees who are being cared for by their benevolent American overseers), he asks his medical staff to open four bottles of French wine—one for each of the deceased men—and share a toast in their memory. Fans of M*A*S*H might find their own memories of earlier episodes triggered by such a toast, which was offered up with slight variation in the episode "Too Many Cooks" (8.01), the penultimate scene of which shows the main characters gathering at the Officer's Club and sharing a bottle of Scotch after Potter has read a touching letter sent by his wife, Mildred. Scenes showing the characters raising their glasses in a toast recur throughout the history of M*A*S*H, as highlighted in episodes such as "Aid Station" (3.19), "The Grim Reaper" (6.12), "Stars and Stripes" (8.14), and "Heroes"

(10.19). These moments—social rituals that are contained within an oft-repeated, equally ritualistic narrative structure that is unusual but not unique to M*A*S*H (as a half-hour television comedy-drama)—attest to the healing power of alcohol, which serves an important role in the lives of medical personnel as well as soldiers.

Connected to its ability to strengthen bonds between people from different social classes and cultural backgrounds, liquor can also reveal otherwise sub-merged aspects of character, as evidenced in "Hot Lips and Empty Arms," an epi-sode from M*A*S*H's second season. Besides featuring a toast scene, this episode shows the inebriated head nurse Major Margaret Houlihan (Loretta Swit) doing something that she rarely does: She opens up about her personal feelings to express her dissatisfaction with Frank Burns (her on-and-off lover). This would be echoed in "Major Ego," an episode from M*A*S*H's seventh season which shows the same loose-lipped woman confiding in B.J., who learns of her pent-up sexual desires and readiness to move forward after her break-up with the money-grubbing Don-ald Penobscott (Beeson Carroll). Despite the fact that her mother is an alcoholic kleptomaniac (something we learn in the episode "Bulletin Board"), Margaret's willingness to toss back the bottle contributes to her newfound respect for and friendship with the perpetually soused Swamp-mates.[28] In particular, she opens up in a more honest, forthcoming way with Hawkeye, who is only half joking when he says that he has "taken gin intravenously."[29] Gradually, after an initial period of antagonism, the two become close friends; and alcohol—a narrative device that sometimes halts episodic plot progression for the sake of "character-building" and interpersonal connection—contributes to this developing comradery, one that is often capped with a toast.

A toast brings the episode "Mr. and Mrs. Who?" (8.09) to an end, providing narrative symmetry to a story that begins with the sight of Major Charles Emerson Winchester III (David Ogden Stiers) returning to the camp with a hangover. The Harvard graduate's disheveled and unshaven appearance is at odds with his typ-ically refined demeanor, suggesting that he did other things during his weekend trip to Tokyo besides attending a medical seminar. Once he ambles away from the jeep and makes his way to his cot, he unpacks his bag to reveal black stockings and rolls of undeveloped film. "I attended some sort of party at the hospital," Charles sputters, concluding that he must have fallen victim "to the insidious blandish-ments of a rowdy surgical staff." However, he is unable to recall anything specific about his excursion. It is only thanks to Corporal Max Klinger (Jamie Farr), who develops the rolls of film showing "Major Disaster" wearing a lampshade on his head (a cliché of public drunkenness) and dancing with an unknown woman, that Charles is able to piece together the puzzle of that weekend. Because he drank too many bowls of sake punch, he apparently got married to a woman who is now expected to arrive at the 4077th in pursuit of her husband. Once "Mrs. Winchester" (Claudette Nevins) gets there, though, she explains that they are not really married, since the ceremony was performed by the hotel bartender. This information brings a sigh of relief to the man who has undergone serious "bottle fatigue" over the course of this episode.

Although they share hot tea while recalling their time in Tokyo, the episode concludes with the image of the main characters toasting their success in figuring out the solution to a patient's mysterious bout with Korean Hemorrhagic Fever, a disease that attacks the kidneys and which, ironically, makes the sufferer (a man named Shaw, who is confined to a bed in post-op) thirsty. "Please, don't say 'drink,'" Charles had earlier told Shaw, who then asked, "You got it too, Doc?" Charles's reply—"No, my pain, regrettably, is self-inflicted"—would seem to indicate that liquor brings anguish rather than comfort to the men and women of the 4077. However, as they raise their glasses in the final scene, a celebratory mood settles over the camp, suggesting once again that the social experience of alcohol injects levity and goodwill into a space otherwise laden with death and misery. As a book-ending device—and following the narrative logic of the sitcom formula—the toast scene in this and other *M*A*S*H* episodes ensures a return to the "natural" state of things. That is, what might be seen by some commentators as a potentially disruptive activity (particularly in the military) is in fact the glue that keeps the social status quo intact, bringing equilibrium back to a narrative ironically premised on the mental and physical disequilibrium unique to the wartime experience; an experience that sometimes necessitates the use of alcohol for "self-medication" and "trauma-buffering."

It is only when Hawkeye's alcohol dependency interferes with either his professional duties or his romantic liaisons that he begins to seriously reassess its role in his life. For instance, after a drinking binge leaves him hungover in the episode "Fallen Idol," he is unable to operate on Corporal Walter "Radar" O'Reilly (Gary Burghoff), who was wounded en route to Seoul (sustaining injuries as a result of taking shrapnel while driving a vehicle). And why was the company clerk undertaking such a perilous journey to the South Korean capitol? Because Hawkeye himself had encouraged Radar to see the city, where he might sow his oats and "become a man." That idea, which recalls a similar comment in *Gomer Pyle U.S.M.C.* (when Sergeant Carter enthusiastically remarks that the childlike Private Pyle has "grown up" upon graduating from vanilla malts to alcohol in the episode "Show Me the Way to Go Home"), has long persisted as part of television's "alcoholic imaginary," the medium's reliance upon recurring tropes that affect the public perception of drinking. Once a hero to Radar, the guilt-ridden Hawkeye is now seen in an entirely new light. Only at the end of this episode, when both men order Grape Nehi soft drinks from the bar, are the two able to see eye-to-eye. Equally troubling for Hawkeye is his inability to sustain an erection in bed, one of the many subplots presented in "Some 38th Parallels" (4.20). Recalling the Painless Pole (John Schuck)'s predicament in Altman's 1970 film, this development—referred to by Hawkeye as "the Big Couldn't"—nevertheless differs insofar as the onus for such a failure falls on the hero's heavy drinking. It also provides Hawkeye, who has been "getting nasty notes from [his] liver," one of his many reasons to give up alcohol on the show.

Another nasty note—his previous month's bar tab of $38.20—compels Hawkeye to go off drink for a week in season eight's "Bottle Fatigue." From its first scene until its final moments, this episode devotes a significant amount of screen time to the topic of alcoholic consumption, and thus deserves special consideration. It begins with Hawkeye, B.J., Charles, Margaret, and Colonel Potter trudging into the officer's club at a "quarter past catatonic." Physically drained after a full night of OR work, the gang attempts to "synchronize [their] exhaustion" through alcoholic means. As in so many previous episodes, images of drinking thus establish this episode's point of narrative equilibrium. Potter remarks, "At times like this, I feel a debt of gratitude to that old Kentucky gent who discovered that you can do more with barley than make soup." Charles, ever the blueblood, tells his commanding officer that bourbon is "the Grape Nehi of alcoholic beverages." In keeping with his fastidious demeanor, he prefers something more "elegant," such as cognac, to which Potter replies, "Who gives a rat's hat? So long as it numbs the noggin." Igor (Jeff Maxwell), the bartender, promptly passes a double Scotch to Margaret, while B.J. receives a gin and tonic and Potter gets his bourbon neat. When Hawkeye first lays eyes on the bar tab that Igor gives him, he says, "I can't be responsible for this. I must have been drunk at the time." In fact, this is "just the tip of the ice cube," for he also has to worry about the charges that have accrued at the camp's other watering hole, Rosie's bar. Winchester tries to calm Hawkeye, telling him that even his "own alcoholic consumption has been elevated since [he] landed in this leper colony." The others, however, cannot help but laugh when the surgeon says that he is giving up alcohol for a week, telling them in earnest, "I want to prove to myself that I can do it." The scenes that follow thus bring narrative *disequilibrium*, or a disruption of the typical state of affairs at the 4077, something that only alcohol can set right by the end of the episode.

Against the expectations of his friends, the doctor's experiment in sobriety actually succeeds, but not without driving everyone crazy with his "teetotaling tantrums." Ironically, being on the wagon ruins cleanly shaven Hawkeye's chances of getting Nurse Mendenhall (Shelley Long) into bed, for his ill-timed temperance lecture brings their romantic dinner to a premature end. The penultimate scene,

coming after an intense situation in the OR (where a North Korean patient bran-
dished a grenade in fear), shows the beleaguered bunch of doctors and nurses once
again bellying up to the bar in the Officer's Club, where—recalling the episode's
first scene—they order glasses of bourbon and gin and tonic. However, even as this
scene adheres to the standard sitcom formula of coming full circle, bringing order
to a diegetic universe temporarily filled with disorder, it breaks from narrative tradition in a subtle yet significant way. Having given up his sanctimonious attitude
in light of their dangerous standoff with the Communist soldier, Hawkeye holds a
glass of Scotch in his hand and pauses before putting it back on the bar, saying that
he will drink again when he *wants* to, not when he *needs* to.

Episodes shown prior to "Bottle Fatigue," particularly "Period of Adjustment"
(8.06) and "A Night at Rosie's" (7.24), had already established the fact that almost
everyone in the camp turns to alcohol as a means of personal relief and bonding
with others. In the aforementioned "End Run," Radar proclaims his masculinity
in Rosie's Bar by telling B.J. that his liver is no longer a "virgin" (a comment that
recalls an earlier episode, "Springtime" [3.06] in which the company clerk, having
just lost his virginity, says, "I think I've just been slaked!"). Even Potter follows
the path of his younger predecessor, Blake, sharing several swigs of Hawkeye's
whiskey-filled canteen in "The Colonel's Horse" (5.12) and getting so drunk in
"Last Laugh" (6.04) that he falls down like a fool. More dignified is the colonel's
aforementioned toast to his World War I buddies in "Old Soldiers," an episode in
which drinking to the memory of fallen friends is deemed an acceptable act for an
old-timer like Potter, who somehow manages to maintain the dignity of the Service and the decorum of the OR without ever sacrificing his humanity or sense of
humor. Less acceptable, at least in the eyes of many doctors and nurses in the 4077,
is the inability of Margaret's friend, Captain Helen Whitfield (Gail Strickland), to
stay sober in "Bottoms Up." Written by Dennis Koenig and directed by Alan Alda,
this episode from season nine is significant in many ways. It begins by establishing
the long friendship between the two nurses, who play cards in the women's barracks and reminisce about their younger days. One of the best medical personnel
in camp, Helen (who used to be a "party girl") reverts back to the habit she gave
up years ago, turning to alcohol as an escape from the daily grind. This begins to
affect her work in the OR, where, suffering from a hangover, she makes mistakes
in front of Potter and the others. After being found by Klinger in the supply tent
downing a bottle of whiskey, the closet drinker is eventually "outed" by Margaret,
who yells, "People's lives are at stake!"

Besides showing the challenges involved in going off the bottle (Whitfield
gets "the DTs," melting down in the mess tent before finally cleaning up her act),
"Bottoms Up" also allows Margaret to turn the tables on Colonel Potter, a man

2.5. Margaret's friend, Captain Helen Whitfield, gets "the DTs" when trying to go off the bottle in the *M*A*S*H* episode "Bottoms Up." © 20th Television

she so admires and respects that she typically assumes a subservient position with him. Here, however, she barks in Potter's face that he has employed a "double stan-dard" with regard to drinking in the camp (meaning that it is naturally assumed to be okay for men but unpardonable for women). In a scene that recalls the final moments in "Fallen Idol," Houlihan and Potter put aside their temporary differ-ences and order Scotch and water at the bar. "Hold the Scotch," Margaret quickly adds, reflecting the way that the socially conscious television series became a more sobering depiction of sobriety throughout the late-1970s and early-1980s—a time when the drinking age in most states was raised following news reports about teen-age traffic fatalities and increased drug use in high schools. Originally airing in March of 1981, "Bottoms Up" is indicative of the tonal shift that had begun occur-ring in *M*A*S*H* as the series shifted away from outright comedy toward serious drama. The strong presence of alcohol in this episode suggests that literal and figurative intemperance was the order of the day.

In his book *Watching M*A*S*H, Watching America*, James H. Wittebols per-suasively argues that alcohol is integral to this television show's comical yet socially conscious storylines,[30] which would become less satirical, more politically cautious, near the end of its eleven-year broadcast. He points toward late-run episodes such as "Taking the Fifth" (9.09) and "Blood and Guts" (10.13), which indicate that the textual linkage between drinking and sexist attitudes in the military had not dissipated since the 1972 pilot episode. In "Taking the Fifth," Hawkeye the seducer goes so far as to use a rare bottle of Bordeaux to lure one of the camp's nurses into his arms, a form of sexual bribery and questionable foreplay that ultimately fails. Similarly, "Blood and Guts" focuses on a visiting U.N. war correspondent, the gregarious, Hemingwayesque Clayton Kibbee (Gene Evans), who woos the camp's women and writes romanticized, fabricated accounts of American bravery on the battlefield after drinking one too many bottles of Scotch. Initially resentful of Kibbee's encroachment on his territory, Hawkeye is forced to put aside his jealousy once the legendary journalist is wounded and requires medical attention. Kibbee's alcohol-induced irresponsibility is to blame, not only in terms of embellishing dishonest stories of wartime adventure for an oblivious readership back home in the States, but also in terms of crashing B.J.'s motorcycle while on a drunken joyride. Bleeding profusely but too hung over to feel the full extent of the pain, the character falls from grace and becomes a figure of pity rather than envy. Chastened from his humiliating experience, Kibbee ultimately makes amends by writing what the characters believe to be a more honest, *more sober*, account of military life for the daily newspaper *Stars and Stripes*.

As Wittebols points out, prior to that episode's January 18, 1982, broadcast, several American newspapers and magazines (e.g., *Parents* magazine, *US News and World Report*) had begun running alarming accounts of teenage alcoholism and the increase in traffic fatalities resulting from drunk driving. Into the early 1980s, such reports fanned the flames of parental paranoia and fed into legislative and public health attempts to regulate alcohol use among young adults, many of which were couched in the simplistic rhetoric of Nancy Reagan's "Just Say No" anti-drug crusade.[31] Moreover, television writers also began exploiting this hot-button topic, as evidenced by "Alex Moves In" (7.01), a 1981 episode of the CBS sitcom *One Day at a Time* (1975–84), and "DUI," an episode of the NBC medical drama *Quincy, M.E.* (1976–83), which aired that same year. In the latter show, the title character (played by Jack Klugman) leads an anti–drunk driving campaign after a lawyer kills a pedestrian while speeding through Los Angeles in a Rolls-Royce. If the "meatball surgeons" in *M*A*S*H* had been loveable lushes during the early-to-mid-1970s, TV increasingly turned "lousy drunks" into figures of public condemnation rather than identification, a trend of the late-1970s and early-1980s summed up in the words of a police officer in *Quincy, M.E.* who wishes "there were some way we could stop them . . . once and for all." Thus, by the time the episode "Trick or Treatment" (11.02) was broadcast on November 1, 1982, the image of a soldier dealing with wounds coming not from combat but from a drunk-driving incident (in which Corporal Hrabosky, played by a young Andrew Dice Clay, backs into a Korean chicken coop only to find himself on the run from military police) provided evidence of the television series'—and the nation's—changing attitudes toward alcoholic revelry.

Significantly, the early 1980s witnessed a concerted effort on the part of government officials and military leaders to strengthen existing preventative measures while implementing harsher punitive responses to alcohol- and drug-use among enlisted men and women. Military historians have argued that this policy change was in part a response to the crash of a jet on the USS Nimitz's flight deck on May 26, 1981 (killing eleven sailors and three marines, autopsies of which showed evidence of marijuana use among some of the sailors and nonprescription antihistamine use by the Navy pilot).[32] Partially because of that aircraft carrier incident, the Department of Defense created a ten-point program "to control drug abuse that called for increased drug testing, discharge of repeat offenders, improved rehabilitation programs, and a massive education effort."[33] Existing policies, which were primarily aimed at rehabilitating substance abusers, underwent revisions that indicated greater emphasis on prevention and disciplinary actions. Besides instituting tests to measure the presence of alcohol in individuals seeking entrance into the armed forces, the US military began mandating that on-base driving privileges be revoked if a serviceman or servicewoman was convicted of driving while intoxicated (DWI).[34] The DoD's "zero tolerance" policy (which, in its harshest form, could lead to the discharge of soldiers) was highlighted in December of 1981, when the US Navy launched its own "War on Drugs,"[35] the rhetoric of which suggested that military branches were toeing the line drawn by members of the Reagan administration. Not coincidentally, two meetings, convened by the Deputy Assistant Secretary of Defense for Drug Abuse and Alcohol Prevention, were held at the White House in 1982—conferences that brought together nationally recognized experts in toxicology for the purpose of further refining and standardizing "minimal levels for both screening and confirmatory testing."[36]

While events such as these would affect the culture of alcohol that, for decades, had been an entrenched part of military life, it is difficult to claim that they dramatically impacted televisual representations in programs concerning the United States armed forces.[37] For example, the critically lauded ABC war drama *China Beach* (1988–91) broached the subject of substance abuse on more than one occasion, focusing on US medical staff stationed at the 510th Evacuation Hospital in Đà Nẵng, Vietnam. Like their predecessors in the Korean War series *M*A*S*H*, these beleaguered army doctors and nurses frequently turned to the bottle to deal with daily setbacks and the trauma of incoming wounded. Although an ensemble series, one character—the camp's head nurse, Colleen McMurphy

(Dana Delany)—is often singled out, both narratively and critically, as someone whose many contradictions ("a woman proud of her composure and careful in her moral convictions, compassionate but capable of a scathingly condemning glance," according to one commentator) hint at the complexities of the wartime experience and the irrational rationale that leads people to drinking.[38] Referred to by Michael Saenz as a "feminized, Irish Catholic version" of Hawkeye, McMurphy is a central figure not only because she represents *China Beach*'s unusual focalization (shifting the narration from the war film's usual priorities, organized around displays of masculinity, to women), but also because she personified the "mordant irony" that had come to typify cultural productions concerned either with the dark legacy of Vietnam or with the enduring presence of alcohol in military life.[39] If *China Beach* succeeded, as Saenz and other critics claim, in undermining "vainglorious heroism" and portraying war "as a vast and elaborate conceit," then a part of that success can be attributed to its televisual forerunner *M*A*S*H*, which made it possible for Americans to question their own complicity in the creation of a damaging and reductive social imaginary.

According to Charles Taylor, the expression "social imaginary" refers to "the ways people imagine their social existence, how they fit together with others, how things go on between them and their fellows, the expectations that are normally met, and the deeper normative notions and images that underlie these expectations."[40] Common understandings and common practices, shared by many individuals, congeal into "normative" (ideologically entrenched) values and might lead to institutionalized forms of discrimination, exclusion, and othering. As Bill Nichols points out, once a "collection of prejudicial images [are] assigned to different groups within the social dynamics related to power and hierarchy," the social imaginary begins to look more and more like a means of licensing both institutional racism and sexism, among other things. Similarly, thanks to televisual and other types of cultural representations (including, but certainly not limited to, *M*A*S*H*), a kind of alcoholic imaginary has come into existence over the past half-century, one that reflects the contradictory values that society attributes to drinking as both a recreational/relaxing pastime and as a potentially addictive behavior to be stamped out. It is telling that TV viewing, another entertaining experience associated with both positive and negative effects, should be the means by which so many people's understanding of the alcoholic imaginary has been formed.

James Wittebols asserts that, over the course of its eleven-year broadcast, *M*A*S*H* reflected changes in the way that "real-world America" viewed alcohol consumption. Although such transformations "are probably evident in most programming of the 1970s," Larry Gelbart and Gene Reynolds's creation was particularly attuned to the attitudinal shifts occurring at a time when the negative consequences of substance abuse (among the nation's youth as well as within military contexts) were making headlines in US newspapers and magazines. However, as Wittebols also correctly claims, M*A*S*H "presents a nuanced perspective, neither underplaying nor exaggerating the fact that alcohol and drugs in general have problematic aspects."[41] This, I argue, is what distinguishes the series and makes it all the more relevant today, in a culture that has become ever more attuned to televised images of inebriation (on network sitcoms such as *The Drew Carey Show* [ABC, 1995–2004], *Two and a Half Men* [CBS, 2003–15], and *How I Met Your Mother* [CBS, 2005–14] as well as critically lauded cable dramas like *Rescue Me* [FX, 2004–11] and *Mad Men* [AMC, 2007–15]).

Why do military personnel use alcohol? Often for the same reasons that non-military individuals partake in spirits: to relieve stress; to cope with boredom; to distract oneself from one's loneliness or sense of isolation; to compensate for a lack of other recreational activities; or simply because they enjoy the taste and find its affects appealing.[42] However, the men and women serving in the US Armed Forces sometimes face challenges that few noncombatants and civilians are asked to endure, and thus turn to drink as a means of dealing with the psychic dislocation of war and familial separation. M*A*S*H presents viewers with a type of ritualized, militarily contextualized drinking that is unique to the wartime experience, but understandable to anyone who has ever sought a source of relief from pain. Yes, sometimes alcohol is merely used for recreational purposes in the series; for instance, to spice up an otherwise boring game, as in the episode "George" (2.22), when the surgeons play checkers with shot glasses—each jump entailing a throwback of the drink. And yet, while the clownish doctors may down bottles of beer in the Officer's Club and call out for sacramental wine at the sight of an attractive nurse, they are also "responsible professionals dealing with terrible causalities under great stress,"[43] an aspect of M*A*S*H that lifts it above many other examples of televisual insobriety, even as it contributes to a conflicting set of social values; that is, to an alcoholic imaginary that continues to change with each new cultural representation.

Show Me the Way to AA

> If I want spiritual advice, I'll get drunk with the chaplain.
> —the "rule-and-regulation-breaking" Major Boyington,
>   speaking frankly to one of his superiors, in the pilot
>   episode of *Baa Baa Black Sheep*

Beyond the sitcoms mentioned above, one could point toward many other examples of military-themed TV episodes as signs of the public's often-contradictory attitudes concerning drinking and drunkenness. For instance, future explorations of this subject would surely benefit from looking at the World War II–set comedy-drama *Baa Baa Black Sheep*, which aired on NBC stations between 1976 and 1978. As the cultural historian A. Bowdoin Van Riper notes, this "heavily fictionalized version of the exploits of a U.S. Marine Corps fighter squadron" not only harkens back to earlier TV programs such as *Combat!* (ABC, 1962–67), *Twelve O'Clock High* (ABC, 1964–67), and *The Rat Patrol* (ABC, 1966–68), but also recalls studio-era films produced during and after the Second World War.[44] Small-unit dramas such as *Wake Island* (1942), *Destination Tokyo* (1943), *Battleground* (1949), and *The Sands of Iwo Jima* (1949) each showcase an ethnically mixed, ragtag group of enlisted men who, under the leadership of "a hard-nosed commanding officer" or "a tough-minded veteran sergeant," manage to put aside their differences (e.g., "wisecracking New Yorker," "boastful Texan," "painfully innocent Midwestern farm boy," "skirt-chasing musician from California") for the sake of standing strong against a common enemy. Male comradery, teamwork, and other homosocial relations are thus emphasized, not only in scenes pitting these films' American heroes against German or Japanese soldiers and sailors, but also during the lulls between fighting—quiet interludes when the men let down their guards and open up to one another. Over the spread of thirty-five hour-long episodes, *Baa Baa Black Sheep* spills over with such scenes, balancing the spectacle of aerial combat—footage of which was taken from earlier Hollywood war films and WWII documentaries—with the combined comedy and drama of interpersonal relationships. But it does so with greater emphasis on the kind of casual and heavy drinking that, as Nick Mansfield and other historians argue, has been a part of many countries' military cultures since at least the beginning of the nineteenth century, but which was largely kept offscreen during the 1940s.[45]

In his book *Soldiers as Workers: Class, Employment, Conflict and the Nineteenth-Century Military*, Mansfield states that the British army's "main social problem" during the 1800s, exacerbated by "disproportionate free time" (relative to the amount of time its units were deployed as front-line combatants), was "excessive drinking of alcohol in reaction to boredom."[46] One could easily transpose that historically specific assessment onto the many images of liquor consumption witnessed in both *M*A*S*H* and *Baa Baa Black Sheep*, which each go to great lengths to show why military personnel, be they medical staff or fighter pilots, might partake in spirits. As discussed earlier, several reasons are given as textually inscribed justification for the potentially dangerous activities that the main characters of these shows resort to when blowing off steam or seeking relief from both the eventful and uneventful moments of wartime work. It should be stated, however, that these programs of the 1970s, watched by millions of viewers at a time when seemingly everyone in the US military could "get away with being blasted" (in the words of one retired Air Force lieutenant colonel), steered clear of outright condemnation, opting instead for a more nuanced, if still-contradictory, set of appeals. Indeed, these television productions were not that dissimilar from their 1960s sitcom predecessors in turning a blind eye to the manner in which heavy binge-drinking might encourage criminal acts and desertion, which Mansfield calls "the perennial problems of army life" (regardless of time period or national affiliation).[47]

One thing that distinguishes TV shows of the 1970s and 1980s from their forerunners from previous decades is the increasingly prominent role that Alcoholics Anonymous—a mutual aid support group whose current membership numbers in the millions—plays in narratives about the reform or rehabilitation of addicts. Notably, an early spoken reference to AA occurs in a military-themed episode of the working-class sitcom *Laverne & Shirley* (ABC, 1976–83). Titled "What Do You Do with a Drunken Sailor?" (5.05), this episode, which originally aired on October 18, 1979, concerns a young man in the Navy who, dropping in on his younger sister while on shore leave, is revealed to be an alcoholic. The sailor in question, Bobby Feeney (Ed Begley Jr.), has largely kept his addiction hidden from Shirley

2.6. Bobby Feeney, a sailor visiting his sister and her best friend while on shore leave, is encouraged to seek help for his drinking problem in this episode of *Laverne & Shirley*, one of the first sitcoms to promote the therapeutic appeals of Alcoholics Anonymous. © Miller-Milkis Productions

(Cindy Williams), though she begins to suspect that he has a problem (based on his erratic behavior). Her suspicions are confirmed when a friend waitressing at a pirate-themed bar (which Bobby frequents, despite it being off-limits to military personnel) tells her how he has passed out in the latrine four nights in a row. When confronted by his sister and her pal Laverne (Penny Marshall), Bobby denies that he has a problem and says that he can "handle it." "I don't drink like *him*," he tells her, making reference to his father, a man whose alcoholism apparently factored into his deceitful, possibly abusive relationship with their mother years ago. After blowing up at Shirley (who, once so proud of her older brother, is now forced to push him out of her life), he begins to see how much pain he has caused her, leaving him few options other than to pick up the AA brochure that she left for him and to dial the telephone number on it. When the person on the other end of the line answers the call, Bobby introduces himself in the standard parlance of Alcoholics Anonymous, telling her his name and saying, "I'm an alcoholic."

As we shall see in the next chapter, that spoken line, in addition to Shirley's contention that "alcoholism isn't just a problem, it's a *disease*" (an idea she picked up from the AA pamphlet), is also part of a social imaginary that, up to this point, I have presented only an incomplete picture of. Indeed, in order to fully explain how the alcoholic imaginary creates a horizon of expectations with regards to images of heavy drinking and its aftermath, it is necessary to look at those cultural productions in which recovering addicts reflect on their bad behavior and perform their *sobriety* before groups of their peers (i.e., other men and women who have likewise resolved to "fight their demons" through a twelve-step program in which God is referenced as a key to their salvation). In the same way that Bobby, without the support of loved ones and the quasi-religious fellowship provided by Alcoholics Anonymous, "ain't got a prayer" (to quote Laverne), the characters who populate more recent television series are often shown to be lacking the inner strength or personal resolve needed to kick their addictions on their own. Hence the need to bring them into a cult-like communion with others who not only share their stories of suffering as part of AA's group catharsis but also, in the manner of a standup comedian, employ self-deprecating humor, which is "both common and crucial" to that organization's culture of therapeutic recovery.[48]

3

The Big Book on the Small Screen

Alcoholics Anonymous, Standup Comedy, and Television's Road to Recovery

> Every day, a part of me wants to drink again. Every morning I wake up and I wonder: Today will I embrace Step Seven and ask for help to overcome my shortcomings, or will I kiss my miserable children goodbye, lock myself in the garage, and take down 40 ounces of drug-store vodka before lunch?
>
> > —recovering alcoholic Jean Brockmire Glasscock (Becky Ann Baker) to her brother Jim (Hank Azaria) during a poorly planned intervention for him in a Season Two episode of *Brockmire* (IFC, 2017–20)

> Great. I'm having a breakdown and you're making jokes.
>
> > —Bonnie (Allison Janney) to her Alcoholics Anonymous sponsor Marjorie (Mimi Kennedy) after being told that she can fight the urge to drink by simply helping other people, in a Season Two episode of *Mom* (CBS, 2013–present)

To the casual observer, Alcoholics Anonymous meetings would not appear to offer many comedic possibilities for television showrunners and writers, given the seriousness with which the subject of addiction is typically presented in popular culture texts. Indeed, in the US American context, cultural representations of insobriety tend to be quite "sobering" accounts of the physical dangers of heavy drinking or the emotional and psychological consequences resulting from such activity, as anyone who has watched the films *Days of Wine and Roses* (1962) and *Leaving Las Vegas* (1995) can attest. As such, alcoholism and the long road to recovery undertaken by millions of people in the United States have been seen as difficult topics best left to dramatists, documentarians, and other fact-driven, truth-seeking purveyors of what Bill Nichols has termed "discourses of sobriety,"[1] lest the struggles of addicts and binge-drinkers be trivialized or reduced to a punchline. However, in recent years, several TV comedies have mined humor from a social problem that has been scientifically framed as either a learned behavior that can be "unlearned" through abstinence or a progressive disease that can be treated (if not "cured") through medical intervention. Examples of this trend include network sitcoms from the 1990s and 2000s, such as *Murphy Brown* (CBS, 1988–98), *The John Larroquette Show* (NBC, 1993–96), and *Malcolm in the Middle* (Fox, 2000–2006), as well as premium cable and web series from the past dozen years, such as *Shameless* (Showtime, 2011–present), *Girls* (HBO, 2012–17), *BoJack Horseman* (Netflix, 2014–20), *Flaked* (Netflix, 2016–17), *Love* (Netflix, 2016–18), and *Single Drunk Female* (Freeform, 2022–present), in which the familiar phrase "My name is [_____] and I'm an alcoholic" is spoken by characters in moments of honest self-appraisal and loosely organized fellowship alongside other recovering addicts. Most notable among this crop of contemporary programs featuring scenes set within AA meetings is the situation comedy *Mom* (CBS, 2013–present).

Episode after episode, this unassuming yet wickedly acerbic multi-camera sitcom invites viewers into a setting that, for much of television history, had only occasionally been spoken about—not visually depicted—for fear that the onerous task of going through a twelve-step program or the prospect of hearing a character's potentially triggering accounts of alcohol-induced pain might be too heavy a burden for this ostensibly "light," laughtrack-reliant genre to carry.[2] On multiple occasions throughout this series' nearly decade-long broadcast, men and (mainly) women are shown gathering together at AA meetings, taking personal inventories of their shortcomings, publicly admitting to themselves and others of past wrongs, and trying to make amends with those whom they have hurt as a result of their substance abuse. By habitually returning to this site of communal sharing, *Mom* and a few additional examples of what might be termed "discourses of *insobriety*" are thus contributing to the cultural entrenchment of an international association whose shockingly low "success rates" (between 5 and 10 percent) belie its nearly century-long evolution into the world's most popular example of religiously imbued addiction treatment (with a global membership of 2.1 million).[3] But, in uprooting Alcoholics Anonymous from its theological base (grounded in Christian fundamentalist orthodoxy and a "Calvinist style of redemption" that cofounders Bill Wilson and Robert "Bob" Smith inherited from the nondenominational Oxford Group in the 1930s),[4] US comedy programs present only a partial view of a "cult-like" organization that, despite its popularity, remains veiled in semi-secrecy. Moreover, they brush aside some of the common complaints that have been leveled against AA, which, according to its harshest critics, has held a virtual monopoly on the addiction treatment industry and become so synonymous with "therapeutic recovery culture" that more effective scientific alternatives (including those based in cognitive and behavioral psychology) often go unnoticed by people most in need of medical attention.[5]

In this chapter, I use the growing number of spoken and visual references to Alcoholics Anonymous in US television series as evidence not only of Americans' general acceptance of twelve-step programs as a core feature in the rehabilitative care of addicts, but also of a larger cultural shift in representations of insobriety as a problem that can be exploited for its comedic and dramatic potential. Comedy and drama combine in several of the TV shows under consideration, including network series for which the "Very Special Episode" (or "VSE")—once a textually and tonally distinctive break from the norm—has become a more commonly occurring feature than in previous years, one that is integrated into message-heavy or controversy-courting programs with relatively little fanfare. The heyday of the VSE was the 1980s and 1990s, decades that coughed up literally sobering episodes of *Growing Pains* (ABC, 1985–92), *Full House* (ABC, 1987–95), *The Hogan Family* (NBC, 1988–90; CBS, 1990–91), *Saved By the Bell* (NBC, 1989–93), and *Clueless* (ABC, 1996–97; UPN, 1997–99) that, with varying amounts of self-righteous earnestness, deal with the potentially deadly consequences of drunk driving.[6] Typically capped with a PSA-style epilogue in which the actors step out from behind their characters to deliver a lesson to audiences who are encouraged to learn more about the dangers of underage drinking or of getting behind the wheel inebriated (the "number one killer of young people in America," according to one of the performers in *Clueless*'s "None for the Road" [3.15]), these installments of TV series otherwise geared toward frivolity and humor evince a moralizing impulse that is not in keeping with the generally light tone of other, "non-special" episodes. And they do so in the manner of a textual "intervention," interrupting the flow of a series through such rhetorical maneuvers and thereby calling attention to the VSE's constructedness as a hermeneutic object.

Not coincidentally, friends and family members of hard-partying teenagers or adult alcoholics are shown staging interventions in several "Very Special Episodes" of 1980s and 1990s programs, including *Family Ties* (NBC, 1982–89), *My Two Dads* (NBC, 1987–90), *Blossom* (NBC, 1990–95), and *Party of Five* (Fox, 1994–2000). The latter show is a single-camera, teen-driven family drama (rather than a multi-camera sitcom) lacking a laughtrack or the sound of an in-studio audience's reaction. Notably, *Party of Five* includes several spoken and visual references to Alcoholics Anonymous, which one of the five Salinger kids begins attending after his siblings confront him about his heavy drinking. In the episodes following Season Three's "The Intervention" (3.20), we see Bailey Salinger (Scott Wolf) discussing the negative and positive aspects of AA meetings, criticizing the organization's

3.1. During the heyday of the "Very Special Episode" (the 1980s and 1990s), it was not unusual to see the cast members of sitcoms breaking character (and breaking the fourth wall) to solemnly deliver a public service announcement at the end, as happens in this alcohol-themed episode of *Clueless*. © Cockamamie

neo-religious atmosphere (where "everybody sits around and talks about how you have to believe in a higher power [and] . . . surrender yourself to God") but also finding consolation in the company of others who, despite their own skepticism, are willing to take a "Leap of Faith" (to borrow the title of another episode from that third season). The trauma of having recently lost not one but two parents (who, as audiences learn in the show's pilot episode, died in a car crash caused by a drunk driver) is a prominent feature of *Party of Five*, which revolves around the orphaned characters' often-painful efforts to rebuild their family (with college-aged Bailey, the second-born son, stepping into the role of caretaker before his alcohol dependence worsens). But cocreators Christopher Keyser and Amy Lippman also make room for humorous takes on the performative protocols of AA, including its urging of members to introduce themselves by first name only; something that Bailey feels that he has to "practice" before doing it at an actual meeting. He says as much to Sarah (Jennifer Love Hewitt), his off-and-on girlfriend whose life he jeopardized while driving under the influence (in the episode "Hitting Bottom"

[3.21]). After she is released from the hospital where she was recovering from a car collision, a smile flickers across Sarah's scarred face as she reminds Bailey about the *anonymous* part of Alcoholics Anonymous. This moment of levity illustrates how comedy and drama frequently mix whenever such therapeutic discourse is broached for the sake of confronting addiction.

"Performing Sobriety" and "Eavesdropping on Somebody Else's Therapy"

> AA goes against everything that I believe to be good and pure in this world . . .
> It's a cult, I tell ya, just like the Moonies or the homosexuals or the elderly.
> —Karen (Megan Mullally) to Grace (Debra Messing)
> in a Season Seven episode of *Will & Grace* (NBC,
> 1998–2006, 2017–20)

In a scene from "One Gay at a Time" (7.03), an episode of *Will & Grace* that—like many others aired prior to its September 30, 2004, broadcast—generates humor from the snarky putdowns and antics of the vodka-swilling supporting character Karen Walker, this longtime advocate for intemperance confronts a friend who has been attending Alcoholics Anonymous meetings. In typically tactless fashion, she tells Grace (who quotes AA catchphrases like "Easy Does It" and "Let Go and Let God") that the organization is full of "nutjobs." Grace, who had mistakenly stumbled into her first AA meeting during an earlier scene (similar to the blunder made by Judd Hirsch's title character in the pilot episode of the same network's *Dear John* [NBC, 1988–92]), then explains why she has kept going back. In addition to the membership's free coffee and donuts, Alcoholics Anonymous seems to her "like therapy," just what she needs in the aftermath of her recent divorce. "But instead of paying," Grace continues, "they just ask that you give a donation, which I'm not going to do because I'm not an alcoholic." According to her, those two things—free therapy and free food—are the closest a Jewish person will get to "hitting the lottery," one of many satirical remarks to generate laughter from the in-studio audience during this scene. As if to remind us of the sitcom genre's cyclical structure as well as its moralizing tendencies, this episode of *Will & Grace* concludes with another tête-à-tête between the two friends, only now Grace expresses guilt about having encroached upon a space reserved for actual alcoholics. "I know I shouldn't have been there," she tells Karen, "But there's something really nice about having all those people around who would listen."

A similar sentiment is conveyed by the protagonist of another NBC sitcom, *30 Rock* (2006–11), when Liz Lemon (Tina Fey), the head writer of a late-night sketch comedy, explains to her show's producer Pete (Scott Adsit) why she has been attending her boyfriend Floyd (Jason Sudeikis)'s AA meetings (despite her not being an addict). "It was like eavesdropping on somebody else's therapy," she says in the episode "Fireworks" (1.18), which partially revolves around the question of whether Liz will "fake being an alcoholic" for the rest of her life if it means continuing to gain access to Floyd's deepest, darkest secrets (i.e., hearing him "pouring his guts out" to strangers). When pressed by Pete on this issue, Liz responds with a mixture of uncertainty and parody, appropriating yet another AA catchphrase when she tells him, "I'm going to take it one day at a time." Nevertheless, like Grace, who sheepishly admits that she was wrong in pretending to be an alcoholic, the main character of *30 Rock* does the ethically responsible thing and fesses up to deceiving her boyfriend, but not without also resorting to Karen's reductive "crazy-talk" and referring to herself as a "nut-log." Liz's self-deprecating swipe at her own sanity, labeling herself "Anne Heche–crazy" while revealing some of her most embarrassing moments to Floyd (including getting "sexually rejected by not one but two guys who later went to Clown College" and pooping her pants at a Country Steaks all-you-can-eat buffet), ironically puts her in league with the men and women who have used the "safe space" of AA meetings as if it were a comedy club; a place where the "wreckage" of a person's past can be cleared out through laughter. This is something that Melvin Pollner and Jill Stein discuss in their study of "humor and the construction of selves in Alcoholics Anonymous," and which I will return to at a later point before reflecting one last time on comic drunks and the performance of insobriety on the small screen.[7]

First, though, I want to provide a historical frame through which to make sense of an organization that, to politely paraphrase the naysaying cohosts of *Penn & Teller: Bullshit!* (Showtime, 2003–10), is often described as nonsense. Rather than attempt a thorough assessment of Alcoholics Anonymous from the vantage of a cultural historian who, like many others to have written about this quasi-evangelical group, remains skeptical about its methods if not its aims, I wish to begin this chapter on the comic construction of drunkenness as a paradoxically amusing yet depressing type of "bad behavior" by looking at the uncanny parallels between AA meetings and comedic contexts where the line between joke-telling and truth-telling blur. "The truth hurts," if I may borrow an old adage; but the equally clichéd idea that "laughter is the best medicine" has fueled countless scenarios in which fictional characters cope with the pain of withdrawal or personal loss by opening up to others *performatively*, and often with humorous self-deprecation, much like standup comics do on stage. We see this not only in sitcoms like *Mom*, which I will return to momentarily, but also in dramatic programs where Bill Nichols's notion of representational "sobriety" (which the film theorist associates with certain techniques in documentary filmmaking that might heighten an audience's sense of objectivity or a feeling for the "real") is discernible.[8]

Consider, for instance, "Easy Does It" (6.15), an episode of the Emmy Award–winning police procedural *Cagney & Lacey* (CBS, 1982–88) that shows the title characters—a couple of upstanding, occasionally compromised members of the NYPD's 14th Precinct—going undercover as part of their investigation into a string of robberies at Alcoholics Anonymous meetings. For one of the two female protagonists, Christine Cagney (Sharon Gless), this brief stint as a boozer is not much of a stretch, as she has been following in her "hard-drinking Irish cop" father's footsteps and, throughout the sixth season, has begun to let liquor cloud her judgment in the line of duty.[9] When she and her partner, Detective Mary Beth Lacey (Tyne Daly), enter an AA meeting being held in an elegantly appointed conference room in midtown Manhattan, a recovering alcoholic named Hal (Mike Chieffo) is wrapping up his public testimony of being sober for a year ("doing it 'one day at a time,'" he says, quoting the organization's well-known slogan). He is quickly followed by another speaker—an upper-middle-class woman named Laura (Sandra J. Marshall)—who stands at the podium to deliver a similarly affirmative message to the audience seated before her. Following the customary opening, in which the character states her first name and identifies her affliction ("My name is Laura, and I'm an alcoholic"), she begins by remarking that "this is not all easy because I like to drink." She then corrects herself, replacing the word "like" with a term befitting her condition: "I *love* to drink." Hearing this, the other AA members chuckle understandingly. Reverse-angle shots reveal her audience to be in an agreeable mood, smiling and nodding their heads as she continues:

> The guys told me I could drink like a man. Hearing that meant more to me than I had "dynamite legs" or "pretty eyes." Drinking like a man was part of my image. But I never drank on the job in my life. It never interfered. Of course, I did drink *after* work to unwind. But I didn't unwind. Man, I *unraveled*!

At this point, Laura's audience laughs, not because her statement is inherently funny but rather in shared recognition that one person's adverse experience of inebriation is not unlike other people's battles with the bottle. This—the reciprocal interplay between speakers and listeners who switch roles and take comfort in the fact that they are not alone in their individual suffering—is one of the reasons why Alcoholics Anonymous rose in popularity as part of a mutual help movement beginning in the 1940s. Following the 1939 publication of Bill W.'s "Big Book" (which, as AA's "bible," would eventually go through several reprints in multiple languages),[10] that decade kicked off with a string of public relations crusades designed to convince Americans that habitual drunkenness could best be dealt with not through the aversion therapy experiments of previous generations (including medically unsound treatments such as colonic irrigation, prefrontal lobotomies, and spinal puncture), but rather by giving oneself over to a community of other addicts and, most controversially, to a "higher power."[11] As Joe Miller, author of *US of AA: How the Twelve Steps Hijacked the Science of Alcoholism*, notes, the PR efforts of former sanitarium patient Marty Mann—herself a recovering alcoholic who gave seminar talks on behalf of the organization throughout the 1940s as part of a multi-city marketing campaign—were largely responsible for Alcoholic Anonymous's "explosive worldwide growth" in the years that followed.[12] And it was then when her and her male colleagues' central message that alcoholism is a disease rather than a moral defect gained traction through cultural representations like Universal Pictures' 1947 film *Smash-Up* (on which Mann served as a script consultant).

Penned by the soon-to-be-blacklisted screenwriter John Howard Lawson (from an original story by Dorothy Parker and Frank Cavett) and helmed by Stuart Heisler (a studio director known for his commitment to social justice issues), *Smash-Up* is noteworthy for a few reasons. First, it was theatrically released the same year that Congress passed the Alcoholic Rehabilitation Act and the Federal Council of Churches recognized alcoholism as a disease, and just a few months prior to the publication of Dr. Benjamin Karpman's scientific study *The Alcoholic Woman* (1948).[13] This would suggest an amenable, receptive context for what seems to have been a very timely film, although producer Walter Wanger had trouble convincing the script-checkers at the Production Code Administration of its suitability as a female-driven follow-up to Paramount's *The Lost Weekend* (1945), director Billy Wilder's equally unflinching, Academy Award–winning look at alcoholism. While well-received at the time of its publication, Karpman's book, like Wanger, Lawson, and Heisler's motion picture, has since been scrutinized as a problematic representation of female drinkers, or what the psychiatrist refers to as "a *certain* type of alcoholic woman" (e.g., one whose "abnormal" social behavior is a manifestation of subconscious sexual desires).[14] Gabrielle Glaser, author of *Her Best-Kept Secret: Why Women Drink and How They Can Regain Control* (2014), notes how Karpman, in his somewhat lurid description of his patients' debauchery whenever they were soused (e.g., their lesbian tendencies, nymph-like naughtiness, etc.), evinces no compassion "for the broken childhoods, the lost siblings, the physical abuse, or the sexual violence" that led those women to the bottle in the first place.[15] Adhering to the moral guidelines set by the PCA, *Smash-Up* does not venture into such salacious territory. However, the film's contradictory appeals as an entertaining piece of fiction meant to educate the masses about the harmful effects of excessive drinking (on women and their families) make it a notable addition to the postwar re-imagining of alcohol as "mom in a bottle" (to borrow the famous phrase of another psychiatric physician, Edward A. Strecker, whose 1946 book *Their Mother's Son* was published a few months prior to the film's release).

Subtitled "The Story of a Woman," *Smash-Up* includes a passage of dialogue in which yet another medical expert with something to say about female patients, Dr. Lorenz (Carl Esmond), tells the husband of the main character (a nightclub singer played by Susan Hayward) that she is "the victim of a disease" for which "there is only one cure: to give up liquor entirely." In much the same way that diabetics "have to reject sugar and take insulin," the doctor continues, "alcoholics must give up alcohol, live without it." This dialogue, along with the protagonist's comment near the end of the film, when she explains "I had to hit rock-bottom before I could change," indicates some of the ways that *Smash-Up* makes its characters mouthpieces of the organization for which Mann was the most vocal spokesperson during the 1940s. In fact, it was through her efforts as both a proponent of AA and the founding executive director of the National Committee for Education on Alcoholism (NCEA), and thanks to this and a few other postwar Hollywood productions, that "pathological intoxication" (to borrow the lingo of the day)[16]— once thought to be the curse of skid-row bums and moral degenerates—came to be seen as a public health crisis that was not restricted to the working class and which affected *women* as well as men. Like the motion picture that bears her advisory imprint, Mann's speeches—including one briefly featured in a *March of Time* newsreel short from 1946 (entitled "Problem Drinkers," which shows footage of an actual AA meeting, albeit populated with Hollywood extras)—made it possible for millions of Americans to reimagine the alcoholic as someone deserving of sympathy rather than scorn. She also contributed to shattering some of the widespread misperceptions of women as being either unaffected by heavy drinking or, as in the case of Karpman's study, unfairly stigmatized for behavior that is more likely to be excused when performed by men.

"Performance," in fact, is an apt term through which to begin making sense of a film like *Smash-Up*. This is not only because the main character, Angie, is an entertainer who seeks solace in the bottle when her career on the stage stalls out, but also because the gender stereotypes associated with maternal melodramas are magnified over the course of a narrative in which she forgoes her professional ambitions for the sake of her marriage to another, more successful singer and becomes a neglectful mother as a result of her chronic boozing. In heightened melodramatic fashion, the film begins and ends with scenes that frame the lengthy flashback as an all-too-familiar tragedy of a woman's fall from grace and which reveal the nearly fatal consequences of Angie's bad behavior (under the pretense of illness). Bookending shots show the bedridden woman flanked by hospital staff and family members who cast a pitying gaze at her heavily bandaged face, disfigured after she has drunkenly dropped a cigarette and burned down her house. As downbeat and harrowing as this story of maternal sacrifice and female suffering is, *Smash-Up* is almost comical in its exaggerated flaunting of inebriated performativity, not to mention its straight-faced commitment to showing the deleterious effects of a woman "drinking like a man" (and then paying the price for that transgression). Nevertheless, this cultural production, along with Marty Mann's own scripted performances as a recovering alcoholic speaking on behalf of AA, laid the foundation for subsequent cinematic and televisual attempts to deconstruct a social imaginary that had largely neglected to account for women's differently embodied experiences as addicts.

Looping back to *Cagney & Lacey*, which debuted thirty-five years after the theatrical release of *Smash-Up*, one must remember that this was not the first TV series—not even the first cop show—to feature a scene set inside an Alcoholics Anonymous meeting. It had been preceded by a Season One episode of *Hill Street Blues* (NBC, 1981–87; "Jungle Madness" part 2 [1.17]) that similarly hinted at the rigors involved in policing New York City streets while maintaining one's sobriety in the presence of endless temptation. But this more narrowly focused, female-centric program differs from cocreators Steven Bochco and Michael Kozoll's male-dominated ensemble series (which Jonathan Nichols-Pethick calls a "sobering" drama sprinkled with dark humor)[17] in its brief but meaningful incorporation of diegetic laughter during the scene described above; one in which a woman (rather than a man) connects with her audience by way of amusing anecdotes about the severity of her addiction. Far removed from the stereotypical personifications of dipsomania seen in earlier television shows (including a few that I will return to in the second half of this chapter), Laura, like real-life recovering addict and fellow blue-blood Marty Mann years earlier, breaks the masculinist mold of alcoholic representations if not the patriarchal, goal-oriented dictates of the twelve-step program (which calls for a religious adherence to its founders' rules and an acceptance of one's ultimate powerlessness in the grips of this disease). She thus serves as a source of combined identification and inspiration for other women, be they fictional characters like Christine Cagney (who, in the wake of her father's death and throughout much of Season Seven, begins attending AA meetings) or viewers of this show who might likewise laugh or nod in recognition of their own foibles.

Though spirits are often high in *Cagney & Lacey* and a generally affable vibe emanates from the small cast of supporting characters (including the precinct's resident male chauvinist Victor Isbecki [Martin Kove] and its genial supervisor Lieutenant Bert Samuels [Al Waxman], who is hospitalized with a heart-related health scare in the episode referenced earlier), the show—like most police procedurals produced in the United States—maintains a somber tone. The series' disposition toward seriousness is all the more acute during its final seasons, leading up to and following the tragic death of Christine's alcoholic father, Charlie (Dick O'Neill), in the two-parter "Turn, Turn, Turn" (6.21 and 6.22). Given *Cagney & Lacey's* "sobriety" as a cultural production that adopts a serious-minded "just the facts" approach to crime-solving, that fleeting moment of audible laughter in "Easy Does It" stands out as a rare instance of jocularity in an otherwise dramatic show that touches on subjects ranging from alcohol addiction, breast cancer, and reproductive rights to child pornography, date rape, and sexual harassment in the workplace.[18] Despite its status as a feminist show that, to the delight of Gloria Steinem and other fans, "stuck—often bravely—to its liberal guns" during a deeply conservative cultural moment (that of the Reagan era),[19] *Cagney & Lacey* hews to the aesthetic protocols of the male-dominated genre that have been around since the days of *Dragnet* (NBC, 1951–59, 1967–70).[20] In doing so, it proves to be as contradictory as the social imaginary that it contributed to during its original broadcast, a time when the task of juggling opposing views on alcoholism (as either a sign of an individual's self-indulgence or a diagnosable disease) within a single episode was more feasible than rewriting "the rules of the cop show" and creating "something that looked more or less like real life on television" (which *Cagney & Lacey's* most vocal supporters, including Steinem, claimed it did).[21]

Besides referencing a famous AA catchphrase, the cautionary title of that episode insinuates how a certain amount of restraint is needed in order to bring potentially controversial subjects to light on network television. Indeed, "Easy Does It" was an unspoken mantra of mainstream cultural production prior to the airing of *Cagney & Lacey*, especially with regard to topics such as alcoholism that are at least partly distinguished by *excess*, or the idea that "too much of a good thing is never enough." Those words, spoken by Christine during a scene in which Mary Beth, who has been patient in the face of her partner's obstinance, hands her an AA brochure, amplify an earlier comment that likens heavy drinking to being "a kid in a candy store." That analogy, reminiscent of Lucy Ricardo (Lucille Ball)'s drunken statement that Vitameatavegamin tastes "just like candy" (in "Lucy Does a TV Commercial" [1.30]), prompts Mary Beth to remind Christine that "too much candy can make you *sick*," the latter word furthermore dredging up the "illness" discourse that medical doctors had been propagating during the time of *I Love Lucy's* original broadcast.

Additionally, Christine's remark that "too much of a good thing is never enough" reminds me of Todd McGowan's notion that addiction is a form of excessiveness that leads to social exclusion. In his book *Only a Joke Can Save Us*, McGowan underscores the relationship between comedy and addiction, arguing

that the ostracism that typically results from the latter is complemented by the pity
with which onlookers view those whose loss of control denotes a contrasting *lack*.[22]
"Addicts are not funny," he maintains, though "we can laugh at representations
of addiction." How is this possible? According to McGowan, laughter emerges
"when the representation highlights the coincidence of lack and excess in the
figure of the addict."[23] As pointed out in the previous chapters, a comic drunk
within a given film or television episode *might* be an addict (as in the case of W.C.
Fields's character Egbert Sousé in *The Bank Dick* [1940]), but he or she has been
constructed, or cobbled together, from a corpus of existing texts, within a comedic
frame where lack and excess come together to humorous effect (in contrast to the
tragic figures in *The Lost Weekend, Days of Wine and Roses, Leaving Las Vegas*,
and other dramatic tales that keep those two conditions separate).

Not all drunks are bums "laying in gutters," as Mary Beth reminds her partner near the end of "Easy Does It," though she admits to being surprised by how
"put-together" everyone at the AA meeting looked. Laura, the polished-looking
woman who can inspire laughter among her peers by laughing at her own foibles
in the aforementioned scene, might lack the excess associated with the comic
drunk. But she is just as bound to a performative tradition—that of the recovering
addict as now-sober truth-teller—as those who play up their *insobriety* in a physically exaggerated manner. In much the same way that Christine will eventually
do throughout the final season of *Cagney & Lacey* (when the newly promoted
detective trumpets her ability to move "through this [AA] program like a house on
fire"), Laura thus performs her sobriety in a way that accords with Kathleen Anne
Flynn's conceptualization of Alcoholics Anonymous as "theater," or as a space in
which to dramatically act out deeply personal experiences for the sake of social
transformation.[24]

In her ethnographic study "Performing Sobriety: Story and Celebration in
Alcoholics Anonymous," Flynn draws from one-on-one interviews as well as firsthand observations of open-speaker meetings of AA (in addition to larger events
such as "festivals, anniversary meetings, and gratitude dinners") to isolate some of
the key features of this contradictory mode of private-public performance.[25] Frequently taking place in catacombic spaces (e.g., church basements, community
centers, etc.) at regularly scheduled times each month, group meetings are secre-
tive social rituals in which long-established tropes associated with addiction are
repeated with slight variation by individuals who must first learn the language
and structure of "AA talk" before walking that talk. As Flynn explains, "members
are given an extended turn to tell their personal recovery stories" after stating the
customary introduction. From that point they might proceed to deliver a "drunkalogue" (wherein the "humorous or pathetic" aspects of past drinking experiences

are acknowledged) before explaining how they "hit bottom" and eventually out-ran their demons thanks to a "spiritual awakening" that led them down a path toward recovery. Not all AA speeches contain these elements, of course. But even "newcomers" are generally able to acclimate themselves to the rhetorical moves and discursive flows of interpersonal communication unique to Alcoholics Anonymous by picking up on these patterns, these performative techniques enacted at local meetings by so-called "oldtimers."[26] Notably, the author, alluding to the latter group's tendency to joke about painful moments, quotes one oldtimer's three pieces of advice, passed down from his sponsor: "Don't drink, go to meetings, and keep your sense of humor." That final bit of instruction is particularly relevant to the discussion at hand, given comedy TV's tendency to treat the very idea of addiction treatment as a kind of communal talking cure; one in which speakers muse on the darkest episodes of their lives with mordant irony and self-deprecating wit, and often to the audible amusement of their listeners.

Comic "Drunkalogues" and Self-Deprecating Humor

> I had to stop drinking alcohol because I used to wake up nude in front of my car with my keys in my ass.
> —standup comedian Robin Williams, making light
> of his history of alcoholism, in *An Evening at the*
> *Met* (1986)

The American Addiction Foundation's website makes the following connection between Alcoholics Anonymous speakers and standup comedians:

> The best AA speakers are often really funny. You may find yourself leaving the speaker meeting with the feeling that you just enjoyed a standup comedy act. Many people in recovery have a dark sense of humor and we mainly laugh at ourselves . . . It's easy to laugh when somebody at the podium cracks a joke about, for instance, going to jail and being the smelliest bum in the holding cell. You may be shocked to hear the whole room laughing about something most people wouldn't find very funny.[27]

The website's insistence that, "despite the seriousness of problem drinking and the austerity of AA's public image," humor plays an "important role in recovery" (and is therefore a "significant part of the program") echoes the arguments put forward by Melvin Pollner and Jill Stein in their study of the "construction of selves in Alcoholics Anonymous."[28] "To talk about oneself," Pollner and Stein explain, is to bring one's identity as a recovering addict into being, and the tendency among AA members is to "include humorous commentary on wayward or shameful actions" when spinning a narrative before a group of their peers. Paraphrasing Norman Denzin, the authors emphasize that, without some degree of self-mockery (be it spontaneous or prepared in advance), a speaker "will not have learned the full meaning" of being a part of the organization and might not connect with his or her audience through the healing power of laughter in quite the same way. As they state, "In laughing with others at the absurdities and profanities of the alcoholic self, one is immersed in a powerful display of consensual affirmation of the appropriateness of the distinction. In effect, laughter divides the self as it displays the unity of the group."[29]

It is not just humor but a *specific type* of humorous discourse that builds rapport and engenders fellowship among AA members. In the words of Pollner and Stein, "[T]ales of ineptitude, impropriety, and disorientation serve as resources for constructing both individual and collective identity."[30] Thus, the ability to laugh at oneself—to make light of one's past indiscretions or inadequacies—proves to be instrumental not only as a means of demonstrating one's eventual "transcendence" or ability to overcome and distance oneself from alcohol-related setbacks, but also in strengthening group cohesion and encouraging others to do the same. Ironically, the risible nature of such talk, which can "yield positive gains in both the humorist and the audience," can be said to simulate the effects of alcohol as a social lubricant, an aspect of AA meetings that the authors note when highlighting yet another paradoxical aspect of recovery (which is always ongoing, never fully realized, and thus an unachievable goal).[31] Ultimately, there can be no transcendence without *descendance* (or abasement) in the first place, and the "dirty, wild, aggressive, and uncivilized" part of the alcoholic self "can never be completely exorcised," although the recovering self seeks to do that very thing, "one day at a time."[32]

The American Addiction Foundation's example of someone standing at an Alcoholics Anonymous podium and cracking a joke about "going to jail and being the smelliest bum in the holding cell" is noteworthy, for it ushers in the abject undercurrents of the recovering addict, whose self-deprecating humor sometimes dredges up truly horrifying memories of urine- and vomit-related accidents. Here I am reminded of a monologue performed by comedy legend Robin Williams, whose 2009 *Weapons of Self-Destruction* television special finds him reflecting back on his past experiences of being "ethanol challenged." Telling the audience members who have gathered at Washington's D.C.'s posh Constitution Hall that there are several ways to tell if someone is an alcoholic, Williams proceeds to enumerate a few "warning signs," beginning with a very un-posh joke that "after a night of heavy drinking, you wake up fully clothed going 'Hey, somebody shit in my pants!'" This reference to defecation, like Williams's memory of taking a dump in someone's tuba after a particularly hairy bout of liquor consumption (in his 1986 standup comedy film *An Evening at the Met*), illustrates how the trickster-like identity of the recovering addict is partially founded upon scatological humor and a loss of dignity or self-respect that attends such embarrassing acts.

In an essay about the correlation between abjection, addiction, and self-deprecating humor, media scholar Philip Scepanski discusses an "unusual monologue" delivered by Craig Ferguson during an episode of his Peabody Award-winning late-night talk show.[33] Aired on February 20, 2007, that episode of *The Late Late Show with Craig Ferguson* (CBS, 2005–14) featured the same "long, rambling, and conversational" style of observational wit for which the comedian is known. But it also marked a departure from previous episodes by giving him the opportunity to fess up to some fairly embarrassing moments from his alcoholic past that continue to haunt his recovering self (a decade-and-a-half into his sobriety). Fifteen years earlier, at the age of 29, Ferguson woke up above a London pub on Christmas morning (where he had passed out after an all-night bender), "soaked in urine, but unable to remember the source of the fluid."[34] Having suffered a black-out, or what Robin Williams once referred to as "sleepwalking with activities," the Scottish-American TV host can only *hope* that the pee in which he found himself was his own (and not someone else's). His uncertainty about the matter, drenched in pathos, elicits nervous laughter from the audience, who soon go quiet as he details how he wanted to kill himself that Christmas morning. Were it not for an Irish barman who convinced him to stay at the pub (rather than shamble over to the London Tower Bridge, where he was planning to commit suicide), Ferguson would not be here today—a sentiment that is indeed unusual in the context of a late-night comedy program.

However, as Scepanski points out, "comedies are awash . . . in all manner of grotesque fluids," and "popular culture is full of examples of how piss, shit, vomit, blood, and other abject material can be funny."[35] Jokes about death and dying are also abject in the sense that they tend to be expelled from polite conversation, not unlike the way that bodily fluids are flushed away for the sake of maintaining some semblance of cleanliness and order in the universe. Comedy is not only a way to metaphorically reclaim the "urine, feces, and other bodily matter" that we shed, but also, as Ferguson tells his audience, a means of attacking "powerful people" (including "politicians, and the Trumps, and the blowhards") rather than individuals whose vulnerabilities are directly correlated to chronic conditions, such as substance abuse, which cannot be conveniently "cured" through a twenty-eight-day stint in rehab.

By making himself "the butt of the joke," and by admitting to having suicidal thoughts ("I want to kill myself today"), Ferguson paints himself as "vulnerable," a trait that he shares with other recovering alcoholics, including wealthy celebrities whose own foibles he had mocked mercilessly in the episodes leading up to that monologue. Although he references, by name, Britney Spears (whose head-shaving antics, post-rehab, were grist for the late-night comedy mill), the idea that audiences might find a recording artist's or television star's fall from grace simultaneously tragic and funny has circulated in American popular culture since the days of Sid Caesar, a comic pioneer from the 1950s whose career, according to one commentator, "was sabotaged by his drinking and bad behavior."[36] Like Ferguson would do years later, the star of *Your Show of Shows* (NBC, 1950–54) and *Caesar's Hour* (NBC, 1954–57) owned up about his self-destructive tendencies, admitting (in his 1983 memoir *Where Have I Been?*) to having spent a large part of the 1960s and 1970s—a "20-year blackout"—drinking two bottles of Scotch a night on top of barbiturates and tranquilizers. In the words of Frank Rich, who conjures the double meaning of expulsion bound up in the abject, "If Mr. Caesar was not also a master of vomiting up his liquor before it reached his liver and kidneys, we might have long ago mourned his passing."[37]

Opening up about a painful aspect of his life in much the same way that Sid Caesar does in his autobiography, Ferguson lets the audience in and gains their sympathy. But he also, as Scepanski notes, adopts "a rhetorical maneuver that ultimately gives him a biographical and ethical authority to speak on these issues," so much so that his parting words about the role of rehab and the effectiveness of communicating with other recovering addicts carries a great deal of weight.[38] Ending his drunkalogue with the remark that "the only way [he] could deal with it is to find other people who had similar experiences and talk to them" (a not-so-veiled reference to Alcoholics Anonymous, which "doesn't cost a thing" and—located near the front of the telephone book—is "very easy to find"), the comedian performs what amounts to a PSA for AA, doing as much as any celebrity has (before or since) to extol its merits as a safe space for people like him.

One need only to watch the pilot episode of the sitcom *Mom* to see how an Alcoholics Anonymous meeting might assume the appearance of a comedy club, or at the very least resemble other spaces in which laughter denotes the release of tension among individuals who recognize their own problems in the words of another recovering addict. Midway through this episode, Christy (Anna Farris), a divorced mother of two who has been sober for 118 days, stands before her peers and says that the past four months have been the worst of her life. On paper, that statement is not likely to engender much more than a smirk. But when performed by Farris (the star of the show) it is greeted with laughter: that of the people seated before her, which is layered atop that of the studio audience. The same mirthful response accompanies the protagonist's comment that her mother—also a former

3.2. On multiple occasions throughout the eight-season run of *Mom*, Bonnie (a recovering addict) and her daughter Christy (who likewise has a history of drug and alcohol abuse) stand at podiums during AA meetings and deliver monologues that sound like stand-up comedy routines. © Chuck Lorre Productions

drinker and drug user who was selfish and neglectful toward her kids—was her "only role model" growing up; a woman who taught Christy "how to beat a cavity search and still feel like a lady." "Thanks for letting me share," Christy remarks by way of conclusion, telling her fellow AA members "how comforting it is to be in a room with people who are just as screwed up" as she is. Applause rings out as she steps away from the podium and returns to her folding chair, making way for the next speaker whose words are soon drowned out by those of another woman, seated behind her: "Aren't you a little old to be blaming all of your problems on your mother?" This, it turns out, is our introduction to Bonnie (Allison Janney), Christy's mom, who likewise attends Alcoholics Anonymous meetings in hopes of righting the wrongs of her past and healing the emotional wounds that she has caused her daughter. And, like Christy, this other maternal figure will, from the first season of *Mom* until its most recent one, use her time at the podium to purge herself of pent-up hostilities and perform her sobriety humorously.

Take, for example, the opening scene of "Thigh Gap and a Rack of Lamb" (3.02), an episode from Season Three in which Bonnie assumes the now-familiar position at the podium, launching into a comedy routine about her recent relapse (following the death of her boyfriend Alvin [Kevin Pollak] near the end of Season Two). She proudly shows off her driver's license, recently given back to her by the State of California after she had gone to jail for a DUI, and then tells the crowd that "four months picking up trash on the side of the highway" has taught her two

3.3. Like other episodes of *Mom*, "Thigh Gap and a Rack of Lamb" reveals how the simmering problems between mother and daughter erupt in public settings (like AA meetings) as frequently as they do at home. Here, Christy gives Bonnie an earful from a seated position that is reversed from that of the pilot episode (when Bonnie did much the same thing to Christy). © Chuck Lorre Productions

things: "It's never okay to drive under the influence" and "No one looks good in an orange vest." Bonnie wraps up her AA talk by thanking the people who helped her through this difficult period in her life: Marjorie (Mimi Kennedy), an older cancer-survivor who often provides sage advice as Bonnie's sponsor; Jill (Jaime Pressly), a wealthy younger woman whom Christy sponsors; and Wendy (Beth Hall), the most recent addition to the group whose weepy outbursts will become a running gag throughout the remainder of the series. When she returns to her seat, Bonnie gets an earful from her daughter, who, leaning forward, thinks that she should have been thanked as well (at the very least for holding Bonnie's hair back all those times "when she puked"). Notably, the position of the two main characters' seats is the same as that in the pilot episode's AA meeting, only reversed, indicating *Mom*'s situational continuity season-to-season as well as the frequent flipping of roles between mother and daughter as they grow closer to—and more supportive of—one another over time.

A smaller support group, comprised of fewer than a dozen AA members, appears near the end of "Thigh Gap and a Rack of Lamb." Arranged in a circle, the women listen to Christy's description of how liquor once made all of her problems disappear ("vodkacadabra," she says, waving an invisible wand), along with "a lot of jobs, a few boyfriends, one husband, and the years 2002 through 2008." Now that she is sober, though, she admits to having no easy way to cope with her feelings of maternal inadequacy, brought on by the prospect of losing her son to her ex-husband (a former pot-dealing "asshat" who, to her annoyance, has gotten his life back in order after meeting another woman). As Christy wraps up her comically infused list of complaints, a woman in her late teens or early twenties opens the door and enters the room. The visible black eye and bruise on her face brings a sudden end to the studio audience's laughter. Introducing herself to the group as Jodi (Emily Osment) and saying, with some hesitation, "I guess I'm a drug addict," she opens up about her recent run-in with her boyfriend, who reacted violently when she told him that she wanted to get clean. "I have no problems," Christy whispers to Marjorie, who is seated beside her; a remark that highlights how one person's potentially traumatizing experience can put another person's relatively minor misfortunes into perspective. Significantly, Jodi first appeared in the opening scene of this episode, during Bonnie's considerably more upbeat story of getting her driver's license back and overcoming her addiction to pain killers. The young woman's reappearance in the concluding scenes thus suggests the relative ease with which a person can find solace in the company of other addicts and, more specifically, smaller support groups like this one.

A Bar Without Alcohol and a Church Full of Sinners

> "AA's been around for years. It's helped a lot of people get over their addiction."
> "No, it hasn't. They've just traded one addiction for another. Their life goes from being all about drinking to being all about AA. The only difference is, when it's all about drinking, they're more fun."
> —Brian (voiced by Seth MacFarlane), trying to convince Lois (voiced by Alex Borstein) that Alcoholics Anonymous is a waste of time, in a Season Nine episode of *Family Guy* (Fox, 1999–present)

Although *Mom* showcases the positive effects of Alcoholics Anonymous, which its main characters attend on their own free will, a number of other television programs use AA meetings as a way to temporarily "trap" people within a program of recovery that is used as punishment for their bad behavior, including misdemeanors and felonies. We see this, for instance in episodes of TV comedies such as *Roseanne* (ABC, 1988–97), *South Park* (Comedy Central, 1997–present), and *Single Drunk Female* as well as dramatic series such as *Masters of Sex* (Showtime, 2013–16), which revolve around characters who are ordered by court to attend AA meetings after getting DUIs. In the *Family Guy* episode "Friends of Peter G." (9.10), the title character and his talking dog are sentenced to thirty days of Alcoholics Anonymous after causing a public disturbance at a local movie theater

3.4. Seated with their backs to the audience during an AA meeting, Brian and Peter quickly see that what this sad, judgmental place needs is some alcohol—one of many paradoxical "solutions" to the problem of addiction featured in this episode of *Family Guy*. © Fuzzy Door Productions

(where, under the influence, they destroyed private property). Brian, a self-described "social drinker," thinks that this punishment does not fit his crime, and rails against the organization, which asks that its members relinquish their independence and give themselves over to a higher power. He also notes that AA itself can become something of an addiction to those with "nowhere to drink without being judged."[39] Peter, too, believes that he and his canine companion are victims of a judgmental society. "*We* don't got a problem with our drinking," he says, before concluding that "It's *everybody else* who's got a problem with our drinking."

Brian and Peter's epiphany prompts them to take crates of beer to their next AA meeting, to the initial consternation of its attendees, who soon put down their defenses once Brian convinces them that they can shield their loved ones from pain by simply doing their drinking in this safe, nonjudgmental space. "You can't hurt 'em if they don't know you're drunk," he says, before declaring this—the Quahog Community Center—their new "sanctuary." It does not take long, however, before a noise complaint is called in to the police, who send a patrolman down to the community center to investigate. Seeing the cop car pull up to the curb outside the building, the drunken revelers quickly transform the space a second time, turning what looked like a bar into a Christian church; complete with pews, statues of Jesus, and a podium where Peter—now dressed in the garb of a puritanical preacher—speaks to his congregation about the evils of alcohol.

3.5. Having earlier transformed the Quahog Community Center (where weekly AA meet-ings are held) into a bar stocked with alcohol, Peter and his "congregation" are forced to quickly change the setting once more—this time into a place of worship—when police officers arrive on the scene. © Fuzzy Door Productions

At this point, the episode itself transforms into a showstopper, with the major and minor characters singing a comical version of an already-funny song ("Mr. Booze") that was originally recorded in 1964 by Bing Crosby, Dean Martin, and Sammy Davis Jr. for the film *Robin and the 7 Hoods* (1964). Featuring the lyrics "You will wind up wearing tattered shoes if you mess with Mr. Booze" and "You'll feel better once you've testified," the musical number draws attention to some of the physical characteristics of the comic drunk archetype long entrenched within the alcoholic imaginary while gesturing toward the idea that Alcoholics Anonymous is a contemporary iteration of that "old-time religion" that Tennessee Ernie Ford once sang about. Ironically, just as he tells his fake parishioners to "cleanse" themselves on the "path of righteousness," Peter will come to heed his own preaching once he gets into a drunk-driving accident and a black-robed figure of death (voiced by Adam Carolla) shows him what his life will look like if he becomes a total alcoholic (burning his family members with his cigar and having extramarital sex with his boss in a public restroom). However, rather than swear off the sauce completely, he learns how to drink sensibly, in moderation, by the end of "Friends of Peter G.," suggesting the middle-of-the-road approach taken by the creators of *Family Guy* and other television shows that occasionally take up the topic of alcoholism.

Returning once again to *Mom*, we can see that many of its Alcoholics Anony-mous scenes oscillate between tonal registers, balancing the frequently lighthearted banter of the main characters with sobering accounts of domestic abuse, rape, and other forms of misogynistic violence that are just as dangerous to a woman's mental, physical, and spiritual wellbeing as the addictions for which they are seeking treatment. The quasi-mystical "mind, body, and spirit" model of recovery that AA's official literature promotes (and which a small minority of its adherents claim to have achieved),[40] can be only minimally effective if the various problems that either lead to or result from substance abuse—and which, some critics claim, are endemic to the organization's masculine culture (where "silence, discretion, and anonymity are the rule")—are left unattended.[41] Colloquially known as the "13th Step," sexual predation within Alcoholics Anonymous has been openly discussed by former members whose experiences as newcomers to the program were forever tarnished by lecherous oldtimers making inappropriate comments and/or advances.[42]

Likened by one former member—a thirty-one-year-old marketing executive named Laura who was interviewed by Kristen McGuiness for the online addiction and recovery journal *The Fix*—as "a bar without alcohol,"[43] an AA meeting is where romantic connections might be made, as demonstrated in another *Cagney & Lacey* episode ("Land of the Free" [7.15]) that shows Christine talking up a handsome plumber in just such a place. More than one episode of *Mom*, including "A Pirate, Three Frogs and a Prince" (3.05), reveal the lengths that Bonnie and Christy will go to find a man, using Alcoholics Anonymous as testing grounds for developing techniques in flirting. Similarly, episodes of *Cybill* (CBS, 1995–98; "Cybill, Get Your Gun" [3.05]), *It's Always Sunny in Philadelphia* (FX, 2005–12; FXX, 2013–present; "The Gang Gives Back" [2.06]), and other sitcoms show men hitting on women at AA meetings or making sexual overtures in a way that calls into question its status as a "safe space." Through such representations, including the aforementioned "Friends of Peter G." episode (in which Brian, horny and inebriated, leaves the AA meeting with a woman he has just met), we can see that Alcoholics Anonymous is potentially rife with sexual misconduct. This is an issue that the voluntary organization's leaders have largely avoided addressing over the years, and which might endanger some members' sobriety or lower their self-esteem even further if left unaddressed.

The Netflix original series *Flaked*, created by and starring Will Arnett as a recovering alcoholic in his forties living in the bikini-filled Venice neighborhood of Los Angeles, points toward the ways in which men who have been sober for some time (or who, as in Chip's case, falsely claim to be dry) might use the power of their position to take advantage of younger people seeking spiritual guidance or practical pointers. We see this, for instance, in the opening scene of "Horizon" (1.02), an episode that begins with an AA meeting coming to an end and Chip sharing words of advice to two newcomers. Telling the women, who appear to be nearly half his age, that "there's really only one 'honest,' but lots of 'truths,'" the main character (who gives off the somber yet feel-good vibe of a self-help guru but who, in reality, has been deceiving his best friend and other AA members with claims of being off the bottle) invites them to his stool-making shop should they "ever want to talk about anything." While this is not an obvious pick-up line, it is easy to see that this doubly deceptive, shaggily charismatic man (who, it is later revealed, has actually been lying about being an alcoholic) is hitting on women through well-rehearsed philosophical mumbo-jumbo in a communal space that is supposed to be safe, but which, in the words of some commentators, begins to look more and more like a "dangerous religious cult" to the outside observer.

Besides gesturing toward the kinds of flirtatious encounters or "hook-ups" that sometimes occur at AA meetings, *Flaked* is noteworthy for the way that it presents the protagonist's sobriety as a *performance*, complete with recitational speech acts that are indeed part of his "act." The opening seconds of the pilot episode string together close-up shots of a few objects—an ashtray filled with cigarette butts, a wedding ring being nervously spun on an elderly man's finger, a bowl of medallions bearing the phrase "Keep Coming Back," a Styrofoam cup filled with coffee—that make the scene's physical setting seem almost tactile, endowing it with a lived-in feeling that might be familiar to anyone who has ever habitually attended such a gathering. Soon, the camera widens our view of the space, showing a shadowy room where several people sit, attentively drinking in the words of the main character whose distinctive voice is at once booming and intimate, a whisper magnified by microphone into this resounding oratory:

> I came to Venice by accident. Let me rephrase that: I came to Venice *because* of an accident. Ten years ago, I killed a man. It was my fault. There's no excuse for it. See, when it's left up to me, my best thinking, well, my best thinking tells me that it's okay to get loaded and get behind the wheel of a car. And that's what I did. I took another human being's life, and in the process destroyed what was left of mine. But the people in these rooms, you got me sober. You got me back on my feet. Which is just as well as I walk everywhere now.

At this point, Chip, who has yet to actually appear on screen, jokes that "the State of California no longer thinks it's a good idea for me to drive," a comment—similar to Bonnie's remark about her driver's license in *Mom*—that generates laughter from his audience. "You taught me to be humble, to be honest, *brutally honest*, about who I am and what I'd done," he says, concluding that his fellow AA members "taught me that if I really wanted to help myself, I had to stick my hand out and help others."

On first blush, this is all that Chip appears to be doing in the aforementioned scene from the episode "Horizon": lending a helping hand to two newcomers who just happen to be conventionally attractive young women hanging on his every word. However, subsequent scenes in the series reveal the extent of Chip's mendaciousness as well as the ulterior motives that have led him to masquerade as a recovering alcoholic, using AA as part of an elaborate ruse in which he is able to protect his wife Tilly (Heather Graham), from whom he is separated (but not divorced). In a plot twist that tests the limits of narrative plausibility, and which is one reason why *Flaked* has failed to garner the same positive reviews of other darkly comedic programs featuring scenes set in AA meetings (such as the critically lauded *Terriers, Maron* [IFC, 2013–16], and *Brockmire* [IFC, 2017–20]), it is revealed that the deadly drunk-driving incident that Chip references in the pilot episode's opening scene was actually Tilly's fault. *She*, not *he*, had been behind the wheel when the victim—not coincidentally, the brother of Chip's current girlfriend London (Ruth Kearney)—was hit. Significantly, our clearest clue that the nominal hero of this show has not been honest with his fellow Alcoholics Anonymous members, who make him their unofficial "mayor" of Venice Beach, comes in the final episode of Season One, after he has given a nearly verbatim speech to the one he gave in the pilot episode (only this time during a neighborhood council meeting that is held in the same community center where the AA gatherings have taken place). With slight modification (changing a few words here and there for dramatic effect), he spins his tale of taking another person's life while driving under the influence, and even manages to spark laughter upon introducing himself as if standing before a group of other recovering addicts: "Hello, I'm Chip, and I'm an alcoholic."

While he manages to inspire many of the folks who have gathered to hear him speak as part of a "Save Venice" initiative (bringing together local business owners threatened by the city's gentrification and development measures), Chip angers his best friend Dennis (David Sullivan), who now sees through his ruse. As the two walk home following the council meeting, Dennis sarcastically remarks, "That was a hell of a speech . . . Especially the part about the accident. That never fails to impress in the rooms . . . You paint such a great picture, almost as if it *really* happened." Dennis sees that Chip has simply been putting on an act, but in such a lackadaisical fashion that he comes across as *genuine*, like the real article. Much of that authenticity can be attributed to actor Will Arnett's performance, which is rooted in his own experiences as a recovering alcoholic whose stated goal in making *Flaked* was to shed "a little light on [his] relationship" with sobriety, "which at times has been tricky at best."[44] There is, then, a kind of performative doubling-up of *lies as truths*, a layering of fictions based on the biographical facts of the funnyman's heavy-drinking past (including his five-month bender and thoughts of suicide, all of which, according to Arnett, came back to haunt him during the production of *Flaked*, when he suffered a relapse before getting back on the wagon). Learning this about Arnett—an actor best known for playing the self-absorbed magician-showman G.O.B. in *Arrested Development* (Fox, 2003–6; Netflix, 2013–19) and for lending his distinctive voice to the title character in *BoJack Horseman*—complicates a straightforward reading of the critically lambasted series as being nothing more than a long con on his and co-creator Mark Chappell's part; a duplicitous form of storytelling that strings its audience along and is as mendacious as its main character. Indeed, knowledge of his experiences as a member of Alcoholics Anonymous might illuminate why Arnett took umbrage at the many reviewers who complained about the show's inaccuracies and shot back with his own revelation that Chip's real yet performed struggle with sobriety was "happening in real-time" to the actor.

Around the same time that he was working through his own experiences as an alcoholic in *Flaked*, Will Arnett starred in another Netflix comedy-drama that featured AA meetings. Or, rather, an animated version of the actor, anthropomorphically transformed into a talking horse, introduces himself during a group session as someone who has struggled to outrun his demons and has let his thirst for fame—on top of his thirst for liquid intoxicants—cloud his judgments over the years. During the sixth and final season of creator Raphael Bob-Waksberg's *BoJack Horseman*, Arnett's equine character finally hits rock bottom and goes to rehab, but he is so haunted by his past that he pursues psychotherapeutic healing in the company of other recovering addicts. Starting with "The Face of Depression" (6.07), BoJack begins attending AA meetings, but six episodes later (in "The Horny Unicorn" [6.13]) he has become so ostracized by society—for what his own lawyer vaguely refers to as "untoward behavior"—that even the safe space of Alcoholics Anonymous becomes "a tough room" (lingo that will be familiar to anyone who has watched a standup comedian "bomb" on stage or fail to entertain an audience). As a former sitcom star who has seen his celebrity status fade and career opportunities disappear, BoJack suffers from depression, which is made more acute once his friends abandon him and his fans turn against him, labeling the shamed celebrity a "ginormous dick weasel" (to borrow the words of one late-night comedy host in the show, voiced by Samantha Bee). His tragic fall from grace recalls the content of gossipy episodes of *E! True Hollywood Story* (1996–present) or tell-all biographies about the entertainment industry's most notorious boozers and abusers (e.g., Charlie Sheen, Lindsay Lohan, and other film and television stars who have become embroiled in showbiz scandals).

3.6. Suffering from depression after a series of personal and professional set-backs, the title character in *BoJack Horseman* looks for healing at an AA meeting only to encounter a "tough room" (similar to that of a comedy club where the audience is hostile toward the performer). © Tornante Company

Ironically, brief moments of sobering tranquility present themselves in places where authentic experiences are revealed to be fabrications or fictions, as when (at the end of "The Face of Depression") BoJack wanders into a church in Horse-berg, a Puritan reenactment town outside Washington, D.C. Sitting in a pew, he watches the pastor—also a horse—deliver a speech that sounds eerily similar to AA talk. "It is only when we show ourselves forgiveness and mercy that we truly live a life of grace, that we are reborn," the preacher tells his congregation, who begin repeating the phrase "Peace be with you" to one another as the service concludes. BoJack joins in on the handshaking and well-wishing, and the pastor cannot help but notice that this newcomer appears to have "found some solace in our show." The fact that this thirty-minute reenactment—the same length of a sitcom episode—is just a *simulation* of a centuries-old church service does not detract from its meaningfulness as a theatrical approximation of something real and tangible; a substantive coming to grips with one's unmet need for serenity or spiritual wholeness. Notably, besides this concluding scene of self-actualization, which fades out to the accompaniment of James Henry Jr.'s song "Take Me Down Easy," an earlier moment in the episode foregrounds the important role that *performance* plays in the character's life. No longer able to find gainful employment in the entertainment industry, BoJack applies for a teaching position at Wesleyan University, hoping to use his previous training as a sitcom actor to his advantage as a drama professor. This further highlights the kind of work that is required to perform one's sobriety in the church-like setting of an Alcoholics Anonymous

3.7. In the Puritan reenactment town of Horseberg, BoJack experiences a moment of grace and spiritual communion in the company of other churchgoers, in the Season Six episode "The Face of Depression." © Tornante Company

meeting. Such work might just "save" BoJack, giving him a second (or third) lease on life while making something as "silly" as a sitcom (or a reenactment show) seem more relevant or soul-stirring than its critics would like to admit.

With *Flaked* and *BoJack Horseman*, Will Arnett adds his name to a long list of actors who have channeled their real-life experiences as recovering alcoholics and turned their chosen profession into a potentially rehabilitative means of dealing with addiction. From Robert Young, famous for playing the kindhearted patriarch in *Father Knows Best* (CBS, 1954–55, 1958–60; NBC, 1958–60) as well as the wise family practitioner in *Marcus Welby, M.D.* (ABC, 1969–76), to John Goodman, who drank heavily throughout the final seasons of *Roseanne* and during the making of *The Big Lebowski* (1998), scores of Hollywood's onscreen talent have sought help from Alcoholics Anonymous over the years. However, an equally large number of creative artists in the film and television industries—including Charlie Sheen (flippantly described by one professional psychologist as a "human train wreck") and Roseanne Barr (Goodman's highly opinionated costar on the sitcom that bears her name)—have vilified the organization, saying that they "hate" AA.[45] In the preceding pages, I have suggested a few of the reasons why one might adopt a hostile or skeptical attitude toward twelve-step programs. But I have failed to fully convey the rationalization of those who support AA's mission and methods, and who—as representatives of the film and television industries—have used the spotlight of celebrity as a way to spread its founders' religiously imbued message of hope. As John Larroquette muses in one of the many speeches that he performed as an advocate for AA during the 1990s and 2000s, being in a business "where people are paid to satisfy" stars' egos is "a real dangerous place for an alcoholic to be," and there are countless examples of TV actors who succumbed to substance abuse as a result of their work (as he did during the production of the military comedy-drama *Baa Baa Black Sheep* [NBC, 1976–78]).[46] Nevertheless, Larroquette's profession has given him a platform to connect with other people from various walks of life who have fallen victim to "demon rum," and to explain how he—an atheist who grew up Catholic—can reconcile his love of *The Big Book* with his skepticism toward the existence (if not the idea) of God.

Although Larroquette, a New Orleans–born actor best known for his Emmy-winning role as the sex-obsessed prosecutor Dan Fielding in NBC's *Night Court* (1984–92), is not a standup comic, his command of the podium will be evident to anyone who has ever listened to him hold court during an Alcoholics Anonymous meeting, spinning tales of his misadventures as a Catholic school boy-turned-troublemaker into comedy gold. During one such performance, recorded for posterity in the 1990s (and available for listening today through publishers of spoken-word recordings), Larroquette opens up about the intergenerational history of dependency that has severed family ties and led to the premature deaths of loved ones, explaining that he too would be dead were it not for AA. With self-lacerating wit, he describes some of the lowest points in his life, prior to achieving sobriety in the early 1980s (when he first happened upon *The Big Book*), including all-night benders that ended with him sleeping in a pool of carport oil and missing out on his children's earliest years. These and other admissions of bad behavior draw gales of laughter from his audience; a testament not only to Larroquette's gift as a raconteur but also to this organization's conduciveness to humor as a mode of rehabilitative discourse. For him, one of the benefits of being part of AA comes from acknowledging "that someone else could teach [him] something about [his] own life," and that having humility about such things can lead to "real, permanent spiritual awareness."[47]

From the Alcoholic Imaginary to the Cult Imaginary

> "Young man, do you know anything about the 12-Step Program?"
> "Yeah, and I also know a thing or two about cults. I was the leader of one for a while."
>
> —Fourth-grader Stan Marsh (voiced by Trey Parker) to an Alcoholics Anonymous group, in a Season Nine episode of *South Park*

Around the same time that John Larroquette began participating in Alcoholics Anonymous speaking engagements, sharing details about the circumstances that led him to hit rock bottom years earlier, the actor starred in another sitcom, one bearing his own name in the title. Over the course of four seasons (between 1993 and 1996), *The John Larroquette Show* charted the highs and lows of a recovering addict whose situations and spoken lines recall many of the actor's real-life testimonies, suggesting that he and series creator Don Reo sought to bring authenticity to his role as a night-shift manager of the St. Louis bus depot. His character, John Hemingway, introduces himself—to his fellow AA members and to the TV audience—in the opening seconds of the pilot episode. Every episode thereafter begins with an opening credits sequence that presents a montage of moments from his days as a hard-partying barfly before he found his way to AA. Notably, a sign for Alcoholics Anonymous is shown in close-up at the end of that title sequence, indicating in a very direct way how the organization would be integrated into the series. Indeed, half of the first season's twenty-four episodes are conceptually linked to the precepts of the Twelve Steps, including the principle that one should make a "fearless moral inventory" of oneself in addition to asking a higher power to remove one's "shortcomings." The star was aware that *The John Larroquette Show* "wasn't really prime-time network comedy material" (as he stated during an interview),[48] and NBC executives' decision to schedule it opposite ABC's "ratings blockbuster" *Roseanne* "could drive TV viewers to drink" (in the poorly chosen words of one reviewer). Gradually, Hemingway cleans up his life, moving out of a low-rent flophouse into an upscale apartment and mending his relationship with his con-artist mother. Accordingly, the show—initially described by TV critics as "biting," "dark," "edgy," "sarcastic," and "somewhat risqué"—became more mainstream or risk-averse after its first season, though Alcoholics Anonymous remained a recurring part of the main character's day-to-day struggles with recovery.

Significantly, the Season Two episode "A Cult to the System" (2.11) calls attention to the questionable levels of quasi-religious veneration given by AA members to its founding "Book" and to the kind of steadfast devotion—bordering on mania—that would be stigmatized if it were directed at a "false god" or charismatic cult leader. The episode concerns Hemingway's son, Tony (Omri Katz), who has recently joined the Church of the Sacramental Light, or what his father refers to as a "fanatical religious cult." Telling his secretary at the bus depot, Mahalia (Liz Torres), that he believes that people should "find their own paths, make their own mistakes," he immediately undercuts that sentiment by saying that whenever he hears the word "cult" he thinks "Waco." Trucking in language that brings another social imaginary—a "cult imaginary"—into focus, Hemingway refers to his son, who is wearing a white flowing robe and a top knot, as "Sabu" before scolding him for falling victim to the "oldest scam in the book." Asked to give 70 percent of all of his assets and earnings to a group dismissively referred to as the Knot Heads, Tony is being exploited by its leadership and thus robbed of his free will, something that takes place in numerous other television shows of the 1990s (as seen, for example, in the simply titled episode "The Cult" [3.18] from the third season of *Matlock* [NBC, 1986–92; ABC, 1992–95]).

However, the young man turns the tables on his father, pointedly asking, "What about the cult *you're* in?" A look of confusion flashes across Hemingway's face. When asked what he means by that statement, Tony continues: "AA, that's kind of a cult, isn't it?" At this point, the protagonist, who has been calling the Knot Heads "dangerous," goes on the defensive, telling his son, "It's totally different. First of all, AA saved my life. And secondly, it doesn't ask me to give 70 percent of my salary, and it certainly doesn't ask me to renounce my son." The scene ends with Tony posing the rhetorical question "What if I asked you to quit? What if I asked you to choose between the Program and me?"—leading his father to admit that he was wrong to make fun of Tony's religion and that he has let his addiction to his own source of spiritual salvation (Alcoholics Anonymous) get in the way of his other relationships (to friends and family).

Coincidentally, around the same time that Larroquette was turning to AA as a solution to his drinking problem (in the early 1980s), he guest-starred in an episode of the sitcom *Mork & Mindy* (ABC, 1978–82) that showed him barking out orders to a group of religious "fanatics" called the Utopians. Appearing midway through "Alienation" (4.09), after the overgrown, half-Orkan son of the title characters (played by the fifty-something comic legend Jonathan Winters) has run away from home and joined a cult at the airport, Larroquette's black-robed Baba Hope embodies many of the stereotypes that have become an indelible part of television's cult imaginary. In fact, Baba Hope is not a charismatic cult leader but rather a second-in-command spokesperson for the group's founder, Baba Love. Throughout the second half of the episode, the latter remains an offscreen figure of combined benevolence and intimidation who exerts God-like power over his flock of followers, forcing them to divest themselves of all worldly possessions (e.g., "jewelry, money, second-trust deeds"). Predictably, Mork (Robin Williams) and Mindy (Pam Dawber) are successful in diverting the Babas from their mission and saving their middle-age son Mearth from a life of servitude at the group's Oregon retreat (an obvious reference to the facilities at Rajneeshpuram, built in that Pacific Northwest state by followers of the Indian guru Bhagwan Shree Rajneesh).[49] Telling him that it "takes a lot of courage" to be different from everybody else, these unconventional parents communicate a parting message—to Mearth and to the audience—that is utterly conventional. Nevertheless, in acknowledging that the

Utopians offer a "safe" alternative to the "joyous confrontations" of the real world (e.g., "hypocrisy, violence, nuclear holocausts, and overbearing salespeople"), Mork and Mindy point toward the dystopian conditions from which many people seek relief in the company of others. In the next section of this book, I explore these and other paradoxical features of the cult imaginary.

PART TWO: TV's Cult Imaginary
Comic Cultists, Pathologized Fandoms, and the Rhetoric of "Crazy" Talk

Very Crazy Episodes

Cultivating Misconceptions about Cults
on American Television

> Your religion is laugh-out-loud stupid . . . Your religion is a goofy fruit off the ha-ha bush.
>
> > —Andy (Andy Richter), a writer of technical manuals,
> > to his officemate Byron (Jonathan Slavin), a newly
> > recruited "Zumanist," in a Season Two episode of
> > *Andy Richter Controls the Universe* (Fox, 2002–3)

> You must not ridicule something just because it's different.
>
> > —high-schooler Arnold Horshack (Ron Palillo) to
> > his mother (Ellen Travolta), who has labeled him
> > a "religious fanatic," in a Season Three episode of
> > *Welcome Back, Kotter* (ABC, 1975–79)

The above line of dialogue from an episode of the short-lived American sitcom *Andy Richter Controls the Universe,* spoken by the title character to a co-worker who has found personal meaning and self-confidence in a fictional cult, is merely an exaggerated variation of the kind of verbal assaults often directed at members of new religious movements; men and women who, in the wake of Waco and other well-publicized tragedies, are widely thought to be susceptible to brainwashing, coercion, and destructive actions that might also threaten the lives of nonbelievers. Although Byron has adopted a promising new perspective on life (one that "promotes kindness," in his words), as a Zumanist both his beliefs and his god ("a beautiful sheep that lives in the sky") are subjected to endless ridicule. Such unmitigated disdain for a seemingly unbelievable belief system is consonant with the general tenor of anti-cult messages in the media, which can be said to reflect widespread opinions among television viewers. Indeed, as Jane Dillon and James T. Richardson point out, societal attitudes about cults are decidedly reductive, and the term itself functions as a dismissive "four-letter word" in contemporary parlance, one that likely triggers stereotypical images and associations in the minds of many people.[1]

In his attempt to balance the scales and offer a critically informed, unbiased account of the ways in which new religious movements have been demonized in American popular culture, Lorne L. Dawson points toward some of the most common stereotypes attending this phenomenon, including that of the young, gullible, maladjusted "loser" who finds a "safe haven in the controlled life of a cult."[2] According to Dawson, much of the hostility and prejudice that continues to be directed against cults as spaces of "exotic and dangerous 'otherness'" stem from "the success of the anti-cult movement," initially organized in the United States and other developed nations beginning in the 1970s, not long after the followers of Charles Manson—collectively known as The Family—participated in a series of appalling murders throughout the summer of 1969, including that of Holly-wood actress Sharon Tate. The Manson Family trials that transpired the following year brought worldwide attention to the twisted motives of this doomsday cult, which took its cue from a Beatles song ("Helter Skelter") purportedly prophesying the coming of a race war between African Americans and Caucasian Americans. With an X etched into his forehead during the trial (a mark that would later be replaced with a swastika), Manson embodied all that was dangerous about cults at that pivotal moment in history, when general anxieties morphed into outright fears spilling out from that Los Angeles courtroom and spreading into the coun-try's heartland.[3]

From that point forward, grassroots efforts to return recently indoctrinated converts to conventional family life grew over time, and by the end of the 1970s "an element of professionalism" emerged in the anti-cult movement, "as per-manent staff were hired, efforts were coordinated, concerted legal actions were launched, and full-time 'deprogrammers' began to ply their trade."[4] The decades that followed witnessed the further solidification of the anti-cult movement as well as the entrenchment of public perceptions about those individuals who, in exper-imenting with alternative religions, exhibited behavioral changes that mimicked "the symptoms of mental illness."[5] The young men and women who had become converts (many of them well-educated) were thought to run the risk of changing into "zombie[s] enslaved to . . . unbalanced and immoral cult leader[s]."[6] Contrib-uting to that image of zombified youth, the publication of numerous articles about "violent cults" during the 1970s, 1980s, and 1990s fed into people's worst fears, with aberrant cases falsely identified by journalists as representative instances of cultic belonging.[7] More recently, Scientology and the writings of the American science fiction author L. Ron Hubbard have served as the source of much critical (and comical) discourse in the media, owing in part to the popularity of the Church's many current and former celebrity-members, including Tom Cruise, Kirstie Alley, John Travolta, Leah Remini, and Isaac Hayes, as well as to the controversies surrounding its business operations.[8]

Running parallel to this pathologizing of emergent religions in the press was an attendant increase in the number of cultic representations on the small screen, with television sitcoms and dramas contributing to a reductionist discourse that merely exacerbated public distrust, apprehension, and fear. As we shall see, "cult" itself has since become a kneejerk signifier in popular media representations; a way for writers and producers of TV programs (that might themselves become objects of adulation or devotion) to distance themselves from fans who are sometimes sneered at in the press due to their unconventional consumption practices. Despite the fact that it derives from the Latin *cultus* (meaning "adoration" and "care") and has historically been linked at once to the idea of cultivation or refinement as well as worshipful devotion to a deity,[9] as a pejorative term "cult" continues to serve as a kind of cultural shorthand for all that is "deviant" in audience formations and "dangerous" in new religious movements. As Hillary Robson states, the concept of the "dysfunctional" fan was brought to the forefront of popular culture throughout the 1980s and 1990s, "suggesting that 'cult' is always a negative term, resulting in mass suicides à la Heaven's Gate, brainwashing, polygamy, spousal abuse, or religious sacrifice."[10]

Because of its continued notoriety, Heaven's Gate, which Robson alludes to, needs little in the way of contextualizing commentary. However, it is worth pointing out that the members of this San Diego–based group, led by co-founder Marshall Applewhite (who, years earlier, had launched it as a Book of Revelations–inspired cult with his nurse, Bonnie Nettles, and encouraged his followers to prepare for an Earthly "evacuation" once an assembly of higher beings arrived on the planet), were frequently referred to as "Trekkies" in the mainstream American press. This was due in part to a message worn on its doomed members' all-black clothing—"Heaven's Gate Away Team"—as well as reports that they had been avid science-fiction fans prior to their mass suicide in March of 1997. The deaths of those thirty-nine people, including Applewhite himself as well as the brother of actress Nichelle Nichols (one of the stars of the original *Star Trek* television series), occurred around the time that the Hale-Bopp comet was at its brightest, when it was thought to be accompanied by an alien spacecraft trailing behind it. After police officers arrived on the scene at the group's Rancho Santa Fe mansion (March 26), they not only found the decomposing bodies of those who had overdosed on Phenobarbital, but also discovered evidence that these people had been sci-fi cultists, fans of Gene Roddenberry's groundbreaking program about space travel.[11] Moreover, the Heaven's Gate members were revealed to have been avid computer users, using the medium to spread the "gospel" of their sixty-five-year-old leader. Besides integrating "all manner of *Star Trek* lore into their daily lives," the Heaven's Gate members thus formed what Paul Virilio has referred to as a "cybersect," one that was not so different, according to the French cultural theorist, from pan-Islamic terrorist groups steeped in the histories of decolonization and mass immigration.[12]

Putting aside that odd comparison, Virilio's word choice, prompted by the centrality of computer-mediated communication within Heaven's Gate, is one of a host of terms employed by theorists to categorize this and other groups. Throughout this chapter, I will use the words "cult," "alternative religion," "fringe religion," and "new religious movement" interchangeably when referring to real and fictional organizations that exert considerable power over their followers in comedic and dramatic television series. However, these much-debated expressions are not equal, in terms of the value placed on them in critical communities; nor do they carry the same connotations within cultural productions that exploit the salacious aspects of parasocial belonging and magnify aberrant cases of (self-)destructive behavior for the purpose of gaining that most valuable of commodities: the audience's attention. Just as comedy and drama often collide in narratives where conflicts between the forces of "good" and "evil" are laughably over-the-top, so too do the above terms slide into one another as near-synonyms for the kinds of borderline belief systems that lack the institutional longevity of more traditional faiths. As will become apparent, additional terms attach to the catchall category of "cult," and critics still resort to dismissive language when describing activities that, to outsiders, look "crazy."

"Batshit Crazy" and "Belief-Shaming"

> I would propose that there's no such thing as a cult. "Cult" is a judgment word used to talk about somebody else's tightly knit religious group. Nobody in the world belongs to what they see as a cult.
> —Professor James Tabor (David Grant Wright) to
> radio personality Ron Engelman (Eric Lange) in an
> episode of the TV miniseries *Waco* (2018)[13]

A standard, if somewhat problematic, definition of the term "cult" is supplied by the counseling psychologist Michael D. Langone. He describes it as "a group or movement exhibiting a great or excessive devotion or dedication to some person, idea, or thing, and employing unethically manipulative techniques of persuasion and control designed to advance the goals of the group's leaders, to the actual or possible detriment of members, their families, or the community."[14] Robert L.

Snow, a commander of the Indianapolis Homicide division, expands this definition, albeit in an alarmist fashion, stating, "Cults, along with being centered around the veneration of a living being, use manipulative techniques in recruiting and fund-raising, use high-pressure thought reform techniques to indoctrinate their members . . . demand total and complete obedience from all cult members, and manipulate and use cult members (through free work, excessive donations, sexual favors, etc.) for the benefit of cult leaders."[15] Compounding the hysteria surrounding new religious movements is the notion that such characteristics are *standard* features found in nearly *all* examples, an idea put forth by American deprogrammer Rick Ross (executive director of the Ross Institute for the Study of Destructive Cults, Controversial Groups and Movements), who argues that "a *typical* cult has a charismatic, unaccountable leader, persuades by coercion and exploits its members, economically, sexually or in some other way."[16] It is not surprising, given the excessively dramatic underpinnings of such descriptions, that the term "cult," when compared to other expressions, is more likely to be heard in mainstream media productions, from network television series to commercial motion pictures, and has become a pejorative way to denote "a deviant religious organization with novel beliefs and practices."[17]

Another word, "sect," has also accrued negative associations, thanks partly to television programs in which it is used either as a homophonic pun for "sex" (as happens in the "Reverend Sanford" [6.18] episode of *Sanford and Son* [NBC, 1972–77]) or as a way to castigate obscure offshoots of established religions (as happens in the "Get a Clue" [6.06] episode of *Castle* [ABC, 2009–16]). Unlike a cult, which distinguishes itself as a novel set of attitudes about this world and possibly other worlds (prior to or after death), a sect is "a deviant religious organization with traditional beliefs and practices."[18] According to Rodney Stark and William Sims Bainbridge, its distinctiveness lies in its relationship to the mainstream religion from which it has split (owing to differences in adherents' interpretation of sacred texts), and that separation or schism hints at the antagonism between the two. Its Latin origins remind us that "sect" refers to a "school of thought" about the divine, hence its usefulness in distinguishing between denominations of a single faith-based group whose canonical teachings might differ considerably (e.g., Baptists, Lutherans, and others within the Christian faith). Regardless, the manner in which the term is integrated into TV series as a synonym for "cult" tends to obscure its etymological roots and has contributed to its negative connotations over the years.

The most famous example of that slippage is "The Joy of Sect" (9.13), an episode of *The Simpsons* (Fox, 1989–present) that shows Homer (voiced by Dan Castellaneta) and his family as well as their friends and neighbors in Springfield becoming members of a group called the Movementarians. Lacking a clear relationship to any one established religion, and headed by a Leader who promises a life of bliss (on the distant planet of Blisstonia) to those who give up all their possessions during their stay at a slave compound outside the city limits, this group is, for all intents and purposes, a *cult* and not a sect. However, those two words are used interchangeably as markers of the dangers awaiting brainwashed converts within a "way-out and wrong religion" (to borrow the words of TV news host Kent Brockman [voiced by Harry Shearer] before he too gets sucked into the Movementarians). Well known to many media scholars and television historians, this satirical take on both underground and mainstream religions in creator Matt Groening's animated hit was not the first instance of TV writers painting a dark picture of sectarian practices bordering on cultism. Indeed, an episode of the newspaper drama *Lou Grant* (CBS, 1977–82) did much the same thing, though it at least acknowledged that deprogramming might lead to a life of greater *unhappiness* and isolation compared to the sense of spiritual oneness and interpersonal connection fostered by a schismatic religious group.

Simply titled "Sect" (1.18) and aired on February 6, 1978, that Season One episode of *Lou Grant* follows the "script" of most cult-themed narratives, insofar as it revolves around a college-aged man from California who has traded in his teenager's threads for the saffron robes and shaved heads of the Hare Krishnas. Officially known as the International Society for Krishna Consciousness, this group steeped in the Vedic scriptures of the Bhagavad Gita has been a mainstay of humorous discourse ever since its founding in 1966 (under the leadership of the spiritual guru A. C. Bhaktivedanta Swami Prabhupada). From images of robed devotees calling out for donations at LAX in the Zucker Brothers' *Airplane!* (1980) to a spoof of that same airport scene in the aforementioned "Joy of Sect" episode of *The Simpsons*, the Hare Krishnas have remained a go-to laugh-getter, based in part on their physical appearance as well as their public chanting, dancing, and proselytizing, all of which has been mercilessly mocked in motion pictures and television series; as Homer does when he says, "This, Bart, is a *crazy* man," directing his son's attention to a stranger promoting "Krishna consciousness" at Springfield airport.

Notably, the word "crazy" is spoken numerous times throughout the *Lou Grant* episode, once the title character (played by Ed Asner) gets embroiled in his friend's effort to rescue his son from the Hare Krishnas. Speaking to a husband-wife team of deprogrammers, including a veteran of the Korean War who claims to know a thing or two about brainwashing, Lou asks the couple if they *really* thought their daughter—a former cult member who has since been "saved"—was out of

4.1. In this episode of *The Simpsons*, a member of the Hare Krishnas appears at an airport where Bart and Homer soon encounter a fictional cult group called the Movementarians. Bart's gullible dad informs him that this strange-looking man promoting spiritual awakening and higher consciousness is "crazy"—one of the most commonly uttered words in American TV's cult imaginary. © 20th Television Animation

her mind before being forcibly brought back to her bland middle-class existence. Explaining to the newspaper man that "all cults are the same" insofar as they rob people of their free will and money, Bill and Shirley Ballard (William Boyett and Jean Gillespie) paint their child's predicament with broad strokes and state, "We tried to talk to her about how *crazy* she had been acting, but most of the time we couldn't get near her." Throughout this scene, the Ballards' daughter Kim (Melissa Newman), a woman in her twenties, is sitting between them on a sofa, silently soaking up this anti-cult discourse. She is forced to hear her parents describe her as not only "crazy" but also a "little girl" who has returned to her rightful place (as "Kimmy") in this infantilizing domestic unit.

Although I will return to the theme of infantilization when I introduce yet another survivor of cultish indoctrination and servitude—the main character in Netflix's *Unbreakable Kimmy Schmidt* (2015–20)—a bit later, it bears mentioning here that all the talk of Kimmy's "crazy" behavior in this episode of *Lou Grant* is echoed by the title character's friend at the fictional Los Angeles Tribune, Charlie Hume (Mason Adams), when he asks a judge to weigh in on his son Tommy (David

Hunt Stafford)'s state of mind. Ultimately, Charlie's legal counsel concludes that the young man, who has adopted the moniker Vishnu Das, is within his constitutional right "to make a fool of himself . . . or to find salvation." This important passage of dialogue reminds us that "Sect" was originally broadcast one year after a landmark Supreme Court of New York ruling that called the International Society for Krishna Consciousness a "bona fide religion" with deep historical roots in India, rather than a heretical "cult."[19] Equally significant is a statement made by one of Lou's colleagues at the Tribune, a reporter named Joe (Robert Walden) who is skeptical about anti-cult foundations like Parents for Freedom. As Joe remarks near the end of the episode (in a scene leading up to Charlie's acceptance of Tommy's religious conversion), "I think that any kid who survives sitting in front of the tube for eighteen years and isn't interested in whiter teeth, fresher breath, or moister cat food probably is *not* a likely target for brainwashing." This assertion, like the concluding scene in "The Joy of Sect" that shows the Simpsons mindlessly watching a TV program on their own network (Fox), points the finger at television as a medium capable of indoctrinating "highly suggestible types" like Homer. For all of this self-incriminating commentary, however, these episodes and many more like them would continue to overstate the "craziness" of Hare Krishna types as well as other, more nefarious examples of parasocial belonging.

In the years since "The Joy of Sect" first aired (on February 8, 1998), several more cultural productions have resorted to the rhetorical moves described above in order to mock the foolishness of anyone who might join a new religious movement for reasons that are actually justifiable (when looked at objectively). Indeed, "crazy" continues to pop up in critical assessments of groups like the House of Yahweh, the Rajneeshees, the Cosmic People of Light Powers, the Brethren, and the Moonies—five of the six candidates vying for "History's Craziest Cult" in an episode of the History Channel's *Join or Die with Craig Ferguson* (2016) (which ultimately picked the Peoples Temple Agricultural Project, better known as "Jonestown," as the winner of that dubious honor). Tellingly, the host of that humorous TV panel show gestures toward the hypocrisy that attends such discussions, telling his studio audience, "We're allowed to laugh at cults for their beliefs, which is odd to me because you can't fat-shame people, you better not, and you can't sexual preference shame people, you better not. But you *can* belief-shame people." And, without the least hint of irony in his voice, Ferguson spends the better part of thirty minutes doing just that: shaming individuals who might have turned to those or other cults as a result of difficult life circumstances. Given the fact that religion itself is a system of unproven postulations of reward "based on supernatural assumptions,"[20] it is surprising that so few cultural productions besides *The Simpsons* have extended their satirical critiques of unbelievable beliefs to more orthodox groups. On the other hand, such equal-opportunity offending is not so surprising, since advertisers and broadcasters generally steer clear of anti-religious discourse even as they support programs with anti-cult messages (with one important exception, according to Craig Ferguson, who tells his audience that the Church of Scientology is *not* among that episode's list of "craziest cults" because they have "very powerful lawyers").

In recent years, TV critics have adopted such rhetoric when discussing the programs in which new religious movements appear. An example of this can be seen in the title of *Daily Beast* contributor Nick Schager's review of *Wild Wild Country* (2018). Promising readers a probing look "Inside Netflix's Crazy Sex-Cult Docuseries," Schager draws attention not only to the outlandishness of the red-robed Rajneeshees (i.e., followers of the controversial Indian guru Bhagwan Shree Rajneesh who built an agricultural commune in Oregon in the early 1980s), but also to the idiosyncratic features of a documentary series that makes a spectacle of that group's most scandalous acts. Several viewers of *Wild Wild Country* followed critics' lead in calling out the "craziest" aspects of this spiritual collective and posting online comments that humorously reveal their shock and disbelief upon seeing what transpired at Rajneeshpuram under the supervision of the Bhagwan's personal assistant Ma Anand Sheela. From election-rigging, immigration fraud, and wiretapping to assassination attempts, mass poisoning, and weapons-stockpiling, the many incidents of criminal behavior covered in the Netflix series are at once ridiculous and serious. At times they are literally incendiary. For instance, a sequence near the end of the second episode, pieced together from TV news coverage, details how a Portland hotel owned by followers of the Bhagwan was bombed in 1983, setting up a fierce standoff between the sannyasin-outsiders who had settled in Wasco County a couple of years earlier and the small community of ranchers who had been living in the neighboring town of Antelope since birth (though the latter had nothing to do with the bombing). Because of its built-in bizarreness as a media event, this "flat-out crazy and fascinating chapter in American history" naturally lends itself to comedy,[21] so it was not a surprise to see the creators of the IFC mockumentary series *Documentary Now!* (2015–present) take that new religious movement as the inspiration for its spoof of cult-themed cultural productions.

Partially inspired by motion pictures such as *The Source Family* (2012) and *Holy Hell* (2016), but largely indebted to the formal and stylistic elements on view in *Wild Wild Country*, the two-part episode "Batshit Valley" (3.01 and 3.02) lifts subtext to the level of text, unambiguously announcing its intent to foreground the "craziness" of cult members as a *construct*, a lure to snag audiences drawn to sensationalistic accounts of people behaving badly or irrationally in the name

4.2. Through staged yet intentionally degraded (and seemingly "real")
footage of fictional Father Ra-Shawbard—an obvious reference to the
controversial Indian guru Bhagwan Shree Rajneesh—speaking to his
congregation of followers, the parodic mockumentary series *Documentary Now!* reminds viewers of the prevalence of charismatic cult leaders
in media coverage of the 1970s and 1980s. © Broadway Video

of spiritual fulfillment. Significantly, in his review of this third-season opener of
Documentary Now!, a critically lauded comedy that, by that time (in February
of 2019), had gained a "cult following," *Entertainment Weekly* contributor Dan
Snierson begins by noting how appropriate it is for creator and writer Seth Meyers
to turn his "off-kilter lens" on this subject.[22] He then quotes Meyers, who says that
he has "always been fascinated by cults and the people who join cults and the law
enforcement officers who try to end cults."[23] Starring Owen Wilson as the long-
bearded, Bhagwan-like Father Ra-Shawbard and Michael Keaton as an FBI agent
who uses him as a mole, "Batshit Valley," according to Meyers, "has all of that,"
but it also features the kind of stereotypical representations that might encourage
viewers to belief-shame cultists for doing the very things that pop culture fans take
pleasure in (and which sometimes result in similar labeling/shaming).

Today, the expression "new religious movement," coined by Eileen Barker (a
professor at the London School of Economics), is generally preferred by social
scientists over the more contentious term "cult."[24] However, as Matt Hills argues
in his important study of fan cultures, that latter term, while "negatively charged

within current constellations of meaning," nevertheless remains useful as designation of the ways in which communities built around particular types of religious worship, ceremony, and ritual are marginalized in the culture.[25] Its functionality springs in part from its etymological base, its earlier connection to the kind of adoring attentiveness to an object of devotion that many hardcore fans of pop culture texts appreciate and even emulate. As Cornel Sandvoss states in his equally significant study of fan cultures, "[I]t comes as no surprise that the notion of cult has enjoyed popularity with academics and scholars who are under particular pressure to legitimize their own consumption patterns in relation to educational capital."[26] This is not to suggest, however, that new religious movements are inherently akin to media cults. Indeed, as Henry Jenkins states, "there are more differences between fandom and religion than there are similarities, and similarities extend to any social organization that serves multiple functions in the lives of its members and becomes a site of meaning and emotion."[27] Nor does it mean that we should construe "religiosity" as a stable, unchanging, essentially affected but unthinking (non-critical) form of piety; as an excessive show of one's predisposition to being "taken in" (or "duped," to use a term central to the study of media audiences) by charismatic leaders or cultural producers in an increasingly secularized world. Rather, as Hills argues, attention should be focused on the ways in which fan cultures "draw on the discourses" of other stigmatized groups,[28] including religious organizations "with novel beliefs and practices."[29]

I seek to go one step further, though, in substantiating Hills's claim that, when circuitously passing between "different contexts of use" (from "the sociology of religion" to the "study of media processes and fan cultures in contemporary society"),[30] cult discourses allow us to perceive the interconnectivity of disparate communities, each bound by similar rules and unique languages (dotted with passwords or shibboleths) that dictate how identity might be fashioned from various scraps of culture in the first place. Like David Chidester, who has explored the actual use of the terms "religion" and "cult" by people seeking to make sense of their increasingly mediated lives, I am interested in the "performative extensions" of those terms into the arenas of popular culture production, consumption, and reception.[31] Television programs in particular serve as complex, contradictory sites of meaning where interpellating strategies are employed by producers to "hail" viewers into receptive modes and imaginary scenarios, never more so than in episodes revolving around cults and other communities defined by their devotion to an exclusive or unorthodox system of beliefs, or what Janja Lalich calls a "totalistic ideology."[32] With this in mind, let us turn to some of the recurring representations of cults in American television programs of the past sixty years.

Totalistic Ideology: Fixed Ideas about Fringe Religions and Their Followers

> I've been involved in a number of cults both as a leader and a follower. You have more fun as a follower, but you make more money as a leader.
>
> —Creed Bratton, a creepy quality assurance director, in
> a Season Four episode of *The Office* (NBC, 2005–13)

In addition to the many investigative documentaries and news reports on the subject that have aired on broadcast and cable networks (including The History Channel's *Decoding the Past: Dangerous Devotion* [2006] and The National Geographic Channel's *Inside a Cult* [2008], which both aim to educate the public about past and present splinter groups such as Strong City and the Worldwide Church of God), dozens of fiction-based TV programs have mobilized the imagery of cults for *narrative* purposes, foregrounding often-mystical, quasi-religious and/or ritualistic group activities in ways that build upon earlier representations in American popular culture. Discounting *Ramar of the Jungle* (1952–54), a syndicated adventure series set in "exotic Africa" that, in typically racist fashion, pitted Caucasian physicians and research scientists against dark-skinned crocodile cults and devil-worshippers,[33] the first televisual representations of the subject can be traced back to "The Chinese Hangman" (1.06) and "Mr. Paradise" (1.33), episodes of *Peter Gunn* (NBC, 1958–60) and *77 Sunset Strip* (ABC, 1958–64), respectively. These and other crime dramas of the late–Eisenhower era put forth protagonists who were occasionally hired to investigate the corruption and/or disappearance of people affiliated with cults. "Mr. Paradise," an episode from May 1959 whose title derives from the name of a character seeking to build a new, utopian community called Eden, was among the first to show private detectives going undercover to infiltrate a cult, one that uses mesmerism and other brainwashing strategies to snare new recruits. "The Chinese Hangman," on the other hand, proffered the novel idea of a cult leader hiring the hero (in this case, dapper gumshoe Peter Gunn [Craig Stevens]) to track down a former member of the community who has absconded from the country with a large sum of money. In an early scene of this episode, before Gunn catches up with the beautiful woman in Spain, Ahben Vanesku (Theodore Marcuse), the bald, robed, ethnically amorphous cult leader, tells one of the lieutenants, "We are not a cult . . . We are a *cosmic oneness*." This combination of assertion and denial, coming from an individual who tries to mislead the police (who are investigating an apparent suicide) and to claim a celestial spot in the afterlife despite his misdeeds, likewise set the template for subsequent representations in the years that followed.

Some of the most noteworthy representations along these lines are found in episodes of the science fiction series *The Twilight Zone* (CBS, 1959–64) and *The Outer Limits* (ABC, 1963–65), which were produced at the height of the Cold War, and which feature paranoia-inducing storylines about brainwashing, invading alien life forms, and the specter of nuclear annihilation. Such subject matter, when grafted onto the imagery of cults, assumes greater associational complexity in the context of a postwar American culture becoming increasingly wary of mass-think and the threats to individualism presumably posed by Communism. Moreover, these pioneering programs introduced millions of viewers to a set of representational practices and textual discourses that would, over time, become engrained features of the "cult imaginary," an expression I use to connote the power of television series and other forms of cultural production to construct and perpetuate stereotypes about new religious movements, creating in the process a kind of uncritical/unthinking consensus around topics of which few people have any firsthand knowledge.

For instance, in a Charles Beaumont–penned episode of *The Twilight Zone* titled "The Howling Man" (2.05), the male protagonist—an American scholar named David Ellington (H.M. Wynant)—is on a walking tour through unnamed parts of Europe when he spots a medieval monastery in the distance. Seeking refuge from the pouring rain, he runs into the castle and is quickly confronted by the "Brothers of Truth," a group of religious zealots described by the mysterious title character (who is locked in the basement) as "outcasts, misfits, cut off from the world because the world won't have them."[34] Ellington, however, uses another word to describe this truth-seeking community, which has managed to imprison Satan himself within the cloistered confines of that sanctuary: He calls them a "cult." The hero's deployment of that term essentially codifies the socially marginalized "misfits" as being amenable to deviant behavior, even though it is soon revealed that the Brothers' actions, while unorthodox, have temporarily removed evil from the world by imprisoning the howling devil in the bowels of the castle.

Framed as a flashback set in the aftermath of World War I, the story (which a much older Ellington has been sharing with a hotel maid) presents the viewer with contradictory messages about cults and their members, suggesting that any parasocial formation defined in part by doctrinal difference, geographical isolation, and/or the presence of a charismatic leader (like Brother Jerome, played here by the cultish character actor John Carradine) is to be viewed with a paradoxical mixture of detached skepticism and vested interest. Indeed, Ellington serves as a model of attitudinal mutability for the television show's audience members, who are encouraged to adopt a similarly incredulous perspective vis-à-vis the cult community only to discover, by the end of the flashback, that the "truth" (an oft-spoken word in this episode) of the Brothers' behavior has been lost on the disbelieving maid. Like the initially doubtful, eventually committed storyteller before her (a man who, through sheer perseverance, and in order to expunge his guilt of having freed Satan from that monastery, has managed to track down and imprison the malicious agent of destruction), she frees the howling man in the episode's penultimate moments, capped by host Rod Serling's closing narration (itself a viewer-directed rhetorical invitation to see beyond the ordinary).

Another important *Twilight Zone* episode, one that features the interwoven themes of religious zealotry, mass think, individual guilt, and the potential for human obsolescence, is "The Old Man in the Cave" (5.07). Adapted from Henry Slesar's short story "The Old Man," this entry in the show's fifth season focuses on a small community of nuclear holocaust survivors who have been passively accepting advice on how to build a better future from their titular leader, an unseen oracle who instructs them on the protocols of avoiding fallout and planting healthy alternatives to contaminated canned food. Giving this "essentially postapocalyptic story" a "mechanical twist," Serling reveals that the "old man," after a full decade of dispensing useful information, is actually a *computer,* not a person. This alarms Major French (James Coburn), the head of a regional constabulary who arrives at the farming commune and—"suspicious of any authority figure outside his control"—sets about to expose the Old Man as a fraud.[35] As an allegorical narrative that deals with the theme of authoritarianism and the disciplining of citizens into obedient subjects of their government, this episode is significant as a Cold War–era representation of cult-like behavior, culminating with a display of mob mentality that is unleashed once the stragglers lose faith and discover the truth.[36] Leading up to the moment when they "kill" the sophisticated machine (destroying it "in an orgy of violence"),[37] we are given an opportunity to reflect on the contradictory impulses of the community and are invited to compare this group of undernourished folks to cult fans, who are similarly sustained—kept *alive*—by communication technologies yet are believed to be prone to manipulation.

After *The Twilight Zone* ended its original broadcast run, additional episodes devoted to the subject of cults appeared throughout the 1960s, in such domestic and international crime and espionage programs as *The Saint* (ITV, 1962–69), *The Man from U.N.C.L.E.* (NBC, 1964–67), and *Mission: Impossible* (CBS, 1966–73). As Joseph Laycock notes, a key episode from that period is "The Groovy Guru" (3.15), a satire of hippie culture from the third season of *Get Smart* (NBC, 1965–69; CBS, 1969–70).[38] Broadcast on January 13, 1968 (over a year before the Manson Family murders), this installment of creator Mel Brooks and Buck Henry's spoof of the spy genre revolves around a radio personality who uses that audio-based medium to reach dozens of kids around the Washington, D.C. area before shifting over to a more wide-reaching, multisensory form of mass communication—television—in his bid to brainwash the nation's youth. "Do you have any idea how much damage ten million teenagers could do to this country?" asks the Chief (Edward Platt) of the US counterintelligence agency CONTROL, to which the show's protagonist, Maxwell Smart (Don Adams) replies, "I thought that they had *already* done it." Also known as Agent 86, Max—a clean-cut government employee who works tirelessly to bring down an international organization of evil called KAOS—is very much part of the Establishment, making him a natural enemy of this episode's titular villain. As "the leader of a religious movement that seems inspired by Hinduism," the Groovy Guru (Larry Storch) comes across as an Orientalist stereotype; a "yellowface" throwback to the kinds of racialized representations seen at the beginning of the decade, in Cold War thrillers like *The Manchurian Candidate* (1962). Like the Communist Chinese captors in that film, the Groovy Guru uses hypnosis on his captive audience. Ensconced in his recording booth at the Temple of Meditation and Inner Peace, he seeks to put the nation's youth on his twisted "wavelength" (through subliminal messages in rock music) so that they will "attack all the squares" and thus clear a path for KAOS to take over the country. In the words of Laycock, "Asian religion and mind control are juxtaposed" in this episode of *Get Smart*, a Cold War TV comedy that takes parodic potshots at the counterculture and suggests that young people are at risk of being exploited for—and targeted through—their media addictions.[39]

Several American sitcoms of the 1970s offered up episodes exploring the corrupting influence of new religious movements on impressionable young minds, mobilizing the subject for comedic as well as instructional purposes. For example, in "The De-Programming of Arnold Horshack" (3.07), an episode of the Brooklyn-based "ghetto comedy" *Welcome Back, Kotter* (ABC, 1975–79), a young woman formally known as "Miss Debbie Rothenberg of Forest Hills" but now named Khali Kalu has lured one of the Sweathogs into a cult with vaguely Orientalist trappings.[40] Changing his name to Abu Kareem Hasan, Arnold (Ron Palillo)—a bumbling class clown who now appears in flowing yellow robes, shaking a tambourine and bearing flowers—explains the rationale behind his religious conversion to his classmates at the fictional James Buchanan High School. He tells them that he was pulled into this community of cultists because Khali Kalu told him that he was "beautiful." As the most gullible and socially inept member of the Sweathogs, someone who stands apart from the others due to his diminutive size and geeky proclivity to wheeze when laughing, the former Arnold Horshack is thus drawn to the teachings of "the great prophet" Baba Bebe for purely personal reasons, as a means of boosting his self-esteem. Soon, news of Arnold's seemingly life-altering decision spreads through school, reaching the ears of Principal Woodman (John

4.3. The Sweathogs (Vinnie, Freddie, and Juan) along with their wisecracking teacher try to convince newly converted cult member Arnold to see the error of his ways and return to his "normal" life as a geeky teenager in a 1977 episode of *Welcome Back, Kotter.* © Wolper Productions

Sylvester White) (the basis, it would seem, for Principal Blackman [Greg Holli-mon] in *Strangers with Candy* [Comedy Central, 1999–2000], another program that has devoted an episode to the subject of cults). Marveling at Baba Bebe's ability to brainwash lots of people, Mr. Woodman remarks, "My kind of guy!"

A very different attitude emerges once Arnold's mother learns about his conversion, with Mrs. O'Hara (a name she has taken through remarriage) greeting Arnold with the words, "Look who it is: My son, the religious fanatic!" Admonishing her for this remark, Arnold responds, "Mother, you must not ridicule something just because it's different." Her barbed reply—"I'm not ridiculing it because I don't understand and it's different, I'm ridiculing it because it's *crazy*"—effectively foregrounds the cultural predisposition to deride that which seems extreme or nonsensical to members of the mainstream. Those members include non-followers like the rationally minded Mr. Kotter (Gabe Kaplan), who states near the end of the episode, "That's not religion, that's *slavery*." The teacher's rhetorical maneuver in these closing moments anticipates the kind of negative commentary spoken by characters in contemporary sitcoms of the past quarter century, such as *The*

Wayans Bros. (WB, 1995–99) and *King of the Hill* (Fox, 1997–2009),[41] as well as crime and courtroom dramas such as *Law & Order* (NBC, 1990–2010), an episode of which ("Apocrypha"[4.07]) features multiple conversations between grizzled detectives about the cult that has sprung up around Daniel Hendricks (Sam Robards), a former military officer who, like a true charlatan, became the founder of the Acherusian Temple.[42] On numerous occasions, the New York cops, who are investigating this "grand Poobah's" possible connection to a car bombing incident, tell themselves (and thus remind the viewer) that the followers of Hendricks are "brainwashed," "lonely," "vulnerable," "manipulated," "mentally defected" and "powerless to leave," and that what they belong to is neither a "congregation" nor a "church" in the proper sense.

Like those dismissive asides uttered by Detectives Briscoe (Jerry Orbach) and Logan (Chris Noth) in *Law & Order*, the teacher's remark in *Welcome Back, Kotter* also forestalls the possibility of dialogic dissent, something he normally encourages in the classroom, but which in this case is kept in check through a commonly shared understanding that cults and even hippie communes (like the one that Gabe's wife, Julie Kotter [Marcia Strassman], briefly joined as a teenager in Nebraska, before getting kicked out for doing her nails) are fundamentally different from officially recognized, long-established religions. Ultimately, Mr. Kotter and the gang manage to convince Arnold to leave the cult, thus restoring narrative order by episode's end while dialing the show's moral compass away from the offscreen outsiders back toward the titular teacher. In the concluding moments, the reinstalled member of the Sweathogs modifies the Baba Bebe mantra, proclaiming, "What will be . . . *is happening right here!*"

The same type of scenario—impressionable young man lured into a cult only to be rescued by his friends toward the end—plays out in an episode of the Watts-based *What's Happening!!* (ABC, 1976–79). Titled "Rerun Sees the Light" (2.18), this story too features a group intervention, with the main characters trying to deprogram one of their friends after his brief dalliance with a hippy-like commune. The religious group in question is the Baba Ram Baba Cult, headed by a High Priest (Oscar DeGruy) and High Priestess (Jonelle Allen) who have fooled members of their flock to part ways with their money. As in the aforementioned episode of *Welcome Back, Kotter*, a young woman is responsible for bringing the protagonist into the fold; in this case, it is the High Priestess, who calls herself "Life-is-Love" and who extols the virtues of Mother Nature (symbolized by a head of lettuce called "Ralph").[43] In truth, she is a con artist named Wanda whom Freddie "Rerun" Stubbs (Fred Berry) has met on the corner of 5th and Le Brea, where she was singing and—in keeping with the representation in *Welcome Back, Kotter*—shaking a tambourine. Drawn to her message of living a wholesome and healthy life, free from unnatural or processed foods and committed to educational attainment, Rerun—a Twinkie-addict and two-time high school flunkie—commits fully to his new life, shaving his head and adopting the name "Abu Waseer Rotundo" (which, he informs his friends, translates as "Large Happy One Who Sucks the Lotus"). Later, after Rerun overhears the High Priest and High Priestess mocking their followers as "dupes," he, Dwayne (Haywood Nelson), and Raj (Ernest Thomas) as well as Raj's mother, Ms. Thomas (Mabel King), who pretends to be "Mother Nature," reveal the sham to his fellow Baba Ram Baba members, all of whom get their money back in the episode's penultimate scene.

These episodes are representative, not unique, insofar as they incorporate iconographic motifs associated with traditional Eastern religions and reflect widespread perceptions about cults as shadowy organizations that manipulate their indoctrinated members, exploiting the latter's capacity to donate time and money to advance the goals of group leaders. Other, less humorous American and British television programs from the 1970s, including nearly-forgotten series such as *Special Branch* (ITV, 1969–74) and *James at 15* (NBC, 1977–78), feature episodes that similarly show young characters being persuaded to sell off their valuable possessions as new recruits in vaguely New Age organizations guided more by material acquisition than by the possibility of spiritual transcendence. Significantly, both of the aforementioned sitcom episodes—"The De-Programming of Arnold Horshack" and "Rerun Sees the Light"—were originally broadcast in the late-1970s (October 13, 1977, and February 11, 1978, respectively), at a time when fringe religions, though a relatively benign presence in American cultural life, were being described by medical doctors, psychologists, and social workers in increasingly alarmist language. For example, Dr. Eli Shapiro, writing in 1977, called "destructive cultism" a "sociopathic illness, which is rapidly spreading throughout the US and the rest of the world in the form of a pandemic."[44] Accordingly, toward the end of the decade, darker thanatological themes began to creep into televisual representations, including those that were unleashed in the wake of the most famous cult-related tragedy in modern history: The Jonestown Massacre.

Rather than delve into the complexities of this well-documented instance of mass persuasion, which began when the Indiana-born founder of the Peoples Temple, Jim Jones, moved his congregation of followers from California to Guyana and which culminated with the suicides of nearly 1,000 members (brought about when they ingested cyanide-laced beverages at the behest of their leader), I will simply probe the effects that it had on television programming. In the immediate aftermath of this tragedy, which occurred on November 18, 1978, CBS executives opted to postpone the network's airing of a *Hawaii Five-O* episode ("The Miracle Man" [11.11]) dealing with a group of brainwashed people being duped by a TV preacher. Originally scheduled to air on November 23, that episode was replaced with a presumably less upsetting one ("The Pagoda Factor" [11.08]) once details about the Jonestown murders reached the United States, initiating a new stage of televisual representations and forever associating that most "child-like" or innocent of drinks (Kool-Aid, or rather Fla-Vor-Aid laced with cyanide) with the murderous intentions of Jones and other cult leaders.[45] From that point forward, after a brief period of relative silence on the subject during the early 1980s,[46] the insidious aspects of cults—especially Satanic cults—figured heavily on American TV, pushing to the periphery the more comedic elements on view in programs like *Sanford and Son*, *Welcome Back, Kotter*, *What's Happening!!*, and *Mork & Mindy* (ABC, 1978–82), at least until the 1990s.

During the mid-to-late 1980s, only a few television programs—masculinist action-adventure series including *The Fall Guy* (ABC, 1981–86), *The A-Team* (NBC, 1983–87), and *Airwolf* (CBS, 1984–86)—dared to tap into the cult imaginary, devoting stand-alone episodes to the subject of destructive fringe religions, which are themselves destroyed or wiped out at the end of each story through the efforts of technologically savvy male heroes.[47] However, the past three decades have been especially fertile in terms of the proliferating, contradictory discourses provided by contemporary TV programs, be they situation comedies (such as *Anything But Love* [ABC, 1989–92]), police procedurals (such as *Criminal Minds* [CBS, 2005–20]), fantasy series (such as *Sabrina, the Teenage Witch* [ABC, 1996–2000; WB, 2000–2003]) or science fiction series (such as *Stargate SG-1* [SCI-FI, 1997–2007]). Significantly, it was in the mid-1990s when a host of shows—from *Melrose Place* (Fox, 1992–99) to *Millennium* (Fox, 1996–99)—began to graft conventional iconography of the past to a kind of ongoing extradiegetic commentary concerning contemporaneous events in the United States and abroad. That development occurred in the midst of widely televised events, including the 1993 Waco siege that pitted federal agents against David Koresh and his followers, as well as shocking news reports of money laundering and mass suicides involving members of the Swiss-based Order of the Solar Temple in 1994. In March of 1995, members of Aum Shinrikyo (a new religious movement in Japan) carried out a Sarin gas attack in a Tokyo metro station, killing twelve commuters and injuring dozens more.[48] Then came the revelation, in 1997, that members of the San Diego–based Heaven's Gate cult (a mixture of UFO theories and Christian doctrine) had committed voluntary castration and eventually suicide so that its followers' souls would be transported to a higher plane of existence. Each of these four cults would become fodder for dramatic television series episodes produced in the months and years that followed, and in many cases those events would be conflated and/or linked to previous tragedies, including the Jonestown Massacre.

This tendency to conflate different cults is epitomized in "Inheritance" (3.12), an episode of the NBC crime drama *Profiler* (1996–2000). Toward the end of this stand-alone story (one that is not part of a serially plotted, ongoing narrative), Samantha Waters (Ally Walker), a member of the FBI's Violent Crimes Task Force, interrogates a former cult leader currently incarcerated at the Georgia State Psychiatric Center, hoping to determine why several people with the same rare blood type (who are revealed to be his children) have been killed in recent months. During their meeting, which is staged like the scenes involving agent Clarice Starling (Jodie Foster) and imprisoned serial killer Hannibal Lecter (Anthony Hopkins) in *Silence of the Lambs* (1991), the clearly deranged man (someone who "is more popular than ever," according to another detective, who has "counted six websites, a dozen fan clubs, [and] rap artists recording his manifesto") tells Samantha, "I have had hundreds of names—Jimmie Jones, Koresh, Heaven's Gate. These are facets. These are permutations. I am in every man." Such a comment, which would be repeated with slight variations in other TV programs of the 1990s and 2000s, should serve to remind viewers of the problematic ways in which distinct neo-religious groups are conflated or presented monolithically in the culture at large.

Besides *Profiler*, several other North American programs with strong fan bases have included direct references to Jonestown, Waco, and Heaven's Gate (among other non-fictional cults). For example, in a flashback-filled episode of *The Dead Zone* (USA Network, 2003–7), a paranormal suspense series based on Stephen King's 1979 novel of the same title, psychic investigator Johnny Smith (Anthony Michael Hall) tries to prevent a potentially deadly confrontation between the FBI and a religious group headquartered in North County, Maine. Known as The Seekers, this Christian commune is led by Nathan Carter (J.R. Bourne), a man who—believing himself to be a prophet—has renamed himself Cyrus. When Johnny arrives at the compound, he is confronted by a state police officer, who asks, "Does the name Waco ring a bell? Ninety people lost their lives." At first, the protagonist is hesitant to believe that Cyrus has been brainwashing his flock of followers. When later asked by a judge what his initial impression of the group was, Johnny replies, "It didn't seem like a cult at first, it was more like a *family*," one that simply wanted to be "left alone" so that its members could practice their beliefs in peace. However, the hero finally sees the light once he discovers that the compound is filled with explosives, realizing that, whenever "Carter turned a switch," they—the produce-growing Seekers—"all became pod people." Intoned in voiceover, this comment suggestively sutures together a metaphor associated with the Cold War communist scare of the 1950s (as exemplified in the original *Invasion of the Body Snatchers* [1956]) and the police officer's earlier reference to Waco, a recent event that continues to stand in for or epitomize all that is perilous about parasocial communion.[49] Significantly, the title of this *Dead Zone* episode—"Vortex" (5.08)—not only denotes the turbulent atmosphere outside the compound, where federal agents fire their guns at the armed cult members inside (a showdown compared by one character to "Armageddon"), but also suggests the intertextually dense mixture of narrative and thematic elements that came into play in contemporary television programs of the 2000s, when real and fictional cults were combined or conflated and, perhaps surprisingly (albeit only occasionally), revealed to be *less corrupting* than the mainstream society that has so frequently demonized them.

I will pull at this thread in the next chapter, which is partially devoted to an episode of *Veronica Mars* (UPN, 2004–6; CW, 2006–7) titled "Drinking the Kool-Aid" (1.09). However, it is worth mentioning here that this provocatively titled episode (departing slightly from the young protagonist's ongoing, season-long investigation into the murder of her friend and former high-school classmate Lilly Kane [Amanda Seyfried]) foregrounds the hypocrisy of those who wish to "save" highly suggestible recruits from woodland retreats that are comparatively safer, more spiritually fulfilling spaces of personal growth than the "normal" lives they left behind. Specifically, this episode shows Veronica (Kristen Bell) tracking down another teenager, Casey Gant (Jonathan Bennett), who has sought a healthy alternative to his overbearing parents and the dog-eat-dog world in which they reside (that of the fictional Neptune, California) in the company of other social outcasts. Creator Rob Thomas's contrarian view of parasocial belonging—his series' foregrounding of the positive effects of leaving mainstream society behind for less crassly commercial or dehumanizing pursuits—is not unlike the temporary happiness experienced by the title character in "Mr. Monk Joins a Cult" (6.11), an episode of the comically inflected detective series *Monk* (USA Network, 2002–9) in which an obsessive-compulsive private investigator experiences temporary relief from his debilitating symptoms in the controlled setting of a cult compound. However, in a textual move that departs from the generally affirming, optimistic portrayal of cult life in *Veronica Mars*, this episode of *Monk* rehashes the idea that, ultimately, a resistance to or rejection of rational thought is at the root of any person's desire to be part of such a parasocial formation, as illustrated in Mr. Monk's statement, "I love not thinking. I'm so tired of thinking." It is a comment that he utters after renouncing his former profession, but before he has been deprogrammed back into his former *intelligent* (if still child-like) self.

In his study of American pop culture's stereotypical depictions of cults, Joseph Laycock alludes to the propensity in contemporary television comedy—animated sitcoms in particular—to freely combine elements from several new religious movements, as part of a postmodern move to foreground the laminate surface of representations in the absence (or perpetual deferment) of any ultimate meaning. His examples include the aforementioned "Joy of Sect" episode of *The Simpsons* and the "Chitty Chitty Death Bang" (1.03) episode of *Family Guy* (Fox, 1999– present), which present viewers with a pastiche of "highly publicized incidents," including thinly veiled references to the Erhard Seminars Training (founded by self-help guru Werner Erhard in the early 1970s), Heaven's Gate, the People's Temple, Scientology, and the Unification Church. According to Laycock, these literally cartoonish depictions of cults should not be brushed off as disposable evidence of TV's failure to take new religious movements seriously. Instead, they should be looked upon as proof of popular culture's tendency toward "convergence," or the linking of "numerous banal features of well-known NRMs [new religious movements] back to the most sensationalized events" of decades past.[50] That transhistorical dimension of the cult imaginary has only strengthened in recent years, thanks to animated series such as *Brickleberry* (Comedy Central, 2012–15) that adopt a more aggressive form of satire than their predecessors.

"Woody's Girl" (2.03), an episode of the latter program, offers a smorgasbord of familiar tropes, taking the viewer from a seemingly innocent scene of the title character—head ranger of Brickleberry Park Woodrow Johnson (voiced by Tom Kenny)—doing stress-relieving meditation and yoga with his girlfriend Astral (voiced by Grey Griffin) to a much darker vision of sexual occultism, one in which she dances provocatively inside a circle of hooded men (i.e., her "quirky," cloak-wearing "church friends"). While the young woman bumps and grinds in praise of Lord Targissian, God of the Universe (whose "alien seed" might fill their "vessels" once he descends by spaceship), Woody turns to his furry friend Malloy (an anthropomorphized bear voiced by Daniel Tosh) and remarks, "Hey, it makes more sense than Catholicism." His comment draws attention to another double standard specific to a social imaginary that props up charismatic leaders as "either con artists or suicidal maniacs" preying on "the foolish, gullible, and lonely," but refrains from pointing toward similar power dynamics within bona fide religions whose arcane rituals and supernatural premises are just as deserving of mockery as those found in cults.

Although the characters in many television programs go to great lengths to distinguish between mainstream belief systems and fringe religions, there have been a few exceptional instances in which such distinctions are problematized, as when, in "The Joy of Sect" episode of *The Simpsons*, Bart (voiced by Nancy Cartwright) states, "Church, cult. Cult, church. So we get bored somewhere else every Sunday." This humorous take on the inherent similarities between officially recognized theological traditions and alternative faiths is reminiscent of Barbara Ehrenreich's comment that "forty-eight people donning plastic bags and shooting

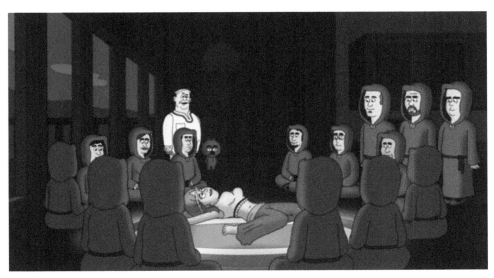

4.4. Astral, a member of a sex cult devoted to the teachings of Lord Targissian, bumps and grinds to the pleasure of several hooded men in this episode of *Brickleberry*. © Comedy Central and DAMN! Show Productions

themselves in the head is a 'cult,' while a hundred million people bowing before a flesh-hating elderly celibate is obviously a world-class religion."[51] Ultimately, the aforementioned episode of *Brickleberry*, after portraying the cultists as lemming-like disciples with bizarre sex fetishes, reveals that their beliefs are actually well-founded. In fact, their mothership finally arrives in time to transport them to a "higher existence" (where they will eat jumbo shrimp to their hearts' content). Nevertheless, the fact that Woody makes that Catholicism joke right after a cultist saunters into frame wearing a handmade diaper, nipple tassels, and colander hat, spouting gibberish about his love for Lord Targissian, highlights how the *cultists'* weird rituals are the main target of satire in this and other TV comedies. Such representations, I have suggested, are no less "cartoonish" in live-action programs that promote a secularist skepticism toward "peculiar groups" led by "con artists or suicidal maniacs" preying on the "foolish, gullible, and lonely."[52]

Healthy Secularist Skepticism and a Rationally Religious Relationship with TV

> Surely one more depiction of new religions as crazy and abusive can't be *that* bad. But we cannot underestimate how little Americans actually know about new religions, or how much damage misconceptions about minority religions can do.
> —Megan Goodwin, "Don't Be Tooken in by *Kimmy Schmidt's* Cult"

"You can't believe everything you hear." These cautionary words, spoken by Raj to Rerun upon learning of the "fly-by-night" Baba Ram Baba religious cult (in the aforementioned 1970s sitcom *What's Happening!!*), might remind readers to take the cultural representations outlined above with a grain of salt. Just as people should be encouraged to adopt a healthy skepticism vis-à-vis the promises that are made by charismatic leaders and the fringe religions that they represent, so too should we be hesitant to embrace or uncritically accept the anti-cult messages disseminated through television narratives, which reproduce well-worn stereotypes and, with few exceptions, create binaristic distinctions between insiders and outsiders. Notably, Raj's levelheaded comment is considerably softer than the many derisive outbursts sprinkled throughout cult-themed episodes of contemporary sitcoms, such as *Everybody Loves Raymond* (CBS, 1996–2005) and *Andy Richter Controls the Universe*. In the former series, the title character's big-boned, large-hearted brother, Robert (Brad Garrett), temporarily joins a community called "Inner Path" and, in the opening scene of the episode "The Cult" (7.01), rhapsodizes about his new and improved outlook on life.

"This is a beautiful day . . . There's a new Robert in town," the once-morose, now-beaming, baritoned brother remarks upon entering Raymond's kitchen, wearing a floral-pattern shirt that is one grass skirt short of turning him into a Polynesian volcano dancer. After learning that Robert joined the group at the behest of his dopey friend Gerard (Fred Stoller), Raymond's wife Debra (Patricia Heaton) muses, "But isn't Gerard an idiot?" This is the first of many sarcastic remarks in *Everybody Loves Raymond* linking cult membership to weak minds or mental deficiency, with the words "stupid" and "nutjob" being repeated several times toward the end of the episode, and with Debra stating outright, "Robert is so impressionable" (to which Raymond responds, "Yeah, he's a dope, so what do we do?"). Even prior to visiting an Inner Path meeting, Raymond informs Robert that "it's like a scam or something." Insisting that "it's not a cult," Robert explains that Inner Path is "just a bunch of people who want to see me happy, who happen to care about me." Although laden with reductive assumptions about cultic membership, this episode of *Everybody Loves Raymond* is partially redeemed at the end, due to its writers' decision to cap the story with a coda in which the male members of the Barone clan (Ray, Robert, and their father Frank) are shown mindlessly following prescribed patterns of behavior in front of the TV while conversing about free will—something obviously missing in this scene, which ends with the men marching, much like cult members, to the dinner table in robotic lockstep.

"Ties That Bind" (2.11), a cult-themed episode of the aforementioned crime drama *Profiler*, is significant here, not only because its title crystallizes the

4.5. Frank berates his eldest son Robert, who has become a "Pathist" (a member of the vaguely New Age group Inner Path) in a 2002 episode of *Everybody Loves Raymond* titled "The Cult." He sarcastically tells Robert, "It's so nice that my son's head is filled with crap . . . What you need is a good kick in the pants!" © Where's Lunch and Worldwide Pants

combined sense of connectivity and constriction that fans might feel in their own interdependent yet frequently isolated roles as "cultists," but also because it identifies one of the reasons why people join such communities in the first place. After being taken by van (a ubiquitous means of cultic transportation) to an agricultural commune guarded by men with machine-guns, the female protagonist—undercover FBI forensic psychologist Samantha Waters—is asked by the new "minister of intelligence" at the compound if she has ever felt lonely.[53] "Do you ever feel that the people around you don't speak or feel like you do?" inquires the cult leader, a question to which Sam responds in the affirmative and which effectively frames the competing discourses that characterize televisual representations of new religious movements, be they the kind of benign groups on view in shows like *Family Guy,* which depicts, in one episode, Peter Griffin as the founder of the First United Church of the Fonz (named after his favorite television character); or more dangerous cults like the one in "Ties That Bind," a group responsible for a series of ritualized murders in the Atlanta area. Diegetically inscribed in the person of a young woman, Maurine Hughes (Rhonda Dotson), who successfully invites Samantha to a group meeting (telling her, "I promise it is *safe*"), this interpellating drive to lure audience members into similarly fraught yet safely detached positions should not obscure the fact that TV's hypothetical scenarios speak to our own desire to belong to (and be metaphorically "tied" together within) an imagined community. Still, most televisual representations of new religious movements draw from a limited repertoire of images and merely rehash conventional storylines.

This is true not only of formulaic sitcoms and crime dramas but also of more unconventional small-screen fare. For example, Netflix's streaming comedy *Unbreakable Kimmy Schmidt*, widely praised for its edgy humor and ironic, feminist take on gender politics, revolves around a young woman striving to acclimate herself to a life of "normality" after spending fifteen years inside a bunker (where she had been imprisoned as a member of Savior Rick's Spooky Church of the Scary Apocalypse). The first scene of the pilot episode ("Kimmy Goes Outside!" [1.01]) shows the 29-year-old title character (Ellie Kemper) decorating a Christmas tree alongside three other women, all conservatively decked out in pompadour hairstyles and long-sleeved prairie dresses. Calling one another "sister," the women—who bear no physical similarities and thus appear to be biologically unrelated—celebrate the holiday as a family through song, changing the lyrics of "O Tannenbaum" to reflect their identity as members of a doomsday cult: "Apocalypse, apocalypse! We caused it with our dumbness." In the words of Megan Goodwin (who has written about the show), "Popular culture has conditioned viewers to expect cult members to look like these women,"[54] and it furthermore comes as no surprise that the darkness of their isolated enclave is soon illuminated by a SWAT team that breaks through the heavily fortified barrier to rescue these helpless victims of the Reverend Richard Wayne Gary Wayne (who, played by Jon Hamm, does not appear onscreen until the eleventh episode). Putting out a hand while bathed in the harsh yet heavenly light of day, one SWAT team member appears as a kind of savior figure in his own right, hoisting Kimmy and her cohort (whom the press calls the "Indiana Mole Women") from their underground lair into the world above. Deliriously spinning around to take in the glorious sight of small-town Durnsville and surrounded by news reporters (who reveal her personal story to the larger public), she is utterly enthralled by, yet wholly unprepared for, the post-cult life that awaits her in New York City.

Significantly, Kimmy's "wide-eyed wonderment" of seeing the Big Apple after spending a decade-and-a-half inside the bunker rang true to many online reviewers, including individuals whose own past experiences with fringe religions resembled the life she left behind. For example, Flor Edwards, in her personal reflection on "What *Unbreakable Kimmy Schmidt* Gets Right" about life in a cult, discusses the years she spent as a former member of the Children of God (CoG), an organization that dates back to the late 1960s and which is today known as The Family International.[55] Labeled a "sect" by the FBI and a "cult" by the New York attorney general's office as well as others familiar with its most disturbing practices, the

4.6. In the pilot episode of *Unbreakable Kimmy Schmidt*, the title character—one of the four "Indiana Mole Women" to have been kidnapped and kept underground by Reverend Richard Wayne Gary Wayne—beams brightly upon being rescued by a SWAT team and stepping outside the bunker. © 3 Arts Entertainment

CoG has been hounded by child-molestation allegations for years and was finally investigated by US and international government officials once former members began to share their accounts of sexual abuse and incarceration during the 1990s. Though his group bears only passing resemblance to Savior Rick's Spooky Church of the Scary Apocalypse, the CoG's founder, David Brandt Berg, is said to have exuded a creepy charm as a heavily bearded, messianic leader in the mold of the Old Testament's Moses, and the many accusations of pedophilia leveled against him prior to his 1994 death bring to mind the most unsavory aspects of Reverend Richard Wayne Gary Wayne (the "senior prophet and CFO" of Kimmy's cult). Although Edwards acknowledges that the sunny disposition of the main character and the show as a whole might strike some audiences as being incongruent with earlier discourses surrounding apocalyptic cults, its depiction of the challenges involved in adjusting to a "normal" life in New York City (a world of intoxicating sights and sounds for which Kimmy was initially unprepared) is "strikingly spot-on" to her and other former CoG members who have left their restrictive "Family" behind.[56]

Despite this and similar claims of representational accuracy and putting aside the fact that the creators of *Unbreakable Kimmy Schmidt* (Tina Fey and Robert Carlock) borrowed elements from several real-life kidnapping stories (including that of Elizabeth Smart, "the confirmed inspiration for the hit Netflix series"),[57]

Goodwin remains skeptical of its "females are strong as hell" messaging. Specifically, she draws attention to the show's dichotomous characterization of cult members "as either men determined to victimize and abuse women (like the Reverend) or women too physically or mentally weak to escape an exploitative situation, detained by force or too dumb to disbelieve."[58] According to her, the show, while laudable as a parodic, pop-culture-savvy take on sitcom formulas, "echoes and amplifies a broader cultural narrative that links end-times religiosity with sexual abuse and women's vulnerability, inadvertently reinforcing a dangerous American conviction that women like Kimmy—and her real-life counterparts, women members of 'cults'—need saving by outside forces."[59]

Particularly problematic, at least from Goodwin's perspective, is the symmetry between onscreen images of cultic attire and the kind of clothing worn by female members of the Fundamentalist Church of Jesus Christ of Latter-day Saints (FLDS), or rather an apocalyptic subset of that Mormon denomination known as Yearning for Zion (YFZ). Using their theology to justify plural marriage, the 500+ members of the latter community sought to raise their families peacefully and await the savior's second coming on a 1,700-acre ranch in Eldorado, Texas. Within a year of their arrival, however, "state representatives attempted to pass a bill targeting FLDS by name as a sexually suspect fringe religion."[60] Lacking any evidence of abuse, the authorities were initially unable to pursue their goal of entering the polygamists' compound by force and pushing them out. However, in March of 2008, a phone call was received by a local domestic violence shelter. Though it was later revealed to be a hoax, that hotline message sparked a large-scale "rescue" operation the following month. Falsely claiming to be a sixteen-year-old victim of physical abuse held against her will at the YFZ Ranch, the woman who placed that call—thirty-three-year-old Rozita Swinton of Colorado Springs—concocted the kind of horrifying story that the authorities had been seeking, prompting them to send in heavily armed law enforcement officers and SWAT-team snipers. In the aftermath of that controversial raid, the Texas Department of Family and Protective Services "initiated the largest government detention of American children in the nation's history," with over 430 minors separated from their parents and taken into state custody. Though the compound's leader, Warren Jeffs, was eventually "convicted of two felony counts of child sexual assault and sentenced to life in prison,"[61] many commentators argue that the events of 2008, which were "prompted by a single, unsubstantiated allegation of abuse," constituted a form of religious persecution that "resulted in further trauma" for the members of FLDS.[62]

While all of this might seem to be tangential, or little more than additional evidence of Joseph Laycock's contention that "cults in popular media are usually exaggerated pastiches of real NRMs,"[63] such historical context helps us to understand how a given social imaginary can have material consequences in the lives of those most directly affected by cultural representations. Indeed, it is with that contextualizing framework in mind that Goodwin calls into question *Unbreakable Kimmy Schmidt*'s seemingly harmless yet duplicitous depiction of sister-wives being "saved" from "a lecherous and charismatic huckster using religion to dominate and exploit women." Not only has "Americans' assumption that members of minority religions need saving" led to an "alarming number of civil rights violations" in recent years, but TV shows like this distract audiences from the most likely scenarios for sexual assault and domestic abuse, which occur not inside cult compounds but at home, at the hands of family members and close associates. As Kimmy herself acknowledges, "the worst thing that ever happened to [her] happened in [her] own front yard," a line that unfortunately is overshadowed by other exchanges calling attention to the dangers and "craziness" of cults.

As I have attempted to indicate through an overview of cultic representations on the small screen, fiction-based television programs have contributed to many of the prejudicial attitudes and misperceptions people have about alternative religions in the United States. While a handful of episodes produced over the past half-century have admirably gestured toward some of the underlying reasons why people join such groups (pointing toward principal and secondary characters' needs for companionship or fellowship),[64] most onscreen depictions pivot on a set of problematic assumptions about the nature of parasocial belonging, which is too often shown to be a result of the kind of indoctrination, brainwashing, and/or conditioning that robs individuals of their identities or capacity to make informed choices about their lives. A typical TV episode about the subject operates within a limited range of narrative possibilities, lurching predictably forward from early scenes in which friends or family members express concern about the behaviors of a loved one who, having joined a cult, must be "saved" or brought back to their previous lives as properly functioning members of society. Such acts of "secular salvation," performed by either third-party interventionists (police investigators, federal agents, etc.) or family/friends themselves, often necessitates "undercover" work as well as the actual crossing of barriers, iconographically rendered through the visual recurrence of gates, guard towers, and/or razor wire outside compounds that are almost always situated in harsh desert landscapes.

The prevalence of such images verges toward parody in many programs, as when, in an episode of *Knight Rider* (NBC, 1982–86; "Sky Knight" [4.04]), the protagonist—undercover detective Michael Knight (David Hasselhoff)—drives his anthropomorphized car "Kitt" into the southwestern part of a Southwestern state (Cactus, Arizona) and pulls up to a cult compound surrounded not only by a fence and reinforced steel walls but also by a mine field. This motif was subsequently spoofed in "The Joy of Sect" episode of *The Simpsons*, showing the area outside a commune littered not only with mines but also alligators, barbed wire, and—in a nod to the British cult TV classic *The Prisoner* (ITV, 1967–68)—a big, blobby defense balloon visually reminiscent of the Rover. Another example of the physical danger posed to the heroes in such narratives can be found in an episode of the Chuck Norris series *Walker, Texas Ranger* (CBS, 1993–2001). Titled "In the Name of God" (2.03), it shows Norris's gun-toting character forced to enter a cult compound surrounded by a 10,000-volt electric fence, the boundary separating "insiders" (the members of the New Canaan "Heaven" compound) and "outsiders" (detectives, district attorneys, Texas Rangers, etc.). "You're still just a child," yells the father of an eighteen-year-old member of New Canaan. His words, directed at his pregnant daughter, illustrate how consistently television series have relied on demeaning, infantilizing strategies of representation, with cultists being no smarter than kids and with charismatic leaders (such as Deacon John Bodie [Franc Luz], a Bible-thumper who is guilty of statutory rape in this episode) rendered as embodiments of "pure evil" preying on innocent youth.

The opening voiceover narration in "Children of Jamestown," an episode of *The A-Team*, provides a perfect—indeed, *perfectly parodic*—distillation of the narrative trajectory and motivic elements on view in most fictional stories concerning the subject of cults. Spoken by John "Hannibal" Smith (George Peppard), the graying, cigar-chomping leader of the titular mercenary group, these words read like a summary of so many other cultural productions premised on the prospects of male heroes rescuing female converts from the clutches of dangerous cults. The offscreen protagonist states: "In the hills of Redwood, California, five miles from the Oregon border, a maniacal religious cult leader named Martin James has been keeping his youthful followers isolated from the outside world, controlling their minds by terror and intimidation. The A-Team has been hired to rescue one of them, a girl named Sheila Rogers." In less than fifteen seconds of screen time, the full range of traditional representational strategies brought to bear on alternative religions has been strung together into two sentences, reminding audiences that distance and isolation ("five miles from the Oregon border") as well as binaristic tensions between the familiar and the unknown, safety and danger, old men and young women, are operationally linked to viewer expectations and genre satisfaction.

Like the "highly suggestible" Homer Simpson, who, in "The Joy of Sect," turns to a cult "for mindless happiness" only to discover that he had the nurturing nuzzle of beer all along, the title character in *Andy Richter Controls the Universe* calls attention to that which, though often ignored by viewers, is in their direct line of sight (seated as they often are before the television set, where, as

Emily Edwards states, audience members are "relaxed, rested, and comfortable" and thus in a potentially "receptive" position vis-à-vis "cult messages").[65] Telling his Zumanist friend Byron (Jonathan Slavin) that there are other things besides religion and sex that give life meaning, Andy reminds him, "There's drinking and watching TV." Framed in such a way, and given its propensity to demonize that which runs counter to established theology or is deemed socially aberrant in some way, television might be even more beguiling or misleading than the representatives of fringe religions who so often appear as secondary characters in stand-alone episodes. As the title character in the Canadian comedy program *The Red Green Show* (CHCH/CBC, 1991–2006) tells his goofy nephew, Harold (Patrick McKenna), upon encountering an alien-fixated religious group gathered outside his hunting lodge (in the episode "Cult Visit" [8.05]), "Cults are full of followers, they have no independent thought, they go to these pointless meetings . . . they all dress the same." The fact that Red (Steve Smith), whom the cultists mistake as their leader, and Harold, who tried to infiltrate the cult, are both decked out in matching khakis, red and black suspenders, and plaid shirts (their standard attire, a form of social costuming from which they rarely depart) during the delivery of this typically dismissive statement reveals the hypocrisy to be found in charges against groups whose members appear to be "nuts" (to borrow the Canadian handyman's term). "These cult members are a lot easier to deal with than normal people. They do anything I want," he says to the in-studio audience, whose collective laughter at that moment audibly registers how prone *all* people (even ostensibly "normal" ones) are to mass-think and behavioral manipulation in a culture that increasingly, distressingly, promotes consensus at every turn.

5

"Drinking the Kool-Aid" of Cult TV

Fans, Followers, and Fringe Religions
in Strangers with Candy *and* Veronica Mars

> Television . . . helps monitor the boundary that separates customary religion
> from deviant faith.
>
> — Lynn S. Neal, "'They're Freaks!' The Cult Stereotype
> in Fictional Television Shows, 1958–2008"

> We're all entitled to our own religions, Veronica.
>
> — Keith Mars (Enrico Colantoni) to his daughter
> (Kristen Bell) in a Season One episode of *Veronica
> Mars* (UPN/CW, 2004–7)

Since the early 1960s, when the groundbreaking science fiction programs *The Twilight Zone* (CBS, 1959–64) and *The Outer Limits* (ABC, 1963–65) first sprang up on America's televisual landscape, "cults" (or what many sociologists refer to as New Religious Movements [NRMs]) have been the occasional subjects of TV series that would themselves become objects of ritualistic viewing and quasi-religious devotion among fans. As descendants of those classic anthology series, contemporary programs like *The X-Files* (Fox, 1993–2002), *Dark Angel* (Fox, 2000–2002), *The Dead Zone* (USA, 2003–7), and *The 4400* (USA, 2004–7) have featured stand-alone episodes devoted to heretical religious sects, and in doing so have self-reflexively solidified their own cult status by way of representational strategies that simultaneously legitimize and pathologize the prospects of parasocial belonging. In addition to these sometimes sympathetic if paranoia-inducing portrayals, a more satiric take on fictional and real religious movements can be found in particular episodes of animated and live-action comedies, such as *The Simpsons* (Fox, 1989–present; "The Joy of Sect" [9.13]), *Martin* (Fox, 1992–97; "In Search of . . . Martin" [3.01]), *Rocko's Modern Life* (Nickelodeon, 1993–96; "Schnit-Heads" [3.02]), *Everybody Loves Raymond* (CBS, 1996–2005; "The Cult" [7.01]), *South Park* (Comedy Central, 1997–present; "Two Guys Naked in a Hot

Tub" [3.08]), *Tenacious D* (HBO, 1999–2000; "Road Gig" [1.06]), *Futurama* (Fox, 1999–2003; "Hell is Other Robots" [1.09]), *Family Guy* (Fox, 1999–present; "The Father, the Son, and the Holy Fonz" [4.18]), *Andy Richter Controls the Universe* (Fox, 2002–3; "Holy Sheep" [2.04]), and *Parks and Recreation* (NBC, 2009–15; "End of the World" [4.06]). These episodes often mobilize the conventional iconography of cults discussed in the previous chapter (e.g., charismatic leaders, brainwashed followers, fortified compounds, etc.) to challenge or deconstruct societal perceptions of the "other," the outsider whose membership in a community of "insiders" is something to be ridiculed (at best) or scorned (at worst). Yet, in taking such a stance, they also perpetuate stereotypes that serve to reinforce mainstream audiences' condescending attitudes toward those who partake in unconventional media consumption practices; fans whose "irrational" infatuations or fixations threaten to turn TV into a totemic object not unlike the sacred articles that are held to be central to both traditional faiths and NRMs.[1]

This chapter picks up where the previous one left off, exploring some of the contradictions bound up in this cultural phenomenon and taking two exceptional US television series—*Strangers with Candy* (Comedy Central, 1999–2000) and *Veronica Mars* (UPN/CW, 2004–7)—as complementary case studies through which to measure the relationship between cults and cult TV. If cults are made up of followers who live in an "extreme" or unconventional manner (often under the guidance of a charismatic leader), then cult TV is at least partially defined by a level of fan devotion that has been discursively framed by media scholars and journalistic reviewers as being similarly spiritual or steadfast in nature, yet can also be gauged through the lens of material culture.[2] Although significantly different from one another in terms of tone, characterization, and generic affiliation, *Strangers with Candy* and *Veronica Mars* share an interest in the cliquish formations of American high school life that divide students into warring camps of insiders and outsiders. Moreover, each is an ensemble series fronted by an unconventional female protagonist who stands out from the crowd yet insinuates herself into the private lives of classmates and teachers. Beyond that, both programs contain pivotal episodes in which the ritualistic practices of fictional cults are presented ambivalently, as a source of humor yet also as a gateway through which our protagonists pass on their way to self-discovery. That journey, I argue, has extraordinary resonance for fans or followers of these programs.

As stated by Jonathan Gray in his work on "affect, fantasy, and meaning," TV "followers" are viewers who are "most involved and most actively implicated in their consumption."[3] Gray's assessment of fan practices and "communities of interest," with its focus on implicature and involvement, builds upon the conceptual framework established by Henry Jenkins, Matt Hills, Will Brooker, and other media scholars with a vested interest in fandom as a site of cultic interaction, collective knowledge, identity formation, and hermeneutic rerouting.[4] For Gray, the push-pull relationship between individual acquiescence to the affective allure of a televisual text and communal resistance to encoded messages or dominant ideologies is worthy of exploration, especially in light of recent industrial changes that have turned the loyalty of fans into a much sought-after commodity in the era of multi-platforming and synergistic cross-promotion. As television programs designed to attract "cult audiences," *Strangers with Candy* and *Veronica Mars* deserve scrutiny as steadfastly "worshipped" texts conducive to the kinds of meta-consumptive discourses and fannish practices that might shed light on culturally entrenched attitudes related to neo-religious activities. With their female protagonists each finding temporary sanctuary amongst a group of welcoming strangers, these series suggest that there are *positive* aspects of cultic belonging, the likes of which rarely surface in other television series concerned with pathological behavior and pragmatic resistance or insistence upon one's individuality.

For example, in parts one and two of the two-episode *Strangers with Candy* storyline "The Blank Stare" (2.08 and 2.09), forty-six-year-old freshman Jerri Blank (Amy Sedaris)—unable to find love or compassion at home or in school—hesitantly joins a society of flower children in search of those intangible things, one whose seemingly despotic father-figure is no more of an authoritarian dictator than the intimidating principal at Flatpoint High, Onyx Blackman (Greg Hollimon). Indeed, the latter's tactics of thought-control, including his efforts to institute a dress code "in order to enhance [the students'] individuality through conformity," prove to be more troubling as a manifestation of mainstream conditioning than anything that transpires at the Safe Trap House (the cult compound where, initially, Jerri had been kept against her will). In much the same way, the seaside town of Neptune, home to the rich and famous as well as the decadent and depraved in *Veronica Mars*, is much more dangerous than the comparatively "normal" Moon Calf Collective, a woodland retreat whose most recent member, Casey Gant (Jonathan Bennett), is being sought by his parents and investigated by our heroine in the episode "Drinking the Kool-Aid" (1.09). Arriving mid-way through the series' first season, this episode offers a more nuanced, less satirical portrayal of cult communities, one that effectively capsizes the dialectical relationship between the familiar and the unknown, normality and pathology. An idiomatic expression linked to the drug culture of the 1960s (in particular the lifestyle of excess made famous by Ken Kesey's Merry Pranksters), as well as the mass-suicide of Jim Jones's followers in the tragic Jonestown Massacre of 1978, "Drinking the Kool-Aid" is a playfully suggestive title for so sober a representation, one that invites viewers to see beyond the insidious implications of cult worship and acknowledge their own devotion to television programs as a similarly unorthodox kind of orthodoxy.

In the following sections I analyze the two aforementioned episodes within a comparative textual framework that acknowledges commonalities (or shared thematic preoccupations) as well as differences at the semantic and syntactical levels. What these differences reveal is the increased willingness of today's cultural producers to diversify their representational practices and plunge below the signifying surface of culturally entrenched images. In the case of creator Rob Thomas's *Veronica Mars*, besides bringing to light less-stereotypical aspects of cultic belonging, "Drinking the Kool-Aid" proves useful as a means of isolating oft-repeated but overlooked narrative elements in the series as a whole. The episode thus shows how prone the otherwise quick-witted, levelheaded main character (played by Kristen Bell) is to lapses in critical judgment, missteps made in the early stages of her fledgling career as an investigator and based on widely shared biases and preconceptions. Similarly, the overtly parodic representational strategies in *Strangers with Candy* open up opportunities for spectatorial self-scrutiny—invitations to see one's own prejudices or misperceptions embodied in the grotesque caricatures that populate this most freak-filled and fringe-friendly of cult TV series. Before discussing the textual side of these and other television programs, I wish to highlight the extratextual discourses—the critical commentary surrounding *Strangers with Candy* and *Veronica Mars*—which suggest that a correlation between media fandom and neo-religious absorption can be and, indeed, *has been* made.

Pathology and Participation: The Competing Discourses of Cult TV

> "What kind of place is this?"
> "Oh, it's just a collective, cooperative, community-service-operation-outreach-program project.
> "Okay, as long as it's not a *cult!*"
> —dialogue between protagonist Jerri Blank (Amy Sedaris) and her new "friend" Rebecca (Emma Bowers), a flower-selling member of a messianic cult, in *Strangers with Candy*

One noteworthy element in the critical rhetoric surrounding *Veronica Mars* is the use of the word "cult," which TV reviewers have habitually deployed in their effusive commentaries extolling the virtues of a series that, to borrow Joss Whedon's description of Rob Thomas's creation, is "the *Harry Potter* of shows." This phrase, provided by a small-screen auteur increasingly drawn to big-screen undertakings and intimately familiar with the fannish activities of hardcore audience members, is included in Darren Devlyn's article about *Veronica Mars* for the Melbourne-based *Herald Sun*. After quoting Whedon, Devlyn states, "It seems fitting that *Veronica Mars* has been hailed the cult successor to *Buffy the Vampire Slayer*."[5] Like Devlyn, Malene Arpe, a writer for the *Toronto Star*, refers to *Veronica Mars* as a "cult hit" nurtured by a "devoted and rabid fan following," before going on to situate the allusion-filled series within a televisual lineage that includes *Buffy the Vampire Slayer* (WB/UPN, 1997–2003), *Twin Peaks* (ABC, 1990–91), *The O.C.* (Fox, 2003–7), and *Freaks and Geeks* (NBC, 1999–2000).[6] "Not since Buffy relocated from The WB has UPN seen a heroine with such *cult* appeal," muses Jennifer Armstrong in a short piece for *Entertainment Weekly*, her words not only highlighting how prone writers were during the first season of the series to position it in close critical proximity to other programs kept afloat by the cult-like responses of fans, but also indicating the ways in which that quasi-religious fervor can extend beyond the series to denote an actor's appeal.[7] An example of this can be found in Rachel Chang's interview with actress Kristen Bell for *Cosmo Girl*, in which she states that *Veronica Mars*—a "cult hit" (to borrow her words)—is making the show's star a "cult icon in the sci-fi world," despite the fact that it does not contain the kind of iconographic elements or textual genre trappings associated with science fiction or telefantasy.[8]

That same rhetorical maneuver on the part of newspaper reviewers can be detected in the critical response to *Strangers with Candy*, a television series created by Paul Dinello, Stephen Colbert, Mitch Rouse, and Amy Sedaris that, almost immediately after its debut on Comedy Central in April 1999, was referred to as a "cult comedy" in the pages of *Rolling Stone* and a "small cult series" in the pages of the *Washington Post*. Peter Rainer, writing in 2006 for the *Christian Science Monitor*, states that the series has "spawned a cult-like following" since appearing on DVD and being adapted into a feature-length motion picture (whose theatrical release occurred that year).[9] On the same date that Rainer's article appeared (July 7), an anonymous writer for the *San Francisco Chronicle* similarly indicated that *Strangers with Candy* has "attracted a cult following."[10] "Cult followings are hard to shake," writes a reviewer for the *Washington Times*, a comment that should remind us of the dedicated ways in which fans attend to their favorite cultural productions, be they compelling teen dramas about murder in an affluent community or intentionally cheesy spoofs of afterschool specials from the 1980s that hinge on grotesquely caricatured portrayals of adolescent longing.

As Sara Gwenllian-Jones and Roberta E. Pearson acknowledge in their Introduction to the edited anthology *Cult Television*, defining "cult TV" is a difficult task, one fraught with epistemological complications insofar as scholars often loosely apply the term to "any television program that is considered offbeat or edgy, that draws a niche audience, that has a nostalgic appeal, that is considered emblematic of a particular subculture or that is considered hip."[11] Despite the slipperiness of this concept, it is safe to say that a basic definition of cult television would encompass any program that attracts a small yet devoted following and which transports those viewers to a "fictive elsewhere."[12] Of course, "small" is a relative term. Millions of people around the world watch the classic and contemporary versions of the British sci-fi series *Doctor Who* (BBC, 1963–present). But the number of viewers for that show is still tiny, percentagewise, when one takes into consideration the *total* number of TV viewers who could tune in to the program if they were so inclined (and if it were marketed to them in the way that other, more popular shows, like *Friends* [NBC, 1994–2004], have been). Throughout its initial three-year run in the United States, *Veronica Mars* regularly ranked around 145 in the Nielsen Ratings (out of roughly 160 shows), making it one of the least-watched network television series in the country, but one of the most *devotedly watched* by a small percentage of the audience.[13] "Excessive devotion," a concept with religious overlay,[14] which Xavier Mendik and Graeme Harper refer to as "a ritualistic form of near obsession,"[15] is a common characteristic of both cult films and cult television programs.[16]

Like many cult films, a cult TV show like *Strangers with Candy* or *Veronica Mars* can be appreciated and enjoyed even after several repeat viewings by an audience that derives intense pleasure from it.[17] It is something that viewers hold close to their hearts and form a strong emotional attachment to. Indeed, the intense pleasure that cult television generates is akin to what Roland Barthes refers to as "jouissance."[18] Cult television is thus often characterized by the intense relationship a fan has to the object of their devotion, a kind of fetish object to be viewed repeatedly and which can be couched within a material context.[19] That is, fans will often go beyond the text proper to seek out various paratextual incarnations of it, not just on videotape or DVD, but also as represented on posters, notebooks, t-shirts, and other examples of the series' ancillary market and transmedia promotional universe.[20]

Moreover, imminently quotable television shows like the original *Star Trek* (NBC, 1966–69) and *Monty Python's Flying Circus* (BBC, 1969–74) have been referred to by media scholars such as Henry Jenkins and Marcia Landy as *participatory texts*. As with cult films and theatrical performances like *The Rocky Horror Picture Show* (1975), audiences of cult TV series will often ritualistically "act out" their pleasure by "memorizing dialogue, practicing gestures, [and] wearing costumes." Such mimetic expressions on the viewer's part, Susan Purdie argues, constitute the ritual-like dimensions of cult spectatorship, even if the participatory actions (e.g., snapping rubber gloves, shouting rehearsed lines, and throwing toast at the screen during a midnight viewing of *Rocky Horror*) are not overtly "associated with any religious belief."[21] This idea corresponds with Chris Gregory's notion that a cult TV program such as *The Prisoner* (ITV, 1967–68) can be thought of as a "sacred text" by its most ardent viewers—men and women who turn to "priests" (or "experts") from their own ranks and experience the show as a series of "intensely ritual" encounters with cultdom itself (a reflexive experience facilitated by certain episodes of the British series, such as "Free for All" [1.04], which seem to "parody the 'religious' [aspect] of TV watching").[22]

Ritual and participation, as performed extensions of cult films and television programs, thus ascribe greater cultural value and resonance to works that might have been overlooked by mainstream viewers upon their original transmission. Here it should be emphasized that the term "mainstream" is itself problematic as a counterbalance against which to distinguish subcultural sensibilities as something inherently oppositional or confrontational. Nevertheless, it still usefully serves as a reminder that members of alternative taste cultures frequently construct their identities as viewers of offbeat or edgy television shows through the latter's "supposed *difference* from the mainstream," from commercial cultural productions which attract mass—as opposed to niche—audiences.[23] What might seem like gibberish to some audience members (such as the character Duncan Kane [Teddy Dunn]'s pangrammatic comment, "Quick Wafting Zephyrs Vex Bold Jim," in the *Veronica Mars* episode "Clash of the Tritons" [1.12], or fan acronyms such as "VMVO," indicating the protagonist's voiceover) are in fact discursive means of gaining entry into an otherwise "gated" community of Web-surfing followers. In a way, the oft-repeated iconography of cult compounds—the cordoned-off spaces devoted to neo-religious activity and worship that can be seen in many televisual representations—is itself a kind of ritualized practice on the part of cultural producers, one that feeds into a deeper social severance pitting "mainstream" against "fringe." But such separatist partitioning is also what lends each imagined community a degree of specificity, with fans embracing the idea of difference and proudly wearing their shared yet distinctive identities—e.g., "Candy Asses," in the case of *Strangers with Candy* followers, and "Cloud Watchers," in the case of *Veronica Mars* followers—as badges of honor.[24]

Like members of fringe religions, fans of cult television series such as *Star Trek* "have been consistently maligned as 'brainless consumers' and infantile, desexualized 'social misfits' dedicated to the 'cultivation of worthless knowledge' over 'devalued cultural material.'"[25] Alluding to the work of Jenkins, Jeffrey Sconce, in his study of the destructive path of the Heaven's Gate group and the concept of "textual transcendence," draws attention to the ways that both religiously fervent followers of charismatic leaders and fans of *Star Trek* are "often accused of being unable to distinguish fantasy from the real world."[26] However, while "Trekkies" (or "Trekkers") might become so obsessed with the object of their shared fascination as to "lose themselves" in "a permanent haze of syndicated televisual reality," the members of Heaven's Gate are reported to have actually suspended belief in reality itself, "leading to any number of potentially hazardous 'conversion' experiences" and unleashing a torrent of fictional televisual representations once news coverage died down in the late-1990s and narrative discourse became the operative means of making sense of the senseless for years to come.[27]

It is helpful to consider a Season Six episode of *CSI: Crime Scene Investigation* (CBS, 2000–2015), which not only offers an emblematic depiction of fringe religions and the "deceitful" men who lead them, but also naturalizes or further establishes transtextual associations between media fandom and fringe religions. Entitled "Shooting Stars" (6.04), this self-contained storyline concerns the search for a missing cultist in the Nevada desert, a man who might have killed eleven other members of a small religious group initially thought to have committed mass suicide. When the show's main Las Vegas criminologists, Gil Grissom (William Petersen) and Catherine Willows (Marg Helgenberger), first arrive at the abandoned military compound/bomb shelter, a series of comments reveals a tendency to blend different cults together while further pathologizing the kind of "irrational" devotion that is often associated with fandom. "What is this place, a mini-Jonestown?" asks the forensics expert Grissom upon seeing eleven corpses on cots inside the bunker. After the camera pans to reveal UFO images on the heavily graffitied walls of the circular compound as well as a twelfth bunk without a body, his female partner alludes to Heaven's Gate and then returns to the subject of Jonestown, saying that the young victims "didn't drink any spiked Kool-Aid."

"This cult was about getting laid," Catherine remarks, a comment that anticipates a later scene at the crime lab, where a fingerprint specialist jokingly remarks that when she starts her own religion, she'll be recruiting impressionable college students. It turns out that one of the dead cult members, a Religious Studies major named Matthew Dickens, was a "hardcore Trekkie." "The guy was a loser," states one of Matthew's former college classmates being interviewed by detective Sofia Curtis (Louise Lombard), who learns that a shyster named Joseph Diamond (Tomas Arana) has been luring susceptible young men and women into a religious community that promises salvation, but which actually drugs them with Ketamine (mixed with vodka) and robs them of their possessions. By linking Matthew's fascination with *Star Trek* and his subsequent activity as a cog in the wheel of a dangerous cult (whose members died, it turns out, as a result of respiratory arrest), this *CSI* episode and several others like it forge a tenuous connection that is made to seem tenable or "natural" through the repeated representations of both groups (media fans and cult members) as misguided and gullible nerds in need of peer recognition or communal fellowship.

Another important episode along these lines is a Season Four storyline of *The X-Files* titled "The Field Where I Died" (4.05). This episode concerns Agents Fox Mulder (David Duchovny) and Dana Scully (Gillian Anderson)'s investigation into the Temple of the Seven Stars, a Tennessee-based cult whose leader, Vernon Ephesian (Michael Massee), is suspected of child abuse and weapons stockpiling. At one point in the episode, Ephesian is referred to as a "paranoid charismatic sociopath . . . obsessed with the book of Revelations." On another occasion, Mulder and Scully's supervisor, Assistant Director Walter Skinner (Mitch Pileggi), expresses concern about the possibility that they will have another Jonestown on their hands.[28] This episode is indicative of the pronounced way in which references to *actual* cults and *real* charismatic leaders (such as Jim Jones and David Koresh, both of whom are mentioned by Ephesian) make their way into fiction-based television programs—something that had not occurred very often before its original broadcast (November 3, 1996), at least, not so directly. What is perhaps most startling about "The Field Where I Died" (apart from Mulder's discovery that he and one of Ephesian's six wives had been lovers in their past lives, during the Civil War) is the overt manner in which the Jonestown Massacre is gestured toward in the penultimate moments, when the members of the Temple are served poisoned red beverages. Originally broadcast by Fox stations in the fall of 1996, this episode anticipates the way that *Veronica Mars*, a cult TV series steeped in intertextual references to previous television programs noted for their own small yet devoted fan bases, acknowledges actual (nonfictional) religious movements of the past, in the tellingly titled "Drinking the Kool-Aid." But, like so many TV episodes that followed it, "The Field Where I Died" also conflates more recent occurrences and NRMs (the 1993 Branch Davidian events, the 1994 Order of the Solar Temple events, and the 1995 Aum Shinrikyo events discussed in the previous chapter) in ways that might deny their historical specificity and, as Lynn S. Neal argues, reinforce "the stereotypical sense that all cults are the same."[29]

In order to illustrate the ways in which the categories of "fiction" and "nonfiction" are blurred in such programming, and to further explicate Neal's notion that the beliefs and actions of NRMs are rendered "interchangeable," it is helpful to turn to the eighteenth episode of *Veronica Mars*'s first season. Titled "Weapons of Class Destruction," this episode features a scene in which Veronica is told by an undercover agent pretending to be a new student at Neptune High that his job at the Bureau of Alcohol, Tobacco, and Firearms (the organization that famously stormed the Branch Davidians' Mt. Carmel compound) involves the monitoring of internet traffic. Ben (Jonathan Taylor Thomas), the young-looking fed, has been fraternizing with a school bully named Norris (Theo Rossi) because he suspects the latter of calling in bomb threats. Prior to learning of Ben's *21 Jump Street*–style undercover work, Veronica spots the two boys initially framed in a long shot with a banner in the background that reads "Culture." Significantly, only half of that word—"Cult"—is visible within the frame. The visual rhetoric of this scene, in addition to Veronica's ensuing remarks (rendered as voiceover) that these two individuals are likely "just biding their time waiting for the moment when they can blow this school mile high," inscribes a sense of foreboding and erroneously suggests that they are working together to inflict Columbine-like harm upon their classmates. A reference to that 1999 high school massacre is actually dropped into a conversation between Veronica and Ben, who tells her that several of Norris's emails contain "red-flag words." When prodded to explain what he means, the agent replies, "'Retribution,' 'bomb,' 'arsenal,' 'gun show,' 'fertilizer,' 'Waco,' 'Columbine.' We think that he's the leader of scores of likeminded misfits who are waiting for his signal to attack."

Again, the carefully scripted yet seemingly stream-of-consciousness dialogue in *Veronica Mars* reveals a willingness to integrate real-world events into its narrative universe. More problematic, though, is the slippage of historical meaning that results from so careless a mishmash of signifiers, with Waco and Columbine being bundled together under the umbrella of global terrorism (connoted by the episode's pun-inflected title). As Lynn S. Neal states, "[B]y using historical elements," the writers and producers of television programs not only contribute to the ongoing conflation and reinterpretation of past events, but also "provide viewers with a way to interpret present or future events."[30] In a post-9/11 world marked by anti-terrorist discourse and widespread fears concerning the global rise of "fanatical" religious movements, "Weapons of Class Destruction" can be said to tap into cultural anxieties that extend beyond the sphere of NRMs and their comparability to cult television fan groups.

Like most *Veronica Mars* episodes, "Weapons of Class Destruction" culminates with a revelation, in this case providing information about the source of the bomb threats while gesturing back to "Drinking the Kool-Aid," an earlier episode containing cultic references. A flashback in the closing minutes reveals that Norris, whom Veronica had suspected of being a would-be school shooter, is actually innocent. Not only did he stand up for Veronica against a bully (who had shot spitballs at her from behind), but he was also framed by Pete (Michael McMillian), another student at Neptune High, who planted fertilizer and a gun inside the trunk of his vehicle. Fans of *Veronica Mars* know that this narrative device—this disclosure of information showing the title character to be fallible and frequently incorrect in her initial assumptions about others—is deployed time and again throughout the run of the series. It thus usefully serves as a rhetorical invitation for audiences to see *themselves* implicated in the heroine's problematic proclivity to judge people by their outward appearances, something that Veronica and her ever-compliant sideman, Wallace Fennel, do upon seeing the t-shirt worn by Norris earlier in the episode, one that reads, "Kill 'em all. Let God sort 'em out."

No less noteworthy is the revelation that occurs in the first season's penultimate episode, "A Trip to the Dentist" (1.21). It seems that Casey Gant, a character who had been introduced in "Drinking the Kool-Aid," has had a change of mind since his previous appearance as a member of the Moon Calf Collective (located on the outskirts of Neptune). Although, in that earlier episode, the once-superficial '09er had developed a respect for nature and a maturity that belied his age as a productive member of the farm collective, Casey has since reverted back to his old ways, telling Veronica that he has gotten his "priorities" straight and has given up the "S'mores and bad folk music." The former cult member's appearance in "A Trip to the Dentist" serves another purpose, however; for he divulges additional details about the previous year's party at classmate Shelly Pomeroy's house, an event that Veronica—by then an ostracized outsider due to her father's handling of the Lilly Kane (Amanda Seyfried) murder investigation—had decided to crash. Unfortunately, that night ended in a blur, with her rum soda being spiked with a roofie-like drug called GBH. When she awoke the following morning, she believed that she had been raped, an assumption that is ultimately proven false (for, in fact, she had engaged in consensual sex with her equally drugged boyfriend, Duncan Kane, the brother of her murdered pal). Audiences learn that it was Logan Echolls (Jason Dohring) who had spiked the drinks that evening, an action that, when combined with the presence of former commune member Casey Gant, gestures toward the cyanide-laced beverages ingested by Jim Jones's followers, lending credence to another '09er's passing remark to Veronica at the party (a comment that she makes after witnessing a girl named Madison spit into the protagonist's cup): "You don't want to drink that."

From Candy to Kool-Aid: Deconstructing the Cult Imaginary

> It's not a cult. It's just a group of lost souls who worship one guy and don't question what he says.
>
> —sarcastic dialogue in a Season Five episode of
> *Sabrina, the Teenage Witch* (ABC, 1996–2000;
> WB, 2000–2003)

In her study of the "occult experience" in American popular culture, Emily Edwards argues that, through repetition, mainstream media representations "tend to validate a certain perception of the world rather than improve it, reiterate old stories rather than initiate new ones, and help to cultivate audiences' perceptions of the world in which they live."[31] According to Edwards, widespread "repetition of similar media texts can have a forceful impact" on viewers, intensifying individual conviction and perhaps leading to social consensus. This idea, developed by George Gerbner, Elisabeth Noelle-Neumann, and other media scholars who have argued that "living with television" contributes to the "cultivation of shared conceptions of reality,"[32] is especially relevant with regards to the obstinacy of negative audience perceptions about cults, despite the fact that the situational circumstances unique to TV viewing (wherein individuals are "relaxed, rested, and comfortable in front of their home televisions" or computer screens) might engender a "more receptive" position vis-à-vis "cult messages." As Edwards states, during the 1980s a number of cultural critics "worried that media or 'electronic churches' were replacing traditional worship," while others writing about media influence believed that "more channels might lead to wider exposure for cults."[33] And yet, even as paranormal subjects and folklore-inspired stories about supernatural beings have become ever more abundant in popular culture texts since the 1980s (for instance, *Buffy the Vampire Slayer, Angel* [WB, 1999–2004], and *Supernatural* [WB/CW, 2005–20]), little has changed about people's attitudes toward new religious movements and cultic belief systems, which largely remain objects of condemnation, ridicule, and scorn in the United States.

Notably, in her study Edwards cites an episode of the live-action telefantasy series *Sabrina, the Teenage Witch* (ABC/WB, 1996–2003) as an example of the contradictory appeals of a cult TV program that warns young people "about the dangers of cults" even as it "reiterates the idea that a 'real witch' does not proselytize."[34] Titled "Welcome, Traveler" (5.07), the episode concerns Sabrina (Melissa Joan Hart)'s attempt to unmask a leader of a bogus New Age religious group as a fake. The man, a self-proclaimed witch named Jim Thom (Richard Kline), is indeed guilty of misleading his flock of followers, including Sabrina's college roommate Miles (Trevor Lissauer). "Get over it," Sabrina tells Miles after he informs her that he feels "connected to other people and the universe" as a participant in this unconventional collective. Significantly, it is through the medium of television that Sabrina—a "real" witch—is able to convince her friend and his fellow "Children of the Stars" that Thom is a phony. In the penultimate scene of the episode, the spell-casting heroine uses her magic to turn on a large TV monitor in the makeshift commune. On the screen, their leader is shown verbally deriding the cultists, the naive men and women who have parted ways with their worldly possessions in return for his "enlightenment." Sabrina's remark, "Get over it," not unlike William Shatner's exhortation to a roomful of male Trekkies that they "Get a life" (in a famous *Saturday Night Live* skit that aired in 1986), ironically stipulates a divestment of interest

5.1. In this cult-themed episode of *Sabrina, the Teenage Witch*, the title character uses a large television set to break the charismatic spell cast over the "Children of the Stars" by their huckster leader, suggesting a correlation between neo-religious devotion, parasocial belonging, and cult TV. © Hartbreak Films

among fans of the actual programs on which these pronouncements air. That is, only by distancing themselves from the texts in which these anti-cult messages are delivered can the most adulatory audience members—the viewers who, like Miles, gain a semblance of "wholeness" through cultic interconnectivity—prevent themselves from succumbing to proselytizing forms of discourse.

Significantly, the same year that the writers of *Sabrina, the Teenage Witch* devoted an entire episode to a fictional cult, providing a conventional narrative set-up and resolution to the story of someone sucked into a bogus religious association, a very different teen comedy deconstructed the traditional televisual tropes associated with this subject. Debuting on Comedy Central on April 7, 1999, *Strangers with Candy* is itself a comic deconstruction of ABC's "After School Specials," which were popular in the United States during the 1970s and 1980s. Delving into sometimes-controversial, socially relevant subject matter (from drug addiction and eating disorders to teenage pregnancy and child abuse), these pedagogically oriented, hour-long dramas are as restrained in their representational strategies as

Strangers with Candy is unrestrained. Occasionally bizarre, frequently grotesque, and "utterly without life lessons" (according to a writer for the *Washington Times*), the taboo-shattering series mobilizes a host of ethnic, racial, and sexual stereotypes and stars rubber-faced comedian Amy Sedaris as a silver-streaked sixties burn-out struggling to fit in as a freshman at the fictional Flatpoint High. As enunciated by Sedaris's bucktoothed heroine in the animated credit sequence that opens each episode, Jerri Blank is a forty-six-year-old ex-con who is trying to start over after a life of larceny, prostitution, and stripping. Once "a boozer, a user, and a loser," this former high-school dropout thus returns to Flatpoint as a means of righting the wrongs of her past. However, as hinted at in the first episode and elaborated throughout the show's three-season run, Jerri is not able to escape the demons of her past, and her present situation as a frequently shunned outsider prone to polymorphous perversity and struggling to fit in is complicated by the fact that Flatpoint is itself a haven for corruption, degeneracy, and vice.

It is against this morally amorphous backdrop that the paradoxically named "Safe Trap House" serves as a sanctuary of relative sanity, albeit one that is run by a leader (simply named "Father") who initially locks Jerri inside the commune against her will. This event takes place in the first half of a two-episode storyline. At the beginning of "The Blank Stare, Part One," Rebecca (Emma Bowers), a flower-bearing member of the cult (the proverbial "stranger with candy"), approaches Jerri in a shopping mall while the latter plays a "President Assassination" video game. A second encounter at the same mall—after the principal of Flatpoint High, Onyx Blackman, has issued a school-wide warning about the presence of an "insidious cult" that preys on "the friendless" and "the weak-minded"—results in Jerri, now acquiescent and hoping to score with Rebecca, accompanying her new friend to an awaiting van. This particular mode of transportation is an engrained feature of TV's cultic representations, as indicated in a passage of dialogue from an episode of the comically inflected police procedural *Monk* (USA Network, 2002–9). Simply titled "Mr. Monk Joins a Cult" (6.11), it begins with the OCD-suffering title character and his assistant, Natalie, investigating the murder of a young girl who was last seen being stabbed by a group of people that left the scene of the crime in a van. "Big silver van, that's what they *always* drive," one of the detectives tells Monk, an acutely observed statement whose truth is born out in the many visual iterations of that iconographic element, from action-packed episodes of *The A-Team* (NBC, 1983–87; "Children of Jamestown" [1.03]) and *Airwolf* (CBS, 1984–86; "Where Have All the Children Gone?" [3.11]) to recent comedies like *Strangers with Candy*.

Although the cultists inside the awaiting van "look like a bunch of zombies," according to Jerri, she climbs in and is transported to the Safe Trap House. There,

5.2. Inside the Safe Trap House, Jerri (Amy Sedaris), the main character of *Strangers with Candy*, meets the leader of the cult, a powerful yet comical figure simply named "Father" (Alan Tudyk). © Comedy Central

after an initial struggle, and despite a growing dissatisfaction with both the lack of kinkiness inside this collective and the cultists' repetitive chanting of a song ("Sit at the Welcome Table," a ditty that is similar to the "Jesus Loves Me" number performed by cultists in *Tenacious D's* "Road Gig"), she begins to fit in. She is even made to feel "beautiful" by her accommodating hosts. Meanwhile, back at Flatpoint High, Principal Blackman is busy instituting a dress code, part of his larger plan to rid the place of individuality. "Never set yourself apart from the crowd. Don't you know there's a cult out there?" says Onyx, his words serving as ironic counterpoint to the Safe Trap House's celebration of difference. Just as the principal's last name is a parodic nod to his racialized identity in the primarily white town of Flatpoint, so too is Jerri's last name laden with significance, suggesting both the moral vacancy at the heart of this community and the ease with which her mind—a blank slate—can be filled with corrupting influences, an idea similarly expressed through the title of a cult-themed episode of the police procedural *Cold Case* (CBS, 2003–10): "Blank Generation."

Ultimately, after Jerri has changed her suggestively empty name of "Blank" to "Sycamore," Blackman and a couple of teachers, Chuck Noblet (Stephen Colbert) and Geoffrey Jellineck (Paul Dinello), as well as her only true friend at Flatpoint High, Orlando Pinatubo (Orlando Pabotoy) (a Filipino American student who is often on the receiving end of her racist remarks), stage an intervention. This development takes place in "The Blank Stare, Part Two," with Jerri being jumped by the Flatpoint faculty, put into a burlap sack, beaten, and dragged to another van. Taking place inside a boiler room, their deprogramming of Jerri is far crueler than anything that transpired at the nonjudgmental Safe Trap House, a truly safe community that, ironically, was threatened by the very presence of this troublemaking outsider (who had poisoned the cultists' water and grain in preparation for an eventually aborted mass suicide). Regardless of the emotional and physical abuse meted out by the deprogrammers, and despite Rebecca's last-ditch effort to save Jerri from these anti-cultists, the protagonist decides to return to the life she left behind at Flatpoint High—a world "where people care enough about her not to care about her." As Jerri muses in the final scene, "If someone tells you that you're beautiful and that they love you, chances are they're just trying to brainwash you into being happy." This seemingly self-defeatist yet perceptive attitude in *Strangers with Candy* verges toward a sentiment voiced in *Veronica Mars*, albeit not by the title character. As Veronica's new journalism teacher, Mallory Dent (Sydney Tamiia Poitier), tells her in "You Think You Know Somebody" (1.05), "Sometimes the lies we let ourselves believe are for our own good."

Significantly, the word "freaks," which Jerri had first used to describe the cult members, might be better applied to those people who have made her "normal" life in the town of Flatpoint such a living hell. From the narcissistic English teacher Mr. Noblet, who mocks the protagonist's appearance in the series' first episode (calling her a "failure" and telling her, "You're only as ugly as we think you are"), to her stepmother (who refers to her as a "hobgoblin" and a "flying monkey"), to the group of cheerleaders who call her a "dumb, no-reading loser" in the Season Two episode "The Blank Page" (2.05) (which reveals that Jerri is illiterate), the men and women of the town draw a line between themselves and the comically flawed anti-heroine. The latter character is continuously beset by problems and tragedies, from her bout with anorexia to the death of her father (a man put into a permanent state of physical mortification by her long absence and the passing of his wife). And yet, despite running a doubles sack race with the ashes of her dead dad, Jerri is no more "warped" (in terms of her outlook on life) than her classmates and teachers. Indeed, the producers of *Strangers with Candy* go to great lengths to frame Jerri's "freakish" behavior against a backdrop of apparent normality, a town that we soon learn is as contradictory as its name ("Flatpoint"). Tellingly, Jerri's encounter with a cult member occurs in a mall, the apotheosis of bland conformity and crass commercialism, where the protagonist drops water balloons on shoppers who display as much, if not more, "mindlessness" as the "wackos" at the hippie commune.

Regardless of whether they are "Movementarians" (the fictional brainwashing cult joined by Homer and his family in an episode of *The Simpsons*) or "Moonies" (the real group of Unification Church members who adhere to the teachings of Reverend Sun Myung Moon), the people who belong to new religious movements in television narratives are almost always described by other characters as "freaks" and "wackos"—two of the most frequently uttered words across the medium's history of cultic representations. It should be noted that the word "freak" is also repeatedly spoken throughout the three-season run of *Veronica Mars*. In fact, it is uttered by a student at Neptune High in an early scene of the series' pilot episode, to describe the title character after she cuts soon-to-be BFF Wallace from the schoolyard flagpole, where he has been duct-taped. A self-described "undesirable," someone who used to sit at a table with the cool kids, "past the velvet ropes" (as she intones in voiceover), Veronica is content to let her "freak flag" fly high, knowing that it will only further distance herself from her former friends. Widely loathed by her clueless classmates (particularly the '09ers, so named to designate those Neptunians who live in the affluent 90909 zip code area), the seventeen-year-old sleuth spends much of her junior year following in the footsteps of her detective father, Keith (Enrico Colantoni), a former sheriff investigating the murder of her best friend, Lilly Kane, and trying to find out why her alcoholic mother, Lianne (Corinne Bohrer), has mysteriously disappeared.

While those long-term goals drive the season-long narrative across a series of episodic developments, stitched together by Veronica's (and the audience's) accumulating comprehension of the details surrounding the main mystery (which harkens back to the central enigma of *Twin Peaks*: "Who Killed Laura Palmer?"), smaller, self-contained plotlines provide opportunities to depart momentarily from that trajectory. As stated, Veronica busies herself searching for her own family member, her missing mother, throughout the first half of Season One. In the manner of a mise en abyme, many self-contained storylines within the larger dramatic arc of the season hinge on Veronica's pursuit (and eventual discovery) of a missing person. For instance, in "The Girl Next Door" (1.07), she has been hired by a married couple, the Williams, looking for their absent daughter, Emily. This anticipates her search for Casey Gant in "Drinking the Kool-Aid." The latter episode, written by Rob Thomas and Russell Smith, loads conventional anti-cultic discourses into its narrative only to capsize traditional representational schemas through a parodic reworking of neo-religious tropes.

After a brief scene at Veronica's home, where Keith has just installed a new waterbed for his daughter, the story begins with a shift in location, taking the viewer to Mars Investigations. Attentive viewers might notice that this noirish office space, where clients unload their problems on Keith, contains a vaguely cult-like image. Visible in the background is the logo for Mars Investigations: a pyramid with an eye. The design of the logo, which suggests divine providence and might further remind audiences of Freemasons, Illuminati, and other secret organizations, assumes metaphorical resonance thanks to its proximity to a poster on which the words "This Is Your God" are written. Soon, a wealthy couple arrives and explains that their well-adjusted son, Casey, has joined a cult, leaving behind his family and friends six weeks ago and selling his Porsche Boxster in the process (although he has continued attending school). The father and mother emphasize that the boy is "definitely not a druggie." He is "secure" and "extroverted"—words that are met with Keith's accurate rejoinder that many fringe religions are filled with well-adjusted people.

Since their son is eighteen, the Gants cannot legally demand his return. However, they are willing to give Keith and Veronica a $5,000 bonus if they manage to convince Casey to leave the Moon Calf Collective or find proof of any illegal activities there. Veronica does much of the footwork in the investigation, seeking information both at school and at the commune. A conference with Casey's ex-girlfriend reveals details about his recent conversion. The '09er explains that she had to "cut him loose" once he renounced "the toxic death style of a late-stage capitalist society" and turned a deaf ear to "the consumer siren song." Although Veronica believes that Casey "looks normal enough," his ex-girlfriend argues that he has become "alien lobotomy boy." Moreover, she suspects Casey of being romantically involved with Miss Mills (Amy Laughlin), his English teacher and the publisher of a literary magazine at school. He has "become one of *them*," the girl concludes, leaving in question whether the "them" refers to members of the "lit mag crowd" or the cult. Regardless, Miss Mills is revealed to be the one who introduced Casey to the Moon Calf Collective.

Despite being given specific orders from Keith not to go there, Veronica takes up Miss Mills's offer and is soon touring the woodland commune, which, in its visual layout and its emphasis on agricultural activities, is strikingly similar to the Juniper Creek compound in HBO's polygamy-themed *Big Love* (2006–11). "I feel like I'm on a movie set or something," Veronica remarks, highlighting the inherent artifice in most cultic representations (be they televisual or cinematic) as well as the mutability of identity in such places, where old names are often replaced with new ones and lives can begin afresh. "We're kind of like a family," says Miss Mills (whose name at the commune is "Miss Holly"), before asking Veronica, "Why

5.3. Casey Gant (Jonathan Bennett), a high-school student who has recently joined a mysterious cult community called the Moon Calf Collective, welcomes the titular protagonist to his new home, in *Veronica Mars*. © Silver Pictures Television and Rob Thomas Productions

don't you stay and join us?" The gumshoe, game for anything, accepts the invitation, and is welcomed with open arms by the leader, Josh (Chris William Martin). Although Veronica is invited to milk Isis, the group's cow, she is warned to stay away from a nearby barn (a reference to "The Joy of Sect" episode of *The Simpsons* in which Homer is given a similar warning). In voiceover, she muses, "Forbidden barn? Check. Implied polygamy? Check. Ladies and gentlemen, we have a cult." An encounter with another young member of the collective, Rain (referred to in voiceover as a "Moonie"), reveals that the place has stayed afloat financially through the growing of "the ultimate cash crop," which Veronica mistakenly believes to be marijuana. However, like so many other erroneous assumptions on her part, things do not pan out as planned or conform to preconceived stereotypes of cultish activity. So taken aback is Veronica by the overwhelmingly "normal" behavior on view in the Moon Calf Collective, which not only puts emphasis on teamwork (in contrast to the conflict-ridden Neptune High) but also profits from the selling of poinsettias (not marijuana) and is nursing an injured horse back to health in the barn, that she thinks to herself, "Enough already with this 'Mellow Incense and Peppermints' vibe! Let's break out the mushrooms and dance naked. Strap on the goat-skull headgear. Sacrifice a few infants. Come on, people, you're cultists. Start acting like it!"

5.4. Veronica's initial suspicions about the Moon Calf Collective are proven incorrect, as this community is "a lot more wholesome and functional" than the seaside town of Neptune (as her father later tells her). © Silver Pictures Television and Rob Thomas Productions

The refusal of the cult members to abide by the "rules" of neo-religiosity on view in other TV programs is a sign of just how unconventional *Veronica Mars* is as a teen-centric television series. After her encounter with the Moon Calf people, initially skeptical and sarcastic Veronica begins to see the value of such parasocial belonging, a transformation in attitude that prompts Wallace to state, "Sounds to me like you've been drinking the Kool-Aid." Although she once believed that Casey had been "weirding out" recently, the fact that he has become a more mature and sensitive student since his conversion suggests to her that the commune might be less corrupting than Neptune High, a school where even the principal, Alan Moorehead, is guilty of nefarious activities. When Veronica apologizes for being a "rampaging jackass," Casey responds, "Have you forgotten who you're talking to? I wrote the jackass Bible, the jackass Koran, the jackass Talmud!" These and other references to mainstream religious texts in *Veronica Mars* provide a structural foundation for the show's many meta-reflexive takes on neo-religious fandom, evidenced in "Ahoy Mateys," a Season Two episode that focuses on Ryan, a self-proclaimed fan of former pirate radio shock jock (and recent bus-crash victim) Marcos, who, as a gay teenager, had been sent by his parents to a "deprogramming camp." The latter individual, as the host of "The Cap'n Krunk Show" prior to meeting a premature death, had developed an intense fan following, one that is referred to as a "weird sorta cult thing" by Veronica's computer-nerd friend, Mac. In keeping with that characterization, Ryan states at one point, "I used to listen to the show, *religiously*."

From its passing acknowledgment of Keith's fanatical passion for baseball player Terence Cook in the episode "Ain't No Magic Mountain High Enough" (2.13) to its allusions to *Battlestar Galactica* enthusiasts in the episodes "Welcome Wagon" (3.01) and "Poughkeepsie, Tramps and Thieves" (3.11), *Veronica Mars* has done more than most other contemporary TV programs to link neo-religious activities and fannish proclivities. The latter episode is particularly noteworthy as a moment in the series when fixed ideas associated with media fandom are prodded for the purposes of exposing how preconceptions can lead the female hero (and the audience) down wrong hermeneutic paths. In this storyline from the third season, one of Veronica's classmates at Hearst College, Max (Adam Rose), asks her to track down a woman whom he had met at a Comic-Con meeting and with whom he has fallen in love. Explaining to Veronica that "it's not all Trekkies and *Star Wars* nerds" at the famous San Diego convention, and that he was there "because [comic-book artist] Dave Gibbons has a new graphic novel that he scripted and drew," Max initially tries to distance himself from the stereotypical image of a fan prone to cosplay and geeking out to science fiction, but soon admits that he "may have drifted into the *Battlestar Galactica* session." "That's where we met," the nerdy classmate states, adding that "her name is Chelsea, and she was in regular clothes, and we started out talking about how the Cylon raiders on *BSG* look like Batman's car when it turns into a plane. But then we started talking about our crappy relationships with our parents, and Chuck Klosterman, and moral grayness."

The first of several revelations in "Poughkeepsie, Tramps and Thieves" is that Chelsea (Brianne Davis) was a prostitute, hired by Max's roommates and coached in the ways of being a *Battlestar Galactica* fan. "That line about the Cylon raiders looking like Batman's car, they fed her that," Veronica informs him, before learning that the woman actually loves Max. This second revelation prompts Veronica to admit, "For what little it's worth, I was totally wrong . . . You two are great together." Then comes yet another narrative disclosure, a scene which reveals that Chelsea (whose real name is Wendy) and her business partner Nicki (Laura Roth), who sports a fake bruise, have apparently been conning people out of their money. As if parodying its own premise as a series that is structurally reliant on Hitchcockian MacGuffins and narrative U-turns, a *final reversal* brings the episode to a close, with Wendy/Chelsea being cleared of any such misdeeds and positioned as someone who genuinely cares about Max (whom she embraces at the end). The repetition of such reversals throughout the series as a whole and this episode in particular reminds audiences that they too should suspend their judgment and look past surface signifiers, if only to more accurately perceive the "truth" of a given situation—a word uttered more than once in "Poughkeepsie, Tramps and Thieves."

This is the message most clearly being communicated in "Drinking the Kool-Aid," which presents a *positive* image of cultic belonging and culminates with Keith's remark to his daughter, "Once you get past all the '60s theme park trappings, that community is a lot more wholesome and functional than—just for example—Neptune is." Unfortunately, Casey has since been apprehended by a black-clad deprogrammer hired by his parents (someone who specializes in "systematic manipulation of social and psychological influence"), setting the stage for the boy's return as a "normal" Porsche-driving member of the '09er community a few episodes later (in the aforementioned "A Trip to the Dentist"). Although Veronica started out believing that "four out of five cult leaders like their handmaidens nubile, flighty, and teetering on the edge of a breakdown," going so far as to surreptitiously sneak a tape recorder into the compound in hopes of capturing some typically "freakish" behavior, by the end of the episode she has decided that the Moon Calf Collective is where Rain—a teenage runaway whose real name is Debbie Meyers and whose photo appears in a Missing Person milk carton display—should *stay*. The episode thus suggests, rather remarkably, that Josh, the Moon Calf leader, might be a better "father" to Rain than her biological or foster parents. That theme is amplified in the secondary storyline, involving Veronica's attempt to determine whether Keith is her real father, going so far as to procure a blood sample from him under false pretenses and sending it to a paternity test lab. Ultimately, these elements of character development add up to a compelling argument for the preferability of surrogate families, including members of cult TV's imagined community, over more traditional domestic units or social groupings.

From Neptune to Venus: Deviating from the "Norm" and Visualizing the "Invisible"

> I'm having candy for dinner!
>> —recently rescued former cult member Kimmy
>> (Ellie Kemper), filling a plastic bag with gummies,
>> in the pilot episode of *Unbreakable Kimmy Schmidt*
>> (Netflix, 2015–20)

Thus far, we have seen how "America's religious margins," including parasocial groups bearing at least faint resemblances to cult TV fans, have been further marginalized within popular culture texts that play up the salacious aspects of becoming part of a closely knit "family" of strangers. In some ways, the television programs in which minority religions pop up are as exploitative as the deliberately deceptive leaders who are so often shown forcibly recruiting new members and coercing young women into sexual acts. As alluded to in the previous chapter, female cult members in particular are placed in vulnerable positions and portrayed as helpless victims in need of rescue. Their reliance on men (including local law enforcement, FBI agents, and SWAT team members) is a recurring trope that, while more prominent in previous decades' shows, is evident in even the most progressive satires and feminist sitcoms being produced today. For example, *Unbreakable Kimmy Schmidt*, a critically adored Netflix series discussed briefly in Chapter Four, is at once a thoughtful yet playful exploration of one woman's attempt to put her traumatic experience of being kidnapped by a cult leader behind her, and another in a long string of infantilizing, sensationalizing narratives that present such characters as child-like adults in need of a man's help.[35]

As Megan Goodwin argues, this candy-colored comedy, in which the title character—stuck in a state of stunted adolescence—rejoices at the prospect of literally consuming candy for dinner (a sign of her newfound freedom as a recently rescued member of Savior Rick's Spooky Church of the Scary Apocalypse), is guilty of reproducing stereotypes and reinforcing "two of the most common assumptions about cults." Those assumptions, according to Goodwin, are that "members are irrational ("brainwashed")" and that "leadership is exploitative, coercing or duping members into surrendering their possessions and/or their bodies."[36] This is not to deny that "financial, physical, sexual, and emotional abuses" occur in new religious movements and other marginalized communities (see, for instance, NXIVM, a not-so-secret "secret society" whose founder, Keith Raniere, was recently convicted of sex-trafficking). But her point is that such mistreatment "does *not* happen because the communities in question are *religious* outsiders," for in fact "abuse happens *everywhere*" (including inside that most sanctified of all sitcom settings: the middle-class home). Indeed, to single out NRMs "as especially or uniquely abusive," Goodwin goes on to say, "is to abdicate responsibility for our broader cultural complicity in the abuse of women and children."[37]

Not surprisingly, TV showrunners and writers are much more inclined to direct our antipathy toward cults as spaces of collective bad behavior than to point out similar forms of cruelty or misconduct within actual families and other, traditionally codified domestic units. Such conventional creative choices, which bespeak a general *lack* of creativity, make *Strangers with Candy* and *Veronica Mars* all the more extraordinary in contrast (given their unconventional takes on the age- and gender-based binaries bound up in the cult imaginary). By focusing on either an older woman who seeks comfort in the kindness of strangers or a young female detective who learns that "saving" a fellow high schooler from a hippie commune might do more *harm* than good, these programs present viable alternatives to the all-too-familiar rescue plots that have been with us for over a half century. They furthermore lend credence to Goodwin's claim that the United States has long been "a space that both fosters and punishes radical religious innovation," born out in the fact that Americans have "enshrined certain religious protections in our founding documents" while also disincentivizing doctrinal differences "deemed too far from the (predominantly white Christian) mainstream."[38]

To a lesser extent, other TV programs have done this as well. Take, for instance, an early episode of the fantasy-based sitcom *Mork & Mindy* (ABC, 1978–82) in which Robin Williams's extraterrestrial misfit, looking for people to befriend beyond his human housemate Mindy (Pam Dawber), enters the orbit of Exidor (Robert Donner), an equally eccentric individual who will eventually become his adoptive father. Before Mork wanders into this street preacher's dingy apartment (the walls of which are spray-painted with the words "Friends of Venus"), we see Exidor taking off his "End is Near" sandwich board and then speaking to a couple of invisible members of his cult (seated in empty chairs). Though he is, in truth, alone, the white-robed prophet carries on a conversation about the impending arrival of a Venusian mothership and the ensuing destruction of this planet, eliciting laughter from the studio audience. This scene establishes the "craziness" of this supporting character, whose recurring presence over the course of the series will turn his "cultness" into a running gag (in much the same way that Jon Hamm's kooky, scripture-misquoting Reverend reappears in *Unbreakable Kimmy Schmidt*). However, upon meeting Mork, who comes in looking for actual friends from Venus, Exidor quickly sees that this potential convert is not just a "true believer" (claiming to have met other aliens) but delusional in his own right. "I had high hopes for you, Mork," the older man remarks, "but *you're crazy!*" He says this after our manic protagonist tells him that the Venusians do not yet have the technology required "to blow the Earth to smithereens." But it is also telling that this comment comes after Mork has put on his own excessively performative show of faith. Pretending to be a Baptist televangelist from the Deep South, Mork—or, rather, Robin Williams—shows how mainstream religions are just as rife with ridiculousness as any cult, thus making visible the idea that satire can be extended further (into the invisible unknown), beyond the relatively "safe" territory carved out by most television series.

In her study of the "cult stereotype" in fictional television programs, Lynn S. Neal argues that mainstream cultural productions play a significant role in reflecting "popular societal views about alternative religions while simultaneously replicating and disseminating them."[39] According to Neal, "stereotypical cult elements, such as fraud, violence, and sexual depravity" have become normalized through

5.5. Throughout its four-year run (from 1978 to 1982), the otherworldly situation comedy *Mork & Mindy* devoted several of its
nearly 100 episodes to the subject of cults. In "Mork Runs Away,"
from Season One, the motormouthed alien played by Robin Williams comes into the orbit of a street preacher named Exidor,
who soon concludes that Mork is "crazy" after the latter does
an impression of a Baptist televangelist from the Deep South. ©
Miller-Milkis Productions

televisual repetition, across a range of generically dispersed programs (dramas,
police procedurals, sitcoms, science fiction series, etc.) that nevertheless share a
consistent point of view vis-à-vis minority religious groups and theological "others."
Among the many means through which textual producers are able to encode these
fictions with dominate messages and "differentiate cults from the norm" (through
the use of strange clothing, remote settings, and oft-repeated images of communal
living), the "strategic use of visibility and invisibility" is perhaps most indicative
of the binaristic tension that continues to characterize cultic representations and
distinguish "dangerous" and "inferior" belief systems from those of conventional
religions. To borrow Neal's words, a "good and godly religion" or theological orientation, such as Catholicism, might be invoked occasionally within the larger
narrative universes of such programs as *The Simpsons*, *Law & Order: SVU* (NBC,
1999–present), and *Boy Meets World* (ABC, 1993–2000), but it remains a relatively
vague, implicit or "invisible" presence in the lives of protagonists whose normalcy
is most apparent when juxtaposed against the very *visible*, explicitly "deviant"
and "delusional" practices of religious outsiders. Although *Strangers with Candy*

and *Veronica Mars* likewise presuppose a normative framework for adducing the main characters' possible religious upbringing, Jerri's and Veronica's respective encounters with "fringe elements" and isolated communities of faith make visible the otherwise "invisible" ideological orientation of contemporary neo-religious representations.

Indeed, the *Veronica Mars* episode "Drinking the Kool-Aid" reveals how dramatically a cult TV series might depart from traditional textual codings of cult members as dupes or dangerous threats to others. If anything, Casey Gant is "saved" by the Moon Calf Collective, only to be deprogrammed back into a spoiled rich kid by the end of the episode. Much the same thing happens in *Strangers with Candy*, with the normal/weird dichotomy collapsing under the weight of so many intentionally clichéd cultic tropes that problematize, rather than legitimize, the medium's conventional representational practices. Indeed, it would seem that "normal is the watchword" in these fan-centric, freak-friendly programs (to borrow Wallace's expression as well as the title of the Season Two opener of *Veronica Mars*), an idea that echoes media scholar Kristen Kidder's assertion that "the search for normalcy is at the very center of *Veronica Mars* and, in many ways, has become synonymous with the show's struggle for truth."[40]

Of course, even these deconstructive takes evince the limitations inherent in the medium, which is said to generate consensus around subjects that few people have little firsthand knowledge of. We therefore should attend not only to the stereotypical images on view in fiction-based programming (including the increased prevalence of mass suicides, previously a taboo topic on US television, in episodes of contemporary dramas such as *CSI: Crime Scene Investigation* and *Salvation* [CBS, 2017–18]), but also to those ideas or events that are *not* typically shown. For example, exit counseling—the oftentimes slow and painful process involved in leaving a cultic experience behind and returning to a socially accepted form of interpersonal relations—is hardly ever depicted in these representations. And, despite its ostensible centrality in several comedic and dramatic series, the actual process of "deprogramming" is rarely shown in detail.

Prior to the 2000s, most televisual representations of cults or NRMs drew from a limited repertoire of images and merely rehashed conventional storylines, making the critical-comedic interventions of recent programs like *Strangers with Candy* and *Veronica Mars* all the more extraordinary in their unconventionality. Since the original airdates of "The Blank Stare" and "Drinking the Kool-Aid," a handful of episodes from other programs, including *Medium* (NBC, 2005–9; CBS 2009–11) and *The Ghost Whisperer* (CBS, 2005–10), have provided "sympathetic and complicated portrayals of alternative religious beliefs and practices."[41] As such, it is important to remember that, just as cult television programs can be thought of as "unfolding texts" replete with a raft of "authors" who contribute to that unfolding through fan fiction and other ritualized/participatory activities,[42] so too does the history of cultic representations continue to evolve, expanding to accommodate alternative viewpoints and non-normative subject positions. Time will only tell if these more balanced portrayals push future productions into untested waters, beyond the shallow and unsympathetic images that have for too long problematically codified and demonized the cult experience on American TV.

Perhaps, with time, more realistic, less sensationalistic depictions will come, counterbalancing the still-widely-held perception of cult members as "crackpots, psychological basket cases, or brainwashed robots."[43] One thing is for certain, though. In this age of economic uncertainty for creative artists working in the television industry, onscreen talent and offscreen labor will continue to approach controversial subjects with caution and care, since losing even a small number of potential viewers or missing out on a sliver of the commercial advertising pie can spell doom for a cable or network project. Though she has seen her own career go belly-up as a result of recent social media gaffes and is hardly one to turn to as a source of sensitive, socially conscious commentary about the "right" and "wrong" ways to represent minorities, TV personnel seem to be heeding the advice of Rose-anne Barr, who—in her 2011 memoir *Roseannearchy: Dispatches from the Nut Farm*—wrote, "Beware of the two-headed monster of politics and religion."[44] It is to the literal and figurative *monsters* of American television—including those played, self-consciously or not, by Barr—and to the political underpinnings of the *monstrous imaginary* (most prominently featured in satires and sitcoms around Halloween time), that I now turn.

PART THREE: TV's Monstrous Imaginary

Comic Creeps, Neighborly Terrors,
and the Rhetoric of Trump

6

Very Spooky Episodes

Intertextual Monsters, Moral Panics, and the Playful Perversions of Halloween TV

I hate Halloween.

> —Adam (Adam Driver), a grumpy New Yorker
> speaking to his fellow road trippers Shoshanna
> (Zosia Mamet) and Hannah (Lena Dunham), in a
> Season Three episode of *Girls* (HBO, 2012–17)

I know that you hate Halloween. But stick with me and I promise you will love it.
> —Charles (Joe Lo Truglio) to Amy (Melissa Fumero)
> in a Season One episode of *Brooklyn Nine-Nine*
> (Fox, 2013–18; NBC, 2019–present)

As a contraction of All Hallows' Eve (referring to the night before All Saints' Day), the annual celebration popularly known as Halloween has been a recurring theme in US television programming since the medium's earliest days as a form of mass entertainment. Although the once-religious, now-secular festival dates back to the ancient Celtic celebration of Samhain,[1] not until the final years of the Great Depression and the early postwar era did its various modern-day connotations (e.g., trick-or-treating, costume parties, haunted houses, etc.) begin to circulate in newspaper articles and via radio broadcasts, soon achieving audiovisual expression through the next major form of American popular culture in the 1950s. It was during the first half of that decade when such disparate TV sketch comedies and situation comedies as *The Jackie Gleason Show* (DuMont, 1949–52; CBS, 1952–57) and *The Adventures of Ozzie and Harriet* (ABC, 1952–66) crystalized some of the many activities that make Halloween unique as a time of potentially transgressive merriment, thus distinguishing it from less taboo-shattering holidays (including the medium's other two seasonal mainstays, Christmas and Thanksgiving).

Typically framed as a temporary relaxation of social inhibitions, whereby revelers—young and old alike—are able to cross lines of decorum through costuming and other forms of camp performance, Halloween can be seen as a kind of "release valve" for the culture at large. It is therefore akin to TV comedy and other forms of humorous discourse insofar as it gives people the chance to satirically mock certain institutions and traditions (religious and otherwise) while "blowing off steam" or relieving the pressures of everyday life (i.e., "pent-up aggressions, anxieties and repressed desires").[2] Though far removed from one another (in terms of their settings and class stratifications), and couched within ostensibly conservative or restrictive generic frameworks (overseen by network executives, regulators, and sponsors), *The Jackie Gleason Show*'s "Halloween Party for the Boss" (2.05), which aired on October 25, 1952, and *The Adventures of Ozzie and Harriet*'s "Halloween Party" (1.05), which aired on October 31, 1952, gesture toward this holiday's playful "perversions" and set the template for future depictions of what the cultural historian David Skal refers to as a yearly event that "turns the world upside down."[3]

In his book *Death Makes a Holiday*, Skal writes that Halloween has historically been the one day when "permission would be granted to mortals to peer into the future, divine their fates, communicate with supernatural entities, and otherwise enjoy a degree of license and liberty unimaginable—or simply unattainable—the rest of the year."[4] Nothing so elaborate or paranormal takes place in *The Jackie Gleason Show* and *The Adventures of Ozzie and Harriet*, but in their own small way these programs demonstrate the ease with which a simple change in physical appearance (such as Ozzie Nelson's choice of a devil costume) can alter one's perception of their main characters as personifications of the presumed threat posed by monstrous others to mainstream society. In the case of the former, Ralph Kramden, the character played by the star and host of *The Jackie Gleason Show* (a forerunner of his more famous sitcom classic *The Honeymooners* [CBS, 1955–56]), destroys an old tuxedo to affect the look of a homeless bum, which he dresses up as in preparation for a Halloween party. After his neighbors Ed and Trixie Norton (Art Carney and Joyce Randolph)—cross-dressing as a flapper girl and a sailor boy, respectively—enter the Kramdens' tiny one-bedroom apartment in Brooklyn, Ralph rips his tux jacket and puts it on, covering the embarrassing Zulu chief costume that his wife Alice (Audrey Meadows) has made for him. Ralph's layered costuming, in which a caricatured image of a white working-class hobo or Chaplinesque tramp rests atop an equally stereotypical representation of racialized otherness (the black Zulu chief), hints at the artificiality of monstrous alterity, its status as cultural construct. The meagerly paid bus driver, whose financial woes are frequently the cause of blustery outbursts and domestic spats with Alice, is able to dress the part of someone lower on the socioeconomic scale by ruining a piece of outerwear that, if left intact, would otherwise signify power and wealth. That this first representation of Halloween costuming on American TV should lean so heavily on the visual coding/clothing of social class is relevant; as is the inclusion of Ed and Trixie's "drag" performances, a gender flip that could only be permitted within the liberating constraints of this most paganist of holidays, which, as David Skal argues, allows for the temporary reversal of "roles and fortunes."[5]

A decade after these episodes of *The Jackie Gleason Show* and *The Adventures of Ozzie and Harriet* aired, Halloween was already becoming something of a televisual touchstone, an annual event paradoxically made more singular yet commonplace by virtue of the increased attention given to it in seasonally themed installments of classic domestic sitcoms such as *Leave It to Beaver* (CBS, 1957–58; ABC, 1958–63), *Dennis the Menace* (CBS, 1959–63), and *My Three Sons* (ABC, 1960–65; CBS, 1965–72). Each of these latter three network programs, like countless others that aired before and after their initial broadcast, mined the cultural imaginary of mid-century monsterdom and made Halloween an increasingly "special" part of the fall television season. For example, precocious middle-class protagonist Dennis Mitchell (Jay North) and his neighbor Tommy Anderson (Billy Booth), primed for a night of trick-or-treating, don grotesque masks in "Haunted House" (3.05), an episode from the third season of *Dennis the Menace*; just as fellow preteen pranksters Chip Douglas (Stanley Livingston) and Sudsy Pfeiffer

6.1. Dennis and his friend Tommy don frightening Halloween masks and scare the ever-agitated Mr. Wilson in "Haunted House," a Season Three episode of *Dennis the Menace.* © Darriell Productions

(Ricky Allen) do in "The Ghost Next Door" (3.06), an episode from the third season of *My Three Sons*.

In these and other domestic sitcoms, characters and audiences alike are "spooked" by the presumed presence of otherworldy beings (hideously deformed monsters, spectral apparitions, etc.) that would not be out of place in that era's science fiction and fantasy programming (e.g., *The Twilight Zone* [CBS, 1959–64], *The Outer Limits* [ABC, 1963–65], *The Addams Family* [ABC, 1964–66], *The Munsters* [CBS, 1964–66]). Such representations, while comparatively tame, are exceptional in their break from normality—the veneer of middle-class sameness that masks potentially "dangerous" or "perverse" ideas and which is prominently displayed in other, non-Halloween-themed episodes of these series. Additionally, these early representations paved the way for more egregious displays of small-screen, Halloween-themed horrors in the years to come, a historical trajectory that ultimately leads to the one American situation comedy which arguably did more than any other—with the obvious exception of *The Simpsons* (Fox, 1989–present)—to "domesticate" that most macabre, death-fixated of holidays, in the process transforming it into the "second-largest seasonal marketing event after Christmas" around the turn of the century.[6]

That television show, *Roseanne* (ABC, 1988–97), is famous for many things besides its annual Halloween installments. At once conservative and progressive, this critically lauded multicamera sitcom, created by veteran TV producers Marcy Carsey and Tom Werner, was initially touted as a reflexive (if not radical) reworking of traditional representations of middle-class and working-class America, foregrounding a closely-knit yet raucously fractured family that was "beset by financial hardships and emotional pain."[7] Taking its title from the name of its unconventional star (Roseanne Barr), this series broke from earlier depictions of domestic bliss—as seen, for instance, in episodes of *The Donna Reed Show* (ABC, 1958–66)—by focusing on an "overweight, loud, and domineering" mom who frequently challenged her husband's and male bosses' patriarchal authority, brashly lashing out at systems of gendered oppression that remain at least partially intact today.[8] In stark contrast to the doting maternal figures on view in *Leave It to Beaver, Dennis the Menace,* and other 1950s and 1960s sitcoms, Roseanne Conner (Barr's character) embodied a new form of primetime feminism during the 1980s and 1990s.[9] However, from a contemporary perspective, she might also be seen as a reactionary throwback to old-fashioned, red-state "family values." This became especially pronounced when both the race-baiting star and her unruly character threw their support behind the 45th US president after his November 2016 election. Tellingly, the much-anticipated relaunch of *Roseanne* in the spring of 2018, coinciding with the rise of a Trump-era social-media politics of xenophobic exclusion and othering, was soon overshadowed by its sudden cancellation in May of that year; an about-face move (initiated by ABC president Channing Dungey) that denied longtime viewers of the program an opportunity to indulge their Halloween fantasies one last time with the Conners.

Before returning to *Roseanne* in the next chapter, which is devoted almost entirely to that series, this chapter explores some of the underlying themes as well as narrative elements at play in many if not all "very spooky episodes" devoted to the holiday. "Play," it turns out, is the operative word; in addition to humor, it is one of the two "dominant tropes of Halloween," according to Nicholas Rogers, a cultural historian who notes the importance of this transitory moment of carnivalesque potential in "promoting different ways of seeing the world" and giving people the opportunity to test the "limits of permissiveness" each year, if only fleetingly.[10] Like an actual carnival, especially one that is aimed at marginalized youth or other subcultures, Halloween provides "a public space for social inversion or transgression" that unsettles older generations of Americans.[11] But, as Rogers is quick to acknowledge, Halloween in its most commercial manifestations also exhibits hegemonic, "homogenizing" tendencies, "as the epitome of North American mass culture" that continues to be exported globally and which feeds multiple revenue streams across different industries.[12] Given his and other scholars' emphasis on humor and play, it is not too big a leap to suggest that situation comedy, which is likewise snagged between contrasting polarities (as a comfortably discomforting cultural form that pleases and perturbs in equal measure), is a natural fit for Halloween, and vice-versa. That is, the yearly festival has found a "home" in the sitcom, an ostensibly conservative genre of highly contrived, ritualized rhetorical figures and morally circumscribed domestic settings that is nevertheless playful and even progressive in its disarming use of humor to "parody power and mock its pretensions."[13] With that in mind, let us turn to some of the distinguishing features of what I call "Halloween TV."

Trick-or-Trope: Horror, Humor, and the Rhetorical Figures of Halloween TV

> Every time a little kid cries in fear, that's Halloween. Every time something repulsive ends up in a mailbox, that is Halloween. As long as you carry the spirit of destruction and vandalism in your hearts, every day is Halloween.
> —Francis (Christopher Masterson), trying to get his younger brother Reese (Justin Berfield) into the holiday spirit, in a Season Two episode of *Malcolm in the Middle* (Fox, 2000–2006)

What, exactly, comprises a "very spooky episode"? What makes Halloween TV so "special," setting it apart not only from other holiday-themed programming (i.e., episodes revolving around Christmas or Thanksgiving, for example) but also from the majority of non-holiday episodes that are broadcast either before or after the final week of October? The calendrical timing of an episode's original or intended broadcast matters, and in fact a few of the entries that are cited in online polls of the "best" or most memorable examples of Halloween TV, including "The Ghost of A. Chantz" (an episode of *The Dick Van Dyke Show* [CBS, 1961–66] that aired on September 30, 1964), "Lucy and the Monsters" (an episode of *The Lucy Show* [CBS, 1962–68] that aired on January 25, 1965), and "Nightmare on Oak Street" (an episode of *The Hogan Family* [NBC, 1986–90; CBS, 1990–91] that aired on November 23, 1987), are not Halloween episodes in the strictest sense, since they feature few direct references to the holiday and were not produced or programmed with the intention of coinciding with it on the calendar. This is not to say, however, that *everything* (or even most things) aired during the week leading up to Halloween concerns the holiday, either directly or indirectly. One need only to recall that *Diff'rent Strokes* (NBC, 1978–85; ABC, 1985–86) and its sister series *The Facts of Life* (NBC, 1979–88), two sitcoms distinguished by their penchant for presenting controversial social issues within "Very Special Episodes" privileging seriousness over humor, each aired only *once* on October 31 (during the 1979 and 1984 fall seasons, respectively), and that neither of those episodes were actually *about* Halloween. Although each of these episodes is still "special," in the sense of being *unusual*—either as the first of a two-part airing (in the case of *Diff'rent Strokes'* "The Adoption: Part 1" [2.08]) or as the only one to have been produced without a laughtrack or live audience (in the case of *The Facts of Life's* "Cruisin" [6.05])—no holiday references are to be found in either of them.

It goes without saying that a Halloween episode is one in which that holiday figures prominently, through the physical integration of conventional iconography within the mise-en-scène (costumes, props, sets, etc.) and with characters talking about and/or performing any of the activities with which it is associated. The "prominently" part of that definition is significant, for there are numerous TV shows in which the common signifiers of Halloween are shown only briefly, or in which the holiday is mentioned casually by individuals whose personal and professional lives are of greater importance—to themselves and within the narrative (subdivided into A, B, and possibly C storylines)—than any concerns with masquerade parties, haunted houses, holiday-related pranks, or neighborhood rivalries between friends and enemies who compete to put on the spookiest "show" through elaborate decorations. For example, "Isosceles Love Triangle" (4.06), an episode of *The John Larroquette Show* (NBC, 1993–96) that aired on October 30,

1996, makes only passing reference to All Hallows' Eve, opting to devote most of its running time to a female police officer's frustration in trying (but failing) to ask the main character, a night-shift manager at a bus depot, out on a date. Although Eve (Elizabeth Berridge), the cop in question, wants John (John Larroquette), the elusive man she has been pining for, to accompany her to a costume party, the latter event is presented as merely an afterthought, tacked onto the concluding scene and, thus, not integrated into the narrative as fully as one would expect in a Halloween episode. For that reason, one might rightly leave this and similar television episodes out of the equation when trying to ascertain precisely *what* Halloween TV is and *how* it functions culturally as a space where conventionally coded signs of bad behavior are given unconventional twists.

In terms of Halloween TV's storehouse of images, its repertoire of rhetorical figures and physical actions, certain signifiers have risen to the surface on more than one occasion, making such episodes simultaneously exceptional (i.e., distinctively different from other non-Halloween episodes) yet predictable (in terms of adhering to audience expectations of what the holiday is supposed to look like). Some visual tropes are in fact dead giveaways about an episode's status as Halloween TV. Consider, for instance, the act of bobbing for apples, a traditional practice that is relatively uncommon outside the domain of this particular setting or time of year, but which is depicted—sometimes humorously, sometimes horrifically—in numerous Halloween-themed episodes, ranging from *The Office* (NBC, 2005–13)'s "Costume Contest" (7.06) to *Supernatural* (WB/CW, 2005–20)'s "It's the Great Pumpkin, Sam Winchester" (4.07). Besides the age-old game of bobbing for apples, other elements of mise-en-scène, including bubbling cauldrons, cackling witches, carved jack-o'-lanterns lit by flickering candles, spiderwebs splayed across darkened doorways, and all manner of deathly symbols—from skeletons and skulls to open coffins and cemetery headstones—are standard features whose repetition, across multiple televisual texts, has ensured a certain visual consistency over the decades.

As such, viewers should not be any more surprised to see costumed trick-or-treaters in an episode of *8 Simple Rules* (ABC, 2002–5) titled "Halloween" (3.06), which aired on October 29, 2004, than they would be in witnessing a similarly dressed bunch of candy-hungry kids in a same-titled episode of *The Cosby Show* (NBC, 1984–92) broadcast nearly two decades earlier, on October 31, 1985. What *will* have changed between those airdates, or across the span of time separating the original broadcast of a much earlier episode depicting kids trick-or-treating (for example, "Halloween Party," from the first season of *The Adventures of Ozzie and Harriet*) and its syndicated rebroadcast (as a rerun) decades later, are the historical contexts in which societal attitudes about that cultural activity are shaped. Thus, while the mere presence of trick-or-treaters—be they the angry, empty-bagged "goblins" threatening the title characters in *George & Leo* (CBS, 1997–98) or the neighborhood kids who are themselves threatened by an old woman believed to be a "witch" in *The Millers* (CBS, 2013–15)—is a tell-tale sign that one is watching a Halloween episode, the discursive framing of the activity necessarily shifts in accordance with larger debates about the perceived dangers to children's safety posed by it.

Bobbing for Bad Apples: Mass Hysteria and Moral Panics

> Halloween is the most important day of the year. It's the one on the Gregorian calendar where you're allowed to go around terrifying children and not be branded a psychopath.
> —Chanel Oberlin (Emma Roberts) in a Season One episode of *Scream Queens* (Fox, 2015–16)

As the "high holy day of candy," to borrow the words of Samira Kawash, Halloween has been a source of consternation for many parents and other adults concerned not only with the physical health of young people (whose hearts, kidneys, livers, and teeth are put to the test by this "annual sugar-fueled ritual") but also about the possibility that kids might come into contact with "bad apples" (figuratively and literally) when unleashed onto suburban and city streets as trick-or-treaters.[14] In her book *Candy: A Century of Panic and Pleasure*, Kawash explains that such collective handwringing, while a relatively recent phenomenon (owing to the fact that trick-or-treating is a fairly modern US invention growing out of the wartime and early postwar eras), has ties to earlier moral and social panics in which irrational, widespread fears had sprung up around the most vulnerable members of society. She mentions, specifically, the image of the "Halloween sadist" that first began to circulate (via news reports and word-of-mouth) in the 1960s, following the notorious case of a California dentist, Dr. William Shyne, who "distributed over 450 candy-coated laxative tablets to the neighborhood children on Halloween" in 1959.[15] Charged with "outrage of public decency," Shyne was singled out as a kind of predatory figure whose very existence threatened the lives of kids (fortunately, the thirty children who were injured as a result of ingesting his "treats" recovered quickly). That initial flareup of public interest in tainted sweets being given to and consumed by kids was soon followed by a full-on tsunami of dread that spread throughout the country during the 1970s—a period when the number of Halloween-themed episodes being produced for the Big Three networks (ABC, CBS, and NBC) increased from previous decades' counts, despite (or perhaps due to) that state of panic.

One such example from that decade is "Haunted" (2.06), an episode of the nostalgically imbued comedy *Happy Days* (ABC, 1974–84) that originally aired on October 29, 1974. That airdate is significant, for it anticipates, by a mere two days, what some cultural commentators have referred to as the most infamous case of Halloween-related poisoning in US history: that of an 8-year-old Texas boy, Timothy O'Bryan, who "died suddenly after eating a cyanide-tainted Pixy Stix."[16] As denoted by its title, "Haunted" largely concerns the irrational fear that Richie Cunningham (Ron Howard) experiences when he steps into a "dusty, cobwebby, and really scary" house—specifically, the old Simpson house—believed to be inhabited by the restless ghosts of its previous owners. But it also acknowledges that there are other, presumably more "rational" or reasonable concerns—within the Cunningham residence as well as the seemingly crime-free Milwaukee neighborhood that surrounds it—about young people's safety during this most fright-filled of holidays. That worry is lent credence by the presence of a gang of leather-clad bikers, who are shown vandalizing Arnold's Drive-In (the local hangout) during this episode's first scene, and is openly expressed in its final scene, well after the supernatural beings lying in wait inside the abandoned house (including a headless body) have been exposed for what they *really* are: as misunderstandings on the part of an all-too-human teenager, who has been the victim of a prank. Sitting down at the kitchen table to inspect her sugary loot from her night of trick-or-treating, Richie's sister, Joanie (Erin Moran), is told by their mother that she cannot eat any candy that isn't wrapped. "Boy, if you can't trust your *neighbors*, who *can* you trust?" the girl asks, to which Mrs. Cunningham (Marion Ross) responds, "Well, there's an awful lot of crazy people around these days."

This line of dialogue, in keeping with the titular theme of the episode, is "haunted" in the sense of containing the residual trace of extradiegetic discourses concerning the threats posed by Halloween-related activities in the 1970s. But these words of maternal wisdom are also haunting insofar as they leave the audience with a feeling of unresolved unease—a decidedly odd sentiment for a normally upbeat situation comedy like *Happy Days*, but one that would linger well into the 1980s. Indeed, in "Fool for Love" (4.01), an episode of *Growing Pains* (ABC, 1985–92) that aired fourteen years later (on October 19, 1988), Carol (Tracey Gold), a teenager who has been left behind by her family members to hand out candy on Halloween, quotes nearly verbatim Marion Cunningham's cautionary advice when she tells a couple of trick-or-treaters (dressed as "Mr. and Mrs. T") that "there are some very creepy people out there who like to hurt little children." Explaining to the dumbfounded kids that they should let their parents "check every single thing" in their candy bags once they return home, Carol unintentionally succeeds in scaring them away—humorously sending them bolting through the front door, screaming into the night—before she can conclude her unsolicited speech about the specific ways that strangers might cause danger ("by putting awful things in their candy, like poison and . . .").

6.2. In this Halloween-themed episode of *Happy Days*, Mrs. Cunningham warns her teenage daughter Joanie not to eat anything that is not properly wrapped, informing the girl that there are "crazy people" in the world who prey on young trick-or-treaters. © Miller-Milkis Productions

Throughout the 1970s and 1980s, reputable publications, including the *New York Times*, encouraged adults to check trick-or-treaters' candy for hidden sewing needles, razor blades, and shards of glass.[17] However, for all of that alarmist rhetoric (summed up by one *Newsweek* reporter's 1975 false claim that "several children have died" and that "hundreds have narrowly escaped injury" as a result of consuming poisoned sweets), the truth about candy-tampering was much harder for many Americans to swallow. A 1984 study by sociologist Joel Best, who "investigated seventy-six press accounts of what he called 'Halloween sadism' published between 1958 and 1983,"[18] revealed that none of the purported cases of candy-tampering held up to scrutiny, and that each of the five most famous incidents over the past twenty-five years was misattributed. Among those incidents was the previously mentioned case of Timothy O'Bryan, whose death, Best pointed out, was brought about not by a sadistic stranger but by Timothy's own father, Ronald. Nicknamed "The Candy Man," Ronald O'Bryan, who was arrested for murder on November 5, 1974, made it "look like the work of a Halloween psychopath so that he could collect several life insurance policies."[19] Coincidentally, Best's report, which was confirmed by several independent studies (including one from the National Confectioners Association) and was further substantiated by the US Food and Drug Administration (which "found no evidence for tampering in over 95 percent of the cases" that its researchers had studied),[20] was published the same year that O'Bryan was executed by lethal injection (on March 31, 1984), between the airdates of two thematically related episodes of George A. Romero's *Tales from the Darkside* (1984–88): "Trick or Treat" (the syndicated horror anthology series' pilot [1.01], broadcast on October 29, 1983) and "Halloween Candy" (from its second season [2.05], broadcast on October 27, 1985). All of this provides a contextual clue as to why some of the most anxiety-ridden episodes devoted to Halloween, beyond those of *Tales from the Darkside*, were produced during that time period, when stories about "broken wrappers and needles in candy bars and rat-poison-coated jellybeans" were contributing to "mass hysteria" on a truly national scale.[21]

Although there are no arsenic-laced goodies to contend with in "Alice's Halloween Surprise" (6.04), an episode of the workplace comedy *Alice* (CBS, 1976–85) that aired on October 25, 1981, it thematizes the then-salient fears of children being abducted, lost, or put into other forms of jeopardy during the holiday season. Specifically, Alice (Linda Lavin), a diner waitress living on the outskirts of Phoenix, grows increasingly anxious waiting for the return of a young boy who has gone missing; not her own son Tommy (Philip McKeon), but rather a grade-schooler named Artie (Evan Cohen) whose father—her romantic interest at the time—has dropped him off at her apartment. After taking Artie, dressed as Darth Vader, trick-or-treating, she returns home and takes off his black mask, only to find a different child (notably, an African American kid named Tyrone [Shavar Ross] whose visible difference from the missing boy is a source of humor, despite the serious nature of this scenario). In typical sitcom fashion, however, the narrative resolves this underlying tension—this sense of Halloween-induced dread—once Artie has been found (sleeping in Tommy's bed the whole time). Variations on this premise of "Alice's Halloween Surprise" would be reproduced over the next four decades, in seasonally themed episodes of other situation comedies where the most pressing "situation" faced by adults is the prospect of losing a child on Halloween.

This happens, for instance, in the Tim Allen vehicle *Last Man Standing* (ABC, 2011–17; Fox, 2018–present), or specifically "Last Halloween Standing" (1.04), one of this series' many odes to the holiday. Here, Allen's character Mike Baxter takes his two-year-old grandson home after a night of trick-or-treating and soon discovers, after removing his skeleton mask, that he has mixed up his Caucasian American family member with an Asian American boy belonging to his neighbors, the Wongs. Other examples can be found in the 1995 episode "Witchcraft" (1.08), from the TV series *Brotherly Love* (NBC, 1995–96, UPN, 1996–97),

6.3. Initiating a trope that would be repeated in several subsequent Halloween-themed sitcom episodes, this moment in *Alice*, when the title character lifts the mask from a young trick-or-treater only to discover that she has brought the wrong kid home, hints at the "stranger danger" phenomenon of the 1970s and 1980s. © Warner Bros. Television

and in the 2002 episode "Halloween Cheer" (2.04), from *George Lopez* (ABC, 2002–7). In "Witchcraft," Joe (Joey Lawrence), another rough-around-the-edges male protagonist (specifically, a twentysomething mechanic who has grown up without a father), returns home from trick-or-treating with his young brother Andy (Andrew Lawrence), only to discover that the kid beneath the white ghost sheet is someone else (this time, an African American girl named Emma [Camille Winbush]). Reassuringly, the two children switch places—going back to their "rightful" locations (safely into the enveloping arms of their biological parents)—before the episode's final moments, which culminate with a PSA-style message to the audience, delivered by the three young stars of *Brotherly Love* (Joey Lawrence and his real-life brothers Matthew and Andrew). Breaking the fourth wall, this trio of actual family members tells us that "Halloween can be scary but should always be safe." "Never ever go home with a stranger," one of the boys states, followed by the other brother who chimes in, "And when you do go out, always wear something bright." This episode's final cautionary line, "Never go trick-or-treating alone," sums up the moral and social panics that have attended Halloween celebrations since the 1970s. Keeping these words in mind, it is easy to see why national efforts to protect young people from the real-world horrors of Halloween have run parallel to televisual mediations on the topics of child abduction and teenage predation, something dealt with most directly in "Fear Strikes Back" (3.02), a bracing episode of *The Facts of Life* (aired a few days after Halloween, on November 4, 1981) in which Natalie (Mindy Cohn), a student at an all-girls school, is sexually assaulted on campus while returning home from a Halloween costume party.

Besides that "Very Special Episode" of *The Facts of Life*, one of the most fascinating case studies in this light is "A Haunting We Will Go" (7.01), the seventh-season opener of *Diff'rent Strokes* that aired in 1984 (a few months after Ronald O'Bryan's execution). This episode begins with gregarious electrician Mr. Owens (John Astin) entering Phillip Drummond (Conrad Bain)'s Park Avenue penthouse and telling the wealthy businessman's adopted son, Arnold Jackson (Gary Coleman), about the old Markwell place, a house rumored to be haunted. This information piques the curiosity of young Arnold and his friends, who naturally decide to visit the place in hopes of putting the question of ghosts—especially those that are purported to "eat little boys"—to rest. When Arnold and his freckle-faced sidekick Sam (Danny Cooksey) arrive there, stepping gingerly on the eerily creaking floorboards, they are greeted by many of the audiovisual tropes associated with "very spooky episodes," including cobwebbed, dust-covered furniture (some of which appear to move on their own accord); exploding glassware; a wheezing organ; cackling, disembodied laughter; and a monstrous green hand that, poking out from behind a curtain, taps Arnold on his shoulder. In an effort to calm his impressionable companion's nerves, Arnold keeps reminding Sam that there is "nothing to be afraid of" and that there are "no such things as ghosts," although he too soon becomes a believer once the latter boy disappears during a sudden blackout. Although he later shows up back at the Drummond household, Arnold's exclamation—"Sam's missing!"—anticipates the title and premise of another *Diff'rent Strokes* episode that aired one year later. Indeed, as a "Very Special Episode" concerned with the growing fears about "stranger danger" (a catchword of the 1980s, when child safety campaigns were increasingly integrated into network programming), the eighth-season opener "Sam's Missing" (8.01) extends the themes of "A Haunting We Will Go" and adopts an altogether more sobering, less humorous, perspective on a subject that has long been a part of Halloween's cultural imaginary. By narrative's end, it is revealed that Mr. Owens and Clarence Markwell (Ray Bolger), the owner of the "haunted" house who is very much alive, have been playing a trick on the kids, and the two of them are eventually held accountable for their actions by the finger-wagging Mr. Drummond and his new wife Maggie (Dixie Carter). Although the handyman has done little more than try to scare Arnold and Sam out of their wits (a far cry from what Donald Brown, the child abductor in "Sam's Missing," threatens to do

6.4. Played with creepy charm by John Astin (of *The Addams Family* fame), the Drummond family's electrician Mr. Owens tries to convince Arnold and Sam that the abandoned house nearby is haunted (or, in his words, filled with ghosts who "eat little boys") in this Halloween-themed episode of *Diff'rent Strokes*. © Tandem Productions

to the titular tyke), Mr. Owens is nevertheless scolded by Maggie, who remarks, "*Shame* on you . . . You're a *bad man*."

On a more humorous, intertextually playful note, the "bad man" of "A Haunting We Will Go" is played by John Astin, well-known to many TV viewers of a certain age as the mustachioed patriarch of the Addams Family. Having played the poetry-quoting Gomez on ABC's 1960s monster comedy *The Addams Family*, Astin imports the broadly theatrical performative flourishes of that role into *Diff'rent Strokes* and thus establishes an intertextual connection to postwar creature features that he and his gothically attired castmates on that classic series embodied over two seasons. During its original run (1964–66), that show's chief competitor was *The Munsters*, rival network CBS's similar attempt to cash in on that era's monster craze. Significantly, the latter black-and-white series is also referenced in "A Haunting We Will Go," during a scene in which Pearl (Mary Jo Catlett), the Drummonds' housekeeper, asks Sam if the Markwell manor looked "like the Munsters' house." In fact, layers of intertextual citations quickly pile up, beginning with a reference to the contemporaneous horror film *Poltergeist* (1982) and culminating with this episode's biggest "reveal": that Clarence Markwell himself is not only alive but also played by Ray Bolger, an aging actor best remembered

6.5. In addition to John Astin, another instance of stunt-casting occurs in "A Haunting We Will Go" when Ray Bolger—an actor famous for playing the Scarecrow in *The Wizard of Oz*—drops in on the boys (who are dressed up as young "Ghostbusters") and therefore extends this episode's intertextuality back to the studio system era. © Tandem Productions

for his role as the Scarecrow in MGM's *The Wizard of Oz* (1939). Sandwiched between these scenes are copious references to yet another film, *Ghostbusters* (1984), which inspires Arnold and Sam to suit up in "ghost fighter" uniforms as they prepare to get "slimed." Given the degree to which intertextuality infuses this and other examples of Halloween TV, it seems appropriate to turn now toward this most engrained feature, citing additional examples in which citation itself is the operative means of generating meaning, both within and across texts.

Cross-Media Intertextuality: Horror Movies and Titular References to TV's Past

> What's the matter? You think that watching too many horror movies will make you into a monster?
>
> > —Larry (Mark Linn-Baker) to his cousin Balki (Bronson Pinchot), who, dressed as a chicken for Halloween, seeks to avoid watching scary movies (because "they are about bad people doing bad things and I believe they put bad thoughts in our heads"), in a Season Four episode of *Perfect Strangers* (ABC, 1986–93)

As a major part of the semantic and syntactic makeup of Halloween TV, costume parties provide opportunities for showrunners and writers to bring forth a panoply of pop culture references that hint at the holiday's built-in intertextuality. Although it is hardly remembered today (and was little seen during its brief broadcast run on NBC), the single-camera sitcom A to Z (2014–15) features a Halloween episode ("E is for Ectoplasm" [1.05]) that cites several better-known classic and contemporary cultural productions (in addition to legendary icons of the early twentieth century, including Charlie Chaplin and Amelia Earhart). Ironically, by doing so, this show, a pastiche of romantic comedy conventions, not only highlights a "crisis of influence" that haunts so many recently produced works but also calls attention to its own *failure* to earn the same accolades or longevity as those to which it pays homage in the guise of costumes (e.g., TV comedies like *Laverne & Shirley* [ABC, 1976–83], crime dramas like *Magnum P.I.* [CBS, 1980–88], sci-fi blockbusters like *Ghostbusters*, and recent cult horror sensations like *Shaun of the Dead* [2004]). Intertextuality is not limited to costume parties, of course, and several satires and sitcoms have found novel ways to integrate references to big-screen thrills and chills, not to mention literally *bloody* types of bad behavior, and in doing so have expanded the range of representational possibilities on the small screen.

For instance, in the "Halloween" (4.07) episode of *Cybill* (CBS, 1995–98), the title character (played by Cybill Shepherd) has been asked to host an all-night on-air telethon in support of a charitable cause and speaks directly to the TV audience in the guise of Glinda the Good Witch, from *The Wizard of Oz*. Seated behind her, several volunteers can be seen answering the telephones and jotting down viewers' pledge donations. Although nameless, these minor characters' costumed presence in the background—playing everyone from Uncle Fester (the baldheaded member of the fictional Addams Family) to Freddy Krueger (the razor-handed serial killer in Wes Craven's *Nightmare on Elm Street* franchise) to Pinhead (the terrifying Cenobite from Clive Barker's *Hellraiser* series)—foregrounds the fact that this fundraising drive is being held on All Hallows' Eve (rather than, say, Labor Day or Thanksgiving). Cybill as "Glinda" also betrays this episode's calendrical setting, for a fake broomstick appears to be drilled into her abdomen, leaving a splash of equally bogus blood on her dress. Prop humor of this kind can be spotted in many other examples of Halloween TV; for example, a large knife is lodged in the blood-spurting chest of Hakeem (Lamont Bentley), a teenaged character who pretends to be the victim of a stabbing and "plays dead" in an episode of *Moesha* (UPN, 1996–2001) (which, like so many other Halloween episodes, eventually builds toward a costume party scene). Similar to that grisly image of bodily harm, the sight of the equally blood-soaked Cybill, an apparent victim of witch-on-witch violence, can be said to "push the boundaries" of what is permissible on network television (at the time of their original broadcast, if not today). But it also fuses seemingly incompatible modes of representation (the comic, the fantastic, and the horrific) while clearing the way for this episode's most glaring incorporation of Halloween-related intertextuality: black-and-white clips of the Universal monster movie *Frankenstein* (1931), which are sprinkled into the show-within-the-show (the "telethon") as ironic commentary on the increasingly ludicrous proceedings.

Besides *Cybill*, other American sitcoms have brought forth direct references to classic and contemporary horror films, forging a cross-media connection that is most pronounced during the Halloween season. Aired on October 28, 1979, the *Mork & Mindy* (ABC, 1978–82) episode "A Morkville Horror" (2.08) followed on the heels of that year's theatrical release of *The Amityville Horror* (1979), incorporating several supernatural elements from the summer hit (including its basic "haunted house" premise). *Square Pegs* (CBS, 1982–83), a coming-of-age comedy about two teenaged social misfits, Patty (Sarah Jessica Parker) and Lauren (Amy Linker), who struggle to fit in at their high school, gestures toward a slasher film released a few weeks before the November 1, 1982, airing of "Halloween XII" (1.05). This episode, bearing a misleading title (which falsely suggests that many other Halloween-themed episodes have preceded it), also alludes to the earlier horror film *Halloween* (1978) through its foregrounding of an assumed stalker's point-of-view. But its scenes of Patty, Lauren, and other girls having a sleepover at the house of their teacher, Ms. Loomis (Catlin Adams) (whose name is another call-back to John Carpenter's classic), are most derivative of *Slumber Party Massacre* (1982), surely the only time that this low-budget cult film has served as the inspiration for a sitcom episode. The misleadingly titled "Halloween II" (4.02), an episode from the fourth season of *Kate & Allie* (CBS, 1984–89), includes a scene in which a teenaged boy named Jason (Ricky Paull Goldin), dressed up as Dr. Frankenstein, asks his friends if they "remember 'that scene' in *Friday the 13th*" as they descend into a darkened basement. Emma (Ari Meyers), his girlfriend (who is dressed as the Bride of Frankenstein's monster), asks, "Which one?," to which Jason responds, "*All* of them." In this brief, seemingly insignificant moment, which invites spectators to reflect on their own genre familiarity ("Do you remember . . . ?"), past and present come together in a subterranean space that is central to the horror film's narrative and thematic focus on characters searching for the "source" of their waking nightmares. Ostensibly carried out to see if anyone has been "fooling around with the circuit breakers," Jason, Emma, and the others' descent into the basement enacts a core theme of the genre while reminding us that "very spooky episodes" are themselves sourced from preexisting cinematic and televisual texts.

For that reason, genre familiarity plays a part in whether audiences will appreciate certain examples of Halloween TV. Sometimes this plays out like a

Scream-inspired meta-commentary about the tropes and conventions of horror cinema, as when supporting characters Trish (Raini Rodriguez) and Dez (Calum Worthy)—best friends to the titular twosome in the Disney Channel series *Austin & Ally* (2011–16)—discuss what it means to "split up" while searching for someone inside a haunted house. Asking Trish if she has "never seen a horror movie," Dez explains that "splitting up" is "when one of the teenagers *gets it.*" The teenager's comment, plus the slashing movement that he makes with his hand across his neck (a universal sign of someone getting murdered), would seem out of place in any but a Halloween-themed episode, especially given the fact that *Austin & Ally* is pitched at a young demographic presumably unfamiliar with self-reflexive horror films like Wes Craven's *Scream* (1996). As exemplified by this Disney Channel offering, in most cases the characters of "very spooky episodes" often do the work of spelling out any references to specific horror films that might otherwise be indecipherable to some viewers. And their dialogue sometimes sounds as if it was written with the intention of having the audience directly confront the horror genre's representational modes (with regard to the issues of gender, race, and social class) as well as its affective dimensions. This is the case in the small-screen version of the 1995 feature-length teen comedy *Clueless* (ABC, 1996–97; UPN, 1997–99), when, following the opening credits of "Trick or Treat" (2.06), Dee (Stacey Dash) and Murray (Donald Faison) discuss the relative merits of a Freddy Krueger Marathon being held at a local movie theater near their high school. Although Dee is of the mind that "those movies are stupid, violent, and degrading to women," her male companion believes that "of all the movie slashers, Freddy has the most progressive attitude." Although she fails to see Murray's logic (i.e., that the villain of the *Nightmare on Elm Street* franchise "hacks just as many men as he does women"), Dee eventually relents and attends the movie marathon before the end of the episode.

An earlier episode, "Aliens" (4.03), from the fourth season of *Perfect Strangers* (ABC, 1986–93), similarly stages a conversation between two characters whose contrasting attitudes toward the horror genre creates a space for spectatorial contemplation about Halloween's cultural function, carving out a part of the year when we willingly confront our deepest fears and entertain otherwise ludicrous ideas. Larry (Mark Linn-Baker), a reporter at the *Chicago Chronicle*, has invited two of his female coworkers to his and his cousin Balki (Bronson Pinchot)'s apartment, where he plans to host a horror movie marathon. The women turn down his offer; one because her mother-in-law is in town ("and why watch movie monsters when you can see the real thing"), the other because she claims to "hate Halloween." This slippage between horror and Halloween is significant, as is the intertextual reference to Alfred Hitchcock's 1960 film *Psycho*, which has made it impossible for this woman to shower alone. This opening scene sets the stage for an ensuing passage of dialogue, this time between Larry and his heavily accented cousin, a former shepherd from the Mediterranean island of Mypos who moved to America three years earlier but remains ignorant about many US customs and cultural references. When he is told that "horror is the *fun* part of Halloween," Balki asks, "Why would anyone want to sit through twelve hours of horrible movies. I could barely make it through *Ishtar*." "No, not 'horrible' movies," Larry explains, "*horror* movies . . . movies that scare you to death." Although specific science fiction and horror films, including *Invasion of the Body Snatchers* (1956), are cited in "Aliens," the titular suggestion of extraterrestrial lives intruding upon the existence of these two "perfect strangers" reflects more generally the tenuous status of Balki. As depicted in an extended dream sequence, the transplanted foreigner is himself an "alien" other—"a strange visitor from another planet" who is shown passing through closed doors like a phantom, shooting lasers from his fingers, and making objects move with his mind. Such fantastical acts or magical feats, though occasionally confined to the world of reverie, daydream, or nightmare, are more likely to occur in Halloween-themed episodes than in "normal" (non-Halloween-themed) episodes lacking the holiday's license to "break the rules" and depart from reality.

In addition to the above visual ingredients, including scenes of trick-or-treating in which anxieties about the wellbeing of children are either deflected and dispensed with or addressed directly, one of the most obvious signs that one is watching a Halloween episode can be found in its title. It should not be surprising to find that many if not all examples of what I am calling "very spooky episodes" sport the word "Halloween" in their titles and/or scripts. This is a tradition, dating back to the 1950s (e.g., *The Jackie Gleason Show*, *The Adventures of Ozzie and Harriet*, etc.), that contemporary screenwriters and showrunners have continued to honor, if also tweak in a knowing, occasionally metatextual or reflexive, way. In that sense, the previously mentioned episodes of *The Cosby Show* and *8 Simple Rules* are not unique in the least, for they call to mind the titular focus on the season's festivities that is discernible within many other programs. Indeed, the unambiguous title "Halloween" can be found in the lists of episodes for such disparate TV shows as *Hangin' with Mr. Cooper* (ABC, 1992–97), *Frasier* (NBC, 1993–2004), *Sister, Sister* (ABC, 1994–95; The WB, 1995–99), *Cybill*, *NewsRadio* (NBC, 1995–99), *Suddenly Susan* (NBC, 1996–2000), *Meego* (CBS, 1997), *You Wish* (ABC, 1997–98), *Yes, Dear* (CBS, 2000–2006), *Reno 911!* (Comedy Central, 2003–9), and *Rodney* (ABC, 2004–6), to name a few examples from the 1990s and early 2000s (the heyday of this cultural phenomenon). Slight variations on that straightforward title include: "Happy Halloween" (*Growing Pains*), "Hollow

Halloween" (*Parenthood* [NBC, 1990–91]), "Hammer Halloween" (*Out All Night* [NBC, 1992–93]), "Halloween Story" (*Ned and Stacey* [Fox, 1995–97]), "Halloween Candy" (*Everybody Loves Raymond* [CBS, 1996–2005]), "The Halloween Show" (*Mr. Rhodes* [NBC, 1996–97]), "The Halloween Episode" (*Maybe It's Me* [The WB, 2001–2]), and "Halloween Boo" (*Twins* [The WB, 2005–6]). Similarly, the expression "trick or treat," a reference to the custom of begging for candy, fruit, nuts, and other delectable edibles (first widely practiced between the final years of the Great Depression and the early postwar era),[22] has been used as the title of several episodes throughout the medium's history and across diverse subgenres, from far-fetched "fish out of water" hits of the 1960s such as *The Beverly Hillbillies* (CBS, 1962–71) and *Bewitched* (ABC, 1964–72) to comparatively realistic critical darlings like the HBO cringe-comedy *Curb Your Enthusiasm* (2000–present). Indeed, before the writers and producers of *Roseanne* brought forth their own "Trick or Treat" episode (near the beginning of that show's third season), other scribes had already gravitated toward that title, which was used for Halloween-themed installments of the LA-based crime drama *ChiPs* (NBC, 1977–83), the syndicated horror anthology series *Tales from the Darkside*, and the middlebrow domestic sitcom *Charles in Charge* (CBS, 1984–90).

Other episode titles harken back to Halloween TV landmarks, including what might be the most fondly remembered of all television specials devoted to the holiday: *It's the Great Pumpkin, Charlie Brown* (1966). As a sign of this latter program's perennial status as a holiday classic (sustained through annual rebroadcasts and a bevy of fan-created works that pay tribute to producer Bill Melendez's animated rendering of Charles M. Schulz's *Peanuts* strips), several contemporary shows tip their hats toward it, through episode titles such as "It's the Great Pumpkin, Maestro Harris" (*Guys Like Us* [UPN, 1998–99]), "It's the Gay Pumpkin, Charlie Brown" (*Will & Grace* [NBC, 1998–2006, 2017–20]), "It's the Great Pancake, Cleveland Brown" (*The Cleveland Show* [Fox, 2009–13]), "It's The Great Pumpkin, Phil Dunphy" (*Modern Family* [ABC, 2009–20]), and "It's a Plastic Pumpkin, Louis Huang" (*Fresh Off the Boat* [ABC, 2015–20]). Likewise, although *The Mindy Project* (Fox, 2012–15; Hulu, 2015–17)'s sole venture into the intertextually ripe world of Halloween bears the most straightforward of all titles ("Halloween"), that episode makes copious references to *It's the Great Pumpkin, Charlie Brown*, which the main character—successful New York obstetrician/gynecologist Mindy Lahiri (Mindy Kaling)—ironically admits to having never seen, to the shocked disbelief of her friends and coworkers. Betsy (Zoe Jarman), the receptionist at Mindy's OB/GYN practice, has procured for her a costume modeled after Linus's getup in that animated special, but her boss mistakes it for a Fat Albert costume (a comically self-mocking nod to star Mindy Kaling's refusal to "present herself as a skinny person" or to fit the narrow mold of "white hegemonic beauty norms").[23] The young woman proceeds to summarize the plot of *It's the Great Pumpkin, Charlie Brown*, telling Mindy that "It's the *best*. It's Halloween, and Linus is excited for the Great Pumpkin, who comes every year to bring toys to the good boys and girls." Synopsized in this way, the storyline hints at a slippage between Halloween and Christmas; a "strange conflation" observed by many cultural commentators and which, in the words of Sarah Honeyman, "obscures the threatening tone of trick-or-treat's protection racket" by distracting the audience with a "squash version of Santa Claus, a specter who watches over children to reward the obedient and disappoint the unruly."[24]

It is worth dwelling on the symptomatic meanings of a long-cherished televisual text that has planted its seeds—like those of so many pumpkins—in more recent productions. Tellingly, much of the online commentary about the aforementioned episode of *The Mindy Project* draws attention to the parallels between the unlucky-in-love protagonist, who is still stuck on her married ex-boyfriend Tom (Bill Hader), and the *Peanuts* character whom she is encouraged to dress up as for the impending costume party. In the words of one reviewer, "much like Linus she is waiting around for someone that may never show up,"[25] a condition that is further underlined through the incorporation of jazz pianist Vince Guaraldi's "Linus and Lucy" theme tune—a musical composition familiar to anyone who has watched *It's the Great Pumpkin, Charlie Brown*—during the second of this episode's two montage sequences (showing Mindy racing to get dressed for that night's main event). Ultimately, Mindy ends up forgoing the *Peanuts* character's outfit (a sign that she is leaving Tom behind) in favor of a different costume altogether. Standing opposite her date for the evening, a young sports lawyer named Josh (Tommy Dewey) who shows up at her apartment wearing an Inigo Montoya outfit (a reference to Mandy Patinkin's role in the 1987 fantasy film *The Princess Bride*), Mindy appears in the final scene dressed up as Shelley Long's character Diane from *Cheers* (NBC, 1982–93). This follows another montage sequence in which she models various "mashup" costumes (e.g., "Lil Wayne On the Prairie," "Tinkerbell Tailor Soldier Spy," "Dirty Harry Potter") for her friends—a brief interlude that anticipates a similar moment of combinatory play in the "Louisween" (3.03) episode of *Fresh Off the Boat* when Louis (Randall Park), father of the Taiwanese American Huang family, dresses as "Pete Vampras" (a cross between a vampire and tennis star Pete Sampras). Besides lending even greater intertextual density to the episode, such comedic bits on the part of talented performers of color remind us that cultural mixing is an engrained facet of the holiday.[26]

6.6. Mindy Lahiri (the medical professional played by Mindy Kaling in the situation comedy bearing her name) momentarily becomes "Lil Wayne on the Prairie" while trying on different costumes in the episode "Halloween." © 3 Arts Entertainment

Like *Roseanne* before it, *The Mindy Project* revels in moments of both intertextuality and metatextuality, in which multiple icons of popular culture across different media industries are not simply cited in an ironic way but are creatively combined and even integrated into its own textual DNA. Kaling's trailblazing show (which she created, wrote for, and starred in—the first time a woman of color achieved such "triple threat" success on a network series) is also notably self-aware in its commitment to the conventions of romcom movies and workplace sitcoms.[27] *The Mindy Project* models itself on earlier programs like *Ally McBeal* (Fox, 1997–2002) while moving the ball forward as a progressive feminist take on the obstacles that women navigate in professions that have historically been dominated by men. It is for that reason that many cultural commentators have drawn a connection between Mindy Kaling and Roseanne Barr, who decades earlier cut a carnivalesque figure prone to social faux pas (playing a character that was "loud, abrasive, large and out of control") on her own eponymously named television show.[28] Indeed, both women are as "unruly" as the Halloween festival that has given them and other feminist or queer icons the license to do and say the "unthinkable" on primetime TV.[29] In part, these two stars' carnivalesque performances have been augmented by the intertextual abundance and metatextual self-awareness the comes with the holiday, which, to a certain degree, denaturalizes "hegemonic beauty norms" as well as heteronormative representations.[30] Indeed, as Nicholas Rogers points out, Halloween opens a space for gender play within mainstream society and has been "used to reaffirm the values of feminist and gay cultures."[31] The characters in situation comedies, whether they identify as straight or gay, male or female (or occupy a position outside those constrictive categories), demonstrate this progressive side of the yearly festivities through a form of costuming that is reverentially referential, lovingly harkening back to past icons and performances while poking holes in the social fabric where questions of identity are openly broached.

Slutty Pumpkins: Cross-Dressing, Halloween Drag, and Sexual Objectification

> "You're missing the whole point of Halloween."
> "Free candy?"
> "It's 'come as you aren't' night. The perfect chance for a girl to get sexy and wild with no repercussions."
>
> —Buffy (Sarah Michelle Gellar) explaining one of the perks of Halloween to Willow (Alyson Hannigan) in a Season Two episode of *Buffy the Vampire Slayer* (WB/UPN, 1997–2003)

One of the most fascinating, if also frustrating, aspects of Halloween TV is its tendency to use the holiday as a pretense for seemingly progressive takes on gender dynamics, sexual orientation, and other issues related to identity, only to retreat to a glib, rigid definition of what men and women "are," or "should be." The sheer number of references to "slutty" costumes alone (spoken by characters in *Friends* [NBC, 1994–2004], *NewsRadio*, *How I Met Your Mother* [CBS, 2005–14], *Last Man Standing*, *The Big Bang Theory* [CBS, 2007–19], and *The Goldbergs* [ABC, 2013–present], among many other shows) is enough to make one question the supposedly enlightened worldview of Hollywood screenwriters or the emancipatory function of a seasonal event that is so frequently handcuffed to images of scantily clad, sexually promiscuous nurses and other women. A humorous take on this issue is presented in "Ronnie's Party" (2.10), an episode of the Canadian sitcom *Schitt's Creek* (CBC, 2015–20), which features dialogue between siblings David (Daniel Levy) and Alexis (Annie Murphy) referencing the long-entrenched stereotype of the "slutty nurse" within the holiday's more salacious traditions. Noting the unusually designed scrubs that his sister has put on in preparation for her new job at a veterinarian's clinic, David tells her, "I don't think sex appeal is the guiding principle behind nursing uniforms." In defense of her clothing choice, Alexis responds, "Obviously you've never been out for Halloween." As the kinky horndog Chad Radwell (Glen Powell) tells a fellow college student in

"Pumpkin Patch" (1.05), an episode of the parodic horror comedy *Scream Queens* (Fox, 2015–16), "Halloween is the greatest night of the year [when] even shy, kind-of-homely girls dress up like total sluts. I mean every costume's just a slutty version of something: Slutty teacher, slutty nurse, slutty nun. I saw a girl last year dressed as slutty Al-Qaeda!" Not one to let his fear of getting hacked to death by a serial killer on the loose (the underlying premise of the show's first season) get in the way of enjoying "the sluttiest night of the year," Chad praises the very thing that researchers have criticized for contributing to the sexual objectification of women.[32] As indelibly associated with Halloween "as candy corn and Tootsie Rolls," short, skimpy, tight outfits have been part of this paganistic celebration for many years, according to Suzanne LaBarre, though popular media texts of the past couple of decades have played a significant part in not only turning women into objects of the heterosexual male gaze but also using Halloween as an excuse to bring private matters into the public sphere.

Another, ultimately regressive perspective on the issue of costuming comes into view in contemporary sitcoms like *According to Jim* (ABC, 2001–9) and *The King of Queens* (CBS, 1998–2007), typically resulting in the male protagonist or some other adamantly "hetero" character defensively asserting his masculinity in the presence of gay men or liberal-minded straight metrosexuals whose Halloween outfits (e.g., the clothing of camp-cinematic icons, such as Dorothy from *The Wizard of Oz* or Faye Dunaway as Joan Crawford in *Mommie Dearest* [1981]) hint at the possibility of a holiday-inspired "queering" of the text. For example, in "Dana Dates Jim" (3.07), an episode of *According to Jim*, Andy (Larry Joe Campbell), a plus-sized supporting character whose dating woes are a running gag, attends a costume party in the guise of a generic superhero, complete with red cape, gold boots, and a chintzy headband in the shape of a winged eagle. Spotting a fellow reveler dressed as Raggedy Ann across the room, he approaches and says, "You know, I may be a superhero, but I still like to play with dolls," to which the recipient of this cheesy pick-up line responds, "You know I'm a guy, right?" Awkward tension results, and the momentary silence between the two is plastered over with the eruption of the in-studio audience's laughter. Soon, though, Andy exchanges a firm handshake with the man, falsely telling him that his name is Jim and that this is his house before quickly turning on his heels and exiting the scene.

Similarly, in the episode "Ticker Treat" (4.06), from the blue-collar comedy *The King of Queens*, another superhero—this time a young boy dressed up as one of the Powerpuff Girls (Blossom, whose bright pink uniform codes that character as excessively "feminine")—is the subject of nervous talk concerning his sexual orientation. Specifically, Doug Heffernan (Kevin James), the main character, tries to ease the mounting anxieties of his best friend and fellow delivery driver, Deacon Palmer (Victor Williams), who worries that his young son might be gay (given the latter's choice in Halloween costuming). Telling Doug that he is afraid to go home at night, for fear that he might walk in on Kirby (Marshaun Daniel) "wearing a girdle," Deacon reminds us that a more pernicious moral panic beyond the largely unfounded trepidation over candy-tampering (a topic of public safety debates during the 1970s and 1980s) haunts this holiday, a time when so-called transgressions or violations of social decorum give opponents an excuse for the worst kind of fearmongering. "Take it easy," Doug says to his friend, noting that "just because [the boy] wants to be a girl superhero doesn't mean he's *gay*." His concluding statement on this matter—"You know they say that most drag queens are actually straight"—does little to allay Deacon's doubts about his son's hetero-sexuality, and even less to correct for this episode's tone-deaf approach to a subject that has become increasingly central to Halloween TV's rhetorical and represen-tational modes.

Consider, as well, the "Halloween Story" (1.08) episode of *Ned and Stacey*, which features a masquerade party bringing together two men who must negotiate the other's sexual orientation as a result of their gender-coded costuming. Here, a supporting character nicknamed Rico (Greg Germann), who has been forced to attend the party in the guise of a female nurse, must contend with the grabby advances of a bisexual man dressed as a surgeon, especially after Rico tells him, "I'm a *guy*." Similar same-sex encounters, always played for laughs, occur in other Halloween-themed episodes (especially those of less-than-progressive sitcoms such as *The Norm Show* [ABC, 1999–2001] and *Good Morning, Miami* [NBC, 2002–4]), perpetuating stereotypes not only about female impersonators, crossdressers, and drag queen culture but also about genderqueer people who ironically might look to Halloween as an opportunity for cross-class solidarity and self-expression. The questionable sentiment that "Halloween is to gays what St. Patrick's is to the Irish," familiar to anyone who has studied this most subcultural, yet strangely domesti-cated, of holidays, has solidified into a kind of "truth" for those commentators who either celebrate or castigate its queering potential.[33]

Funnily enough, an earlier scene in *Ned and Stacey*'s "Halloween Story," show-ing the female member of the titular duo (played by Debra Messing) bingeing on junk food while watching a scary movie on TV (a way for this freelance journalist to feed her emotional hunger after having an article turned down), makes direct reference to a sitcom that not only made "very spooky episodes" a much-antici-pated yearly event but also pioneered more progressive forms of non-binary and queerly transgressive representations during the 1980s and 1990s. The television series to which I am referring is the one that I referenced at the beginning of this chapter and will focus on in the chapter that follows: a working-class classic that is mentioned by title, or rather by *name*, when Stacey's sister, Amanda (Nadia Dajani), who is dressed as Glinda the Good Witch from *The Wizard of Oz*, asks the sweatpants-wearing consumer of junk food if she is going to the upcoming costume party "as Roseanne."

7

"Three-Headed Monster"

Queer Representation, Social Class, and the Trumpist Rhetoric of Roseanne

Situation comedy characters are not people who tell each other jokes. They are resonant, believable people who are trapped in lives of not so quiet desperation. Often there is one who rises above the pack to become the focus for the show and I am going to call them the monster character. These people epitomize the worst in human behavior, be they tyrant or whinging fool, callous boss or incompetent husband, gullible moron or pontificating bore. They are people who either do not recognize boundaries or who gaily trample them in their search for personal power.

—Marc Blake, *How to Be a Sitcom Writer: Secrets from the Inside*

Every monster has its weakness.

—Francis (Christopher Masterson), talking to his mother Lois (Jane Kaczmarek) about his evil, racist "grandmother from hell" Ida (Cloris Leachman) in a Season Four episode of *Malcolm in the Middle* (Fox, 2000–2006)

In the wake of Roseanne Barr's racist comment about Valerie Jarrett (former senior advisor to President Obama), which she posted on Twitter on May 29, 2018, the controversial actress-comedian was publicly brought to task for her inflammatory rhetoric and was forced to step away from the recently revived television series that bears her name. Within hours of the tweet, ABC Entertainment president Channing Dungey announced that Barr's remark was "abhorrent, repugnant and inconsistent with [the network's] values," hence the reason why *Roseanne* (ABC, 1988–97)—a sitcom once celebrated for its social consciousness and commitment to working-class values, but now scorned as a hideously deformed mouthpiece for President Trump's "MAGA"-style nativism—was dropped from ABC's primetime lineup and consigned to an early grave.[1] The latter metaphor, which is perhaps more suggestive of cemetery-filled horror films, is an apt description not only of *Roseanne's* precipitous cancellation but also of the titular star's figurative demise in the public eye, one that echoes the rhetorical maneuvers of her most vocal online critics. Indeed, if one word sums up the moral outrage engendered by Barr's racially insensitive barb at an African American woman, not to mention the questionable comportment of this iconoclastic figure within the overlapping spheres of popular culture and political communication, it is "monster."

From the many journalists who called *Roseanne* a "monster hit" (i.e., one boasting "monster TV ratings") in the days following its March 27 relaunch, to fellow cast and crew members (in addition to other industry spokespeople) who have weighed in on her bad behavior (which, in the words of one writer, had already succeeded in "scaring away liberal viewers" from her program),[2] one term more than any other has become so synonymous with Barr that the star's on-air hosting of an earlier reality TV series—the tellingly titled *Momsters: When Moms Go Bad* (Discovery, 2014–15)—should not come as a surprise. Critical recourse to the word "monster" is not unusual when it comes to the discursive framing of working-class characters on American television, a medium that has long treated blue-collar laborers and economically struggling families as freakish miscreants whose "otherness" is the source of often-dehumanizing humor.[3] As Richard Butsch has argued in his historical overview of social hierarchies in US sitcoms, the relative "prestige and privilege" with which middle-class lifestyles are associated in TV programming remain beyond the grasp of low-wage workers; especially so in *Roseanne*, in which the monstrous title character appears to be "content with and unapologetic about" her "low" standing and laughably "bad" taste, but also expresses anger, sarcasm, and volatility toward those who would deprive her of the respect that she ironically believes that her family deserves.[4]

Significantly, Roseanne Barr's much-discussed "monstrosity" had been anticipated by her character Roseanne Conner's fondness for "dressing the part" in Halloween-themed episodes of the series—a "very special" annual event (occurring every fall season during the show's original run, save for its first season) in which various creatures were allowed to come out of the proverbial closet and give voice to otherwise-repressed elements in the culture at large. Whether playing the "Wicked Witch of the Midwest" (in the Season Two episode "Boo" [2.07]) or donning a bloodied shirt as a knife-wielding homicidal maniac (in the Season Four episode "Trick Me Up, Trick Me Down" [4.06]), the comedian habitually literalized the metaphor of monstrosity that has long haunted her onscreen and offscreen personas as a self-described "domestic goddess." Those episodes, in which faked disembowelings, eye gougings, and other kinds of "body horror"

7.1 and 7.2. Beginning with its second season, *Roseanne* couched the bad behavior of its titular lead (played by Roseanne Barr) within the context of Halloween each year, either by literalizing her "monstrous" side (under layers of makeup and prosthetics) or by showing her playfully terrorize friends and family members in the guise of a killer. © the Carsey-Werner Company are performed with devilish glee for neighborhood trick-or-treaters and in-studio audiences, laid the foundation for subsequent television series that use Halloween as an excuse for staging similarly grisly scenes inside cluttered suburban spaces and working-class homes. In the years since *Roseanne* debuted in the late 1980s, several live-action and animated sitcoms, ranging from *Home Improvement* (ABC, 1991–99) and *Family Matters* (ABC, 1989–97) to *Family Guy* (Fox, 1999–present) and *Bob's Burgers* (Fox, 2011–present), have incorporated such horrifying, holiday-based iconography in their own "very spooky episodes," further perpetuating the idea of socially disenfranchised or downwardly mobile Americans as monstrous others.

It should be noted that the aforementioned network and cable programs reside within either one of two categories of cultural production—the multi-camera sitcom and the animated sitcom—that, to varying degrees, each evince a "trash TV" aesthetic. Referred to by John Caldwell and other media scholars as a "zero-degree sitcom style," that aesthetic, combined with the comically grotesque performances on view in *Roseanne* and other television series, contributes to their "lowly" status as well as to the literal and figurative "demonization" of working-class characters therein. Not insignificantly, the multi-camera sitcom, of which *Roseanne* is an example, adopts a shooting style and technological setup that many creative personnel in Hollywood refer to as the "three-headed monster." That expression, unique to the television industry and dating back to the 1950s (when cinematographer Karl Freund, editor Dann Cahn, and other pioneers of the soon-to-be-standardized multi-camera system worked on *I Love Lucy* [CBS, 1951–57]), hints at the longstanding associations between a genre frequently deemed "inferior" to other cultural forms and the lives of "lesser-than" individuals whose problems—the source of so much combined humor and horror—are not always conveniently resolved by episode's end. Although it is probably only coincidental, Roseanne's onscreen hubby Dan (John Goodman) sports a three-headed get-up in the Season Three episode "Trick or Treat" (3.07). Wearing a cheap-looking "Three Stooges" costume, with plastic versions of Larry and Moe's visages to his side and his own noggin standing in for that of Curly, Dan embodies the comically grotesque, excessive way that monstrosity plays out in this and other domestic arenas.

In the first half of this chapter, I will explore this and another important episode of *Roseanne*, "Skeleton in the Closet" (7.06), in hopes of demonstrating how each of them departs from the traditionally moralizing tone of more typical "Very Special Episodes" (e.g., *Diff'rent Strokes'* "The Bicycle Man" [5.16], *Saved By the Bell's* "Jessie's Song" [2.09], etc.). Despite their difference from the norm, however, "Trick or Treat" and "Skeleton in the Closet" both operate along the same teacherly principles of other US sitcoms, instilling valuable lessons about inclusivity, tolerance, and the mutually impacting benefits of celebrating cultural differences across class lines. As contradictory as the "festival of death and life" that inspired them, these episodes are doubly instructive case studies, laying bare the otherwise hidden horrors of America's most venerated of institutions—the traditional nuclear family—while masking the outspoken star's more reactionary leanings (only recently brought to light) behind her progressive political stance on issues related to women's rights and workers' rights. To varying degrees, "Trick or Treat" and "Skeleton in the Closet" reveal the radically denaturalizing potential of Halloween as well as the inherent limitations of network television programming (at least that which is driven by commercial interests and advertiser dollars) in fully representing historically marginalized individuals and groups. The latter includes members of the LGBTQ+ community who, ironically, look to Halloween as a kind of counter-Christmas, a safely "dangerous," prank-filled corrective to more religiously conservative holidays.

Drawing upon the work of Julie Bettie, Kathleen Rowe Karlyn, Tison Pugh, and other media scholars who have explored the feminist and queering potential of this particular television series, I therefore seek to critically intervene not only in the current debates surrounding Roseanne Barr's ultimately self-defeating words and actions, but also in the emerging discourses concerning the very "specialness" of "Very Special Episodes." Sadly, the aforementioned messages about acceptance and respect for others were lost on the titular star, who should have taken them to heart before taking to Twitter in the lead-up to her once-subversive show's cancellation.

The second half of this chapter tackles that issue head-on, but also shifts focus to examine additional examples of the show's yearly Halloween installments in hopes of pinpointing some of the reasons why the Conners, like other working-class families on American TV, might be drawn to an annual celebration distinguished by competition, deception, pranks, roleplay, and the subversion of social norms. To be sure, numerous cultural critics and television historians have already discussed *Roseanne*'s status as a comedy of bad manners about a low-income family, noting that the series "presents working-class characters that are not uniformly 'saints' or 'sinners'" (in contrast to TV's tendency to paint such figures in "a two-dimensional way").[5] However, the show's Halloween episodes provide a unique vantage on its core features as a blue-collar comedy, one that leans into its characters' questionable tastes and allows them to laugh at their own "'trashy' origins and behavior."[6] Other holidays provide similar insights into the Conners' self-conscious staging of family life as a gaudy "monster" in its own right, as demonstrated in the episode "White Trash Christmas" (6.12), which pits them against neighbors who are offended by their tacky yuletide yard decorations (e.g., beer can wreath, cardboard Liberace, neon bar sign, etc.). Indeed, the latter episode has Roseanne proclaim herself the "Goddess of Tacky" and declare that she and Dan actually enjoy "degrading [themselves] for the sheer holiday joy of it." However, Halloween, much more than Christmas or Thanksgiving (another holiday prominently featured in *Roseanne*), is predicated on the playful breaking of taboos. Its centrality to the Conner family's skewering of "class-based norms of good taste" therefore demands consideration if we are to gain a better understanding of the monstrous imaginary as a cultural framework that encourages viewers to demonize and sympathize with working-class characters in equal measure.[7]

"Queens" of Halloween: Wicked Witches and Bad Bitches

> I was doing Halloween since before there were even any gay people.
> —the title character to her business partner, Leon
> Carp (Martin Mull), in a Season Seven episode of
> *Roseanne* (ABC, 1988–97)

"Trick or Treat," a third-season episode of *Roseanne* that was written by Chuck Lorre and which originally aired on October 30, 1990, stands in stark contrast to many of the Halloween-themed shows cited in the previous chapter, mainly because it disrupts their outmoded representations while also thematically unpacking the "discomfort" that one character—Roseanne's husband Dan—experiences when it comes to the subject of homosexuality and "any incipient sign" of his preteen son's "effeminacy."[8] As Tison Pugh argues in *The Queer Fantasies of the American Family Sitcom*, the holidays—Christmas and Thanksgiving included—provide a backdrop for some of this series' most revealing signs of that discomfort, which manifests paradoxically at the moments when lesbianism and other forms of queer desire are expressed; either directly (via the physical attraction between two supporting characters, Nancy [Sandra Bernhard] and Marla [Morgan Fairchild], who were introduced in the fourth and fifth seasons, respectively), or indirectly (via cutaways to Dan, for instance, just as Nancy and Marla lean in for a mistletoe kiss). But it is Halloween, more so than any other celebratory event in the Conners' working-class lives, that most emphatically propels Dan and his more open-minded partner toward a resolution that is truly cathartic, making this "very spooky episode" very special indeed.

Like so many other *Roseanne* episodes, "Trick or Treat" begins with an opening-credits sequence that, in a single shot (accompanied by the show's bluesy, harmonica- and saxophone-driven theme music), encircles the Conner family as they sit around the kitchen table; starting with the main character and then showing her husband Dan, son D.J. (Michael Fishman), daughters Darlene (Sara Gilbert) and Becky (Lecy Goranson), and sister Jackie Harris (Laurie Metcalf). The setting of this title sequence would stay the same for the nine years during which the series was broadcast, although the family's activities would change each season. As an episode from the third season, "Trick or Treat" highlights the Conners' togetherness by way of a "high-stakes" card game, with a pot of pretzels, cookies, and candy in the middle of the table that the titular star scoops up to the tune of her trademark cackling laugh. Tellingly, the first scene that immediately follows the opening credits is likewise set around the kitchen table, only this time it is an all-male group of poker players—Dan and his belching, beer-guzzling friends—who form a social unit whose bubble of hypermasculinity is breached once Roseanne and Jackie enter the scene, breaking up their sexist fraternizing. Soon, young D.J. swoops in wearing his Halloween costume, a black witch's outfit—"complete with broom, long pointy nose, and red sparkly shoes"[9]—that draws a look of concern on Dan's face. After sending his son upstairs to his bedroom, Dan informs his wife that "witches are girls," not boys. "Witches are *women*," Roseanne corrects him, and then explains to her husband that D.J. got to pick his own costume this year. Clearly agitated, Dan wishes that his child had picked something "normal" (i.e., less "sissy") to wear as a trick-or-treater who will be seen by their neighbors ("like a vampire or a nice axe-murderer").

This is hardly the first occasion in which Dan and Roseanne have an argument over family matters. Throughout the initial nine-season run of the series, spousal

7.3. To the dismay of his father and to the amusement of his mother, D.J. dresses as a "girly" witch in the Season Three episode "Trick or Treat." © the Carsey-Werner Company

flareups occur frequently, though the couple maintains a loving and supportive relationship that sustains them through periods of financial uncertainty. Only on rare occasions does Dan's frustration with his wife boil over into physical anger, as happens in the episode "Canoga Time" (1.11), when—bickering over the tastelessness of their home's decorative knickknacks—he begins destroying their furniture and tossing out Roseanne's belongings in the front yard. He does much the same in "Fights and Stuff" (8.25), after she confronts her overweight husband—just released from hospital (where he recovered from a heart attack)—about his dietary regime; only this time Dan says and does things that he will deeply regret (and which cannot be quickly forgiven or forgotten through makeup sex). Flipping over the coffee table in a fit of rage and raising his voice in a manner that was, *and still is*, unusual within the sitcom genre, Dan calls Roseanne a "controlling bitch," one of the harshest things he has ever uttered (although he uses the same misogynistic language to describe Nancy in "Halloween V" [6.06]). He then tells her, "I wish I had never mar . . . ," but stops short of crossing that very *un*-matrimonial threshold. This painfully realistic domestic spat comes to an end once Roseanne picks up a Godzilla toy—a small tchotchke that has been visible in their living room since the first season—and hurls it into the television set. The sound of the TV screen shattering puts a final exclamation point on a scene that likewise shatters the conventions of situation comedy and puts a literal monster in the electronic box. This latter metaphor, lifted up to the denotative level by a female character who has been called worse things than "bitch" (within anti-fan discourse), harkens back to the critical discourse of the postwar era analyzed by Lynn Spigel, who notes that cultural commentators during the 1950s often likened the TV set "to a monster that threatened to wreak havoc on the family."[10]

Returning to "Trick or Treat," we can see that Dan's argument with Roseanne about their son's Halloween outfit is relatively mild in comparison, and that the holiday itself functions as a kind of release valve in their marriage, which at times seems more like a back-and-forth tug-of-war. But the excessiveness of his sarcastic remark about their son (who, dressed as a witch, would be better costumed as a "nice axe murderer") is in keeping with the verbal outbursts that occur in "Canoga Time," "Fights and Stuff," and other episodes, and is further accentuated by the next scene, which picks up with a phone conversation between Becky and her offscreen mother, now at work. While speaking on the phone, the young girl, shown from her left side, turns to reveal the right side of her body, which is covered in (fake) blood. One of her eyeballs also appears to have popped out, a bit of prop humor that might remind viewers of other instances of "body horror" on the small screen (for instance, the obviously plastic axe blade that has settled into the torso of Alex [Bonnie Somerville], the female lead in the short-lived sitcom *In-Laws* [NBC,

2002–3]). Such images can be said to "push the boundaries" of what is permissible on network television (at the time of their original broadcast, if not today). With only one side stained with viscera, Becky's prom dress (which is almost as gross as her sister's *Alien*-inspired stomach-bursting costume) connotes the two-sided nature of the main conflict that drives a wedge between husband and wife in "Trick or Treat." Eventually, Roseanne and Dan resolve their differences in opinion about D.J.'s clothing and come together as a stronger married unit—husband and wife, or rather husband and *husband*—during the episode's final scenes.

Set in an old-fashioned, wood-paneled bar, those concluding moments show Roseanne in cross-dressing mode, decked out in a lumberjack's camouflage hat, plaid shirt, and khaki jacket. She and Jackie have taken shelter in the dive after her car has broken down, and she is nervous because she is "the only person here in a costume"—a statement that is particularly ironic given that the female protagonist, in traditional male truck-driver's garb, looks like most of the men in the bar (hinting at the fact that their own masculinity is something of a put-on or performance). Later, after she has insulted and drawn the ire of a group of braggarts playing pool, Dan arrives on the scene and rescues her from "a fight with an aggressive boor."[11] When the latter individual asks him why he is sticking his nose in their business, Dan steps closer to Roseanne and responds chivalrously, saying, "He's my *husband* . . . Anyone that messes with him messes with me." This radically transgressive moment is capped with a final exclamation point: the sight of the seemingly same-sex couple kissing. Although this gender-bending scene from *Roseanne* is something of a ruse, a "mask" like the one worn by the bearded, burly title character (insofar as it covers up the reality of a heterosexual, rather than homosexual, embrace), it nevertheless proves both "the perversity of heterosexuality and the fundamental normativity of homosexuality," at least as much as that is possible "within the protocols of network television and its ostensible family hour."[12] Thus, "Trick or Treat," and to a certain extent the star of the series as a whole, serve as a "privileged site of homoerotic presence," according to Tison Pugh, one that would have been much less apparent or explicitly visible were it not for the playful "perversions" unique to Halloween TV.

Not surprisingly, the series would return to the queering potential of the holiday in another Halloween-themed episode, the tellingly titled "Skeleton in the Closet," from Season Seven. Once again, cross-dressing revelers come to the fore in scenes showcasing the performativity of gender, with Roseanne dressed up as the stubble-faced musical legend Prince (whose all-purple outfit is mistaken for that of Barney the Dinosaur) opposite Dan's more rigidly masculine emulation of Western film icon John Wayne. This admittedly odd couple descends on the Lanford Lunch Box, a sandwich spot that she and Jackie co-own along with business

7.4. "Trick or Treat" builds toward a provocative moment when Dan, stepping in to protect his wife (dressed as a burly man) from a barroom fight, plants a kiss on her in full view of the bar's patrons. © the Carsey-Werner Company

partner Leon Carp (Martin Mull), who is throwing a Halloween party there. As a proudly gay man, Leon labels himself the "Queen of Halloween" (which "everyone knows . . . is *our* holiday") and has made every attempt to *not* turn this queer-friendly soiree into one of Roseanne's "lame little lodge parties." But because Leon has invited many of this small but apparently liberal-minded town's LGBTQ+ community to the gathering, Jackie's husband Fred (Michael O'Keefe) shows up in a state of duress, fearful—as Dan, mimicking The Duke, likewise is—that gay men will spend the night hitting on him. For his part, Leon tries to calm Fred's nerves, reassuring him that "we don't bite," to no avail, as the Batman-suited straight man leaves the party prematurely.

Partly because "Fred doth protest too much" (to borrow the words of Roseanne's bisexual friend Nancy), but also because one of his friends, a drag queen, informs Roseanne that her brother-in-law has been living a lie this whole time, she soon believes that he is "gay, gay, gay, gay, gay" (or, as she sums up, the "gayest"). Fred's homosexuality would appear to be confirmed in the episode's penultimate scene, in which Roseanne and Jackie find their husbands in bed together, interrupting what looks to be a lovers' tryst. However, in keeping with the Conners' knack for outlandish Halloween tricks, this moment of *coitus interruptus* is simply the culmination of everyone's "long con," or what Dan, now beaming, calls the "all-time greatest prank in the history of the universe." The truth is revealed when Jackie begins giggling uncontrollably and Leon and Nancy (dressed as Hillary Rodham Clinton and Marilyn Monroe, respectively) burst out of the bedroom closet to declare, "We're everywhere!"

As Lynne Joyrich notes in her brief assessment of "Skeleton in the Closet," *Roseanne* was "at the forefront of queer representation throughout its network run," perhaps never more so than in this episode. However, as Joyrich points out, this seemingly progressive installment highlights "the way in which US television both impedes and constructs, exposes and buries, a particular knowledge of sexuality."[13] This idea is made more evident if one takes into consideration the second of the two pranks being played on Roseanne in this episode, which concludes with a shot of her overbearing mother Beverly (Estelle Parsons) (who will eventually come out as a lesbian during the show's ninth season) removing her wig to reveal a nearly bald head, with only a few wisps of tangled hair left. As one beauty salon stylist had informed Roseanne earlier in the episode, children tend to inherit their mothers' hair (or lack thereof), and this brazen display of maternal baldness in the final scene cuts the main character to her core. Throughout much of this episode—and at various points throughout the series—Roseanne has grappled with the prospect of her elderly mother passing away, as well as with her own aging anxieties. Thus, "the uncertainties of sexual bodies" (those of actual and pretend queer people in this episode) merge with "the uncertainties of aging bodies," and it is clear that the extended Conner family (including Darlene's former boyfriend David [Johnny Galecki] and Becky's husband Mark [Glenn Quinn]) is eager to "mock both fears" with devilish glee.[14]

Indeed, "Skeleton in the Closet" ends with a "literal unmasking" that complements its metaphorical one, showing Dan, Jackie, and the other family members joining Bev in her baldness by removing their own wigs, leaving Roseanne in a state of shock. Refusing to go down without a fight, and never one to be beaten in a game of one-upmanship, she resorts to an even greater prank than the ones they have pulled on her, and promptly blows up their house with dynamite that she had stashed away beneath the kitchen sink. In the words of Joyrich, "discovering that Dan is gay," which overlaps with Roseanne's discovery that her mother is bald, "would be tantamount to exploding the familiar and familial TV diegesis," and that "bringing what typically exists outside TV's representational space into its core creates an epistemological crisis that threatens, both literally and figuratively, to blow this space up."[15] In this way, "Skeleton in the Closet" is representative of the problematic tendency in Halloween-themed episodes to dangle the prospect of queer desire and non-heteronormative subject positions only to erase or annihilate said representations by treating the image of same-sex couples as a sight gag or as the punchline to an elaborate prank or juvenile joke. This—one of the paradoxes of Halloween TV more generally—serves as a reminder that, for all that it did to give "voice to those pushing back against a socioeconomic system that demanded greater sacrifices and offered fewer rewards for working families," *Roseanne* was not the fully inclusive show about marginalized communities that its makers might have intended it to be. And though its Halloween-themed episodes boldly go where few other programs before or since have ventured, their naked (dare I say "bald") disregard for the niceties of more tastefully appointed holidays proves to be something of a ruse in hindsight; a "long con" prank pulled on former fans of the show by a politically reactionary star who has since used a different form of mass communication—that of social media—to explode her own myth and reveal the "monster" beneath the mask.

Acting Like Kids and Breaking All the Rules: Halloween and the Working Class

> All monsters are human. *You're* a monster.
> —Sister Jude Martin (Jessica Lange) in a Season Two
> episode of *American Horror Story* (FX, 2011–present)

Privileging tricks over treats, *Roseanne* embraces the orderly disorder or carefully structured chaos of Halloween, never more so than in the trippy, misleadingly titled Season Eight episode "Halloween: The Final Chapter" (8.05).[16] Lacking a central plot and structured as a series of tangential mini-episodes, including encounters with unusual trick-or-treaters (such as former *Tonight Show* sidekick Ed McMahon, who shows up at their door toting an oversize Publishers Clearinghouse jackpot check), this hallucinatory installment of the series plays out like a stream-of-consciousness dream narrative, jumping from [1] a spooky family séance at the kitchen table in which Dan is overtaken by the spirit of Elvis; to [2] an extended scene of Roseanne and Jackie battling one another with flashlights and syrup bottles (all while dressed as a gypsy woman and wicked witch, respectively); to [3] another stab at otherworldly communion by way of Ouija board; to [4] a suite of flashbacks to previous Halloween episodes (rendered as her memory of better times while lying in a hospital bed); to [5] a concluding tie-dye dance musical number in the hospital's delivery room, where Roseanne gives birth to a baby boy she christens Jerry Garcia (in honor of the Grateful Dead's lead guitarist, who somehow spoke to her from the beyond when she was in a Demerol-induced haze). Sprinkled between these bizarre segments are now-dated jokes about the O.J. Simpson trial (which had reached a verdict three weeks prior to the airing of "Halloween: The Final Chapter") and still-relevant debates about the best kind of goodies to hand out to the neighborhood's children. Although Dan and Roseanne, childish as ever, contend that sugar-filled sweets are the proper treats, young David, wise beyond his years, insists on filling the kids' Halloween bags with apples, nectarines, and other fresh fruit—a seemingly sensible yet risible thing to do that leads the peeved trick-or-treaters to hurl those healthy yet unenticing snacks back at him. Notably, this is one of several moments in *Roseanne* when the adult members of the Conner clan use Halloween as an excuse to indulge their most juvenile fantasies, as suggested by Roseanne's fond reminiscence (in "Trick Me Up, Trick Me Down") of throwing flaming bags of dog doo-doo onto the next-door neighbor's lawn, and Dan's plan (in "Halloween IV" [5.07]) to moon the town's retirement home and stuff dead fish through people's mail slots (which, he sheepishly admits, is a "childish" activity).

One sign of this series' cultural impact is the prevalence of that "adults-acting-like-kids" theme within more recently produced sitcoms, in which neighborhood competitiveness or friendly familial in-fighting leads characters—many of whom are stuck in arrested development (economically, emotionally, and/or psychologically)—to do things that they would normally refrain from doing any other time of the year.[17] As Roseanne tells David at one point, "This is *Halloween*. It's the one night of the year where you're *supposed* to break all the rules"—words of advice that are meant to prevent the teenaged boy from sitting at home all evening being "good and nice and well-behaved." It is tempting to extend this predilection for seasonal hijinks, performed by individuals who not only embrace but *promote* their own age-defying state of stunted adolescence, into the arena of ostensibly progressive (or "left-leaning") yet oddly problematic programming discussed by Taylor Nygaard and Jorie Lagerwey in their 2020 book *Horrible White People*.[18] Exploring a cluster of recently produced single-camera satires and sitcoms about men and women in their twenties, thirties, and forties who frequently devolve into childish antics even while engaging in very mature, at times salacious activities, from *Girls* (HBO, 2012–17) and *Crazy Ex-Girlfriend* (The CW, 2015–19) to *Casual* (Hulu, 2015–18) and *You're the Worst* (FXX, 2014–19), the authors pinpoint several textual features that, on the surface, seem far removed from the less prestigious blue-collar comedy of *Roseanne*. And yet, these formally innovative, serialized stories of self-obsessed, wildly destructive professionals—primarily "complicated women" seeking romantic and sexual fulfillment as well as creative outlets for their "shocking, revolting, or purposefully heinous" behavior—ultimately center Whiteness (and "white suffering") in much the way that Barr's show did years earlier. But they do so with the added wrinkle of being made after the Great Recession (2007–9) or during the first years of the Trump presidency (2017–20); an era, in other words, "of growing income inequality, highly visible racial inequality and violence, rampant anti-immigrant rhetoric, and persistent gender and sexual discrimination against marginalized communities."[19] This relatively recent crop of shows about horrible white adults acting half their age or being "viciously mean" to others (including members of their own family) nudges viewers to see immaturity and incivility less as character defects than as a general condition that affects millions of Americans who—putting politics aside—might be drawn to these rude, rule-breaking protagonists for their own (very personal) reasons.

For the most part, and with few exceptions, prior to *Roseanne*'s premiere on October 18, 1988, US situation comedies tended to play by the rules as "good and nice and well-behaved" cultural productions, with Halloween episodes giving showrunners, writers, and performers the rare opportunity to "cut loose" or "let their hair down" (only to return to more conventional representations of domestic and workplace relations in non-holiday-themed installments). In a way, the kitschy clutter and narrative chaos of "Halloween: The Final Chapter" and the seven other "very spooky episodes" starring Barr are merely intensified—more fantastical and grotesque—versions of what plays out in her show's 223 non-Halloween-themed installments, which likewise derive their humor from "the incongruity between the Conners' life and that of other families in sitcoms past and present."[20] Ironically, in the years since the airing of *Roseanne*'s two-part series finale "Into That Good Night" (9.24),[21] several US sitcoms have demonstrated its lasting influence, especially around the end of each October. From the relatively comforting depictions of blue-collar life in *The Middle* (ABC, 2009–18) and *Raising Hope* (Fox, 2010–14) to the more extreme visions of working-class squalor and monstrous behavior seen in *It's Always Sunny in Philadelphia* (FX, 2005–12; FXX 2013–present), today's television programming is populated more than ever by characters who "dress the part" of the downwardly mobile or disenfranchised (or what Roseanne herself has called "poor white trash"), and who view Halloween like she did: as an opportunity for potentially enfranchising forms of role-play, including that which blurs the line between genders.

It bears repeating that the creators and writers of *Roseanne* saw in Halloween not only a "cheap" way for members of the working class to taste the metaphorical "treats" that are otherwise unavailable throughout the rest of the year, but also a potential means for minor characters to "express themselves in ways that society usually deems lewd, weird, or inappropriate."[22] As Tyler Curry, a social activist and contributing editor of *The Advocate*, has argued, Halloween has become a kind of "institution" for LGBTQ+ people, many of whom "grew up having to wear a mask" in order to protect themselves from school bullying, parental admonishment, and domestic violence. Although, as Curry emphasizes, today's generation of queer and trans kids might feel less pressured to do so, he and others became "highly trained at hiding [their] true selves" during the 1980s and 1990s (when this show originally aired), making "the celebration of costume and disguise" a much-anticipated occurrence each year. As he states, "The holiday is one that praises all the frights and fetishes that we are told to cover up."[23] As highlighted above, more than one of *Roseanne's* Halloween-themed episodes hinges upon the uncanny effects and fetishistic appeal of cross-dressing, which the star herself performs in Season Three's "Trick or Treat" (in which she pretends to be a burly, bearded truck-driver) and Season Seven's "Skeleton in the Closet" (in which she dresses up as Prince). In these and other installments of her same-named series, Roseanne is "there but not there," a "monster" hiding in plain sight beneath layers of clothing that a drag king might wear on any given night besides All Hallows' Eve. But nothing is ever as it seems in these "very spooky episodes," and looks can be doubly deceiving. This is especially apparent in the aforementioned "Halloween V." Most of this episode's humor derives from the one-upmanship between Roseanne and Dan, her more-than-game husband who is happy to compete against her for the honor of pulling off the most audacious prank.

As any fan of the original series knows, a running gag in this annual celebration is the married couple's back-and-forth battle for Halloween supremacy, something that can only be achieved when one person completely fools the other. This element was initiated in *Roseanne's* first Halloween episode ("Boo," from Season Two), which shows Dan rushing into the kitchen after a terrible woodworking accident, blood erupting in spurts from his apparently severed fingers. By the time "Halloween V" aired in the fall of 1993, audiences would have witnessed even more shocking displays of Grand Guignol–style tomfoolery, making one seriously question Jackie's remark that Dan's bloody hand trick from four years earlier was "the sickest thing [she had] ever seen."[24] In fact, during the opening scene of "Halloween IV," which aired one year prior to this episode, Dan one-ups himself by sticking his hand into the kitchen sink's garbage disposal only to have it cut into shreds by the whirling blades. Unfazed by the fleshy shrapnel shooting out from the sink, Roseanne knows better than to take him seriously, and sees through her husband's sanguinary charade. Yet even she is duped by episode's end, following a series of escalating pranks that culminates with her next-door neighbor's apparent decapitation at the hands of her daughter Darlene (who, like the rest of the family, is in on the twisted joke). Significantly, besides alluding to Nancy's plan for Dan to cross-dress as *Leave It to Beaver* matriarch June Cleaver (despite his discomfort in having to wear high heels) and suggesting that—in nearly shocking his wife to death with the sight of a teenaged girl's decapitation—Dan has gone too far as a prankster this year, "Halloween V" draws attention to the multiple layers of deception or masquerade that make it difficult to locate the "real" Roseanne. It does this through a passage of dialogue that she delivers to her husband in a moment of ironically misleading candor, or truthful trickery: "You never tell people that you *like* that you like 'em. The only people that you ever tell that you like are the people that you actually *don't like.*"

It is important to note that Halloween traditions such as the ones cited above offer more than a release valve for the Conners and other working-class TV families. The holiday's paradoxical appeals—as a largely harmless invitation to confront physical pain and death through the horrifying yet humorously deployed iconography of "rotting corpses, mutilated body parts . . . and skeletons of all sizes"[25]—is one matter worth considering; but so too should the yearly rituals enacted by Roseanne and her cohort be seen as a means of bringing stability and predictability to a family unit that often copes with financial instabilities. Living paycheck to paycheck and moving from one pink-collar service-sector job to another (e.g., shampoo girl in a beauty parlor, home-based telemarketer, secretary at a meat-packing plant, waitress at a shopping mall café, assembly line worker at a factory) in search of the security that seems to have eluded her since before her marriage to Dan,[26] she justifiably looks to Halloween as a source of perverse pleasure, thumbing her nose at institutions that have exploited her. Yet it is also a way for Roseanne to ironically reduce the unpredictability that has largely defined her life up to that point. Halloween, as we have seen, is a means to satirically mock traditions, but it is a tradition in its own right; one that, steeped in odd rituals, has relied upon the repeated cultural enactment of certain tropes in order for it to challenge the primacy of other holidays likewise noted for bringing families together. One trope in particular—the act of dressing up as someone else, so central to the holiday's (and the television medium's) appeals as a form of escapism—has shifted from its initial connotations in 1950s sitcoms such as *The Jackie Gleason Show* (DuMont, 1949–52; CBS, 1952–57) and *The Adventures of Ozzie and Harriet* (ABC, 1952–66) toward more progressive and potentially transgressive notions of gender fluidity in recent years' Halloween celebrations. And, for better or worse, we have Roseanne Barr, the always-controversial TV star, to thank for that.

Treats, Tricks, Trump: Hating Halloween

> I don't know, girl. Halloween. To me, white people in sheets is *not* a good
> time. I *hate* that holiday.
> > —African American student LaDonna Fredericks
> > (Claudette Wells) to one of her white classmates in a
> > Season One episode of *Square Pegs* (CBS, 1982–83)

In the previous chapter, as part of the epigraph, I quoted the words of Adam Driver's character in the HBO series *Girls*, someone who is not alone in vocalizing his strong dislike of Halloween. Another person who expresses a similar sentiment is LaDonna Fredericks (Claudette Wells), the young African American student quoted in the epigraph above, who tells one of her high-school classmates in an episode of the short-lived sitcom *Square Pegs* (CBS, 1982–83), "To me, white people in sheets is *not* a good time. I *hate* that holiday." In part because Halloween is perceived as a moment of temporary "permission" (to do and say provocative things that would be balked at if not outright forbidden any other time of the year), it has been used as an excuse for hateful, bigoted, or simply ill-advised actions and words that harm particular groups already disadvantaged as a result of the United States' long history of institutionalized racism. In recent years, several highly publicized examples of cultural appropriation have provided white Americans with opportunities to reflect on their own privilege and to ponder how the actions of some—including those who wear blackface or attempt to imitate African Americans (as former *Dancing with the Stars* cast member Julianne Hough did in October 2013, when she dressed up as Uzo Aduba's character Suzanne "Crazy Eyes" Warren from the Netflix hit *Orange Is the New Black* [2013–19])—might open old wounds, enflame existing prejudices, complicate contemporary debates about racial justice, and incentivize others to adopt even more injurious forms of verbal or physical abuse in the years to come. Such (perhaps unintended) consequences leapt to mind recently, when the outspoken political commentator Megyn Kelly made on-air remarks about the appropriateness of blackface as part of kids' costumes only to have her daytime talk show *Megyn Kelly Today* (NBC, 2017–18) cancelled the following day (on October 24, 2018)—one week before Halloween and five months after Roseanne Barr's show had been handed the same fateful decision by ABC executives.

Of course, cross-ethnic masquerade is not a recent phenomenon, but has been a fixture of social life in the United States for decades, bubbling up in everything "from Halloween costumes to Cinco de Mayo parties to the Washington Redskins to decorative bindis and other music festival fashion," as Lauren Michele Jackson notes in her 2019 book *White Negroes*.[27] However, while "dressing up as a person of another race to the point of stereotype" has long been seen as problematic, and has increasingly been decried on social media sites where Hough and other TV celebrities feel compelled to apologize for their mistakes, the country paradoxically appears to be "in the midst of forgiving and actively forgetting the surfaced photograph of a state governor costumed in either blackface or Klan robes."[28] With this reference to Virginia's Ralph Northam, whose 1984 medical school yearbook shows him posing in blackface next to a man wearing a Ku Klux Klan outfit,

Jackson underscores the contradictions of a politically divided era when one half of the nation wants to hold people accountable for their actions and words, while the other half seems content to let people in power off the hook for any such indiscretions. Indeed, former President Trump has managed to exert sway with a shockingly large portion of the electorate, even after leaving office, by playing up the rhetoric that *he could do or say practically anything*—including standing in the middle of Fifth Avenue and shooting someone with a gun (which he snidely joked about at a 2016 campaign stop in Iowa)—without losing any of his most diehard supporters.

Compounding the problem, television shows such as *South Park* (Comedy Central, 1997–present), *Family Guy* (Fox, 1999–present), and *American Dad!* (Fox, 2005–14; TBS, 2014–present), which flaunt their status as "equal opportunity offenders" prone to upset both sides of that ideological divide through "politically incorrect" humor, have occasionally used blackface as a cheap if dubious way to get laughs even as they are quick to strategically reframe cross-ethnic masquerade as an ignorant blunder on the part of clueless white characters (as if to remind audiences that the creators of these comedies do not actually *advocate* such representations). In these and other animated sitcoms, such individuals are often just given a good scolding, or, in the case of the *South Park* episode "Summer Sucks" (2.08), which shows the African American character Chef (voiced by Isaac Hayes) coming face-to-face with a town full of ash-covered locals, a good "ass-whooping." Significantly, *Family Guy*'s first Halloween episode ("Halloween on Spooner Street" [9.04]) begins with Chris (voiced by Seth Green), the well-meaning but easily confused son of Lois and Peter Griffin (voiced by Alex Borstein and Seth MacFarlane, respectively), descending the staircase to reveal his trick-or-treating costume—a wildly inappropriate appropriation. To the shock of his mother, Chris is dressed up as Bill Cosby, complete with gaudily colorful knit sweater and a charcoal-covered face that, in her own words, "is racist." The presumably humorous capper of this opening scene comes when Lois instructs her son to "go upstairs and put on that Indian chief costume" that she had intended for him to wear, as if the ongoing discussion around cultural appropriation can accommodate only one set of identificatory claims or sensitivities while ignoring others (i.e., those relating to indigenous people as well as Arab Americans, Asian Americans, Latinos, and other communities concerned with stereotypical uses of culturally specific clothing like Native American headdresses, bindi decorations, hijab, sombreros, dreadlocks, etc. as Halloween costuming). Its very contradictoriness as an episode that props up an antiquated throwback to black minstrelsy as a means of generating laughter only to swiftly condemn such representations as racist makes "Halloween on Spooner Street" a particularly accurate summation of *Family Guy* as a whole.

But the episode also points toward the larger mediasphere of "mixed messages" concerning white Americans' appropriative tendencies that Jackson alludes to her in her aforementioned study—tendencies toward insensitivity and offensiveness that are especially prominent around Halloween time.[29]

Throughout the genre's history, this calendrical event (described in an episode of *The Norm Show* as "your basic Satanic holiday") has been harshly criticized by numerous characters in sitcoms that nevertheless use it has an excuse to break from representational norms. Some people, such as Minnie Driver's overbearing maternal figure Fiona in the short-lived comedy *About a Boy* (NBC, 2014–15), complain about the unhealthy indulgences of Halloween, a "made-up American holiday" that, in her words, was "invented to encourage obesity and diabetes." Other naysayers, such as the title character in *Everybody Loves Raymond* (CBS, 1996–2005), have simply grown tired of being victimized by neighborhood trick-or-treaters who, armed with toilet paper, vandalize personal property and interrupt family time (including Ray [Ray Romano]'s long anticipated night of lovemaking with his wife Debra [Patricia Heaton]). On a related note, one might have an aversion to this annual night of revelry due to some traumatic experience from the past, as alluded to by Paul Provenza's character Patrick in *Empty Nest* (NBC, 1988–95) and by Paul Reiser's character Paul in *Mad About You* (NBC, 1992–99), the latter explaining to his wife Jamie (Helen Hunt) that, as a sixteen-year-old high schooler, he was attacked by big burly ten-year-old triplets (the Escobar brothers) who did not "respect" his Superman costume. Similarly, when asked to explain why he "can't stand Halloween," Patrick in *Empty Nest* opens up about a painful moment from his childhood when, at the age of 5, he was beaten up by older kids who mocked his Little Orphan Annie costume. Such dialogue, while suggestive of the way in which Halloween can temporarily emancipate men and women (or boys and girls) from the constrictive dictates of gender, reminds us that a conservative public backlash often accompanies any attempt to subvert the white heteronormative status quo. As such, Adam's comment "I hate Halloween," though spoken by a straight, cisgender Caucasian American man living in New York City, is a justified response to the reactionary attacks—verbal and otherwise—so often directed toward marginalized, historically disenfranchised communities throughout the country.

That backlash is literalized—lent horrifying corporeal expression—in the aforementioned "Halloween V," from *Roseanne*'s sixth season. The episode begins with Nancy hauling a holiday prop into the Lanford Lunch Box, where she deposits it onto a table. This is no ordinary prop, however, but a life-sized "dead guy" that Roseanne will use to scare customers inside the eating establishment. Putting the darkly painted mannequin into a seat at the bar, the protagonist complains that it does not look as realistic as she had hoped it would, and proceeds to repeatedly stab the fake customer in the back with all the force and savagery of a slasher film villain. As she does so, the brown head of the slumped figure bangs against the countertop, revealing to the camera deep gashes across its face. Those physical marks indicate that this is not the first time that this uncannily lifelike yet "dead" object—a Halloween plaything used for these white characters' amusement—has been subjected to violent acts. The cuts and bruises also suggest the brutality visited upon African American bodies several years prior to this episode's October 26, 1993, airing, decades before and after the turn of the twentieth century (when white lynch mobs terrorized black people throughout the United States). Such cruelty, aimed at communities of color, has continued well into the twenty-first century, making the prospect of revisiting this otherwise "harmless" episode from a contemporary vantage (with the benefits of historical hindsight and in the midst of a growing number of deaths resulting from police brutality) unnerving, to say the least.

7.5. Propping up a dark-skinned mannequin atop a stool at the Lanford Lunch Box, where it will be used as a Halloween prop, Roseanne proceeds to stab the physically damaged figure several times in a demonstration of brutal force that, from a contemporary vantage, is horrifying. © the Carsey-Werner Company

I will return to the topic of racial terrorism as well as the structural inequalities and fear of the other that have long been part of the monstrous imaginary in the next chapter. However, it bears mentioning here, in this chapter devoted to *Roseanne*, that the star's recent fall from grace—brought on by her ill-advised use of a public forum (Twitter) to spread conspiracy theories and launch personal attacks against Democrats—has fundamentally altered our present-day understanding of her past work. Indeed, several critics and audiences, including those who once appreciated Barr's socially progressive vision of a working-class family held together by its members' mutual support for one another (in the absence of government support), have grown disillusioned with her public persona, especially once she aligned herself with President Trump. Referred to by Elena Alvarez (Isabella Gomez), a young lesbian feminist-activist in Norman Lear's multi-camera sitcom *One Day at a Time* (Netflix, 2017–present), as "that monster in the White House," Trump has, since the days of his racially biased real-estate dealings, tallied a long list of discriminatory actions that undermine his claim of being "the least racist person" in the world. As someone who made explicitly bigoted remarks on the campaign trail (for instance, calling Mexican immigrants "criminals" and "rapists") and openly pandered to white supremacists while in office, he has behaved (and tweeted) in a beastly manner; thus making Roseanne's gravitation toward him and his race-baiting MAGA rhetoric a deeply troubling manifestation of her decade-long slide into regressive politics. From comparing an African American woman to an ape to posing for a photo shoot dressed as Adolf Hitler "removing a tray of burnt gingerbread men" from an oven,[30] Barr has in fact lowered the bar for contemporary purveyors of political humor, though her *monstrosity*—as a disruptive cultural embodiment of social anxieties in the age of Trump—has been lifted from subtext to text in recent years. This is apparent in the first episode of *Roseanne*'s 2018 revival.

Packaged and programmed by CBS executives as the show's tenth season, that relaunch begins with "Twenty Years to Life" (10.01), an episode that picks up after Darlene has moved back home to live with her ageing parents (following a separation from her husband David). Darlene brings with her two kids of her own: surly teenaged daughter Harris (Emma Kenney), whose disrespect toward her elders prompts Roseanne to call her an "entitled little bitch," and genderqueer pre-teen son Mark (Ames McNamara), whose flamboyant outfits make Dan visibly uncomfortable. In addition to tracking the socioeconomic travails of being a single mother or, in her equally cash-strapped sister Becky's case, being a recently widowed waitress willing to sell her eggs in order to put a down payment on a house, this and the eight episodes that follow it spend a considerable amount of time with the younger Conners. But "Twenty Years to Life" also pivots on the simmering anger between the show's other two siblings: Roseanne and Jackie. Within minutes of the opening scene, it is revealed that the two women had a falling out in the aftermath of the 2016 presidential election, and Trump's victory has spurred Jackie to wear Nasty Woman shirts and pink "pussy" hats in a show of solidarity with feminists around the country. While Roseanne calls her sister a "snowflake," Jackie returns the compliment by referring to this unrepentant Trump supporter as a "deplorable"—a word famously uttered during an election-season fundraiser by Hillary Clinton (who is referenced on numerous occasions in this episode).

"Twenty Years to Life" is unusual in its foregrounding of a family's emotionally heated discussion of political disagreements, which threaten to tear at an already-frayed relationship that, ultimately, is mended by episode's end. The sisters "hug it out," in typical sitcom fashion, once Jackie apologizes to Roseanne for implying that she was a "right-wing jackass" and Roseanne—short of saying "sorry" herself—forgives her. Despite its conventional ending, however, the episode makes space for a dialectical to-and-fro between someone who claims that she voted for Trump because "he talked about jobs" and promised to "shake things up," and someone who has little patience for Americans who "wrap themselves up in the flag and cling to their guns." Since the 2016 election, other contemporary TV comedies have directly referenced—or taken satirical aim at—President Trump, including *Broad City* (Comedy Central, 2014–19), *Unbreakable Kimmy Schmidt* (Netflix, 2015–20), *One Mississippi* (Amazon Video, 2015–17), and the recently relaunched *Will & Grace* (NBC, 1998–2006, 2017–20), which spends much of its ninth-season opener, "11 Years Later" (9.01), poking fun at the Trump administration, with jokes about "fake news," senior counselor Kellyanne Conway, and the campaign-rally chant "Lock Her Up" sprinkled liberally into the script. But no other recent sitcom, with the possible exception of *Black-ish* (ABC, 2014–present), which devoted the episode "Lemons" (3.12) to a thoughtful discussion of what Trump's victory—or Clinton's loss—might mean to African Americans, looked so intently at the internal familial strife brought about by that election, the result of which (according to Jackie) has "[torn] America apart and [brought] the world to the brink of nuclear apocalypse."

Speaking of apocalyptic endings: As mentioned earlier, the original run of this working-class sitcom came to an end on May 20, 1997, when the one-hour series finale "Into That Good Night" (9.23 and 9.24) aired. Or, rather, that double-barreled episode, watched by 16.6 million viewers, was the first of *two* finales, followed twenty-one years later by a second conclusion that capped a tenth-season revival of the show. Having already discussed the reasons for the sudden cancellation of that *final* final season, including the controversial star's racist remarks on Twitter (for which she would later apologize, calling them Ambien-induced "bad jokes"), I wish to conclude this chapter by considering how her influence on the monstrous imaginary continues to make itself felt despite—or, rather, because of—those missteps. Not surprisingly, Roseanne's highly publicized blunders led to her character's death and prompted a slew of critical putdowns whose rhetorical excess nearly matched that of her own online screeds. In the days and months following her show's cancellation, several cultural critics as well as creative personnel in the television industry drew upon the language of horror films while tossing dirt atop her grave, pointing out how unacceptable her May 29, 2018, tweet (directed at Valerie Jarrett, former senior advisor to President Obama) was, and using words like "appalling," "horrible," and "loathsome" to describe her political views (including her support of Donald Trump and of far-right conspiracy theories such as QAnon).[31] For instance, Kenya Barris, the creator of *Black-ish*, referred to Barr as "a fuckin' monster" not long after the network's entertainment president, Channing Dungey, brought a premature end to his show's Tuesday night lead-in. Satirically imitating other executives' question about Roseanne's behavior ("Why is this monster killing villagers?"), Barris provided the most obvious response: "Because that's what a monster does."

The legitimate anger that drove Barris to make that remark is not unlike the antipathy that many Americans feel toward the then-occupant of their nation's highest office. Moreover, the rhetorical maneuvers through which the monstrous imaginary is stretched to accommodate such emotionally fueled criticism of political figures are noteworthy. Not long after the 2016 election results came in, Tony Fratto, a former assistant Treasury secretary in President George W. Bush's administration, stated that "we'll be putting a monster in the White House."[32] More recently, Michael Cohen, Trump's longtime personal lawyer who has since been sentenced to three years in federal prison (after pleading guilty to campaign finance violations), used the M-word to describe his former boss, claiming that the president's efforts to delegitimize Joe Biden's 2020 electoral college victory are further evidence of a bigger "con job" that he has been playing on the American public since before the previous election.[33] Jennifer Finney Boylan, a contributing writer for the *New York Times*, similarly called Trump a "monster who feeds on fear," owing to his tendency to spin falsehoods designed to make US citizens afraid "of immigrants, of transgender people, of one another."[34] Putting a parodic spin on President Franklin Roosevelt's first inaugural address of March 4, 1933, Boylan begins her opinion piece by declaring that "the only thing Mr. Trump has is fear itself" and then ends it by putting a further spin on it: "The only thing we have to fear is Trump himself."

Such rhetoric turns him into a modern-day, real-world extension of the "wellworn trope in horror fiction about the Monster Who Feeds on Fear." Citing examples such as "The Tingler" (the parasitic creature from director William Castle's 1959 film of that title), the Scarecrow supervillain in the *Batman* franchise, Pennywise the Dancing Clown from Stephen King's 1986 novel *It*, and the shapeshifting boggart from J.K. Rowling's *Harry Potter* stories, Boylan spins an encompassing web of intertextual references to put Trump in his place as a figure of justified derision whose notoriously thin skin (with regard to attacks on his character, business dealings, and misuse of the government's executive branch for personal gain) suggests one way to defeat this "monster." Indeed, as she notes, besides using legal action against the president, who is "famous for having no sense of humor," activists should take up comedy and satire as their weapons, for these have the power to peel "the masks off liars" and reveal the truth.[35] Though salted with malice, Barris's joke about Barr as a rampaging "monster"—like other comedians' humorous yet heartfelt comments about Trump—is in keeping with that spirit of comedy-as-protest and can be seen as a means of removing the proverbial mask in pursuit of the truth.

Only slightly less offended by Roseanne's behavior than was Barris, Ernest Owens, who posted an op-ed piece on CNN's website within hours of her tweet, called out ABC executives who "should never have been willing to work with an offensive comedian whose horrific statements were well known." Unlike Barris, though, Owens admits to feeling "conflicted on killing off a show" with such a "phenomenal cast" (including Laurie Metcalf, Sara Gilbert, and John Goodman, all reprising their roles from twenty years earlier). Owen's use of the term "kill" to denote the manner in which a television program might meet a swift end is telling, for it reminds us of the way that troublesome actors, including series headliners, are sometimes "written out" of casts while highlighting how onscreen and offscreen acts of bad behavior bring together complicated questions of morality and mortality. In recent years, those questions, sometimes woven into storylines, would have been evident to anyone who has watched *Two and a Half Men* (CBS, 2003–15) and *House of Cards* (Netflix, 2013–18) before and after their respective leads' forced departures. Much like Charlie Sheen and Kevin Spacey, whose characters died as a result of the stars' "dangerously self-destructive conduct" (including, in Spacey's case, allegations of sexual assault that lend extratextual meaning to fictional President Frank Underwood's scandal-ridden administration), Barr was forced to watch her same-named onscreen persona succumb to an offscreen death due to her inflammatory social media posts. The publicly shamed star's tweets (which took aim not only at retired government official Valerie Jarrett but also at billionaire investor George Soros) were, as Billy Nilles points out, less injurious to other parties than what Bill Cosby, Louis C.K., and other famous men with careers in TV comedy have done. But the result of her unconscionable behavior is the same, leading Nilles to state that "laughing along with them for a lighthearted 22 minutes has suddenly come to feel untenable."[36] In the end, Barr's character was revealed to have died as a result of an opioid overdose following knee surgery, a narrative solution to the problem of her offscreen bad behavior for which the show's writers had unwittingly prepared by including copious references to pain medication and drug dependency throughout its tenth season.

Before she was "killed off," Roseanne managed to squeeze in a few final references to herself as a "monster," including a moment in the episode "Dress to Impress" (10.02) when, warning her gay grandson's new elementary school classmates not to pick on him because of his "girly" outfit, she says, "I'm a white witch." It is a humorous remark that plays on the age disparity between speaker and listeners, and which echoes her earlier one-on-one chat with Mark, whom she hugs (in support of his clothing choices) and asks, "Kinda scary talking to your old grannie, huh?" Responding that he is "not afraid" of her, the young boy is told that he should just "give it time"—a scene-ending button that reflects the extradiagetic discourses surrounding the star's slippery standing over the past twenty years. Moreover, as a sign of the long shadow that she casts over *The Conners* (ABC, 2018–present) (the renamed "offspring" of *Roseanne* that marched on without her), additional allusions to monstrosity have continued to spring up in recent episodes, including "Halloween and the Election vs. the Pandemic" (3.02). This latest take on holiday-themed shenanigans deftly weaves together a subtle critique of the Trump administration's mishandling of the COVID-19 pandemic (which, at the time of this episode's airing on October 28, 2020, had claimed over 220,000 American lives) and the many visual components that make this annual event such a special occasion in the Conners household. Once again, Mark, now speaking to Dan about a bully at school who has mocked mask-wearing and other coronavirus protection measures, utters the phrase "I'm not afraid." Later, Darlene's child explains to her why he got into a fight with that bully (who is quoted as saying that "wearing a mask is just a way to scare people into staying home"). Mark says that "it felt good to talk back"—a statement that surely would have made his grandmother proud.

Because the mayor of Lanford has cancelled neighborhood trick-or-treating due to the pandemic, Dan, Becky, Jackie, Darlene, and her new boyfriend Ben (Jay R. Ferguson), who is dressed as Frankenstein's monster, decide to recreate the experience inside the house, giving Mark and his younger cousin Mary (Jayden Rey), the African American daughter of D.J., an opportunity to literally taste the holiday in the absence of a traditional celebration. Behind each bedroom and bathroom door of the Conner household is an opportunity for either a "trick" or a "treat," and Jackie—dressed as a wicked witch—serves as the kids' tour guide through this house of horrors. This episode, which revolves around different kinds of masks (including the blood-smeared facial covering that Mary wears as part of her nurse's costume), concludes with a conversation between Darlene and Dan in which their political differences are put on the table. Telling his daughter that the two sides of the political divide each think that their opponents are stupid, and that a failure to meet in the middle or simply talk to one another is "the kind of mentality that's ruining the country," Dan puts forth a position of compromise that would have been harder to imagine during his wife Roseanne's life. Candy, too, is put on the table: the kids' sugar-filled Halloween haul, which has been dumped out of their bags and turned into poker chips for the adult members of the family. "Oh my god, you people are *real monsters!*" Mark exclaims upon seeing his Kit-Kats, Lemonheads, and Three Musketeers bars being gambled away without his consent. It is a fitting ending to an episode that reminds us of the need to participate in national and local elections at a moment when perceived and actual threats to democracy gain a stronger foothold on the nation.

8

"Ugly Americans"

Animating Monsters, Demonizing Others, and Racializing Fear on American Television

You know, Halloween is fast approaching. The day when parents encourage little boys to dress like little girls, and little girls to dress like whores, and go door to door, browbeating hardworking Americans into giving them free food. Well, you know what, western Ohio? We've lost the true meaning of Halloween: *Fear.* Halloween is that magical day of the year when a child is told their grandmother's a demon who's been feeding them rat casserole with a crunchy garnish of their own scabs. Children must know fear. Without, they won't know how to behave. They'll try Frenching grizzly bears or consider living in Florida. So, moms, skip trick-or-treating this year, and instead sit your little toddler down and explain that Daddy's a hungry zombie, and before he went out to sharpen his pitchfork, he whispered to Mommy that you looked delicious.

—Sue Sylvester (Jane Lynch), speaking to the viewers of
WOHN News as part of her segment "Sue's Corner,"
in a Season Two episode of *Glee* (Fox, 2009–15)

You white monster, shut up!

—Amy Schumer, imitating a Latino woman speaking
to a Caucasian woman, in a Season Two episode of
Inside Amy Schumer (Comedy Central, 2013–16)

In her book *The Celebration of Death in Contemporary Culture,* Dina Khapaeva draws attention to some of the contributing factors that led to an increased public interest in—or rather insatiable appetite for—thanatological content during the second half of the twentieth century. Death, she argues, has become a pronounced, pervasive theme in US popular culture over the past six decades, as evidenced by the postwar spread of "sadistic urban legends" (e.g., "The Bunny Man," "The Hook," "The Killer in the Backseat"), the reporting of grisly murders committed by serial killers since the 1970s (e.g., John Wayne Gacy, Ted Bundy, David Berkowitz), and the more recent emergence of "dark tourism" (to travel destinations associated with historical tragedies) and "murderabilia" (i.e., collectibles related to violent crimes) within industries catering to the morbidly curious.[1] Khapaeva also gestures toward wave upon blood-splashing wave of slasher movies produced after the original theatrical release of John Carpenter's *Halloween* (1978), a contemporary classic of that horror subgenre whose title points toward yet another source of our collective fascination with the grim reaper.[2] A contraction of All Hallows' Eve (referring to the night before All Saints' Day), the annual celebration popularly known as Halloween had been imbued with ghoulish connotations long before Carpenter's low-budget film scared up $47 million at the domestic box office, luring audiences into darkened theaters with the promise of lurid material and forever linking that titular touchstone on the Christian calendar with the lethal actions of a suburban stalker preying on babysitters and other unsuspecting victims. Indeed, earlier big-screen evocations of Halloween's disarming charms could be witnessed in everything from *I Was a Teenage Werewolf* (1957) to *The Little Girl Who Lives Down the Lane* (1976), two of the many motion pictures that extended the ghastly and ghostly associations of the yearly festival, which dates back to the ancient Celtic celebration of Samhain, into the modern era.

Moreover, in the days between *Halloween*'s October 25, 1978, Kansas City premiere and the nationwide celebration of All Hallows' Eve that occurred one week later, a number of television series—from the rural family drama *The Waltons* (CBS, 1972–81) to the musical-comedy smorgasbord *The Muppet Show* (1976–81), not to mention largely forgotten primetime programs like *Flying High* (CBS, 1978–79)—devoted episodes to the holiday. In fact, it was there, on the small screen, where Halloween's paradoxical appeals—as a largely harmless invitation to confront death through the horrifying yet humorously deployed iconography of "rotting corpses, mutilated body parts . . . and skeletons of all sizes"[3]—had already garnered the attention of TV audiences prior to the slasher film's theatrical release, in "very spooky episodes" that were as contradictory as the once-religious, now-secular "festival of death and life" that inspired them.[4] Of course, nothing as terrifying as a masked killer lurking in the shadows and shrubbery of an otherwise peaceful small-town community, or as graphic as Michael Myers's brutal massacre of sex-starved teenagers, can be found in the seasonally themed installments of classic domestic sitcoms such as *Leave It to Beaver* (CBS, 1957–58; ABC, 1958–63), *Dennis the Menace* (CBS, 1959–63), and *My Three Sons* (ABC, 1960–65; CBS, 1965–72). However, as discussed in Chapter Six, these and other programs that aired before and after their initial broadcast mined the cultural imaginary of mid-century monsterdom and made Halloween an increasingly "special" part of the fall television season.

This chapter extends some of the arguments of the previous two in order to flesh out what I call the "monstrous imaginary." Doing so, I hope, will clarify why this televisual trope (with roots in much earlier storytelling traditions, including ancient myths, legends, and folktales) is such an enduring part of the medium's mixed cultural heritage. The strange resilience of monstrosity as a rhetorical figure attests to our paradoxical compulsion to replenish, or keep well-stocked, the onscreen arsenal of threats aimed at our very existence. Frequently grotesque in its physical makeup, and potentially unfathomable from a psychological perspective, the monster escapes our cognitive grasp as disturbingly as it breaches social and corporeal boundaries. As a cultural construct, it serves many purposes, including that of making social anxieties and moral ambiguities a bit more manageable, more legible, in much the same way that clowns, fools, and jesters have done since the time of ancient Greek comedy (when jokes about death and other grave subjects were habitually performed on stage). Comedy and horror are, in fact, two sides of the same genre coin insofar as they allow us to hold contrasting views of a single phenomenon simultaneously while helping to normalize the idea of "abnormality" through the repetitive foregrounding of either humorous or horrifying incongruities. At once strange and utterly familiar, aberrant and wholly expected, the monster haunts comic tales as frequently as it does terrifying ones. Its ubiquity, however, does not necessarily lead to comprehension on the part of today's audiences, who remain as flummoxed by or fearful of the thing as they have always been.

Death, of course, is the big boogeyman—the source of most people's deepest fears. But other social anxieties lay at the feet of the monster, which lends figural expression to the loss of control—over oneself and one's environment—that ironically worsens with age and despite gaining greater knowledge or "mastery" of the world. As the Irish philosopher Richard Kearney notes, "[I]t is precisely because we are beings who *know* that we will die that we keep on telling stories, struggling to represent something of the unrepresentable, to hazard interpretations of the puzzles and aporias that surround us."[5] The monstrous other, our closest approximation to that unrepresentable Real, brings a semblance of security to the always-interpreting self, even as it reminds us of our inescapable "fragility and fallibility" as subjects imprisoned by our own mortality and morality. According to literary historian Tina Marie Boyer, it is the means through which the protagonists of strangely comforting yet disquieting stories, from the novels of H. P. Lovecraft and Stephen King to the video games and motion pictures in the *Silent Hill* and *Resident Evil* franchises, are able to "reorder the meaning of their existence and the knowledge of their world in the face of a menace that cannot be grasped nor understood."[6] "We all have a sense of an ending," Kearney writes, "and one of the reasons our lives are in quest of narratives is because we know that our existence, like the stories we tell, will come to an end."[7]

Beyond this knowledge of our imminent demise or "finitude," the monster ushers in a host of associated meanings, all resting upon a fundamental assumption of difference; namely, that between Self and Other. Racialized alterity or otherness has been a mainstay of comedy TV's monstrous imaginary for decades, and the increased presence of more accurate, less offensive representations in contemporary programs should not distract us from the long history of bigoted and xenophobic depictions of different ethnic groups and foreign nationals in American popular culture more generally. Historically demonized if not always portrayed as literal vampires, werewolves, zombies, and other fantastical creatures, ethnic minorities and "foreigners" occupy a vulnerable position within mainstream cultural productions, including sitcoms that attempt to squeeze laughter from stereotypes that are not just outdated, objectionable, and even harmful but also visually *grotesque* in their excessiveness. However, a few television comedies have moved the marginalized figure of the monster from the periphery to the center of prejudicial discourse, and not just in Halloween-themed episodes that are annual exceptions to the "norm." In doing so, they shine a spotlight on ostensibly nonconforming individuals who would otherwise be excluded from the benefits of middle-class prosperity and the commercially advertised "good life," or simply kept at a safe distance by those seeking to maintain the status quo.

In the second half of this chapter, I will say a few words about two such programs—*The Addams Family* (ABC, 1964–66) and *The Munsters* (CBS, 1964–66)—which put a humorous spin on the assimilation narratives that have traditionally colored the immigrant experience in the United States. Both of these black-and-white comedies present a dichotomy between conventional and unconventional modes of domestic living that is as stark as their monochromatic cinematography. By showcasing numerous instances in which outsiders (i.e., the so-called "normals" who nervously enter and quickly exit the main settings) are thrust into sudden, uncanny proximity to their own hideous prejudices vis-à-vis the peculiar occupants of those houses, *The Addams Family* and *The Munsters* hold a mirror up to society and call out people's tendency to judge others based on their physical appearance or perceived eccentricities. But, like the other social imaginaries discussed in this book, the monstrous imaginary, which these and other TV programs have helped to construct, is the kind of weirdly distorting reflective surface typically found in carnival funhouses; allowing us to laugh at *ourselves* as much as others, or at least to see how we too might be rendered as misshapen forms subject to ridicule.

My choice of those two sitcoms as case studies will seem sensible, if uninspired, to anyone who has viewed just a few episodes, or who is simply aware of their centrality to the "monster craze" that swept through the United States during the 1960s (a decade bookended by the theatrical release of Alfred Hitchcock's genre-redefining thriller *Psycho* [1960] and the death of the silver screen's most famous interpreter of Frankenstein's monster, Boris Karloff). Although subsequent TV comedies have foregrounded fantastical creatures and supernatural scenarios since the spring of 1966, *The Addams Family* and *The Munsters* are unique as catalyzers of a decades-long cultural movement to domesticate monsters, to bring them out of the shadows and into the suburban environs that are otherwise reserved for comparatively straightlaced, upwardly mobile middle-class characters who are said to "look like" you and me. That latter point is especially pertinent to the study of satires, sitcoms, and social imaginaries as mirror-like distortions of an already-warped reality. As Jeremy G. Butler states, "Because characters typically assume human form, because they *look like us*, *talk like us* and, in some sense, *behave like us*, it is easy to mistake characters for real people, with real lives beyond the boundaries of their television programs."[8] One can certainly take issue with such claims, and question the rhetorical underpinnings of the seemingly inclusive but exclusionary pronoun "us," especially since the diegetic universe of American television has *never* accurately reflected the demographic diversity of the audience's world (across a spectrum of human differences, including age, ethnicity, gender, physical ability, political affiliation, religious or ethical values, and sexual orientation). But the fact remains that televisual narratives employ interpellating strategies that put spectators "in place" and encourage identification with certain subject positions, including that of literal and figurative monsters whose "weird" behavior or unorthodox (vaguely "European") approach to modern American living presents a vicariously experienced alternative to conventional social mores.[9]

For all their outward edginess and macabre humor, the households at the heart of *The Addams Family* and *The Munsters* are fairly traditional as the kind of loving, mutually supportive social structures promoted in postwar domestic comedies. Indeed, as Lorna Jowett and Stacey Abbott state, "Despite their strange appearance, both the upscale Addams and the blue-collar Munsters are close families, with parents supporting and nurturing their children, and husbands and wives demonstrating enduring marital love."[10] Still, despite their adherence to conventional codes of morality in mid-century America, the main characters in these programs stand out from their sixties sitcom peers by virtue of their many idiosyncrasies and unthrottled passions (including a then-unprecedented amount of sexual chemistry between Gomez Addams [John Astin], a "Latin Lover" of Castilian extraction, and his Vampira-like wife Morticia [Carolyn Jones]) as well as their embodiment of Old World values that suggest ethnic, immigrant, and/or working-class backgrounds at odds with the genre's middle-of-the-road representational politics. They even have, as Stephen Tropiano claims, "definite gay appeal," in that they represent "the 'other' kind of American family," made up of "domesticated ghouls . . . who thought *they* were normal and everyone around them was odd."[11]

Interestingly, two episodes of the gay-friendly sitcom *Roseanne* (ABC, 1988–97)—"Dream Lover" (3.10) and "Stressed to Kill" (4.09)—hint at the kind of influence that *The Munsters* and *The Addams Family* had on subsequent generations of television programming, including those of the past thirty years that similarly pivot on exclusionary social formations and the rhetorical framing of class-, race-, or sex-based otherness as a specific type of culturally constructed "monstrosity." In the first of those two episodes, Roseanne jokes that her dark-haired son D.J. (Michael Fishman)'s role model is Eddie Munster, the lycanthropic tyke played by Butch Patrick in the classic black-and-white comedy; and in the latter episode she attributes her unhealthy addiction to cigarettes to her earlier addiction to television, having learned to smoke from watching Gomez and Morticia do the same on the boob tube. Like her sister Jackie (Laurie Metcalf), who, in the Halloween-themed episode "Trick Me Up, Trick Me Down" (4.06), attends a costume party dressed as Morticia, Roseanne frequently pays homage to the TV shows she grew up with, including sitcoms that spoofed the white middle-class social imaginary of suburban prosperity and domestic bliss that her own eponymous program took a more comedically incisive scalpel to.

Before circling back to *The Addams Family* and *The Munsters* as well as their "hideous progeny" (i.e., more recent TV shows featuring supernatural and/or strange creatures as the leads), I want to underline the applicability of monster metaphors in the larger context of US political discourse and popular culture more generally. Doing so, I hope, will illustrate the life-and-death stakes involved in being subject to such social imaginaries, which can foster deeply biased, potentially harmful attitudes toward individuals and groups whose very existence is threatened whenever their "kind" is presented on television not just in less-than-flattering ways but as something to *fear*. Because fear, in addition to play, is at the heart of Halloween's contradictory set of appeals, it behooves us to consider this holiday's status as a nodal point in the nation's cyclical narrative of progress and regression; a kind of calendrical reminder that, for all the steps taken in the march toward social justice, the United States cannot outrun its demons or fully unshackle itself from its "original sin." Bentley (Paul Benedict), a white English character in the African American sitcom *The Jeffersons* (CBS, 1975–85), is not entirely incorrect when he muses (in the Halloween-themed episode "Now You See It, Now You Don't" [6.04]) that the things that he loves about the holiday—"the goblins, the monsters, the ghouls"—are "what America is all about." But there is also something disingenuous or at least misleading about Bentley's statement, insofar as his monstrous references to this darkest, most deathly of celebrations obscures a deeper truth about the United States, a nation that (to quote the editors of *YES! Magazine*) was "built on the back of slavery and racism."

The philosopher-journalist Barrett Holmes Pitner states that many Americans like to believe in the "inevitable progression toward racial equality" (something that *The Jeffersons*, a comedy about "moving on up," not to mention the 2008 presidential election of Barack Obama, fed into).[12] Because of this they are unprepared for those times when the nation takes a "step backwards" (which Pitner identifies as Donald Trump's 2016 victory). The commentator, like so many others who have written about the virulent spread of white racism in this country, believes that its citizens' "neglect of the past" have left them "unaware of the severity and scope of our racial tensions," which can be traced back at least to the 1600s (when the first slaves from Africa arrived in America).[13] Indeed, one would need to go back to the earliest years of the transatlantic slave trade to dig up the deepest roots of today's social problems and to begin piecing together a complete picture of television's monstrous imaginary. While something of that order is beyond the scope of my study, I take seriously the words of Derrick Johnson, President and CEO of the National Association for the Advancement of Colored People (NAACP), who, when asked about his opinions of Roseanne Barr following her May 29, 2018 tweet, remarked that it was "reminiscent of a horrific time in our history when racism was not only acceptable but promoted by Hollywood."[14] With that in mind, I wish to open up the historical parameters of this book, as we near the end, to include not only a brief discussion of real-world horrors and racialized fear-mongering, but also a few references to American motion pictures, including the Universal monster movies of the 1930s that would later influence the visual style and underlying themes of *The Addams Family* and *The Munsters*.

It Came from the East: Empire and Orientalism

> Your panic is perfectly understandable . . . Anyone who saw a sea serpent would be terrified.
>
> —The Professor (Russell Johnson) to Gilligan (Bob
> Denver), who claims to have come face-to-face with
> a monster, in a Season One episode of *Gilligan's
> Island* (CBS, 1964–67)

As W. Scott Poole, author of *Monsters in America: Our Historical Obsession with the Hideous and Haunting*, has argued, the monster is not just a rhetorical figure in the United States, a symbolic shorthand for all that has (internally) afflicted or (externally) assailed its citizenry since its Founding Fathers formally severed ties to Great Britain in 1776 (a history that conveniently overlooks the actual horrors visited upon indigenous people through European colonization, beginning nearly three centuries earlier). For Poole, "monsters are *real*," not just "interesting word pictures," insofar as "the metaphors of the American experience are ideas hard-wired to historical action."[15] He lends credence to this claim through copious references to the monstrous imaginary being invoked by English settlers for the purposes of justifying their own terrorizing "enslavement and oppression of native peoples."[16]

That particular social imaginary—that collective mental picture of the New World "as a landscape of horror" (filled with flesh-eating cannibals and other demonic figures who would be brought to their knees by "civilizing" forces)—extended not only to the racist folklore concerning indigenous tribes but also to that of African Americans. The latter's subjugation at the hands of white colonizers and slave-owners is not just a matter of historical record, but also an enduring palimpsest of past crimes against humanity, made all the more relevant in light of recent reports about police brutality and deadly violence directed against Black men and women in Baltimore, Baton Rouge, Ferguson, New York, and other US cities. As Stephen T. Asma argues, "The myth of the black monster has had a prosperous career in the twentieth century, first in the Jim Crow era of public lynchings, then in the reactions to the civil rights struggle, and now in the well-known statistics that one in every twenty black men over the age of eighteen is incarcerated in the U.S. prison system."[17] Past and present are thus brought into uncanny, uncomfortable alignment through the conjuring of real and rhetorical monsters; i.e. those who perpetuate hatred and embody the worst aspects of US exceptionalism versus those on the receiving end of violent acts who, ironically, are deemed "deserving" of such fear and loathing by dint of their constructed otherness.

With tentacles "wrapped around the foundations" of US political history, the monster "draws its life from ideological efforts to marginalize the weak and normalize the powerful, to suppress struggles for class, racial, and sexual liberation, [and] to transform the 'American Way of Life' into a weapon of empire."[18] For these reasons, Poole maintains, the monster resonates as something more than mere metaphor; as a living representation of our otherwise carefully concealed darkness. Certainly, one could point toward a number of historically reverberating incidents in which either interracial or cross-species encounters, veiled in mystery and lent a supernatural aura, contributed to setters' and colonists' fear of human or nonhuman "monsters" (including the so-called "paranormal disappearance" of Sir Walter Raleigh's Roanoke colony in the 1580s). However, the author's best example—the first of many in his book—serves as a useful entryway into a discussion of alterity, celebrity, and the ultimately self-destructive desire to destroy others that not only characterizes Roseanne Barr as both subject and object of public ridicule and scorn (the subject of my previous chapter), but also informs our understanding of the larger social imaginary under consideration in this chapter.

Specifically, Poole cites the now-little-known case of public frenzy resulting from the sighting of a sea serpent off the coast of Gloucester, Massachusetts in August of 1817. As described in *Monsters in America*, that widely reported event led to intense speculation about the creature's possible "meanings" as well as semi-satirical broadsides taking aim at a credulous community of whalers and fishermen who, like flounders inside a net, were swept up in the mass hysteria. Spotted by hundreds of eyewitnesses not once but twice (on two separate days) in the Gulf of Maine, the beast became a topic of conjectural conversation after the *Boston Daily Advertiser*, the *Salem Register*, and other newspapers printed stories of its tremendous size (appearing to measure at least 150 feet in length). The mythic proportions of the monster only grew in the ensuing years, becoming more metaphor than flesh for those who wished to question the logic of people acting inhumanely—becoming monsters themselves—in opposition to difference. Its "many-headed" multi-meaningness as a symbol for everything that threatened the wellbeing of New Englanders (including the recently passed Embargo Act, which had been worrying maritime entrepreneurs at the time of the monster's sighting) makes the thing especially "monstrous," a messy tangle of interpretative possibilities. What is most disturbing about the Gloucester sea serpent, besides its polysemic excessiveness and ultimate unknowability as a signifier, is the speed and eagerness with which would-be-heroes—harpoons at the ready—rushed to kill it. Indeed, destroying the massive animal "was the community's first priority" upon learning of its existence. That fact underscores a recurring theme in the paradoxically regressive story of American progress, demonstrating a "civilized" people's willingness to tame or eradicate the other and thus restore social order through "savage," socially destructive means.

This historical anecdote might seem to have little relevance to the televisual case studies under consideration. However, a number of network programs from the recent and distant pasts have mobilized "sea monster" imagery as part of their representations of racialized fear, highlighting the enduring legacy and viral spread of that New England legend. Take, for instance, "So Sorry, My Island Now" (1.15), an episode from the first season of Sherwood Schwartz's *Gilligan's Island* (CBS, 1964–67).

This episode begins with Gilligan (Bob Denver) fishing for lobsters in a lagoon of the remote Pacific island where he and six other castaways have been awaiting rescue after their charter boat (the S.S. Minnow) veered off course months ago. Up to his chest in the water, the scrawny first mate makes a speedy exit from the lagoon once he comes face-to-face with a sea serpent, which he then frantically describes to his captain the Skipper (Alan Hale Jr.) and the island's resident scientist The

8.1. Gilligan comes face to face with a one-eyed sea monster—
actually, a small submarine piloted by a Japanese sailor who is
unaware that World War II has ended—in this episode of *Gilligan's Island*. © Gladasya Productions

Professor (Russell Johnson) as having "one big eye" and a "long neck . . . covered
with green things." The Professor, who was not around to witness the monster,
calmly informs Gilligan that his panic is a reasonable response to the terrifying
thing that he *thinks* he saw. "Then how come everybody's standing around here
like I didn't see one?" Gilligan asks, to which his more level-headed island companion replies, "Because you *didn't* . . . There is no such thing as a sea serpent.
Sailing men from time immemorial, in Norse legends, in Greek mythology, in
Phoenician times, all thought they saw things that *didn't exist*." The Professor's
words, gesturing back to historical antecedents predating the supposed sighting
at Gloucester in the early 1800s, fail to allay Gilligan's fear, which is revealed to
be both unfounded and well-founded once the lagoon's "beast"—a small peri-
scope-equipped submarine occupied by a Japanese soldier—takes to land in pursuit of prisoners of war. Unaware that the Second World War ended nearly twenty
years ago (owing to a broken radio and transmitter), the sailor is stuck in time, and
the manner in which he is portrayed (by the Italian American character Vito Scotti
in "yellowface") is similarly outdated, a relic from Hollywood's racist past that was
somehow deemed permissible during the 1960s (this, of course, is not surprising to
anyone who has studied the history of Asian and Asian American representations
in US film and television, or simply watched Mickey Rooney's equally offensive
take on Mr. Yunioshi in that decade's *Breakfast at Tiffany's* [1961]).

8.2. Italian American actor Vito Scotti plays the Japanese sailor in "yellowface," presenting this racialized Other as a monster to be feared by the all-white community of shipwrecked islanders. © Gladasya Productions

From the sonic orientalism that musically announces this unwanted guest's otherness (when he opens the submarine hatch to reveal his face, poking up from the water) to the manner in which Vito Scotti performs the character's pidgin English through large prosthetic buck teeth (which, along with his squinted eyes and thick coke-bottle glasses, completes this wartime caricature), "So Sorry, My Island Now" is grotesque on many levels. Although his one-man submarine is mistaken as a one-eyed monster from the deep, it is *he*—the occupant inside who violates the Caucasian Americans' Edenic space of racial harmony—who is clearly made out to be both a mysterious beast from the East and a hot-headed brute (despite his diminutive size). One by one, he captures Mr. and Mrs. Howell (Jim Backus and Natalie Schafer), Ginger (Tina Louise), Mary Ann (Dawn Wells), and The Professor, forcing them into bamboo cages that he has somehow managed to construct during his brief time on the beach. When asked by The Professor how he concocted the makeshift brig, which is booby-trapped with hand-grenades, the Japanese soldier says that he stole the idea from a John Wayne movie—a humorously ironic take on the educational value of WWII propaganda pictures. Eventually, though, Gilligan and the Skipper assume John Wayne's heroic role and rescue their friends while their captor dozes in a tree, letting his bayoneted rifle slip from his grip. Once he awakens and makes a hasty exit, the Japanese villain pilots his submarine "like he's drunk" (to quote the Skipper), but in fact "he not have glasses on" (to quote Gilligan, who has stolen the man's eyewear and now imitates his pidgin English).

As Walter Metz notes in his monograph on *Gilligan's Island*, "So Sorry, My Island Now" is reminiscent of the Warner Bros. cartoon *Bugs Bunny Nips the Nips* (1944), one of the most notorious examples of wartime propaganda in which racial epithets like "monkey face" and "slant eyes" are directed against visually deformed stereotypes of the East Asian other. But its farfetched story is also rooted in reality. There were several actual instances of "Japanese soldiers continuing to fight on remote Pacific Islands long after the war was over."[19] While it harkens back to the past and touches on the theme of war-related trauma, this episode reveals something about the time in which it was made and the mindset of those creative personnel—including series creator and producer Schwartz—responsible for such an indefensible representation. Originally broadcast on January 9, 1965, this episode was notably followed by a similar, albeit shorter, example of onscreen Orientalism one month later, when "Follow That Munster" (1.23), from the first season of *The Munsters*, aired on CBS stations.

Although *The Munsters* attempts to reposition monstrosity as a positive alternative to the representational uniformity that had already come to define the situation comedy, this particular episode features a brief image of Herman Munster (Fred Gwynne), who moonlights as a private detective to supplement his pay from the funeral home where he works, dressed in a traditional Chinese costume and performing Orientalist tropes in a way that rivals the grotesquerie of Mickey Rooney's Mr. Yunioshi. Through huge buck teeth, Herman—wearing a mask upon his own Frankenstein monster visage—mouths the words, "Me no peeping tom, me number one detective" as he intrudes upon a young Caucasian couple's first attempt at a kiss in the park, sending them scampering away in fear. Poking his head out from a bush, the character appears to be a weird mixture of Charlie Chan, Mr. Moto, and Fu Manchu, bringing together the "good" (morally upright) and "bad" (evil) embodiments of Asian and Asian American screen roles made famous during Hollywood's Golden Age of the studio system era (1930s–1940s).

Such problematic throwbacks to the US motion picture industry's past, and to the larger history of insensitive portrayals of racial and ethnic minorities (which predates film and television), make these episodes of *Gilligan's Island* and *The Munsters* symptomatic of the general failure to culturally enact the sociopolitical ideals of equality and inclusivity that would be enshrined that same year in the Hart-Celler Act (better known as the Immigration and Nationality Act of 1965). Abolishing previous decades' restrictive national-origin quotas, this watershed piece of legislation, signed into law by President Lyndon B. Johnson, was especially relevant to Asian Americans, who had grown weary of seeing themselves

8.3. Masks upon masks—or the metatextual layering of performance—is a trademark of *The Munsters* and other television comedies pivoting on monstrosity as a social imaginary. Here, actor Fred Gwynne (who plays a Frankensteinian creation named Herman) sneaks up behind a necking couple in the park wearing the guise of an Oriental detective, complete with stereotypical buckteeth and squinted eyes barely visible behind thick glasses. © Kayro-Vue Productions

reflected in cultural productions as second-class citizens. The passage of the Hart-Celler Act "ushered in a new era of mass immigration" that, in the words of Erika Lee, was "qualitatively different from earlier periods both in terms of volume and in terms of ethnic makeup."[20] Specifically, people from Asia and Latin America, including family members reuniting with loved ones after decades of living apart from one another, assumed a prominent position in what she calls "the racial restructuring of U.S. society" throughout the 1970s, 1980s, and 1990s.[21]

Originally aired on March 11, 1965, just two weeks after the broadcast of "Follow That Munster," the final episode of the Hanna-Barbera animated adventure series *Jonny Quest* (ABC, 1964–65) gave audiences yet another look at a monstrous figure from the East; one that, like *Gilligan's Island* before it, suggests a racially tinged updating of the Gloucester sea serpent legend. Titled "The Sea Haunt" (1.26), the episode begins with the captain of a Dutch freighter, the Star of Borneo, which is carrying precious cargo on the Java Sea, being set upon by a large amphibious creature. High above, seated in a jet plane headed for Sumatra, the eleven-year-old title character (voiced by Tim Matheson), his scientist father (voiced by Mike Road), and the rest of the Quest team receive a radio message informing them to be on the lookout for the disabled ship. Spotting the abandoned freighter below, special agent "Race" Bannon (voiced by Mike Road) lands the plane on its deck, and within minutes of their arrival they find large footprints that Dr. Quest attributes to a "sea-going dinosaur." Soon thereafter, they flip through the pages of the ship's log to glean details about the mysterious creature, a "strange and awful thing," according to the captain, whose written description of the beast ("body covered with scales . . . huge glassy eyes [and] superhuman strength") fill Jonny and his young friend Hadji (voiced by Danny Bravo) with dread. Committed to killing "this monstrous evil," the captain was ultimately unable to protect his crew (who either died or fled on lifeboats), though he did manage to safeguard the "top secret" cargo down below, which Bannon refers to as "what's left of [the Dutch] empire." Before we are granted a view of that cargo—a collection of coffin-shaped crates containing gold bars—the characters come face-to-face with the ship's one remaining crewmember, a Chinese cook named Charlie (voiced by Keye Luke) who has been hiding inside a walk-in ice box. Wielding a large kitchen knife to protect himself from what he calls a "dragon," Charlie switches from Mandarin to pidgin English, telling them that the thing only comes out at night and appears to be afraid of light.

Though a man of science, Dr. Quest is just as prone to rely upon the language of fantasy as the Chinese cook is, calling the creature a "cross between a manticore and a hippocampus . . . two mythical monsters with the heads of one animal, the bodies of another, and tails of fishes or reptiles." Viewers who are familiar with science fiction and horror films of the Cold War era might instead see the thing as a kind of "missing-link" mix of Godzilla and the Creature from the Black Lagoon, two lumbering icons of 1950s cinema that would influence subsequent cultural productions in the decades that followed. Regardless of the name that we might give it, this monster is a slippery signifier of irreducible alterity, something than no one will believe actually exists unless the heroes either capture it or take its photograph. Although they eventually contain the threat and escape with their lives, they fail on those other two counts, as the sea monster slithers back "to the depths from which it came" and Hadji had his thumb over the camera lens at the crucial moment of recording its existence. Throughout it all, Charlie, a "good" Asian, serves rice and fortune cookies to the globetrotting heroes and their orphaned,

8.4. Alerted to the presence of a giant dinosaur-like monster in the Java Sea, the heroes of *Jonny Quest* board a seemingly unmanned ship and stumble upon a Chinese cook. © Hanna-Barbera Productions and Screen Gems

Kolkata-born sidekick (who complains about having to eat the same food he left behind in their previous destination, Singapore). As an infantilized figure of comic relief who is also shown bumbling and stumbling around the ship before falling overboard, Charlie ultimately has to be fished out of the sea by his white saviors. Barely escaping death in the shark-infested waters, the cook, gripping onto the side of the freighter, thanks his "honorable ancestors" and says something that reveals a great deal about the cultural anxieties surrounding "fresh-off-the-boat" foreigners in the lead-up to the 1965 Immigration and Nationality Act: "I should *never* have left my homeland. I should *never* have come to sea. I know better *next time*. By the great Buddha, I know better."

In his study of primetime animation, M. Keith Booker discusses *Jonny Quest* as both a product of the Cold War and a reworking of Milton Caniff's action-adventure comic strip *Terry and the Pirates* (1934–73), which likewise fell prey "to Orientalist stereotyping."[22] In many of the episodes that preceded "The Sea Haunt," the series—created by comic book artist Doug Wildey—gave its heroes multiple opportunities to be small-screen versions of British superspy James Bond, jetting from one exotic, Third World locale to the next in search of adventure. And they did so while continually foiling the maniacal plans of Asian criminal master-mind Dr. Zin, a mad scientist descended from the Mongol Khans (and voiced by white actor Vic Perrin). The recurrence of this "Yellow Peril" villain complements the long string of *other* monstrous others that would appear throughout *Jonny Quest*, from the giant lizards of "Dragons of Ashida" (1.14) to the Himalayan yeti of "Monster in the Monastery" (1.25). At one point in "The Sea Haunt," Jonny says, "All we have to fear is monsters themselves," and his linguistic reworking of Franklin Roosevelt's famous inaugural-speech line sums up the public paranoia surrounding a supernatural, otherworldly threat that was beginning to assume more recognizably human features in popular culture texts. This final episode of the series can therefore be read as the culmination of a "beasts from the East" motif discernible within other TV programs made prior to 1965, as well as a throwback to the mass hysteria that resulted from a creature's sighting off the coast of Gloucester, Massachusetts a century and a half earlier.

Frankenstein's Munster and the Meaning of Mobs

> Great shades of Satan! A lynch mob!
>> —Gomez Addams (John Astin), upon hearing a group of teenagers outside his house screaming for Lurch (Ted Cassidy), the Frankensteinian butler-turned-rock star, in a Season One episode of *The Addams Family* (ABC, 1964–66)

Not coincidentally, the ultimately unsuccessful search for that legendary sea serpent at Gloucester, which spilled over into the following year (when the monster's notoriety as a topic of reportage and scientific inquiry was further amplified through essays, fiction, and poetry), coincided with the initial publication of Mary Shelley's *Frankenstein; or, The Modern Prometheus* (1818). The latter text has done more than any book, before or after, to establish the central yet vulnerable place of the monster in the English-speaking world's popular imagination. Fittingly for an epistolary narrative about the creation of a lumbering, eight-foot-tall fiend, its cultural footprint is deep and wide, and the book's perennial status can be partially attributed to the many "hideous progenies"—theatrical dramatizations, cinematic adaptations, and televisual spoofs—that Shelley's late-Gothic novel has spawned over the years.

Foremost among them is Universal Pictures' 1931 production *Frankenstein*, a film that, along with the same studio's *Dracula* (1931), kicked off that decade's horror craze and lent visual expression to ideas which had earlier been consigned to the page. One theme in particular—society's rejection, expulsion, and eventual destruction of the monstrous Other—is especially pronounced in director James Whale and screenwriter John L. Balderston's version of the story. The film builds toward a climatic confrontation between the titular scientist's unholy invention (played by Boris Karloff) and an angry mob of villagers whose literally incendiary actions in those concluding scenes would have been eerily familiar to anyone who had witnessed racialized violence firsthand, outside the movie theater. Indeed, as the torch-toting residents of the European village set fire to the old mill where the monster has fled (dragging his grave-robbing master, Henry Frankenstein [Colin Clive], with him), one is struck by these images' similarity to real-world attacks against vulnerably positioned ethnic and religious minorities in the years immediately preceding *Frankenstein*'s theatrical release. Despite its foreign setting, the American subtext of this cinematically rendered narrative is clear, and likely would have been transparent to audiences in the early 1930s, for it hints at the lynch-mob mentality that had encroached upon and stolen the lives of those who were too often conceived as "monsters" by the white majority. As such, the beast that is this film's fleetingly beating heart is not unlike the sea serpent that had engendered a desire for violence within a small Massachusetts community over a century earlier.

Naysayers who doubt or question the "racial resonances" of Shelley's story and, especially, Whale's big-screen version of it need only to consult Elizabeth Young's 2008 study *Black Frankenstein: The Making of an American Metaphor*, which makes a convincing case for the patchwork monster's malleability as a symbol of both US foreign policy and domestic race relations.[23] As the title of her book suggests, Frankenstein's monster—though "described as yellow in the novel, painted blue in nineteenth-century stage incarnations, and tinted green in twentieth-century cinematic ones"—bears the accumulated weight of African American history.[24] But, as Young acknowledges, on its square shoulders also sit the problems of the working poor, the unemployed, the homeless, and other unfortunate targets of mass vilification who, inside and outside the African American community, had been rhetorically coded as "monsters" well before the privations of the Great Depression made them wards of the nation-state. Indeed, social class as well as race informs our understanding of this cobbled-together aberration who, clothed in the rags of an impoverished day-laborer and vocally reduced to a primitive assortment of guttural utterances, embodies the objectifying tendencies of early twentieth-century eugenics. It is worth pointing out (as the cultural historians Susan E. Lederer and Angela Smith have done in their respective studies of the subject) that, years before cameras began rolling on the 1931 Universal production, Shelley's creature had appeared in political cartoons as a symbol not only of "mob rule and violence" but also of "the working class, the uneducated, and the Irish."[25] Discourses both complementary and contradictory thus jostled against one another during the latter half of the nineteenth century, eliciting a range of irrational responses that are strangely similar to the knee-jerk condescension coloring twenty-first-century attitudes toward socially marginalized people.

To be sure, Frankensteinian figures of speech, including those that evince a slippage between monster and monster-maker, are not limited to such issues. They also frequently pop up in scientific discourses (including "discussions of stem-cell research, cloning, cosmetic surgery, and genetically modified foods"),[26] not to mention everyday talk in which people express fear or ambivalence over the prospect of giving birth to things that might one day take on lives of their own and usurp or destroy their creators. But the special salience of this late-Gothic tale—or, rather, the Depression-era cinematic retelling of it—as a sadly timeless commentary on racialized violence and class warfare stands out in light of the "the genealogy of Black Frankenstein stories" that Young and other scholars have uncovered. Drawing a line from the insurrectionary rhetoric of *The Confessions of Nat Turner* (1831) to Herman Melville's abolitionist short story "The Bell-Tower" (1855) to the writings of Frederick Douglass (who, in 1860, famously remarked, "Slavery is everywhere the pet monster of the American people"), critics have begun closing the historical gap between the original *Frankenstein* and its most famous offshoot, a film that not only crystalized the image of the title character's monstrous creation but also generically recast the "American iconographies of race, rape, and lynching" that had been established sixteen years earlier, in D. W. Griffith's *Birth of a Nation* (1915).

Elizabeth Young is not alone in sensing a connection between Universal's *Frankenstein* (as well as its 1935 sequel, the same studio's *The Bride of Frankenstein*) and that silent-era historical epic directed by Griffith. The latter motion picture, set during and after the American Civil War (with lengthy passages showcasing the "heroic" efforts of the Ku Klux Klan to suppress the primal urges of former slaves in the Reconstruction Era), has been widely derided as a racist fantasy, a morally repugnant "foundational myth of the monstrous black rapist" that planted the seeds for subsequent stereotypical depictions of African American men. Robin R. Means Coleman has noted *The Birth of a Nation*'s "racialization of Blackness as horror," pointing toward the film's infamous "Grim Reaping" sequence, in which Gus, a lascivious freedman (played in blackface by Walter Long), pursues Mae Marsh's white damsel-in-distress Flora in hopes of making her his bride.[27] Foaming at the mouth and filthy in his tatters, this swarthy ex-slave (whose ruddy complexion and bulging eyes are accentuated through the Caucasian actor's theatrically overdramatic onscreen minstrelsy) conjures a racially charged social imaginary as well as a vision of the working poor whose body bears the brunt of labor's physical tolls. In many ways, the chase sequence in Griffith's film, which leads to Flora's death (the result of her suicidal fall from a cliff) and to a white mob descending vulture-like on Gus, anticipates the monster's dogged pursuit of female victims in Universal's *Frankenstein* and *Bride of Frankenstein*. His is a desire that, according to the racist tautology of the text, must be suppressed if the taboo of miscegenation is to be respectfully observed and rigidly enforced.[28]

Although *The Birth of a Nation* does not fit conveniently into the horror film genre and can be categorized more accurately as a wartime melodrama, its construction of the monstrous Black buck as a source of dread for white America would filter into a variety of cultural productions in later years, becoming a dominant trope in the racist imagining of US history. However, an ironic outcome of this film's initial popularity (as the first motion picture to be screened in the White House) and subsequent reevaluation of its artistic achievements (following its 1992 inclusion in the Library of Congress's National Film Registry) is that it has come to be seen as a "catalyst for the rebirth of the monstrous white nation as a whole" (famously, *The Birth of a Nation* is often referred to as a "recruitment tool" for white supremacy hate-groups like the KKK, neo-confederates, and neo-Nazis).[29] That is, mob mentality rather than the misunderstood outsider came to be seen as the lynchpin for societal ills, a shift in public perceptions—detectable in everything from Fritz Lang's early social problem film *The Fury* (1936) to Don Siegel's Cold War science fiction film *Invasion of the Body Snatchers* (1956)—that did not necessarily entail a complete, welcoming acceptance of others, sympathetic though the latter often are in cinematic and televisual narratives from the mid-to-late twentieth century. One sign of the larger culture's realignment of sympathies—its recalibration of mainstream attitudes vis-à-vis representations of monstrous alterity—was the emergence of TV series such as *The Addams Family* and *The Munsters*, which each took parodic potshots at the suburban myths of inclusion and the good life perpetuated by earlier all-white domestic sitcoms of the Eisenhower era.

Limited space prevents me from fully unpacking these programs' subversion of cultural norms and embracing of nonconformity as a theme that would gather steam over the course of their short (two-season) broadcast runs. However, it behooves us to consider the role that *The Addams Family* and *The Munsters* played in complicating the received wisdom concerning the monster as the ultimate outsider, someone whose "invasion" of a racially homogenous, socially harmonious space—that of the idyllic suburbs—brought with it the associated threats of mob-like behavior on the part of mainstream Americans. Cultural critic Laura Morowitz offers up one of the most compelling portraits of the titular families populating these TV series, which debuted in the midst of a "monster craze" that had begun sweeping across the nation a few years earlier. Before the two programs' first episodes aired on network affiliated stations in the fall of 1964, Screen Gems (a television subsidiary of Columbia Pictures) had packaged dozens of Universal horror films for the purposes of bundled syndication, and the resulting program, marketed as *Shock Theater,* became "an overnight sensation" in Philadelphia and New York in 1957 and 1958, respectively.[30] Those same years brought a legion of low-rent, high-concept motion pictures like *I Was a Teenage Werewolf, Attack of the Crab Monsters* (1957), *The Blob* (1958), *The Fly* (1958), and *Fiend Without a Face* (1958), in addition to more prestigious, if salacious, offerings from England's Hammer Films, including *The Curse of Frankenstein* (1957) and *Dracula* (1958). James Warren and Forrest J. Ackerman's hugely influential magazine *Famous Monsters of Filmland,* described by one historian as "porn for monster fans,"[31] was launched in February of 1958. Besides paving the way for subsequent publications like *Fantastic Monsters of the Films, Castle of Frankenstein, Horror Monsters,* and *For Monsters Only, Famous Monsters of Filmland* helped to make potentially dangerous content "safe" for America's youth, just as Harvey Kurtzman and Al Feldstein's equal-opportunity offender *Mad* magazine was doing for teenagers and young adults immersed in the world of US politics and popular culture more generally. By the time Bobby "Boris" Pickett's novelty song "Monster Mash" reached #1 on the Billboard Hot 100 chart in the last weeks of October 1962 (becoming the unofficial soundtrack of that and subsequent years' Halloween celebrations), the country had been sufficiently groomed for the comically inflected doom that seemed to infect every aspect of Cold War media culture, becoming an indelible part of big-screen and small-screen horrors, from Stanley Kubrick's 1964 pitch-black political satire *Dr. Strangelove or: How I Learned to Stop Worrying and Love the Bomb* to that same year's *The Addams Family* and *The Munsters.*

Morowitz alludes to the "broader context of 'monster' culture" in which the latter two examples of the mid-1960s "magicom" subgenre (which would also include *My Favorite Martian* [CBS, 1963–66], *Bewitched* [ABC, 1964–72], *My Living Doll* [CBS, 1964–65], and *I Dream of Jeannie* [NBC, 1965–70]) were produced. But she, like Helen Wheatley (author of *Gothic Television*), also asserts the need to look back at the previous decade's family-oriented domestic sitcoms (or "domcoms"), such as *Father Knows Best* (CBS, 1954–55, 1958–62; NBC, 1955–58; ABC, 1962–63), *Leave It to Beaver* (CBS, 1957–58; ABC, 1958–63), *The Adventures of Ozzie and Harriet* (ABC, 1952–66), and *The Donna Reed Show* (ABC, 1958–66) as important televisual touchstones whose generic formulas and visible signs of "clean" and "healthy" living (e.g., waxed floors, spotless kitchens, manicured lawns, etc.) would be tweaked by those literally and figuratively dark, freak-populated programs. As Wheatley summarizes, the nostalgically imbued domcoms of the 1950s—an almost mythic yesteryear that was never truly as conflict-free as some TV fans might believe or wish it to be—presented viewers with a "cavalcade of bombastic fathers, hapless mothers and brattish children, getting into 'scrapes' that were resolved by the end of each episode."[32] Doubly conservative in terms of promoting social hierarchies and endorsing stereotypical gender roles while emphasizing the need to return to a state of "normality" or equilibrium by narrative's end each week (an implicit privileging of the status quo), the aforementioned shows taught audiences what it meant to be a *particular type* of American—a white middle-class Protestant American—throughout the postwar and Cold War years. And yet, on occasion, they flirted with nonconformity and highlighted the appeals of Halloween-related "thrills and chills," as when—in an episode of *The Donna Reed Show* that aired on October 12, 1961—Jeff (Paul Petersen), a suburban teenager excited to watch a horror film on TV, proclaims "I love monsters!"

The very suggestion that adolescents and teens might come into contact with potentially dangerous ideas thanks to the 1960s monster craze, exacerbated by peer pressure and against the wishes of their parents, is broached in "Sweatshirt Monsters" (5.35), a fondly remembered episode of creators Joe Connelly and Bob Mosher's *Leave It to Beaver*. Originally aired on June 2, 1962, this episode revolves around young Theodore Cleaver (Jerry Mathers), also known as "the Beav," and his pals Richard (Rich Correll), Whitey (Stanley Fafara), and Alan (Mark Murray) making a pact to wear their recently purchased novelty sweatshirts—each graced with a gruesomely ghoulish face—to school the next day. Emblazoned on the Beav's shirt is a monster with three eyeballs, the sight of which very nearly makes his prim and proper mother, June (Barbara Billingsley), clutch her pearls. "What in the world is *that*?" June asks, unable to make heads or tails of her son's beastly attire. Though he does not answer her question directly, the Beav tries to ease his mother's worries by telling her that "all the guys got one," a remark that ironically suggests that one type of "mass think" (that of adolescent consumers of pop culture collectively buying into a fad) might stand in opposition to another (that of white middle-class adults who would like their children to look and behave a certain way).

The next morning, the boy's father, Ward (Hugh Beaumont), who tells his wife that he is "looking forward to a very serene and orderly day (though, as he grumbles, that "probably means there will be one crisis after another"), sternly informs the Beav that he cannot wear the monster sweatshirt to school. When his son complains that his friends will be wearing theirs, Ward responds in a way that associates the monstrous with the *barbaric*, saying "You're going to school wearing something *civilized*." In a plot development that would be repeated countless times in subsequent stories about teenagers sneaking past parents and trying on new identities outside their homes, the Beav leaves that morning sporting a "normal" button-up shirt, but on his way to school he removes it to reveal the "abnormal"

8.5. In "Sweatshirt Monsters," an episode of *Leave It to Beaver* revolving around midcentury "mass think" and parental concern over the wellbeing of juveniles, a group of young boys agree to wear their latest clothing purchases to school the next day, to the dismay of their teachers and other finger-wagging adults. © Gomalco Productions

clothing beneath. Staged in this way, the potential for "uncivilized" behavior is shown to be lurking just below the surface of even the most respectful of teenagers, whose outwardly conservative appearance or deferential attitude toward figures of authority masks feelings of discontent that find figural expression in the hideously deformed face of the monster.

Once he arrives at school, the Beav sees that his friends have not held up their end of the agreement (as a result of their strict parents doing much the same that his mom and dad had done), and have shown up wearing regular shirts, making his monstrous outfit all the more conspicuous. Stepping into the classroom, he is greeted by the sound of laughter, as his classmates—including Richard, Whitey, and Alan—appear to mock his decision to violate the school's dress code. His teacher, too, takes a disapproving view of this commotion, sending the student to the principal's office. Ward, who accurately predicted a crisis that day, receives news of his son's disruptive activity. Soon thereafter, the "law of the father" comes down swiftly on the Beav, who is forced to leave school early and is given a good scolding in Ward's study. Pointing his finger at his son, Ward tells him that "a thing is either *right* or it's *wrong* and if it's wrong in the first place then it's still wrong, no matter how many people do it." He rephrases that sentiment two days later, during the Beav's weekend-long punishment (when he is forced to stay inside his bedroom), saying in a less agitated tone, "Just remember this: wrong is *wrong*, even if everyone says it's right, and right is *right*, even if everyone else says it's wrong." This prescriptive, black-and-white morality, ostensibly meant to encourage free thought on the part of a young person, enforces a strict definition of good and bad behavior, with the latter ironically being associated with the kind of group think or mob mentality that makes boys like the Beav stick to their social scripts and keep their monstrous sides hidden from public view.

If not exactly "radical," the monster-filled magicoms that followed the 1963 cancellations of *Father Knows Best* and *Leave It to Beaver*, most notably *The Munsters* (which was also produced by Connelly and Mosher), expanded the boundaries of what an "acceptable" nuclear family might look like. And they did so by openly revealing that monstrous underbelly of suburban life that is otherwise hidden inside the bedrooms of America, as well as by directly confronting the xenophobic, "protectionist attitudes" of neighbors who do not take kindly to outsiders or strangers. Statements like "We don't want them wandering over here, if you know what I mean," and "This was a nice neighborhood until *they* moved in," carry overtly racist connotations, and are frequently spoken in the next two case studies under consideration, typically by older members of all-white communities who see the residences of the Addams and the Munsters as eyesores, blots on the suburban landscape, not unlike the monstrous sweatshirt worn by the title character in *Leave It to Beaver*.

In situating their characters not within the sprawling ranch houses of their televisual predecessors or their actual neighbors (where glistening appliances and handsomely attired suburbanites might entice the eye), but inside cobwebbed mansions cluttered with "old world" tchotchkes and other decorative debris, *The Addams Family* and *The Munsters* signaled an unusual approach to ethnic identity and social class. Indeed, as Morowitz points out, "In their preference for the old, the Gothic, the claustrophobic and overstuffed interiors of another age, the shows mount a challenge to the spotless, commodified domain of the suburb," something that would occur years later in TV's ostensibly creature-free but no-less-messy or kitsch-littered homes of working-class Americans, from the Bunkers to the Conners. If the economically challenged characters in such multi-camera sitcoms as *All in the Family* (CBS, 1971–79) and *Roseanne* sometimes behave "monstrously," acting out in ways that conform to longstanding stereotypes about the offensive tackiness or lowbrow vulgarity of working-class Americans, then the actual monsters who inhabit the cramped interiors of these more fantastical magicoms of the 1960s paved the way for such metaphorical associations. And they did so through the literal embodiment of longstanding fears about interethnic mixing and social passing, something enacted with regularity throughout the two-season run of *The*

Munsters whenever "normals" cross the threshold, from exterior to interior, and first encounter the residents of 1313 Mockingbird Lane inside their dilapidated home. Moving from the foyer, past "worn wall coverings" and "sagging couches," into the "dusty velvet parlor" where Herman, his wife Lily (Yvonne De Carlo), his werewolf son Eddie, and Grandpa (Al Lewis) sit like smiling arachnids awaiting their prey, the series' supporting characters—who, ironically, are turned into outsiders by virtue of this spatial arrangement—evince in their own stunned reactions an inability to comprehend the Munsters' "de-evolved, primitive, bestial" characteristics.

The first example of this recurring element can be seen seven minutes into Season One's "Munster Masquerade" (1.01), an episode in which a wealthy young man named Tom (Linden Chiles) pays a visit to Marilyn Munster (Beverley Owen), Herman and Lily's "black sheep" niece (a blonde-haired WASP in her early twenties who is distinguished by her paradoxically "ugly" beauty). The premise of this initial entry in the show's episodic storyline revolves around a masquerade party being thrown by Tom's parents, the influential and powerful Dailys. Ensconced within their elegantly appointed high-rise penthouse, the older couple extend a written invitation to their son's love interest and, begrudgingly, to her extended family. Having never met them, the Dailys are naturally curious and somewhat nervous to see what the oddly named "Munsters" will bring to their members-only social gathering. When Marilyn's suitor, attired in the garb of a Mayflower pilgrim (his get-up for the Halloween-style party), steps into their crumbling, multi-leveled Victorian mansion, he reacts with a mixture of confusion and shock. So too does the second outsider to enter this space, the elderly babysitter who has been hired to watch Herman and Lily's lycanthropic son while they attend the masquerade dressed in their own telling costumes (he as an armor-clad King Arthur, she as a not-so-little Bo Peep). These are the first of several such scenes in the series when "normal" people, indicative of the oppressive conformity that surrounds and indeed threatens the Munsters, can be seen as trespassers invading on *their* territory; a humorously macabre inversion of the traditional conception of monstrosity as that which menaces mainstream society.

When Herman, Lily, and Grandpa finally arrive at the Dailys' apartment, they are greeted at the door by Tom's mother (Mabel Albertson). Her Marie Antoinette outfit sharply contrasts Grandpa's centuries-old Napoleon get-up, but the funniest bit of complementary contradiction comes when we see Mr. Daily (Frank Wilcox) dressed as Frankenstein's monster. His shabby, flea-bitten jacket is in keeping with the spirit of earlier incarnations of the creature (particularly Karloff's), but differs considerably from the host's normally neat appearance (as seen earlier in the episode). Standing next to Herman, whose own Frankensteinian visage has

8.6. Herman wins first prize in a masquerade contest in the first episode of *The Munsters*, though the other revelers mistakenly think that he is wearing two costumes: one (that of a Frankensteinian monster) under another (that of a knight's suit of armor). © Kayro-Vue Productions

been hidden behind a mask, Mr. Daily's made-up monster suggests the show's underlying themes of "role playing and false appearances." As Morowitz notes in her reading of "Munster Masquerade," the "real" is "no less a false façade . . . than the costume," something hinted at when one of the party guests, seeing Herman remove his armored face plate to reveal his monstrous features, remarks that "He's wearing one mask under another mask." Of course, the unsuspecting revelers do not perceive Herman's "true" nature, nor do they react with the fear or revulsion that one would expect to witness in such encounters. Instead, they award Herman first prize in their costume contest, handing him a bottle of champagne as excessively large as his own ungainly body.

Only in the episode's final scene, when Tom revisits Marilyn's family, does the young man actually see them for whom they really are, out of their costumes.

As if struck by a bolt of electricity, Tom jolts in apprehension, his eyes and mouth agape, his pilgrim's wig standing on end. Then, in a flash, he runs out the front door, bringing "Munster Masquerade" full circle by calling back to the episode's first scene, set outside the entrance of their house (near the overgrown garden that surrounds it, much like a white picket fence might in more traditional sitcoms). Notably, it was during that opening scene when viewers were first shown the building's exterior, presented from the vantage of someone who, not yet acquainted with the quirky denizens inside, stands before the front door waiting to be let in—an early sign that *The Munsters* will concern itself with the literal and figurative crossing of boundaries.

This episode—the first of seventy to be aired over *The Munsters'* initial broadcast (not counting two unaired pilots)—anticipates the Halloween-themed storylines that would become such a staple of other television comedies' fall seasons, including those of *Roseanne*. Despite originally airing on September 24, 1964, rather than during the final week of October, it contains many of the elements that one might expect to see in All Hallows' Eve–style celebrations on American TV, from the gathering of costumed strangers to the themes of mimicry and mistaken identity that take on additional meaning in the context of suburban neighborhoods or other environments where social barriers are transgressed.[33] Although Connelly and Mosher did not produce any "official" Halloween episodes during *The Munsters'* two-year run, Grandpa would break out his Napoleon outfit near the end of the first season, as part of his attempt to scare away a home-wrecking company preparing to level the family's house. In "Munsters on the Move" (1.27), he dons his masquerade costume from the pilot episode and fires a cannon at the bulldozer parked in front of their residence, but it misfires (the same "goof," Grandpa says, that he made at Waterloo 150 years earlier). It is a truly revolutionary act, hard to imagine on any traditional domestic comedy set in the suburbs. Thankfully, Herman arrives on the scene just in time, striking fear in the hard hats. A cooler head prevails, with one of the men telling his coworkers that this is "just another one of those Halloween makeups to try to get us off their backs." Rather than scare off the men, though, Herman takes the moral high road, using words that one can imagine Ward Cleaver speaking in Connelly and Mosher's *Leave It to Beaver*, when he tells Grandpa that "right is right" and that the wrecking company, which bought the house, has a legal right to tear it down. "You can't just go around aiming a cannon at everybody without having anarchy. And anarchy is violence. And violence is . . . very naughty," he says, providing a striking contrast to the men's description of this strangely attired family as "radicals [who] will do anything to get their picture in the paper."[34]

Won't You (N)t) Be My Neighbor?:
(Un)Gracious Hosts and Animated Monsters

> Well, there goes the neighborhood.
>
> —Barney Rubble (voiced by Mel Blanc), seeing the
> mountain-shaped house of the ghoulish Franken-
> stones (the latest additions to the prehistoric city of
> Bedrock), in *The Flintstones' New Neighbors* (1980)

Not long after its September 18, 1964, debut, *The Addams Family*, a TV comedy based on the New Yorker cartoons of Charles Addams, offered up its own Hallow-een-themed episode, simply titled "Halloween with the Addams Family" (1.07). In it, two bank robbers fleeing cops on foot are mistaken as adult trick-or-treaters by the main characters, who—ever the gracious hosts—invite them into their home and proceed to scare them witless. The thieves, Claude (Don Rickles) and Marty (Skip Homeier), initially believe the members of the Addams family to be dressed for the holidays. However, in trying to remove the nonexistent mask from man-servant Lurch (Ted Cassidy)'s face, they realize that their get-ups are "real." That word is uttered on several occasions throughout this episode, beginning with a scene showing Gomez trying to capture the essence of Uncle Fester (Jackie Coo-gan) in sculptural form, using his new knife to carve the bald man's likeness into a pumpkin. "Are you sure you're getting the *real* me?" Uncle Fester asks, to which Gomez, whittling away at the jack-o-lantern, responds by assuring him that he seeks to convey "the real, the true, the unadorned you." Such dialogue, along with the robbers' later amazement at the *realness* of this kooky-looking bunch, works to put flesh on the monstrous imaginary, to bring what would otherwise be a meta-phor into actual existence as something tangible. It is one thing to speak of mon-sters, to dream them into being. But physically touching the face of one (as Marty does when trying to see if Lurch is real) is another thing altogether; an uncanny encounter that invites us to imagine ourselves—our fleshy selves—as objects of fear. Ultimately, these two increasingly panicked thieves would prefer being taken away by the police (who show up at the residence during a patrol) than to endure another minute in the company of these oddballs for whom Halloween is a very special time of the year.

Like its rival on CBS, *The Addams Family* generated laughter from the sight of so-called "normals" stepping into the main characters' home and quickly turning on their heels to leave once the strangeness of the place and the eccentricity of its inhabitants come into full view. We see this, for instance, in the first episode of the series, "The Addams Family Goes to School" (1.01), which begins with a truancy officer, Mr. Hilliard (Allyn Joslyn), arriving outside the gate of their mansion on Cemetery Lane. He has come at the request of the Sherwood school board since Gomez and Morticia's two children—Pugsley (Ken Weatherwax) and Wednesday (Lisa Loring)—have not yet enrolled in classes. Even before Mr. Hilliard sets foot inside the house, the eeriness of the setting impresses itself upon him, thanks to a sign on the fence that reads "Beware of the Thing" and a gate that opens and closes on its own. Through him, our onscreen surrogate, we are given a tour of the building's interior, as Wednesday leads the man past the polar-bearskin rug in the foyer and the half-cocked moose-head that hangs above the fireplace to one of her distant relatives, Cousin Farouk (or, rather, his remains as a victim of a swordfish attack). Additional oddities spring up, including Morticia's carnivorous plant Cleopatra, an African strangler that snakes around their nervous guest's neck before he is escorted to Gomez's "train-wreck" playroom. From there he is redirected to the dungeon-like guest room, where the children's uncle and grandmama (Blossom Rock) are throwing knives at a devil statue. This is the last straw for the man, who—like so many of the other outsiders who will enter into the Addams's domain—screams before fleeing in terror. "Weird, isn't he?" Gomez says to Uncle Fester, a line that Morticia will echo near the end of this episode (after Mr. Hilliard has returned to and left their home): "Such a weird little man."

Although it reverses the terms that are typically used to delineate between normal and abnormal behavior, *The Addams Family* nevertheless retains those terms and keeps that reductive binary intact. In doing so, it presents an either-or set of options that is in keeping with the "good vs. bad," "self vs. other" dichotomies that are at the heart of the monstrous imaginary. Tellingly, this pilot episode builds toward a scene in which Gomez and Morticia confront the truancy officer about the "violent" literature that their children have been forced to read at school, including Grimms' fairy tales in which "poor defenseless" dragons are slain by knights and "sweet old ladies" (i.e., witches) are pushed into ovens by "juvenile delinquents."[35] At one point, Gomez even refers to himself and Morticia as "ordinary citizens." This is the first of many instances throughout the series when their ordinariness—though surrounded by architectural and decorative oddities (e.g., the foghorn doorbell, the hangman's noose butler bell, the giant two-headed tortoise, etc.)—is propped up against the weirdness of everyday people, including those who refer to their house as a "creep joint" (in the episode "Green-Eyed Gomez" [1.08]) and as a "madhouse" (in the episode "Wednesday Leaves Home" [1.10]), but who behave in ways that suggest that *they* might belong in a sanitarium.

For instance, in "Morticia and the Psychiatrist" (1.02), Pugsley's parents, like so many other fathers and mothers in more traditional sitcoms, worry that their son has taken up extracurricular activities that might lead to deviant behavior. Their notion of "deviancy," of course, is markedly different from that of the Andersons or the Cleavers, reflecting a need to steer Pugsley away from his newfound interest in joining the Boy Scouts, playing baseball, and raising a puppy through the help of a child psychologist, Dr. Black (George Petrie) (hired because his name "sounds friendly"). In the end, the doctor, who has misunderstood the Addams's request, quits his profession and appears in need of psychiatric evaluation himself. Although their definition of "normal" differs considerably from what situation comedies of the past promulgated, the couple's method of restoring their ten-year-old son to a life of deadly play (with his pet octopus, with a guillotine, inside a mineshaft, etc.) makes them seem quite ordinary as exemplars of parental concern for the wellbeing of a child. Along the same lines, in the episode "The New Neighbors Meet the Addams Family" (1.09), soon after a newlywed couple—"typical" to their core (as young, middle-class white characters)—moves in next door, the word "monstrosity" is spoken by the blonde woman as she peers through the window at the Addams family's residence. A similar dismissal drips from the lips of the raven-haired Morticia, who—upon meeting the couple and learning that, now on the verge of madness, they want to break the lease—says, "We have ourselves some very *peculiar* neighbors." Variations of that line are spoken by characters who detect a similar peculiarity in the Addams family's behavior, suggesting that Gomez and Morticia are just as prone to judge people based on their perceived eccentricities as the latter are.

That theme carried over into the next adaptation of American cartoonist Charles Addams's *New Yorker* drawings, an animated program produced by Hanna-Barbera and televised throughout the autumn of 1973. Simply titled *The Addams Family*, this animated sequel to the live-action series differs from the original in its use of the open road, sending the creepy, kooky, mysterious, spooky, and altogether ooky protagonists (some of whom were voiced by actors from the previous series) far away from their house on Cemetery Lane. Over a single season, the group travels by RV to such destinations as Nashville, New Orleans, New York City, and way out West, where they follow the trail of the nation's "great pioneers," including Wyatt Burp and Silly the Kid. Pitched at a younger demographic than its black-and-white predecessor had been, this colorful set of cross-country excursions was programmed by NBC executives to air on Saturday mornings, rather than during prime time; meaning that its messages about tolerance, inclusivity, and the need to see past another person's physical appearance fell on younger eyes and ears. But it was not the first animated kids' program to tap into the monstrous imaginary, having been preceded by *Scooby-Doo, Where Are You!* (CBS, 1969–70), *Groovie Goolies* (CBS, 1970–72), and *The Funky Phantom* (ABC, 1971–72), in addition

8.7. In this episode of *The Addams Family*, Gomez and Morticia meet their new neighbors, who look on in amazement when they are given a tour of their unusual house and who, ironically, are judged to be the "strange" ones by the usually open-minded protagonists. © Filmways Television

to episodes of Hanna-Barbera's best-remembered, most commercially successful work from the 1960s, *The Flintstones* (ABC, 1960–66).

This latter riff on sitcom formulas, a precursor to *The Simpsons* (Fox, 1989–present) in many ways, is set during a highly fantastical version of the Stone Age, and thus tends to generate humor through the anachronistic incorporation of modern-day concerns (like urban sprawl) and mid-twentieth-century technologies within a world inhabited by cavemen (who ironically do not live inside actual caves) and dinosaurs (who somehow coexist with humans). However, throughout its six-season run on primetime television, *The Flintstones* occasionally introduced scientifically inclined or supernaturally endowed minor characters whose monstrosity became a source of consternation for the prehistoric protagonists. For instance, "Monster Fred" (5.02), which aired on the same night of *The Munsters'* debut

(September 24, 1964), features a mad scientist named Dr. Frankenstone (voiced by Allen Melvin) who subjects our unlucky hero Fred (voiced by Alan Reed) to an experimental mind-transfer operation to cure him of his baby-babbling and amnesia (brought about by a bowling accident). The procedure succeeds in allowing Fred, a boisterous throwback to *The Honeymooners'* Ralph Kramden (Jackie Gleason), to swap personalities and voices with his wife Wilma (voiced by Jean Vander Pyl) and his superstitious pal Barney (voiced by Mel Blanc), suggesting a kind of intersubjective access to other people's interior lives that makes empathy possible. But any suggestion that Fred might become better attuned to the feelings of his friends and loved ones is undermined at the end, once Dr. Frankenstone returns his mind to its proper body. "Thank goodness we're all back to *normal*," Wilma says to her best friend Betty (voiced by Gerry Johnson), a reference to the sitcom's most prominent structural feature: return to the status quo. Despite reverting back to a "normal" state of affairs, however, Fred's string of bad luck continues, as seen in this episode's final scene, in which he is tormented by a vampire whose vehicle has run over his foot.

Indeed, more creatures awaited the Flintstones in the episodes that followed "Monster Fred," including spectral apparitions and his (presumably) dead uncle's ghoulish-looking servants in "A Haunted House is not a Home" (5.07), which aired two days before Halloween in 1964. The Flintstones' most obvious spoof of *The Addams Family* and *The Munsters*, which were themselves parodies of earlier domestic comedies, came two weeks later, when "The Gruesomes" (5.09) aired. Taking its title from the name of a family that moves in next door to Fred and Wilma, this episode provides the clearest example of sitcom characters revealing prejudicial attitudes toward new arrivals within their community. Even more so than the 1980 TV special *The Flintstones' New Neighbors*, which revolves around Fred and Barney's worry that their houses' property values would decrease now that a family of "spooks," the Frankenstones, have moved next door, "The Gruesomes" offers contemporary viewers a vital glimpse into the racialized fear that infiltrated so much of the popular culture being produced at the height of the monster craze. From its first scene, which takes place at Bedrock Realty (where the hearse-driving monsters are looking to buy a haunted mansion), until its final scene, which shows these new residents of the dilapidated Tombstone Manor, Weirdly (voiced by Howard Morris) and Creepella (voiced by Naomi Lewis), staring out their window at their "odd" neighbors Barney and Fred, this episode pivots on the question of whether space can be made to accommodate individuals who do not look or act like the majority of people within a racially homogenous community.

Like Gomez and Morticia before them, Weirdly and Creepella call out the peculiarities of average folks (saying things like "We always manage to get odd neighbors" and "Why is everyone else in the world so odd?"). But unlike their black-and-white predecessors, these characters are marked as "different" from everyone else around them as a result of their physical traits, including their skin color, not to mention their radical departure from conventional standards of beauty. The Gruesomes' abject ugliness, though literally cartoonish, brings to mind theories of the monster as both abnormal and unnatural. Though, like the animal, the monster is believed to be "closer to nature" and farther removed from "culture" (which might explain its modern-day allure to audiences who envy its freedom or lack of restraint), it does not accord with human notions of aesthetic form and therefore strikes us as something that is aberrant. Michel Foucault argued that the form of the monster is "a violation of the laws of society [and] a violation of the laws of nature. Its very existence is a breach of the law at both levels." The French philosopher elaborated this in a lecture on the subject of abnormality, saying that "the monster is the limit, both the point at which law is overturned and the exception that is found only in extreme cases. The monster combines the impossible and the forbidden."[36]

Importantly, several narrative elements in "The Gruesomes" highlight the dichotomy between natural and unnatural abominations, including the fast-grow-ing watermelon seeds that Barney plants (and which spring up immediately) and the storm cloud that hovers over the Gruesomes' moving van, which prompts Fred to muse, "Nature has many strange secrets." With shaggy mop top, fangs, and dark green skin, the Gruesomes' short patriarch, Weirdly, is not obviously "raced" in any way, nor does his thin, long-nosed wife seem to have any clear ethnic identity. But their freakish otherness is partially conveyed through the animators' chromatic tools, making their initial exclusion from the Bedrock community a sign that the bigotry on view in this episode is only skin-deep. Only after the Flintstones look past the surface and adopt a more gracious attitude toward Bedrock's latest arrivals (as Wilma does when she invites Creepella to the school's PTA meetings) are they able to live up to the "Love Thy Neighbor" credo that Barney quotes, and which appears to be this episode's main "message." Ultimately, though, the messages being sent by this and other examples of monster TV are as contradictory as the turns-of-phrase spoken by the Gruesomes in the episode that bears their name. At various points, we hear Weirdly refer to various people and things as being "delightfully morbid," "beautifully rundown," "nauseatingly gracious," and "revoltingly nice," and the manner in which adverbial "badness" or "goodness" is conjoined to its adjectival opposite hints at the paradoxical appeals of the monstrous imaginary.

At once attractive and disgusting, frustrating and comfortably familiar, the monster continues to exert sway over the minds and bodies of today's TV audi-ences, be it the funny type of frightmares on view in comedies like *Holliston* (FEARnet, 2012–13), *Santa Clarita Diet* (Netflix, 2017–19), and *What We Do in*

8.8. As recurring avatars of otherness on the primetime animated hit *The Flintstones*, Weirdly Gruesome and his family of strangely colored monsters were figures of combined derision and fear during the mid-1960s, often bringing out the worst, most xenophobic (and borderline racist) behavior in their Bedrock neighbors Fred and Barney. © Hanna-Barbera Productions and Screen Gems Television

the Shadows (FX, 2019–present) or the scary sort featured in supernatural dramas like *The Vampire Diaries* (The CW, 2009–17), *Grimm* (NBC, 2011–17), and *Sleepy Hollow* (Fox, 2013–17). One contemporary show, creator Devin Clark's *Ugly Americans* (Comedy Central, 2010–12), taps into the textual affordances of animation to bring forth a wide assortment of fantastical creatures, spread out over several ethnic enclaves of New York City; or, rather, an alternate version of that culturally mixed metropolis where the main character—a human social worker named Mark (voiced by Matt Oberg)—works for the Department of Integration. Though he is frequently stymied by government bureaucracy, Mark's job entails helping otherworldly "immigrants" (e.g., blobs, demons, pigeon-headed birdmen, etc.) acclimate to life in the United States, where anti-monster sentiments still run high, four decades after the end of the Zombie War of 1968. In the episode "Blob Gets Job" (1.04), he accompanies his zombie roommate Randall (voiced by Kurt Metzger) to the latter's hometown in New Jersey, where he is eventually "outed" to his parents (including his dad, a zombie-killing veteran of the war who did not know that his son was a member of the walking dead).

While seated in a Jersey diner, the two men—one undead, the other living—discuss the prejudice that most monsters face whenever they leave the melting pot

8.9. Seated at a New Jersey diner, human social worker Mark and his zombie roommate Randall—two of the main characters in the animated cult comedy *Ugly Americans*—discuss the anti-monster hysteria that has swept through the country and led otherwise peaceful, law-abiding citizens to take up arms against those who are literally demonized because of their physical differences. © Augenblick Studios

that is New York City and venture into America's rural areas (where everything, even a zombie's gait, is slower). As they do so, a group of flesh-eating ghouls can be seen in the background, through the window of the diner, and the manner in which they are destroyed by rifle-toting humans (as if it were a game) visibly upsets Mark, who has spent much of his young adult life trying to protect nonhumans. It is a thought-provoking yet gruesome scene—one of many in *Ugly Americans*—that attaches the titular hideousness not to monsters but to those who would destroy or demean (or, more to the point, *demonize*) them. At once forward-thinking in its racial politics (if not its sexual politics) and retrograde in its reliance on long-established tropes, this is just one of many recently produced monster shows that is as contradictory as the "delightfully morbid," "revoltingly nice" TV families that preceded it.[37] Ultimately, in order to make sense of the current fascination with vampires, werewolves, witches, and zombies on American television, one might benefit from looking back at their forerunners from previous generations, if only to see how *fear of the other*—so deeply engrained in this nation's racist past—remains an indelible part of today's monstrous imaginary.

Beyond Bad and Evil

Finding TV's "Good Place"

> You take the good, you take the bad, you take them both and there you have
> the facts of life, the facts of life.
>> —lyrics accompanying the opening theme music of
>> *The Facts of Life* (NBC, 1979–88)

> I don't even know how to respond to that.
>> —Tig Bavaro (Tig Notaro), upon learning that
>> residents of her hometown have renamed Martin
>> Luther King Jr. Day as "Happy Great Americans
>> Day," in a Season Two episode of *One Mississippi*
>> (Amazon Video, 2015–17)

In a recent essay about her experience of growing up in a family of TV industry types (including her father, composer-screenwriter George Tibbles) and then, as a screenwriter herself, working on the production of Whitney Blake and Allan Manings's *One Day at a Time* (CBS, 1975–84), Christine Tibbles McBurney discusses a moment from her childhood when she was taken by her dad to the set of *The Munsters* (CBS, 1964–66). Although she had watched the show on her local CBS station in Los Angeles, Christine was amazed to see that Herman (Fred Gwynne), Lily (Yvonne De Carlo), Grandpa (Al Lewis), and the rest of the family members had blue-green faces, remarking that their "strange, pallid-color" gave them a "deathly glow." As if prompted by the memory of the actors' skin color (which was not discernible to viewers at home, since the show was televised in black-and-white), she muses that "the deep changes that were part of America (and the world)" at that time (during the mid-1960s) might have been "reflected in these stories of 'monstrous' families who just wanted to be loved and were loving and real inside their weird worlds." "Perhaps," the screenwriting veteran states, shows like *The Munsters* and *The Addams Family* (ABC, 1964–66) were "trying to capture the racism and sense of [the] 'other'" that have been "part of our culture from the beginning."[1]

In the previous chapter, I argued that these two sitcoms from the mid-1960s each reveal something about what it feels like for an individual to be discriminated against because of their appearance or behavior. They are shows about monsters, to be sure, living amongst people who wish to see them leave their communities or simply keep their eccentricities hidden from view. But they are also about ethnic and racial minorities whose own lives, culturally and institutionally marginalized yet subjected to surveillance and framed as a "threat" to white middle-class prosperity and security, have been tethered to a social imaginary that can turn deadly in a flash. And yet, one inescapable fact about these two programs is their near-total lack of African American representations, making them overwhelmingly white despite a preponderance of scenes promoting acceptance, inclusion, and the need to take pride in one's own divergence from mainstream societal norms. Such messages, ostensibly anti-racist, come at the cost of denying anyone who is *not* white a shot at the spotlight. As such, one might rightfully question my choice of those two texts as case studies in Chapter Eight, especially since more recent comedies, including creator Devin Clark's animated series *Ugly Americans* (Comedy Central, 2010–12), convey similar messages while at least featuring more diverse casts as well as more overt, taboo-shattering types of bad behavior. However, my intention in spotlighting *The Addams Family* and *The Munsters*, as well as other examples of 1960s programming in which literal and figurative monsters appear fleetingly in stand-alone episodes, was to underscore their centrality to the "monster craze" that partially defined that decade and to furthermore suggest the relevance of that historical context to the current problems faced by minorities in large cities and small towns throughout the United States.

Debuting on different networks within a week of one another in September 1964 (less than three months after President Lyndon B. Johnson signed the Civil Rights Act into law, officially prohibiting discrimination based on race, color, religion, sex, and national origin), these comedies "tapped into the zeitgeist" in a way that few other programs of that era did.[2] As media scholar Jason Mittell notes in his book *Television and American Culture*, the issues of racial integration and civil rights—though foregrounded in 1960s documentary and news images of African Americans' struggles to gain equality in the United States—were rarely broached in popular fictional programming during that decade. On the few occasions in which they were explored within televisual narratives, those issues tended to be "cloaked in allegories," as seen in *The Addams Family* and *The Munsters*, which frequently portrayed "the horrified reactions of white suburbanites [to] a family of friendly 'monsters,'" or what were sometimes referred to (by supporting characters) as "spooks."[3]

One episode of the latter series—"All-Star Munster" (1.17)—stands out for its allegorical suggestiveness as a text that positions Herman as a stand-in for an

African American man. In it, the 7'3"-tall head of the Munsters is mistaken for a basketball recruit at Marilyn (Pat Priest)'s college, which he visits in hopes of clearing up his "normal-looking" niece's tuition problem. Expecting a young man named "Moose" Mallory, who at one point is referred to as "a big dumb ape from the hills" of Kentucky (where he played high school basketball for six years), the Westbury College coach takes one look at Herman and salivates at the prospect of enrolling this athletic specimen on a basketball scholarship. Although he is confused by the coach's insistence that he hit the court before bringing up the subject of tuition with the dean, Herman goes along and demonstrates his skills during tryouts. Making one trick shot after another and dunking the basketball with ease in between showboating, he puts the other players on the court—all of whom are white—to shame.

C.1. In one of the clearest indications that *The Munsters* is allegorically concerned with the (mis)treatment of African Americans, the episode "All-Star Munster" depicts Herman as a "naturally gifted" basketball player whose talent would put an otherwise unremarkable all-white team of college players on the winning path (once he signs a contract and becomes their teammate). © Kayro-Vue Productions

Frantically putting a pen into Herman's hand, the coach tells him that he will "never have to worry about tuition again" once he signs the contract; something that our protagonist hesitantly does only to later regret once he learns about the *real* "Moose" Mallory, a lanky "hick" from the sticks whose socioeconomic status is lower than that of the Munsters. Significantly, when this white college recruit and his hillbilly pa first appear in this episode, arriving two hours late at the bus terminal, an African American woman can be seen behind the counter of a newspaper stand. Were it not for the fact that this is the only moment when a person of color appears in *The Munsters*, it would hardly be worth dwelling on. But her fleeting appearance not only calls attention to the conspicuous absence of anyone who does not racially fit within the show's narrow representational schema, but also reminds us that this episode is putting an allegorical spin on Herman's status

C.2. *The Munsters* can be said to revolve allegorically around the plight of African Americans and other ethnic groups whose racially marked difference is conveyed in the way that white suburban dwellers respond to the title characters. However, black men and women do not actually appear in the program, save for this fleeting moment, when one bystander is confined to the literal backdrop of a scene. © Kayro-Vue Productions

as an exceptional—exceptionally *exploitable*—means for the basketball coach to compete against teams with African American players and win state titles.

As suggested by the title of Charles Pinkney's 2017 book *From Slaveships to Scholarships*, black athletes have long been exploited by predominately white institutions of higher learning, which are part of a modern-day "plantation sports culture." The 1960s saw a significant increase in "the number of young black athletes being recruited to major universities on athletic scholarships to participate in football, basketball, baseball, track and field and volleyball." "For the most part," Pinkney states, "the black athlete was restricted by universities' unwillingness to integrate."[4] Much the same could be said about another institution at that time, television, which failed to measure up to the ideals enshrined in the 1964 Civil Rights Act and tended to limit actors of color, such as Kim Hamilton, Greg Morris, and Rockne Tarkington, to small supporting roles or simply use them as background extras in crowd scenes (as happened frequently in *The Dick Van Dyke Show* [CBS, 1961–66]). Such information helps us to fill in the historical context of "All-Star Munster," which notably aired on January 14, 1965, two days before a group of twenty-one African American players from the American Football League—protesting their unfair treatment by business owners—refused to play in an all-star game to be held in New Orleans. Perhaps it even helps to explain why Herman Munster became an internet sensation in the summer of 2020, over a half-century after he had first tickled America's funny bone as the father of a family of monsters.

In June of that year, only a few days following the tragic death of George Floyd at the hands of a Minneapolis police officer and in the midst of national protests in support of the Black Lives Matter movement, former NBA player Rex Chapman posted a video clip on Twitter that showed Herman offering words of fatherly advice to Eddie (Butch Patrick). In it, the Frankensteinian monster tries to console his werewolf son (who has been bullied at school for his small stature), instilling the lesson that "It doesn't matter what you look like. You can be tall or short or fat or thin, or ugly or handsome, like your father, or you can be black or yellow or white. It doesn't matter. But what does matter is the size of your heart and the strength of your character." Chapman's heavily retweeted clip, taken from the episode "Eddie's Nickname" (1.19), which originally aired two weeks after "All-Star Munster," quickly became viral and led several cultural commentators to weigh in on the contemporary relevance of Herman's words of wisdom. Most critics seemed to appreciate the positive effect that the video clip was having on social media users. Noting how "correct" those words were in the 1960s (and continue to be today), those Twitter users crowned Herman a "Civil Rights activist" and took personal swipes at Donald Trump (writing things like, "Today we learned Herman

Munster is a better role model and leader than the President of the United States").[5] Penning a think-piece for the *Washington Post*, Hank Steuver offered a rare dissenting opinion, emphasizing that this "vital lesson in self-worth and acceptance of others . . . doesn't quite get us where we need to be right now." As he states, "Celebrating Herman's simple wisdom," which equates race with appearance, "is an entirely too facile way of glossing over a moment in which America may at last be at a breakthrough with its own history."[6] Nevertheless, many people seemed to take pleasure in finding a "good place" in which to retreat from the "bad time" that was 2020.

One wonders how many of the Twitter users who celebrated Herman as the anti-Trump have seen "Big Heap Herman" (2.18), an episode from the second season of *The Munsters*. It begins with what looks to be a séance: Herman and his family—wife Lily, son Eddie, niece Marilyn, and Grandpa—sit around a table in a dark room lit by a single candle. With great solemnity he explains that he has summoned them on the stroke of midnight for an "annual Munster ritual," a tradition that has been in their family for over 100 years. Opening a ballot box on the table, he begins reading the results of a recent vote concerning their next vacation destination, one that will be "decided in the democratic manner; a fair, decent, honest American way." Seeing that his choice of Buffalo Valley has been beaten by "the beach," four votes to one, Herman forgets his earlier words about there being "no hard feelings" and throws a temper tantrum. "If I can't go to Buffalo Valley, I don't want to go anywhere," he pouts, before demanding a "recount." Using language that retroactively seems to have been lifted from President Trump's playbook, he intones gravely, "I say that this election was fixed. It's just not fair and it's nothing but a case of crooked politics." Finally, after Herman pounds his fist down on the ballot box until it breaks, Lily tries to soothe the savage beast, telling him that they will be going to *his* preferred destination rather than theirs.

It will perhaps come as no surprise that this 1966 episode originally aired on January 20, a day on the political calendar that marks Inauguration Day (which traditionally occurs every fourth year). Further strengthening the connection between this opening scene of a TV episode broadcast over fifty years ago and the closing chapter on the Trump administration's efforts to undermine democracy through baseless claims of voter fraud are the words that US District Judge Matthew Brann used to describe the president's challenge of Joe Biden's victory. Drawing upon a metaphor that has been useful in a variety of political contexts, Brann called Trump's legal efforts to prevent Pennsylvania state officials from certifying the results of the 2020 election (based on speculative accusations of vote rigging) "Frankenstein's Monster," one that had been "haphazardly stitched together" by a campaign desperate to retain control of the government's executive branch.

As I write these words, three weeks before the 2021 inauguration of Trump's successor, Joe Biden, I find myself reflecting back on the past four years, when much of the research and writing of this book took place and when the very definition of "bad behavior" seems to have changed considerably over a relatively short period of time. I also think about the many producers, showrunners, writers, and performers in the industry who have taken a stand against abuses in presidential power while telling stories about different communities throughout the United States having tough conversations about the beleaguered state of the nation. *One Mississippi* (Amazon Video, 2015–17), a semi-autobiographical comedy created by and starring Tig Notaro, exemplifies this trend. In its Season Two opener, "I Want to Hold Your Hand" (2.01), Notaro, who plays a slightly fictionalized version of herself (Tig Bavaro, a Los Angeles radio host recovering from illness and returning to her family home in rural Mississippi in the lead-up to her mother's imminent death), learns that the small-town residents of Bay St. Lucille and the neighboring city of Biloxi have changed the name of Martin Luther King Day. Now the national holiday will be referred to as "Happy Great Americans Day" because, in the words of one older white member of the community, "you know, it's Robert E. Lee's birthday as well." When another well-meaning but ill-informed lady tells her that she thinks that "it's right that they honor *both* sides," Tig responds with trademark irony, "You mean Good and Evil?"

The protagonist's deadpan remark, withering in its frankness, prepares us for another tense encounter later in the same episode, when her brother Remy (Noah Harpster), a Civil War reenactor, begrudgingly discusses the election of Donald Trump with a young Vietnamese woman on whom he has a crush. Their heated conversation, which takes place on a literal (yet fake) battlefield, is sparked by a rude comment made by another person taking part in the historical reenactment, a man who asks Vicky (Adora Dei), dressed as a Civil War nurse, "Why are you even here?" Telling her that "there weren't any Chinese people" involved in that conflict from the 1860s, the Southerner, also wearing period clothing, has to be corrected about his nation's history. Joking that his and Remy's characters must be "fucking concubines," the man walks away, beer in hand, leaving his friend to answer Vicky's question: "Why is he saying it *now*?" The woman, justifiably angry, answers her own question: "Because he has permission, now, to be racist." When Remy, stumbling over his words, suggests that he is able to look past his friend's faults just as she, a Catholic, is able to "overlook the bad parts" of her religion, Vicky maintains that the two are not the same and puts a question to him that was rarely asked in television comedies prior to 2016: "Who did you even vote for?" The two characters go back and forth, with Remy putting up his hands and telling her not to blame him (because he did not even vote in the election) and Vicky growing testier before she finally calls him "ignorant" for doing nothing "to stop a racist bully from becoming president." Though many fans of *One Mississippi* found "the disintegration of Remy and Vicky's relationship [to be] disappointing," the show has done right by those characters in framing their political discussion as a matter of great, perhaps existential, significance.[7] In this way, Notaro's program is noteworthy for its progressiveness in challenging those who would "honor both sides" or—restated as a Trumpism in the aftermath of the 2017 Unite the Right rally in Charlottesville, Virginia (a Confederate armaments stronghold during the Civil War)—those who acknowledge "very fine people on both sides."

The past four years (2016–20) have been especially good for American television audiences, if not for anyone else who—concerned about the general state of the nation at a time of domestic and international crises—might characterize both the behavior and policies of the former president as being incontrovertibly bad. As suggested by the titles of several recent comedies and dramas, including *Good Behavior* (TNT, 2016–17), *Good Girls Revolt* (Amazon, 2016), *The Good Doctor* (ABC, 2017–present), *The Good Fight* (CBS All Access, 2017–present), *Good Girls* (NBC, 2018–present), *The Good Cop* (Netflix, 2018), and *Good Trouble* (Freeform, 2019–present), TV writers and showrunners are foregrounding a range of positively valenced attributes at a time when such traits appear to be in short supply within the political sphere. Evoking everything from moral righteousness and virtue to the high standards of artistic quality or technical excellence that make certain things—including scripted TV shows—praiseworthy, the word "good" has become a recurring rhetorical figure in televisual fictions; not only as a titular reminder of the ethical conundrums faced by protagonists in the aforementioned programs, but also as part of characters' metaphor-drenched dialogue.

Nowhere is this more apparent than in NBC's critically acclaimed *The Good Place* (2016–20), a high-concept comedy series with dramatic undertones and supernatural flights of fancy that concerns a small group of people who, discovering that they have recently died and gone to the "bad place," strive to become better human beings—more caring, compassionate, and emotionally generous with their true feelings—in order to gain entrance to a decidedly nondenominational heaven. When I watched this show during its original broadcast, throughout the four-year Trump presidency, I could not help but notice the many utterances of the word "good" across several of this series' episodes. In many cases, the word is simply dropped into everyday conversations by the main characters to express their approval of something deemed satisfactory in quality, quantity, or degree (tasty food like Tom Yum Goong soup, grilled eggplant, frozen yogurt, etc.). But it also calls attention to deeds that are benevolent or kind, in addition to serving as a noun for anything that might conform to the moral order of the universe. In that sense, the habitual utterance of the word "good" encourages viewers to grapple with the question of what constitutes virtuous conduct (or what Tim Dant calls a "moral imaginary"); something that is either subtly suggested or openly broached by individuals who, across four seasons, embody the challenges involved in tamping down their own worst tendencies. Described by one critic as not just funny but "necessary" and "vital" as a seemingly far-fetched, afterlife-focused sitcom with demons aplenty, *The Good Place* delivers comforting yet incisive messages "about humanity and redemption," themes that have special resonance in an era of "deep existential dread."[8] But it does so with a critical reflexivity that has become increasingly common in contemporary cultural production, discursively framing its own relative "goodness"—its esteemed place among other examples of "prestige TV"—as a marker of quality that derives from contrasting traits.

Being "Good," Being "Frank"

> We've been asking the wrong question. What matters isn't if people are good or bad. What matters is if they are trying to be better today than they were yesterday.
>
> —Michael (Ted Danson) in a Season Four episode of
> *The Good Place*

Since its debut four years ago, *The Good Place* has racked up numerous critical accolades and industry awards in recognition of its narrative complexity, thematic depth, and groundbreaking audaciousness as a televisual text unlike any other. Though indebted to ABC's cult phenomenon *Lost* (2004–10) and to Jean-Paul Sartre's existentialist stage play *No Exit* (1944), this Emmy-nominated, Peabody Award–winning program created by Michael Schur is wholly unique, offering a humorous, philosophically astute meditation on the challenges of being a good person in an age of rapidly diminishing moral clarity; an era when the highest office in the nation's government is rife with toxic masculinity and racist fear-mongering, and when even the most upstanding citizens' best intentions—as consumers, as social media users, as voters—can have unintended, potentially harmful, consequences for themselves and others. Starring Kristen Bell, William Jackson Harper, Jameela Jamil, and Manny Jacinto as recently deceased individuals who must overcome their outward differences and embrace their common fate as posthumous pawns of demons in the afterlife, *The Good Place* is certainly willing to take risks in terms of departing from generic TV formulas and possibly alienating red-state viewers with its left-of-center perspectives on what ails the nation today.

Season by season, and with unforeseen twists occurring along the way, the series focuses on the occasionally combative but generally cooperative efforts of those four characters—Arizona salesperson Eleanor Shellstrop (Bell), Nigeri-an-Senegalese ethics professor Chidi Anagonye (Harper), Pakistani-British philan-thropist Tahani Al-Jamil (Jamil), and Florida-born amateur DJ Jason Mendoza (Jacinto)—to somehow make their way into the titular (secular) heaven that awaits only the most decent folks, despite a rigged point system. In doing so, and through an elastic time-travel narrative that partially allows them to wipe the proverbial slate clean, *The Good Place* offers valuable lessons on how to go about correcting for past mistakes while charting a path forward, toward a better and brighter future. Indeed, the show functions as a cheery (rather than dreary) form of pedagogical television, and not simply by spending so much time in the makeshift classroom that Chidi constructs for the sake of educating Eleanor. It does this also in the sense of introducing some of the core tenets and foundational principles of moral philosophy to audiences who might not otherwise have access to such teaching (notably, Schur has drawn upon the expertise of actual philosophy professors who vet the show's copious references to Aristotle, Hume, Kant, Nietzsche, and other great thinkers whose work—summarized on Chidi's blackboard—is not necessarily "dumbed down" for TV audiences).

The Good Place is not the first American television program to feature spoken references to those and other philosophers. Classic comedies of the 1950s and 1960s, from *The George Burns and Gracie Allen Show* (CBS, 1950–58) to *Hank* (NBC, 1965–66), include scenes in which the main characters occasionally pontif-icate on the fundamental nature of knowledge, reality, and existence, citing every-one from Socrates, Plato, and Aristotle to Spinoza, Kierkegaard, and Nietzsche. In the case of *Hank*, a campus comedy about a young man illegally auditing classes at the fictional Western State University (where he impersonates different students who are absent from class), highbrow name-drops occur within a college classroom, where philosophy professor Dr. McKillup (Lloyd Corrigan) guides the title char-acter toward a better understanding of himself and the world around him (much as Chidi does for Eleanor in *The Good Place*). But those references also occur "in the wild," outside of educational contexts, where individuals from different social backgrounds conversationally wrestle with weighty philosophical theories (as the gunrunning Irish terrorist Joe Devlin [Clive Revill] does in an episode of *Columbo* [NBC, 1968–78] when he opines about Hegel's definition of tragedy as a conflict between "right and right" rather than "right and wrong," and which the snobbish property manager Jonathan Higgins [John Hillerman] does in an episode of *Mag-num, P.I.* [CBS, 1980–88] when he speaks about "the virtues of dialectic versus symbolic syllogism"). Such moments, however, tend to exist solely as a means of establishing a character's educational training, mental prowess, and/or cultural sophistication, as sometimes occurs whenever Diane Chambers (Shelley Long)—a college graduate working at a bar in *Cheers* (NBC, 1982–93)—shows off her book smarts to her clueless coworker/lover Sam Malone (Ted Danson). In *The Good Place* (another series starring Danson, who plays the demonic architect with a heart of gold, Michael), Western philosophy is central to its underlying themes and is integrated into the unfolding narrative as something of substance (rather than as a superficial aside). And the range of its philosophical references, covering "everything from Jonathan Dancy's theory of moral particularism, to Aristotelian virtue ethics, to Kantian deontology," is unprecedented for an American TV comedy.[9]

Contractualist reasoning in the vein of T.M. Scanlon (whose 1998 collection *What We Owe to Each Other* has been called the show's "ur-text") is especially central to *The Good Place*'s depiction of human beings who bear a moral obligation to acknowledge the value of other people's lives (i.e., to recognize that they are, in the words of a sentient database called Bad Janet [D'Arcy Carden], "good and worthy of respect and not big fat sacks of dookie"). Indeed, the show's morality of "right and wrong" is superimposed atop its portrayal of "good" and "bad" versions of certain characters whose actions would be deemed *wrong*, according to Scanlon, "if a principle that permitted [those actions] couldn't be justified to the affected people in the *right* way."[10] For creator Michael Schur, boiling down "good behavior" and "bad behavior" based on the reason-giving force behind the moral judgment of an action's "rightness" and "wrongness" (relative to affected parties) is the starting point for a discussion of *empathy*, which he has said is the emotional "core" of his series.[11] Having "zero empathy," in other words, lands one in The Bad Place, the show's hellish version of an afterlife where damned souls are tortured endlessly by butthole spiders, nostril wasps, penis flatteners, and other horrors. However, Schur's claim about the empathetic basis for moral judgment does not always accord with his show's depiction of the many silly things that accrue "negative points" in a person's life and lead to eternal damnation.

For instance, having a vanity license plate, "like 'Mama's BMW,' 'Lexus for Liz,' or 'Boob Guy,'" is mentioned in Season One's "Most Improved Player" (1.08) as a criterion for badness, and in the same breath Michael names "murder, sexual harassment, [and] arson" as criminal offenses that are likely to lead one to The Bad Place. People who end up going there, he informs Eleanor (as part of her litmus test in that episode), run the gamut from concertgoers who have paid money to hear the Red Hot Chili Peppers' music to anyone who has taken off their shoes and socks on a commercial airline. Not many of these point-deducting items, save for the criminal offenses that often lead to other people's emotional, psychological, or physical harm, are really indicative of an empathy-based assessment of whether someone has behaved in a virtuous or unvirtuous manner. But by the end of the series, Michael's ideas about his role in the afterlife have "evolved" as a result of his

C.3. *The Good Place* functions as televisual pedagogy, instructing the audience not only how to grapple with weighty philosophical issues but also how to watch TV in a way that is sympathetic to those who have been labeled "bad" as a result of their past actions. © Fremulon and 3 Arts Entertainment

own spiritual growth, going from a demonic fire squid dressed in human skin to an actual flesh-and-blood human who has learned that changing a person's behavior can actually lead to an alteration in that person's moral fiber. Believing that people are capable of self-improvement, he and the other main characters enact the social contract that is central to the show's Scanlon-inspired philosophy and simply help one another, all while striving "to be better today than they were yesterday."

"Humans are b-b-b-bad to the bone," Bad Janet tells Michael in "A Chip Driver's Mystery" (4.06), citing "wars, murders, women in $400 yoga pants . . . refusing to vaccinate their children, [and] vindictive nerds at Apple . . . changing the charger shape again." But, as a personal assistant designed to serve—and mouth the faulty wisdom of—the Eternal Beings of The Bad Place, she is a part of a system that is inherently binaristic, and therefore would not be able to grasp Eleanor's point (articulated near the end of Season One) that "this whole good/bad system is bull-shirt." "There should be a *medium* place for people like me," the female protagonist says, meaning people who kind of sucked, but in, like, a fun, chill way." Television, it turns out, *is* that medium place, one that "is not inherently good or bad," as critics have argued since its earliest days *as a medium*, but rather a complex mixture of different orientations to the larger world that is reflected in its programming.

As the authors of the 1992 study *Big World, Small Screen: The Role of Television in American Society* argue, TV shows "often contain social stereotypes, violence, and other content selected for its immediate appeal to a targeted 'market' of buyers (not viewers) rather than for its utility to a wide range of groups in the society." But people are just as likely to pick up "prosocial forms of behavior" (e.g., "cooperation, helpfulness, sympathy, negotiation in conflicts, and persistence when things get difficult") as they are antisocial forms of behavior, and scholars should be wary of blaming television for societal ills that have been part of the American experience since before the medium's emergence in the 1940s and 1950s.[12] Throughout this book, I have tried to steer clear of media effects models that underline television's "positive" and "negative" influence on viewers. However, it must be said that viewers' use of programming as a source of potentially transformative entertainment and/or education should be kept in mind by scholars looking to study the medium's role in shaping social imaginaries.

In writing this book about classic and contemporary television comedy, I have found inspiration in several trailblazing studies of the medium that have done just that, including David Marc's *Comic Visions: Television Comedy and American Culture* (1989), Darrell Hamamoto's *Nervous Laughter: Television Situation Comedy and Liberal Democratic Ideology* (1989), and Joanne Morreale's edited collection *Critiquing the Sitcom: A Reader* (2002), as well as recently published work on satires and sitcoms that, in their own ways, are just as pioneering as the canonical texts that preceded them.[13] The latter include Michael V. Tueth's *Laughter in the Living Room: Television Comedy and the American Home Audience* (2005), Doyle Greene's *Politics and the American Television Comedy: A Critical Survey from "I Love Lucy" Through "South Park"* (2008), Christina von Hodenberg's *Television's Moment: Sitcom Audiences and the Sixties Cultural Revolution* (2015), Rosie White's *Television Comedy and Femininity: Queering Gender* (2018), and Alice Leppert's *TV Family Values: Gender, Domestic Labor, and 1980s Sitcoms* (2019).[14] Though the "baby" of the bunch, Leppert's book has already contributed much to a better understanding of how previously overlooked or critically disparaged programs, such as *Gimme a Break* (NBC, 1981–87), *Silver Spoons* (NBC, 1982–86), *Webster* (ABC, 1983–87), *Charles in Charge* (CBS, 1984–85, first-run syndication, 1986–90), *Who's the Boss?* (ABC, 1984–92) and *Mr. Belvedere* (ABC, 1985–90), not only reflected the shifting social landscape but also modeled new feminine and masculine ideals (including the "working mom" and the "domesticated dad") during the Reagan era. It, like Mary Ann Watson's more expansive study *Defining Visions: Television and the American Experience in the 20th Century* (2008), thus makes the case that "the medium did much more than just hold up a mirror" to society. In the words of Watson, television's transformative power can be discerned in the way that it provides "social scripts" through which citizens derive "lessons" about what the world outside their domestic sphere "expects from them."[15] Domesticity itself, once an impenetrable shell in the sheltered lives of so many 1950s TV families (e.g., the Andersons, the Cleavers, the Stones, etc.), was opened up or perforated by new possibilities in the 1980s, according to Leppert, whose analysis—a deft blend of textual and contextual decoding of the aforementioned shows (whose relatively progressive attitude toward issues of parenting and childcare is matched by their self-consciousness as metatextual works *about television-viewing*)—served as a guiding light for my own analysis of TV shows that, in their own ways, are like funhouse mirrors, reflecting a paradoxically distorting truth about ourselves and the world around us.

Tellingly, that "funhouse mirror" image, besides popping up in TV comedies like *The Addams Family* (which, in one episode, shows Lurch [Ted Cassidy], a butler modeled after Frankenstein's monster, standing before his own oddly squashed and elongated reflection, looking at it as if it were a stranger), also infuses the critical discourse around certain programs. This is apparent in much of the online commentary surrounding *The Good Place*, which the *AV Club*'s Erik Adams refers to as a "funhouse mirror version of our stupid world" and which *Entertainment Weekly*'s David Canfield singles out as the definitive "funhouse refraction" of the situation comedy genre.[16] Jack Katz, who in 1999 wrote about the "funny mirrors" often found in amusement parks, noted that humor, "while 'natural' to this setting, is far from inevitable in [that] it points to the work that visitors must do in order to construct their emotions."[17] According to Katz and other sociologists who have been influenced by his work, in order for people to take pleasure in the "hyper-elongated" or "fat and squat" versions of themselves contained in a concave or convex surface of that kind, "it is necessary to build a dynamic tension between a person as depicted by the mirror and that person's presumptively normal identity" (which might be farther from that person's "true self" than the monstrous reflection, or, in Katz's words, "the many-headed creature"). Laughing thus emerges from the "interactional pressure" unique to social groupings like families (his main subject of study) and is a way of "turning oneself inside out." "Laughing together," Katz concludes, "family members can hold fast to the conviction that they share a common experience, seeing the same things despite the world's tricky powers of distortion, knowing who each really is despite the monsters each may seem to be in the eyes of others, even as they wander about, for long stretches isolated from each other, in a world of cold, bizarrely reflecting surfaces."[18]

Rereading his words, I am struck by how applicable they are to the idea of television comedy as a mirror-like means for audiences to see themselves as someone else; an image that, in its grotesqueness, can elicit laughter but also fear at what we have become. In this light, I am reminded of one particularly noteworthy episode of a TV show well-known for its characters' outrageous, antisocial behavior. Originally broadcast on February 10, 2016, "Being Frank" (11.06), from the eleventh season of *It's Always Sunny in Philadelphia* (FX, 2005–12; FXX, 2013–present), has been described as "one of the most depraved episodes in the show's history," which is another way of saying that it is one of the most depraved episodes in US television history.[19] In it, Danny DeVito's perpetually frazzled character Frank deals with a string of hostile people and dangerous, potentially life-ending events over the course of a single day, from his angry landlord demanding rent payment and a gang of muscle-bound men accosting him outside a roller rink, to a near-overdose on drugs prior to attending a shiva and his unwitting involvement in a scheme to illegally retrieve an impounded Range Rover. On the surface, that brief synopsis—"wild" by the standards of more relaxed or comforting televisual fare—does not seem all that different from most of the other storylines in this pitch-black comedy about "horrible people" doing "horrible things." Indeed, far worse things have transpired over the show's 154 episodes, including earlier instances when the main characters—Dennis (Glenn Howerton), Dee (Kaitlin Olson), Charlie (Charlie Day), and Mac (Rob McElhenney)—reveal themselves to be "morally bankrupt" both inside and outside the confines of Paddy's Pub (e.g., bribing and kidnapping a newspaper critic who wrote a scathing review of their Irish bar; poisoning the owners of a rival bar; recording a jihadist video in hopes of saving the bar; encouraging underage drinking in the establishment in order to drum up sales; breaking into and destroying other people's homes; impersonating police officers and throwing a Molotov cocktail into a cop car; scamming the IRS by having a funeral for a fake baby; attempting to trigger a soldier's PTSD; forcing their former high-school classmate Rickety Cricket [David Hornsby] to sell cocaine for them and getting him addicted to drugs in the process, etc.).

What sets "Being Frank" apart from other episodes is its use of point-of-view (POV) shots that put us "inside the skin" of the show's oldest, most hedonistic character. In fact, the entire episode is presented from Frank's ocular perspective, forcing us to look at the world through his drug-addled eyes and barely conscious mind. It begins with him struggling to get to his feet one morning after a night of drunken revelry (signified by the Mardi Gras beads near his bed that, initially blurry, gradually come into focus once he puts on his glasses). The shaky handheld camera wobbles as he waddles over to the "toilet," which is really just a couple of paint cans on the floor of his squalid apartment (one of which is for "spillover"). The image of the fountain-like pee pouring into the cans, seen from his POV, is the first clear indication that we will be handcuffed to this "gnome gone bad" for the duration of this frantically paced episode, forced to tag along as he careens from one base activity or extreme situation to the next.[20] Indeed, not only do we wake up with Frank and try to shake off his hangover, but we are forced to endure "every grimy detail" of this typical—typically chaotic—day in his life, which delivers him (and us) to the brink of death on more than one occasion.[21] The first such occasion comes when he eats a bit of his landlord's blackout-inducing snakemeat sandwich, which sends Frank (and us) to the ground when that morsel of food goes down the wrong "pipe." Returning to consciousness in a hospital, we see Frank's hands rise up from the bottom of the screen to grope a middle-aged nurse's breasts as she administers care, and from there we move on to even more troubling subject-object relations in the company of his recently divorced, heavily intoxicated pal Bill Ponderosa (Lance Barber), who, before hitting on a teenaged girl at a skating rink, offers him a dangerous-looking pill and asks, "Does Franken-stein want to come out and play?"

This reference to Mary Shelley's monster, a manmade miracle that has moved far beyond its literary origins to become an all-purpose metaphor in contemporary popular culture, comes to a literal head once we see Frank in the bathroom mir-ror—a reflected image that confronts us with the prospect of our own "descent into madness" as accomplices in his badness. Having ingested a drug-laced dog treat and crushed up a bottle of pills to snort, he stares at himself/us in a moment of hallucino-genic self-recognition and, with muddled lucidity, calls himself/us "Frankenstein."

C.4. Spaced out after downing a drug-laced dog treat and snorting a bottle of crushed-up pills, Frank—perhaps the most dissolute character in *It's Always Sunny in Philadelphia*—looks at himself in a bathroom mirror. However, because this is a POV shot, he appears to be addressing the audience, turning us into unwitting conspirators who are as monstrous as he is. © Bluebush Productions and 3 Arts Entertainment

His facial features, visually distorted as a result of those mind-altering substances, are suggestive of the way that both mental health and morality are made flesh in *It's Always Sunny in Philadelphia*. Indeed, at various points throughout the series' fourteen-season run, the gang's various delusions—Dennis's illusions of grandeur as a self-proclaimed "Golden God," Dee's belief that she can succeed as a comedienne/actress despite a lack of talent, Charlie's dream of romantically hooking up with a waitress who wants nothing to do with him—manifest as corporeal pathologies and physical tics, built up to the point that their bodies eventually break down in "gross" or abject ways (e.g., declining physical health, vomiting, etc.).

Besides literalizing Frank's amorality-as-monstrosity, though, this mirror scene (which itself mirrors an earlier moment when he looked at his own reflection after waking up with a hangover, albeit with fewer toxins in his system), provides an opportunity for spectatorial reflexivity; a calling-into-question of the vicarious pleasure that we sometimes take in watching characters break laws, commit crimes, cross boundaries, and behave in ways that undermine the social contract of mutual respect and virtuous action performed in more uplifting shows like *The Good Place*. Indeed, such pleasure is no less "monstrous" than the "grunting, rutting, sexist, gluttonous old bigot" who stares back at us, though we would hardly call ourselves such things unprompted.

Although there had been previous attempts to structure entire episodes around POV shots, as seen in *M*A*S*H* (CBS, 1972–83; "Point of View" [7.11]) and throughout the run of the British sitcom *Peep Show* (Channel Four; 2003–15), none of those had deposited the viewer into such compromising positions as "Being Frank" does. Although we are encouraged to see Frank as "the worst of the worst," a "moral monster" who, in the words of Adam Henschke, appears to be "without redeeming qualities," he could be said to exhibit virtuous characteristics as a role model of sorts,[22] doing right by his younger friends (in terms of following through with his contributions to their absurd heist plan) and putting his life at risk to protect Bill. He is also someone who lives an authentic, inhibition-free life and who, lacking the self-delusions of his younger accomplices in crime, sees himself for who he really is. Who he is, of course, is a creation, a fantasy, a fiction; albeit one that communicates something truthful about television spectatorship at a time when far *worse* kinds of lies—including those spoken by political leaders and perpetuated by news organizations—have taken hold of sensibilities and undermined the aforementioned social contract. Perhaps it is only coincidental that his name is "Frank," but that word—indicating something that is forthright, honest, open, and direct when dealing with "unpalatable matters"—points toward the underlying *goodness* of characters and cultural productions whose *badness* is only skin-deep.

Notes

Bibliography

Index

Notes

Contemporary TV Comedy

1. Sarah Kreps, "Flying Under the Radar: A Study of Public Attitudes Towards Unmanned Aerial Vehicles," *Research and Politics* (April–June 2014): 1–7; James Ron, Howard Lavine, and Shannon Golden, "No, Americans Don't Support Airstrikes That Kill Civilians, Even When They Target Terrorists," *Washington Post* (May 6, 2019): https://www.washingtonpost.com/politics/2019/05/06/no-americans-dont-support-airstrikes-that-kill-civilians-even-when-they-target-terrorists/.

2. Dom Nero, "Everything About *Barry* Is Strange," *Esquire* (May 7, 2018): https://www.esquire.com/entertainment/tv/a20090096/barry-hbo-bill-hader-review/.

3. Here I am alluding to Brett Martin's *Difficult Men: Behind the Scenes of a Creative Revolution: From The Sopranos and The Wire to Mad Men and Breaking Bad* (New York: Penguin Books, 2014).

4. Michael Curtin and Jane Shattuc, *The American Television Industry* (London: Palgrave Macmillan, 2009), 37, 59.

5. David Susskind, interviewed by Cecil Smith, "Susskind Won't Gamble with Sponsors' Millions," *Los Angeles Times* (September 13, 1959): G2.

6. Curtin and Shattuc, *The American Television Industry*, 59.

7. Curtin and Shattuc, 59.

8. As Michael V. Tueth states, "Milton Berle's drag routines, Red Skelton's drunken characters, and Ernie Kovacs's effeminate Percy Dovetonsils were . . . mild violations of the social taboos of middle America that kept well within the traditions of slapstick and vaudeville comedy." Michael V. Tueth, "Breaking and Entering: Transgressive Comedy on Television," in Mary M. Dalton and Laura R. Linder, eds., *The Sitcom Reader: America Viewed and Skewed* (Albany, NY: SUNY Press, 2005), 25; Michael V. Tueth, *Laughter in the Living Room: Television Comedy and the American Home Audience* (New York: Peter Lang, 2005), 19–33; Gerald Nachman, *Seriously Funny: The Rebel Comedians of the 1950s and 1960s* (New York: Pantheon Books, 2003); and Andrew Horton, *Ernie Kovacs & Early TV Comedy* (Austin: Univ. of Texas Press, 2010).

9. Émile Durkheim, *The Division of Labor in Society*, ed. Steven Lukes, trans. W. D. Halls (New York: Free Press, 2014). See also: Matthieu Béra, "Émile Durkheim: A Biography by Marcel Fournier," *Sociologica* Vol. 7, No. 3 (January 2013): 1–9.

10. Manfred B. Steger, *The Rise of the Global Imaginary: Political Ideologies from the French Revolution to the Global War on Terror* (Oxford: Oxford Univ. Press, 2008), 7.

11. Steger, 7.

12. Tim Dant, *Television and the Moral Imaginary: Society Through the Small Screen* (London: Palgrave Macmillan, 2012).

13. Dant, 194.

14. Dant, 193.

15. Doyle Greene persuasively argues that the "liberal-conservative debate" surrounding Comedy Central's *South Park* is largely "unproductive," owing to the watered-down (over)use of terms such as "liberal" and "conservative," which the creators of the long-running adult animated program (Trey Parker and Matt Stone) have frequently employed themselves when trying to explain their positions on various political matters. Quoting Parker's belief that "all people are born bad and are made good by society" (which co-creator Stone labels a "conservative" statement), Greene points out how easily the duo's politics (and *South Park's* satirical bent) "can be read against the classical liberal philosophy, from which American liberalism, American conservatism, and libertarianism are *all* derived." Doyle Greene, *Politics and the American Television Comedy: A Critical Survey from "I Love Lucy" Through "South Park"* (Jefferson, NC: McFarland & Company, Inc., 2008), 219–20.

16. Beverley Skeggs, Leslie Moran, Paul Tyrer, and Jon Binnie, "*Queer as Folk*: Producing the Real of Urban Space," *Urban Studies*, Vol. 41, No. 9 (August 1, 2004): 1839–56; Robin Pickering-Iazzi, *The Mafia in Italian Lives and Literature: Life Sentences and Their Geographies* (Toronto: Univ. of Toronto Press, 2015).

17. Elizabeth Klaver, *Performing Television: Contemporary Drama and the Media Culture* (Bowling Green, OH: Bowling Green State Univ. Popular Press, 2000), 56.

18. Jürgen Habermas, *Between Facts and Norms: Contributions to a Discourse Theory of Law and Democracy*, trans. William Rehg (Cambridge, MA: MIT Press, 1996). Sociologist Graeme Kirkpatrick defines the term "social imaginary" along similar lines, calling it the "background sense-making operations that make the idea of society and its practical reality possible." Graeme Kirkpatrick, *Computer Games and the Social Imaginary* (Cambridge: Polity Press, 2013), 2.

19. Steger, *The Rise of the Global Imaginary*, 6.

20. In the words of Andrea L. Press, "popular television . . . cannot be said to reflect society, nor should this be its role." What the medium reflects, according to Press, is "a desire to simplify terrains of ideological confusion and contradiction within our society." Andrea L. Press, "Women Watching Television: Issues of Class, Gender, and Mass Media Reception," in Peter d'Agostino and David Tafler, eds., *Transmission: Toward a Post-Television Culture* (Thousand Oaks, CA: Sage Publications, Inc., 1995), 66.

21. Klaver, *Performing Television*, 58–59.

22. Scott Sedita, *The Eight Characters of Comedy: Guide to Sitcom Acting and Writing* (Los Angeles: Atides Publishing, 2006).

23. Catie Cambria, Richard Drew, and Danielle Robinson, "*Mad Men*: Bad Behavior All Around," *The Atlantic* (August 23, 2010): https://www.theatlantic.com/entertainment/archive/2010/08/mad-men-bad-behavior-all-around/61889/.

24. Cary W. Horvath, "Measuring Television Addiction," *Journal of Broadcasting & Electronic Media*, Vol. 48, No. 3 (2004): 378–98. The idea that Don Draper drinks an average of ten alcoholic beverages a day comes from a report put out by the editors of Detox.net and reported in Erin Mosbaugh, "Infographic: How Much Does Don Draper Drink in One Day?" *First We Feast* (March 18, 2015): https://firstwefeast.com/eat/2015/03/don-draper-is-an-alcoholic-infographic#:~:text=According%20to%20Detox.net%2C%20the,164%20drinks%20in%20a%20season.

25. Edward A. Batchelor, "I Was Cured of TV," *Coronet*, Vol. 37 (February 1955): 38–40.

26. Richard Butsch, "Boob Tubes, Fans, and Addicts," in Peter Urquhart and Paul Heyer, eds., *Communication in History: Stone Age Symbols to Social Media* (New York: Routledge, 2019), 285.

27. Lynn Spigel, "Seducing the Innocent: Childhood and Television in Postwar America," in Henry Jenkins, ed., *The Children's Culture Reader* (New York: NYU Press, 1998), 119.

28. John T. Caldwell, *Televisuality: Style, Crisis, and Authority in American Television* [reprint edition] (New Brunswick, NJ: Rutgers Univ. Press, 2020), 56.

29. Spigel, "Seducing the Innocent," 119.

30. Other television shows featuring episodes titled "TV or Not TV" include *The Jetsons* (ABC, 1962–63), *The Andy Griffith Show* (CBS, 1960–68), *Gimme a Break!* (NBC, 1981–87), *Webster* (ABC, 1983–89), *Amen* (NBC, 1986–91), *Full House* (ABC, 1987–95), *Murphy Brown* (CBS, 1988–98; 2018–19), *Doogie Howser M.D.* (ABC, 1989–93), and *Pinky and the Brain* (Kids' WB, 1995–98).

31. Christine Acham, *Revolution Televised: Prime Time and the Struggle for Black Power* (Minneapolis: Univ. of Minnesota Press, 2004), 102–4.

32. Richard Butsch, *The Citizen Audience: Crowds, Publics, and Individuals* (New York: Routledge, 2008), 129–40.

33. Robert Kubey and Mihaly Csikszentmihalyi, "Television Addiction is no mere metaphor," *Scientific American*, Vol. 286, No. 2 (February 2002): 74–80.

34. Butsch, *The Citizen Audience*, 138–39.

35. Butsch, 138.

36. Ted Rall, "Trash TV: Insightful and In Touch with America," *The Baltimore Sun* (April 9, 1996): 59.

37. Butsch, *The Citizen Audience*, 133.

38. David Mirkin, "'Treehouse of Horror V' Commentary Track," *The Simpsons The Complete Sixth Season DVD* (20th Century Fox Home Video, 2005).

39. Matthew Guida, "10 Worst Things That Homer Simpson Has Done," *ScreenRant* (July 8, 2019): https://screenrant.com/worst-things-homer-simpson-done/.

40. Guida, "Homer Simpson."

41. Norman K. Denzin, *The Alcoholic Society: Addiction & Recovery of the Self* (New York: Routledge, 2017), 342.

42. John Gunn and Pamela J. Taylor, *Forensic Psychiatry: Clinical, Legal and Ethical Issues* (Boca Raton, FL: CRC Press, 2014), 217.

43. Evan Elkins, "Excessive Stand-Up, the Culture Wars, and '90s TV," in Chiara Bucaria and Luca Barra, eds., *Taboo Comedy: Television and Controversial Humour* (London: Palgrave Macmillan, 2016), 140.

44. James Davison Hunter, *Culture Wars: The Struggle to Define America* (New York: Basic Books, 1991).

45. Matthew A. Henry, *The Simpsons, Satire, and American Culture* (New York: Palgrave Macmillan, 2012), 3.

46. Elkins, "Excessive Stand-Up, the Culture Wars, and '90s TV," 141.

47. Elkins, 142.

48. Anon., "History of Cable," *California Cable & Telecommunications Association*: https://calcable.org/learn/history-of-cable/

49. Elkins, "Excessive Stand-Up, the Culture Wars, and '90s TV," 140.

50. Doyle Greene, *Politics and the American Television Comedy: A Critical Survey from "I Love Lucy" Through "South Park"* (Jefferson, NC: McFarland & Company, Inc., 2008), 200–201.

51. Lisa Kimmel, "Media Violence: Different Times Call for Different Measures," *University of Miami Law Review*, Vol. 10, No. 3 (2014): 692–93.

52. Robert J. Thompson, *Adventures on Prime Time: The Television Programs of Stephen J. Cannell* (West Port, CT: Praeger, 1990), 43.

53. Newton N. Minow, "Television and the Public Interest," Address to the National Association of Broadcasters, Washington, D.C., May 9, 1961.

54. Susan M. Ruddick, *Young and Homeless in Hollywood: Mapping the Social Imaginary* (New York: Routledge, 1996), 12.

55. Cornelius Castoriadis, *The Imaginary Institution of Society*, trans. Kathleen Blamey (Cambridge, MA: The MIT Press), 149.

56. Dennis Perkins, "*The Good Place* Walks, Finally, Right into the Good Place," *AV Club* (January 23, 2020): https://tv.avclub.com/the-good-place-walks-finally-right-into-the-good-plac-184 1179535.

1. Very Drunken Episodes

1. Simon Critchley, *On Humour* (London: Routledge, 2002); John Morreall, *Comic Relief: A Comprehensive Philosophy of Humor* (Chichester, West Sussex: Wiley-Blackwell, 2009); Steven Gimbel, *Isn't that Clever: A Philosophical Account of Humor and Comedy* (New York: Routledge, 2018).

2. Gimbel, *Isn't That Clever*, 5.

3. Morreall, *Comic Relief*, 92–98.

4. Ted Cohen, *Jokes: Philosophical Thoughts on Joking Matters* (Chicago: Univ. of Chicago Press, 2001), 79.

5. Morreall, *Comic Relief*, 94.

6. Though not as canonical as those three practitioners of ancient Greek comedy (or "Old Comedy," dating from the 480s to 440s BCE), the Athenian actor and poet Crates was credited by Aristotle as being the first to bring inebriated characters to the stage, in plays that were distinguished by their non-iambic meters (in contrast to lampoons) and connected storylines (a distant forerunner to today's TV comedies). Erich Segal, *The Death of Comedy* (Cambridge, MA: Harvard Univ. Press, 2001), 38.

7. Iain Gately, *Drink: A Cultural History of Alcohol* (New York: Gotham Books, 2008), 114.

8. Albert H. Tolman, "Shakespeare Studies: Part IV. Drunkenness in Shakespeare," *Modern Language Notes*, Vol. 34, No. 2 (February 1919): 82–88.

9. Brock Swinson, "Mel Brooks on Screenwriting," *Creative Screenwriting* (January 14, 2016): https://creativescreenwriting.com/mel-brooks-on-screenwriting/.

10. Alex Clayton, "Why Comedy Is at Home on Television," in Jason Jacobs and Steven Peacock, eds., *Television Aesthetics and Style* (New York: Bloomsbury, 2013), 79.

11. Clayton, 88.

12. Clayton, 91.

13. Jeffrey Sconce, "*Tim and Eric's Awesome Show, Great Job!*: Metacomedy," in Ethan Thompson and Jason Mittell, eds., *How to Watch Television* (New York: New York Univ., 2013), 77.

14. John A. Miles, Jr., "Laughing at the Bible: Jonah as Parody," *The Jewish Quarterly Review*, Vol. 65, No. 3 (January 1975): 175.

15. Noël Carroll, *Humour: A Very Short Introduction* (Oxford: Oxford Univ. Press, 2014), 74.

16. Neil Genzlinger, "Realism Splashing a Screen Near You," *New York Times* (March 8, 2014): C5.

17. The excess of hangovers and uncontrollable vomiting has been audibly registered on TV show soundtracks ever since Rachel (Jennifer Aniston) and Ross (David Schwimmer) staggered drunkenly out of a Las Vegas wedding chapel and upchucked offscreen in an episode of *Friends* (NBC, 1994–2004). In fact, years before the double-length fifth-season finale "The One in Vegas" aired on May 20, 1999, a few small-screen comedies brought the sound (if not the image) of someone throwing up into American households, including the fantasy-themed sitcom *ALF* (NBC, 1986–90). In the episode "Tequila" (2.24), the title character—a furry alien from the planet Melmac who has been living in a Californian suburb—tries to keep pace with a "hooch-monger" named Maura (Dorothy Lyman). When he wakes the next morning with a terrible hangover, ALF ralphs up the previous night's liquor and soon pledges to go off the sauce forever. The offscreen sound of him doing the "technicolor yawn" is nearly drowned out by the laughter of a studio audience that—to repeat the argument against comedy as a cultural form that allows people to free themselves "from the customary restrictions of social empathy"—apparently derives pleasure from his misery. See: Franco V. Trivigno, "Plato on Laughter and Moral Harm," in Pierre Destrée and Franco V. Trivigno, eds., *Laughter, Humor, and Comedy in Ancient Philosophy* (Oxford: Oxford Univ. Press, 2019), 14; Michael Billig, *Laughter and Ridicule: Towards a Social Critique of Humour* (Thousand Oaks, CA: SAGE Publications, Inc., 2005), 120.

18. Jen Chaney, "Why Is Everyone Projectile Vomiting on TV?," *Vulture* (March 29, 2017): https://www.vulture.com/2017/03/projectile-vomit-why-is-everyone-on-tv-throwing-up.html.

19. Audra Schroeder, "The Warped Tour: Tim and Eric Perfect the Anti-Joke," *The Austin Chronicle* (April 25, 2008): https://www.austinchronicle.com/screens/2008-04-25/616136/.

20. Segal, *The Death of Comedy*, 8.

21. Segal, 36.

22. Rupert D. V. Glasgow, *Madness, Masks, and Laughter: An Essay on Comedy* (Cranbury, NJ: Associated Univ. Presses, 1995), 302.

23. For more on Charlie Chaplin's nearly career-long impersonation of comic drunks (a routine he first developed while working for the Karno Pantomime Troupe beginning in 1907), see Gerald Mast, *The Comic Mind: Comedy and the Movies*, Second Edition (Chicago: Univ. of Chicago Press, 1979). See also: Yves Laberge, "Representations of Drinking and Temperance in Film," in Jack S. Blocker, Jr., David M. Fahey, and Ian R. Tyrrell, eds., *Alcohol and Temperance in Modern History: An International Encyclopedia*, Vol. 1 (Santa Barbara, CA: ABC-CLIO, Inc., 2003), 234.

24. Glen R. Shepherd, "Alcoholism Can Be Cured," *The Washington Post* (February 4, 1952): B4.

25. Shepherd, B4.

26. Rosie White, *Television Comedy and Femininity: Queering Gender* (London: I.B. Tauris, 2018), 44.

27. White, 46.

28. White, 44.

29. Genevieve Knupfer, quoted in Barbara C. Leigh, "A Thing So Fallen, and So Vile: Images of Drinking and Sexuality in Women," *Contemporary Drug Problems* 22 (Fall 1995): 420–21.

30. Knupfer, 46.

31. Moreover, society's disapproval of women downing a bottle of alcohol (or "tonic," in Lucy's case)—an act that becomes truly taboo whenever she is pregnant—would not sully this episode's reputation since the main character was not with child at the time of its original broadcast (although Ball had given birth to her firstborn, Lucie Arnez, one year earlier). Not until the end of

1952—December 8, to be exact (a date that marks the airing of "Lucy Is Enceinte" [2.10])—would she be forced off the bottle as a result of her pregnancy.

32. Saul Austerlitz, *Sitcom: A History in 24 Episodes from "I Love Lucy" to "Community"* (Chicago: Chicago Review Press, 2014), 202–3.

33. Gately, *Drink*, 420.

34. Gately, 420.

35. Mary Ann Watson, *Defining Visions: Television and the American Experience in the 20th Century* (Malden, MA: Blackwell Publishing, 2008), 180.

36. Sid Caesar, *Caesar's Hours: My Life in Comedy, With Love and Laughter* (New York: PublicAffairs, 2003), 245.

37. In 1950, the average drinker consumed twenty-three gallons of beer. Iain Gately, *Drink: A Cultural History of Alcohol* (New York: Gotham Books, 2008), 419.

38. The vaudevillian roots of comic inebriation are sometimes used by critics to deride a particularly hammy performance, as David Hofstede does in his description of a drunk scene in "The Big Bookie" (9.13), an episode of *Dragnet* (NBC, 1951–59, 1967–70). He says that it "plays like a bad vaudeville routine in the middle of a serious undercover investigation." David Hofstede, *5000 Episodes and No Commercials: The Ultimate Guide to TV Shows on DVD* (New York: Back Stage Books, 2006).

39. Notably, one of Van Dyke's most recent honors was bestowed upon him at the Indiana-based Red Skelton Comedy Festival, where he received the inaugural "America's Clown Award"—a sign that there is a strong connection between the two performers (who, on the surface, look very dissimilar from one another).

40. "Double Agent" (1.16), an episode of *Get Smart* (NBC, 1965–69; CBS, 1969–70), foregrounds the performative aspects of public drunkenness. In it, the protagonist Maxwell Smart (Don Adams), a secret agent working for CONTROL, must impersonate an alcoholic in order to gain the confidence of a rival organization, KAOS. In preparation for this ploy, the Head of CONTROL (played by Edward Platt) gives him an "Absorbo pill" that, if kept in his mouth while drinking, will counteract the effects of the booze and allow him to stay "stone sober." The Chief also hands Max a dirty, moth-eaten coat to help him look like a bum, highlighting the important role that social costuming plays in sustaining the social imaginary under consideration in this chapter. Not long after stepping into a skid row dive frequented by KAOS agents and bellying up to the bar, Max—looking and even smelling like a vagrant—accidently swallows the pill, leading to his very real descent into dissipation. Nevertheless, the performances of that scene are metatextually "stacked," allowing the audience to appreciate Adams's faked inebriation at the same that his bumbling character shifts from pretend drunkenness to actual drunkenness.

41. Vince Waldron, *The Official Dick Van Dyke Show Book: The Definitive History and Ultimate Viewer's Guide to Television's Most Enduring Comedy* (New York: Applause, 2001), 186-87.

42. Waldron, 187.

43. Joanne Morreale, *The Dick Van Dyke Show* (Detroit: Wayne State Univ. Press, 2015).

44. Morreale, *Dick Van Dyke Show.*

45. Kenneth J. Meier, *The Politics of Sin: Drugs, Alcohol and Public Policy: Drugs, Alcohol and Public Policy* (London: Routledge, 2016).

46. James B. Nelson, *Thirst: God and the Alcoholic Experience* (Louisville, KY: Westminster John Knox Press, 2004), 42.

47. Stephen P. Apthorp, *Alcohol and Substance Abuse: A Handbook for Clergy and Congregations* (Lincoln, NE: iUniverse, 2003), 69

48. David Sterritt, *The Honeymooners* (Detroit: Wayne State Univ. Press, 2009), 5.

49. Sterritt, 5.

50. Helena de Bertodano, "Dick Van Dyke: 'I'd Go to Work with Terrible Hangovers,'" *Telegraph* (January 7, 2003): https://www.telegraph.co.uk/culture/film/film-news/9779018/Dick-Van -Dyke-Id-go-to-work-with-terrible-hangovers.-Which-if-youre-dancing-is-hard.html.

51. Ralph and Ed's ability to get "drunk" on grape juice is similar to the mistake made by the main characters in *Beavis and Butt-Head* (MTV, 1993–97), who get wasted after drinking cans of a nonalcoholic beverage (or what the convenience store owner who sells it to them calls "piss water") in the episode "Buy Beer" (6.20). When a police officer administers a sobriety test on Beavis and Butthead, he concludes that the boys are not drunk, just "stupid."

52. Amitava Dasgupta, *The Science of Drinking: How Alcohol Affects Your Body and Mind* (Lanham, MD: Rowman & Littlefield, 2011), 38.

53. Craig MacAndrew and Robert Edgerton, *Drunken Comportment: A Social Explanation* (Eliot Werner Publications Inc., 1969), 165.

54. Steven T. Sheehan, "To the Moon! Working-Class Masculinity in *The Honeymooners*," in Mary M. Dalton and Laura R. Linder, eds., *The Sitcom Reader: America Re-viewed, Still Skewed* (Albany, NY: SUNY Press, 2016), 51.

55. Anon, "Opinion," *New York Times* (November 14, 1987): 26.

56. Mirra Komarovsky, *Blue-Collar Marriage* (New Haven, CT: Yale Univ. Press, 1964), 291. This passage is quoted in Sheehan, "To the Moon!," 51.

57. Chris Murphy, *The Violence Inside Us: A Brief History of an Ongoing American Tragedy* (New York: Random House, 2020), 196.

58. Kathleen Fearn-Banks and Anne Burford-Johnson, *Historical Dictionary of African American Television* (Lanham, MD: Rowman & Littlefield, 2014), 189.

59. David Pratt, "Television," in Scott Martin, ed., *The SAGE Encyclopedia of Alcohol: Social, Cultural, and Historical Perspectives* (Thousand Oaks, CA: SAGE Publications, 2015), 1242.

60. Scott Meslow, "The History of Alcoholism on TV: From Comedy to Empathy," *The Atlantic* (March 20, 2012): http://www.theatlantic.com/entertainment/archive/2012/03/the-history-of -alcoholism-on-tv-from-comedy-to-empathy/254750/. Although he is not mentioned in Meslow's piece, Al Denton, the character played by Dan Duryea in an episode of *The Twilight Zone* (CBS, 1959–64) titled "Mr. Denton on Doomsday" (1.03) represents a very different type of town drunk than Otis. A figure of derision for local townsfolk, this once unparalleled gunslinger in the Old West takes to the bottle after killing a boy in a duel, and becomes so desperate for the taste of alcohol that he allows himself to be mocked while wallowing in the dirt outside a saloon and singing choruses of "How Dry I Am." Here, the scornful laughter of those forcing him to sing for whiskey is countered by the tragic notes of Duryea's performance as well as the spectator's likely response to such jeering.

61. Richard Michael Kelly, *The Andy Griffith Show* (John F. Blair, Publisher, 1981), 50.

62. Fans of 1960s TV comedies will likely recall Larry Storch's most famous role during that decade, as the bumbling Corporal Randolph Agarn on ABC's Wild West parody *F Troop* (1965–67). Notably, this sitcom also featured an affable alcoholic named Charlie (Frank McHugh), referred to by one character as "the fastest drunk in the West."

63. David Everitt, *King of the Half Hour: Nat Hiken and the Golden Age of TV Comedy* (Syracuse, NY: Syracuse Univ. Press, 2001), 168.

64. Robert Lloyd, "'Disjointed' on High Road," *Los Angeles Times* (August 24, 2017): E-4.

65. Wayne Curtis, "The Lost Art of Acting Drunk," *The Daily Beast* (September 24, 2018): https://www.thedailybeast.com/the-lost-art-of-acting-drunk.

66. Curtis elaborates this point, stating, "Brooks's act was refined enough that it often fooled people who weren't in on it. When he showed up on stage or live television, someone invariably thought he was an everyday actor who'd had one bracer too many backstage, then sat on the edge of their seat to see if he'd make it through." Curtis, "Acting Drunk."

67. Cecil Smith, "Drunk Act Lands Series for Brooks," *Los Angeles Times* (September 20, 1972): D17; Jim Murray, "Only Way to Drink," *Los Angeles Times* (June 2, 1972): E-1.

68. Smith, "Drunk Act Lands Series for Brooks," D-17.

69. Murray, "Only Way to Drink," E1; Martin Kich, "*The Honeymooners*: American Dreaming Scaled Down to the American Screen," in Laura Westengard and Aaron Barlow, eds., *The 25 Sitcoms that Changed Television: Turning Points in American Culture* (Santa Barbara, CA: ABC-CLIO, 2018), 24–25.

70. Murray, "Only Way to Drink," E-1.

71. Kich, "*The Honeymooners*," 24–25.

72. Curtis, "The Lost Art of Acting Drunk."

73. In April of that year, NBC gave fans of *The Andy Griffith Show* a chance to revisit their favorite small town with the made-for-TV movie *Return to Mayberry* (1986), which showed Otis, now completely sober, driving an ice-cream truck."

74. Doug Grow, "Drunks Who Once Got Laughs Get Convictions," *Minneapolis Star Tribune* (August 21, 1990): B-1.

75. Warren Breed and James R. De Foe, "Drinking and Smoking on Television, 1950–1982," *Journal of Public Health Policy*, Vol. 5, No. 2 (June 1984): 257–70.

76. That same month and year (January 1971), an episode of *The Brady Bunch* (ABC, 1969–74) weighed in on the matter of smoking, showing Greg Brady (Barry Williams) giving in to peer pressure and accepting a fellow high-schooler's offer of a cigarette in hopes of becoming "one of the guys." Saddled with the alarmist title "Where There's Smoke" (2.14), this heavy-handed episode was one of the first attempts to inject an anti-smoking message into a situation comedy that was meant to instruct and entertain in equal measure, culminating with a lesson learned and the teenaged character's pledge to never lie to his parents. By the end of the decade, that message had become a more common feature of the genre, as illustrated by "Smokin' Ain't Cool" (6.17), an episode of *Happy Days* (ABC, 1974–84). Besides giving her the titular advice, the Fonz (Henry Winkler) tells Joanie (Erin Moran), a high-school junior who has joined the popular cigarette-smoking Magnets, that if she doesn't kick the habit "[her] body is going to dump [her]." Joanie's parents Mr. and Mrs. Cunningham (Tom Bosley and Marion Ross) flesh out the Fonz's critique, reminding her that nicotine-addiction can increase chances of cancer, heart attack, and lung disease. Her brother Richie (Ron Howard) has even harsher words for her, calling Joanie a "stupid little kid" and an "immature little baby" in what amounts to an intervention. Few television series since the airing of *Happy Days* have put forth such strongly worded "tough talk" against teenage smoking.

77. Breed and De Foe, "Drinking and Smoking on Television, 1950–1982," 266.

78. Watson, *Defining Visions*, 181.

79. Breed and De Foe, "Drinking and Smoking on Television, 1950–1982," 268.

80. Watson, *Defining Visions*, 180.

81. Alan Sepinwall and Matt Zoller Seitz, *TV (The Book): Two Experts Pick the Greatest American Shows of All Time* (New York: Grand Central Publishing, 2016), 42–46.

82. Joseph J. Darowski and Kate Darowski, *Cheers: A Cultural History* (Lanham, MD: Rowman & Littlefield, 2019), 51.

83. Darowski and Darowski, 52–53.

84. Anon., "Leno Calls Telecast on *Cheers* 'a Mistake': Drunken Cast Members Ruined *Tonight* Broadcast from Boston Bar, He Says," *Los Angeles Times* (May 28, 1993): https://www.latimes.com/archives/la-xpm-1993-05-28-ca-40740-story.html. This post-finale farewell to the main cast of *Cheers* is reminiscent of the notorious September 20, 1970, episode of *The Dick Cavett Show* (ABC, 1969–75) in which John Cassavetes, Peter Falk, and Ben Gazzara—promoting their latest film *Husbands* (1970)—spend nearly thirty minutes tormenting the show's host, who can barely contain their drunken antics.

85. Quoted in Darowski and Darowski, *Cheers*, 38–39.

86. Bob Beach, "Authority in Storytelling: Comedy Central's *Drunk History*, Intoxication, and the Historian's Craft," *Points* (December 11, 2018): https://pointsadhs.com/2018/12/11/authority-in-storytelling-comedy-centrals-drunk-history-intoxication-and-the-historians-craft/.

87. Beach, "Authority in Storytelling."

2. "Drinking the War Away"

1. William L. White, *Slaying the Dragon: The History of Addiction Treatment and Recovery in America* [Second Edition] (Bloomington, IL: Chestnut Health Systems, 2014), 386.

2. White, 386.

3. David Pratt, "Television," in Scott Martin, ed., *The SAGE Encyclopedia of Alcohol: Social, Cultural, and Historical Perspectives* (Thousand Oaks, CA: SAGE Publications, 2015), 1240–43.

4. Pratt, 1243.

5. Pratt, "Television," 1242.

6. For a discussion of 1970s sitcoms, such as *The Mary Tyler Moore Show* (CBS, 1970–77) and *All in the Family* (CBS, 1971–79), which exemplified the "age of relevancy" by catering to "upscale" audiences and directly confronting topical issues, see Judy Kutulas, "Liberated Women and New Sensitive Men: Reconstructing Gender in 1970s Workplace Comedies," in Mary M. Dalton and Laura R. Linder, eds., *The Sitcom Reader, Second Edition: America Re-viewed, Still Skewed* (Albany, NY: SUNY Press, 2016), 123–24; and Melissa Crawley, *The American Television Critic: A History* (Jefferson, NC: McFarland & Company, Inc., 2017), 60–62.

7. Warren K. Garlington, "Drinking on Television; a Preliminary Study with Emphasis on Method," *Journal of Studies on Alcohol*, Vol. 38, No. 11 (1977): 2199–2205; Jenny Cafiso, Michael S. Goodstadt, Warren Garlington, and Margaret A. Sheppard, "Television Portrayal of Alcohol and Other Beverages," *Journal of Studies on Alcohol*, Vol. 43, No. 11 (1982): 1232–43; Lawrence Wallack, Warren Breed, and John Cruz, "Alcohol on Prime-Time Television," *Journal of Studies on Alcohol*, Vol. 48, No. 1 (1987): 33–38; Lawrence Wallack, Joel W. Grube, Patricia A. Madden, and Warren Breed, "Portrayals of Alcohol on Prime-Time Television," *Journal of Studies on Alcohol*, Vol. 51, No. 5 (1990): 428–37; and Dale W. Russell and Cristel A. Russell, "Embedded Alcohol Messages in Television Series: The Interactive Effect of Warnings and Audience Connectedness on Viewers' Alcohol Beliefs," *Journal of Studies on Alcohol and Drugs*, Vol. 69, No. 3 (2008): 459–67.

8. Published in the journal *Pediatrics* in 1985, Dorothy G. Singer's "Alcohol, Television, and Teenagers" is emblematic of that traditional approach, for the essay focuses on the "modeling" of young viewers' habits through print and TV advertisements and recommends ways that

the entertainment industry might minimize its contributions to underage substance abuse and to the widespread belief that drinking is a "socially desirable" practice. Appearing a decade later in Susan E. Martin's edited collection *The Effects of the Mass Media on the Use and Abuse of Alcohol* (published by the US Department of Health and Human Services), George Gerbner's "Alcohol in American Culture" provides a more discursive approach than those that preceded it by exploring the federal government's regulatory policies, the role of citizen action groups, and self-regulation within the media and alcohol industries. Dorothy G. Singer, "Alcohol, Television, and Teenagers," *Pediatrics*, Vol. 76, No. 4 (October 1985): 668–74.

9. One of the few critical explorations of this otherwise overlooked television series is A. Bowdoin Van Riper, *"Baa Baa Black Sheep* and the Last Stand of the WWII Drama," in Anna Froula and Stacy Takacs, eds., *American Militarism on the Small Screen* (New York: Routledge, 2016), 77–92.

10. Quoted in Jeremy Kuzmarov, *The Myth of the Addicted Army: Vietnam and the Modern War on Drugs* (Amherst, MA: Univ. of Massachusetts Press, 2009), 27; see also: James Westheider, *Fighting in Vietnam: The Experiences of the U.S. Soldier* (Stackpole Books, 2011), 95.

11. J. P. Shanley, "TV: Fun with *Sergeants*: Mac Hyman's Novel Adapted on ABC," *New York Times* (March 18, 1955): 39.

12. Thomas Lisanti, *Hollywood Surf and Beach Movies: The First Wave, 1959–1969* (Jefferson, NC: McFarland & Company, Inc., 2005), 370.

13. Lisa M. Mundey, "'Bilko's Bombers': Anti-Militarism in the Era of the 'New Look,'" in Anna Froula and Stacy Takacs, eds., *American Militarism on the Small Screen* (London: Routledge, 2016), 26.

14. The song "Show Me the Way to Go Home," which this episode of *Gomer Pyle, U.S.M.C.* references, is sung by a captured German soldier (Albert Paulsen) who wishes to demonstrate his admiration for all-things-American in "Forgotten Front," the first episode of the World War II television series *Combat!*. The soldier gets so caught up in performing for his American captor (singing the lyrics, "I had a little drink about an hour ago and it went right to my head") that he momentarily forgets that he is a prisoner.

15. Gordon Arnold, *The Afterlife of America's War in Vietnam: Changing Visions in Politics and on Screen* (Jefferson, NC: McFarland, 2006), 33.

16. Arnold, 33.

17. Robert Bray, Mary Ellen Marsden, John F. Mazzuchi, and Roger W. Hartman, "Prevention in the Military," in Robert T. Ammerman, Peggy J. Ott, and Ralph E. Tarter, eds., *Prevention and Societal Impact of Drug and Alcohol Abuse* (Mahwah, NJ: Lawrence Erlbaum Associates, 1999), 347.

18. James H. Wittebols, *Watching M*A*S*H, Watching America: A Social History of the 1972–1983 Television Series* (Jefferson, NC: McFarland, 1998), 53.

19. John Darrell Sherwood, *Officers in Flight Suits: The Story of American Air Force Fighter Pilots* (NYU Press, 1998).

20. David Pratt, "Television," in Scott Martin, ed., *The SAGE Encyclopedia of Alcohol: Social, Cultural, and Historical Perspectives* (Thousand Oaks, CA: SAGE Publications, 2015), 1242.

21. Pratt, 1242.

22. Pratt, 347. See also Meredith H. Lair, *Armed with Abundance: Consumerism and Soldiering in the Vietnam War* (Chapel Hill, NC: Univ. of North Carolina Press, 2011).

23. John Darrell Sherwood, *Officers in Flight Suits: The Story of American Air Force Fighter Pilots in the Korean War* (New York: NYU Press, 1998), 164–65.

24. Melinda L. Pash, *In the Shadow of the Greatest Generation: The Americans Who Fought the Korean War* (New York: NYU Press, 2012), 201.

25. Michael B. Kassell, "M*A*S*H," in Ray B. Browne and Pat Browne, eds., *The Guide to United States Popular Culture* (Madison: Univ. of Wisconsin Press, 2001), 520.

26. Reference to another unusual mixing of drinks is made in the episode "Deal Me Out" (2.13), in which Radar alludes to the combination of Scotch, gin, and vodka contained in the same bottle of alcohol, a valued possession of Lieutenant Colonel Blake.

27. For more information about the series' mixing of tones and genres, see David Scott Diffrient and Hye Seung Chung, "TV Hybridity: Genre Mixing and Narrative Complexity in *M*A*S*H*," *Quarterly Review of Film and Video*, Vol. 29, No. 4 (2012): 285–302.

28. Airing in November of 1978, this episode ("Major Ego") had been preceded a few months earlier by a similar attempt (on another CBS television program) to demonstrate alcohol's ameliorative ability to unlock troubling yet cathartic memories and to soften strained interpersonal relationships. In February of that year, an episode of *All in the Family* titled "Two's a Crowd" (8.19) brought the normally antagonist characters Archie Bunker (Carroll O'Connor) and Michael "Meathead" Stivic (Rob Reiner) together in a neighborhood bar, the local watering hole formerly known as Kelsey's that Archie recently took over (after mortgaging his house). After the "lovable bigot" and his liberal son-in-law get locked in the stockroom of Archie's Place, they drink booze to pass the time, and this leads to an intimate conversation that reveals the roots of the former's racist, xenophobic attitudes. The laughter of the in-studio audience dies down once Archie divulges secrets from his childhood, indicating that his abusive father beat certain "values" into him—attitudes about ethnic minorities that shaped the character's archaic worldview as an adult.

29. This unique way of "irrigating the innards" (to borrow a euphemism for drinking in "Check Up" [3.07]) apparently inspired Twentieth Century-Fox to license a unique novelty item during the original run of *M*A*S*H*: an IV liquor dispenser bearing both the title of the television series and the name of the studio. Not surprisingly, among the most popular gift items related to the series was a set of shot glasses bearing the "M*A*S*H" logo. See David Scott Diffrient, *M*A*S*H* (Detroit: Wayne State Univ. Press, 2008), 4.

30. Wittebols, *Watching M*A*S*H, Watching America*, 52–54, 107–11.

31. Wittebols, 109.

32. Jacques Normand and Richard O. Lempert, *Under the Influence?: Drugs and the American Work Force* (Washington, DC: National Academies Press, 1994), 129.

33. Bray et al., "Prevention in the Military," 349.

34. Bray et al., 363.

35. Bray et al., 350.

36. Bray et al., 350.

37. Genevieve Ames and Carol Cunradi claim that, while illicit drug use and cigarette smoking in the US military both "decreased significantly over the period from 1980 to 2002, heavy alcohol use did not show the same decline." Heavy drinking (consuming more than four drinks during a single occasion/session) was reported by 27 percent of young adults in the military, according to the authors. Genevieve Ames and Carol Cunradi, "Alcohol Use and Preventing Alcohol-Related Problems Among Young Adults in the Military," *Alcohol Research & Health*, Vol. 28, No. 4 (2004/2005): 252.

38. Michael Saenz, "*China Beach*," in Horace Newcomb, ed., *Encyclopedia of Television* (London: Routledge, 2013), 515.

39. Saenz, 516.

40. Charles Taylor, *Modern Social Imaginaries* (Durham, NC: Duke Univ. Press, 2004), 23.

41. Wittebols, *Watching M*A*S*H, Watching America*, 111.

42. Ames and Cunradi, "Alcohol Use and Preventing Alcohol-Related Problems Among Young Adults in the Military," 252–57.

43. Daniel O'Brien, *Robert Altman: Hollywood Survivor* (New York: The Continuum Publishing Company, 1995), 36.

44. Van Riper, "*Baa Baa Black Sheep* and the Last Stand of the WWII Drama," 77.

45. There are, of course, exceptions to this rule, most notably director William Wyler's *The Best Years of Our Lives* (1946), in which US Infantry Sergeant Al Stephenson (Fredric March) copes with family- and business-related tensions after his homecoming by turning to drinking.

46. Nick Mansfield, *Soldiers as Workers: Class, Employment, Conflict and the Nineteenth-Century Military* (Liverpool: Liverpool Univ. Press, 2016), 74.

47. Mansfield, 201.

48. George H. Jensen, *Storytelling in Alcoholics Anonymous: A Rhetorical Analysis* (Carbondale, IL: Southern Illinois Univ. Press, 2000), 5.

3. The Big Book on the Small Screen

1. Bill Nichols, *Blurred Boundaries: Questions of Meaning in Contemporary Culture* (Bloomington, IN: Indiana Univ. Press, 1994), 47, 67.

2. Alcoholics Anonymous was a topic of conversation in early-to-mid-series episodes of the daytime drama *The Young and the Restless* (CBS, 1973–present), in which Katherine Chancellor (Jeanne Cooper) is introduced as an inveterate drunk who would periodically seek help through the Twelve-Step Program. In the mid-1970s, the topic was also broached in the syndicated spoof of soap operas *Mary Hartman, Mary Hartman* (1976–77), suggesting that producer Norman Lear understood the socially therapeutic function not only of AA but of the TV genre that his show was reflexively parodying—one that has traditionally generated pathos from the spectacle of suffering housewives and career women.

3. Lance Dodes and Zachary Dodes, *The Sober Truth: Debunking the Bad Science Behind 12-Step Programs and the Rehab Industry* (Boston: Deacon Press, 2014).

4. Marc Galanter, *What is Alcoholics Anonymous?* (Oxford: Oxford Univ. Press, 2016), 4–5.

5. Dodes and Dodes, *The Sober Truth*, 2–10.

6. By the mid-1990s, the VSE had become such an ingrained feature of primetime programming—situation comedies in particular—that it was possible for showrunners and writers to make fun of its didactic moralizing, as seen for instance in the back-to-back February 7, 1997, airing of *Beavis and Butt-Head* (MTV, 1993–97)'s "Very Special Episode" (7.06) and "Dumbasses Anonymous" (7.07), the latter showing America's most famous slackers attending an AA meeting to cope with the "problem" of not being able to legally procure booze.

7. Melvin Pollner and Jill Stein, "Doubled Over in Laughter: Humor and the Construction of Selves in Alcoholics Anonymous," in Jaber F. Gubrium and James A. Holstein, eds., *Institutional Selves: Troubled Identities in a Postmodern World* (Oxford: Oxford Univ. Press, 2001), 46–64.

8. Nichols, *Blurred Boundaries*, 47, 67.

9. Ben Bethell, "Cagney and Lacey," in Roger Sabin, ed., *Cop Shows: A Critical History of Police Dramas on Television* (Jefferson, NC: McFarland & Company, Inc., 2015), 103.

10. Susan Cheever, *My Name Is Bill: Bill Wilson—His Life and the Creation of Alcoholics Anonymous* (New York: Washington Square Press, 2015), 127–48.

11. Dodes and Dodes, *The Sober Truth*, 12–13, 129–31.

12. Joe Miller, *US of AA: How the Twelve Steps Hijacked the Science of Alcoholism* (Chicago: Chicago Review Press Inc., 2019), 34–35.

13. Michelle L. McClellan, *Lady Lushes: Gender, Alcoholism, and Medicine in Modern America* (New Brunswick, NJ: Rutgers Univ. Press, 2017), 127–29.

14. Gabrielle Glaser, *Her Best-Kept Secret: Why Women Drink—And How They Can Regain Control* (New York: Simon & Schuster, Inc., 2014), 75–78.

15. Glaser, 78.

16. Anon., "Alcoholism Held Illness Rising Out of Problems," *Los Angeles Times* (October 24, 1947): 13.

17. Jonathan Nichols-Pethick, *TV Cops: The Contemporary American Television Police Drama* (New York: Routledge, 2012), 3.

18. Robert J. Thompson, *Television's Second Golden Age: From "Hill Street Blues" to "ER"* (Syracuse, NY: Syracuse Univ. Press, 1996), 108. See also: Bethell, "Cagney & Lacey," 99–106.

19. Bethell, "Cagney & Lacey," 106.

20. One of the earliest references to Alcoholics Anonymous in a scripted television program occurs in "The Big Search" (6.10), a January 4, 1968, episode of the police procedural *Dragnet* that revolves around a police investigation into the disappearance of two sisters that leads Sergeant Joe Friday (Jack Webb) and Officer Bill Gannon (Harry Morgan) to the girls' father, a recovering alcoholic who is separated from their mother. When asked if he is "on the wagon," the man—a suspect in the case who had been denied visitation rights by his ex-wife—says that the colloquial expression does not reflect his day-to-day reality as someone who does not drink anymore. "I know it's a disease," the man tells the detectives, one for which there is "no cure." Then, unprompted, he says that the "program" in which he has found the power to remain sober for nearly a year really "works." When Friday asks, "Program?" the man explains, "Alcoholics Anonymous. I'm with it and I'm gonna stay with it."

21. Bethell, "Cagney & Lacey," 100.

22. Todd McGowan, *Only a Joke Can Save Us: A Theory of Comedy* (Evanston, IL: Northwestern Univ. Press, 2017), 26.

23. McGowan, 26.

24. Kathleen Anne Flynn, "Performing Sobriety: Story and Celebration in Alcoholics Anonymous," Ph.D. Dissertation (Northwestern Univ., 1994).

25. Flynn, "Performing Sobriety."

26. Flynn, 64–65.

27. American Addiction Foundation website: https://www.americanaddictionfoundation.com/getting-help/types-aa-meetings/

28. Pollner and Stein, "Doubled Over in Laughter," 48.

29. Pollner and Stein, 49.

30. Pollner and Stein, 49.

31. Along the same lines, Philip Scepanski argues that "the language of addiction recovery prohibits the addict from considering themselves to be recovered. Instead, they are always recovering." Philip Scepanski "Addiction, Abjection, and Humor: Craig Ferguson's Confessional Stand-up," in Patrice A. Oppliger and Eric Shouse, eds., *The Dark Side of Stand-Up Comedy* (London: Palgrave Macmillan, 2020), 95.

32. Pollner and Stein, "Doubled Over in Laughter," 46–64.

33. Scepanski, "Addiction, Abjection, and Humor," 80.

34. Scepanski, 96.

35. Scepanski, 82.

36. Frank Rich, "A Funny Man's Sad Story," *New York Times* (October 24, 1982), 7-7.

37. Rich, 7-7

38. Scepanski, "Addiction, Abjection, and Humor," 95.

39. A few television comedies point toward the recursive nature of addiction, or the fact that people who give up one source of combined enjoyment and misery sometimes do so by gravitating toward another addictive substance or pastime. For instance, in *Mom*, Christy kicks her alcohol addiction but replaces it with a gambling addiction, an echo of how Sam Malone (Ted Danson), the main character of the ensemble comedy *Cheers* (NBC, 1982–93), went from being a recovering alcoholic to a bartender with a caffeine addiction and a sex addiction (he starts going to SA meetings at one point in the series).

40. Danny M. Wilcox, *Alcoholic Thinking: Language, Culture, and Belief in Alcoholics Anonymous* (Westport, CT: Praeger, 1998), 112.

41. Claire Rudy Foster, "What #MeToo Looks Like When You're in Recovery," *The Establishment* (April 10, 2018): https://theestablishment.co/what-metoo-looks-like-when-youre-in-recovery-64c0ade43411-2/index.html.

42. Dodes and Dodes, *The Sober Truth*, 129–30.

43. Kristen McGuiness, "The 13th Step: People Who Prey on Newcomers," *The Fix* (April 15, 2011): https://www.thefix.com/content/13th-step.

44. Patrick Ryan, "TV Comedies Get Real About Addiction, Recovery," *USA Today* (March 10, 2016): https://www.usatoday.com/story/life/tv/2016/03/10/addiction-depression-tv-mom-cbs-love-flaked-netflix/81508984/.

45. Elvira G. Aletta, "7 Reasons Charlie Sheen May Hate Alcoholics Anonymous," *Psych-Central* (July 8, 2018): https://psychcentral.com/blog/7-reasons-charlie-sheen-may-hate-alcoholics-anonymous/.

46. John Larroquette, "Alcoholics Anonymous Talk," *YouTube*: https://www.youtube.com/watch?v=ZeuhYV8WqjY.

47. Larroquette, "Alcoholics Anonymous Talk." In a 1988 *LA Times* interview, following his successful bid for a fourth consecutive Emmy Award (for Outstanding Supporting Actor in a Comedy Series), Larroquette opened up about how his "need for alcohol" a decade earlier had overshadowed "everything—his health, his family, his work" before he stumbled upon AA. He also noted that his artistic "heroes"—writers such as Charles Bukowski and actors such as Richard Burton and John Barrymore—seemed to "grab life by the throat and choke it" after giving themselves over to liquor as a kind of "elixir" for success; an idea that ceased to make sense for him as his own professional achievements received industry-wide recognition. Steve Weinstein, "*Night Court*'s Prosecutor Confesses to a Serious Side," *Los Angeles Times* (October 25, 1988): 1.

48. Richard Ouzounian, "John Larroquette: This is a Dark Ride," *Toronto Star* (April 1, 2011): https://www.thestar.com/entertainment/2011/04/01/john_larroquette_this_is_a_dark_ride.html.

49. For more information about the controversies surrounding Rajneesh and his devotees (the "sannyasins"), who took temporary leave of their meditation retreat in Pune (following the Indian government's allegations of drug trafficking, gold smuggling, money laundering, and prostitution) and established a communal city in Wasco County, Oregon (where additional criminal

investigations took place in the early 1980s), see Marion S. Goldman, "Controversy, Cultural Influence, and the Osho/Rajneesh Movement," in James R. Lewis and Jesper Aa. Petersen, eds., *Controversial New Religions* (Oxford: Oxford Univ. Press, 2014), 176–94.

4. Very Crazy Episodes

1. Jane Dillon and James T. Richardson, "The 'Cult' Concept: A Politics of Representation Analysis," *Syzygy: The Journal of Alternative Religion and Culture*, Vol. 3, No. 3/4 (1994): 186.

2. Lorne L. Dawson, *Comprehending Cults: The Sociology of New Religious Movements* (Oxford: Oxford Univ. Press, 2006), 71.

3. Vincent Bugliosi with Curt Gentry, *Helter Skelter: The True Story of the Manson Murders* (New York: W.W. Norton & Company, Inc., 1974).

4. Dawson, *Comprehending Cults*, 7.

5. Marc Galanter, *Cults: Faith, Healing, and Coercion* (Oxford: Oxford Univ. Press, 1999), 5–7.

6. Dawson, *Comprehending Cults*, 5.

7. This is not to dispute accurately reported incidences of indoctrination involving authoritarian methods and physical as well as mental abuse, such as sleep-deprivation and general deception. However, as David V. Barrett, a scholar who prefers the term "alternative religion" to the word "cult," reminds us, "It's all too easy to commit the logical fallacy of generalizing from the particular, saying that because one individual youngster has been damaged by one individual cult, then everyone in that movement is in danger, and that it, and all other 'peculiar' religious movements, must be destroyed." David V. Barrett, *Sects, "Cults" and Alternative Religions: A World Survey and Sourcebook* (London: Blandford, 1996), 279.

8. Despite the fact that there have been dozens of TV representations devoted to the Church of Scientology (its belief system, its history, its founder L. Ron Hubbard, and its members), I have opted not to include many of these in my historical overview. A separate, more detailed study of Scientology's precarious position in American popular culture (as a source of spiritual strength for so many of Hollywood's creative personnel and a source of scripted humor for so many others in the industry) can and should be written. However, it is simply too large an undertaking for this chapter (with an eye toward more general patterns of anti-cultic portrayals in the media).

9. Hillary Robson, "Television and the Cult Audience: A Primer," in Stacey Abbott, ed., *The Cult TV Book* (London: IB Tauris, 2010), 210.

10. Robson, 210.

11. Details of this connection are provided in Jeffrey Sconce, "*Star Trek*, Heaven's Gate, and Textual Transcendence," in Sara Gwenllian-Jones and Roberta E. Pearson, eds., *Cult Television* (Minneapolis: Univ. of Minnesota Press, 2004), 199–220.

12. For more information about the relationship between the religious fanaticism of a "global subproletariat" and the irrational drive toward self-annihilation inscribed in this American Away Team's *Trek*-like beliefs in transcendence, see Paul Virilio, *The Paul Virilio Reader* (New York: Columbia Univ. Press, 2004), 250.

13. This passage of dialogue from the 2018 miniseries *Waco* is similar to former Manson Family member Dianne Lake's view (included in her 2017 memoir) that "No one chooses to be in a cult; no one seeks it out or strives for it. Being in a cult is not something you notice as it is happening—it doesn't matter if you're incredibly self-aware or if you're a teenager who can't see past her own emotions." Dianne Lake and Deborah Herman, *Member of the Family: My Story of*

Charles Manson, Life Inside His Cult, and the Darkness That Ended the Sixties (New York: William Morrow, 2017), 236–37.

14. Michael D. Langone, "Cults: Questions & Answers," *Cultic Studies* (June 7, 2002): www .csj.org/studyindex/studycult/cultqa.htm.

15. Robert L. Snow, *Deadly Cults: The Crimes of True Believers* (Westport, CT: Praeger, 2003), 6.

16. Rick Ross, "Watch Out for Tell-Tale Signs," *The Guardian* (May 27, 2009): https://www .theguardian.com/commentisfree/belief/2009/may/27/cults-definition-religion.

17. Rodney Stark and William Sims Bainbridge, "Of Churches, Sects, and Cults: Preliminary Concepts for a Theory of Religious Movements," *Journal for the Scientific Study of Religion*, Vol. 18, No. 2 (1979): 124.

18. Stark and Bainbridge, 124.

19. Murray Schumach, "Judge Rejects Charges of 'Brainwashing' Against Hare Krishna Aides," *New York Times* (March 18, 1977): 24.

20. Stark and Bainbridge, "Of Churches, Sects, and Cults," 121.

21. Jen Chaney, "*Wild Wild Country* May Be the Craziest Series You Watch All Year," *Vulture* (March 16, 2018): https://www.vulture.com/2018/03/wild-wild-country-review.html.

22. Dan Snierson, "See Owen Wilson as a Cult Leader in Documentary Now's Parody of *Wild Wild Country*," *Entertainment Weekly* (December 21, 2018): https://ew.com/tv/2018/12/21 /owen-wilson-cult-leader-documentary-now-wild-wild-country/.

23. Snierson, "See Owen Wilson."

24. Barrett, *Sects, "Cults" and Alternative Religions*, 16.

25. Matt Hills, *Fan Cultures* (London: Routledge, 2002), 120–25.

26. Cornel Sandvoss, *Fans: The Mirror of Consumption* (Cambridge: Polity Press, 2005), 41.

27. Matt Hills and Henry Jenkins, "Intensities Interview with Henry Jenkins," *Intensities: The Journal of Cult Media*, 2: http://intensities.org/Essays/Jenkins.pdf, 20.

28. Hills, *Fan Cultures*, 122.

29. William S. Bainbridge, *The Sociology of Religious Movements* (London: Routledge, 1997), 24.

30. Hills, *Fan Cultures*, 121.

31. David Chidester, *Authentic Fakes: Religion and American Popular Culture* (Berkeley, CA: Univ. of California Press, 2005), 17.

32. Janja Lalich, *Bounded Choice: True Believers and Charismatic Cults* (Berkeley, CA: Univ. of California Press, 2004), 5.

33. "Escape to the House of the Mummies Part II" (2.04), an episode of the Adult Swim program *The Venture Bros.* (Cartoon Network, 2003–18), similarly revolves around *Ramar of the Jungle*–style exoticism in its depiction of a bloodthirsty Egyptian cult from which the Caucasian heroes must escape.

34. These words in "The Howling Man" recall the opening and closing narrations in "The Invisibles" (1.19), an episode of *The Outer Limits* that features a secret organization whose members "have never experienced love or friendship" and remain unseen by most people.

35. Steven Rubin, *Twilight Zone Encyclopedia* (Chicago, IL: Chicago Review Press, 2018).

36. Underlining the religious connotations of Serling's adaptation, Gabriel McKee calls "The Old Man in the Cave" a "clever science-fictionalization of Exodus 32, in which the Israelites, doubting the religion taught to them by Moses in his absence, flaunt their God's commandments

and worship a golden calf." Gabriel McKee, *The Gospel According to Science Fiction: From "The Twilight Zone" to "The Final Frontier"* (Louisville, KY: Westminster John Knox Press, 2007), 98.

37. John V. Karavitis, "In a Mirror Is Our Image," in Heather L. Rivera and Alexander E. Hooke, eds., *"The Twilight Zone" and Philosophy: A Dangerous Dimension to Visit* (Chicago, IL: Open Court Publishing Company, 2018), 55–66.

38. Joseph Laycock, "Where Do They Get These Ideas? Changing Ideas of Cults in the Mirror of Popular Culture," *Journal of the American Academy of Religion*, Vol. 81, No. 1 (March 2013): 80–106.

39. Laycock, 80–106.

40. It should come as no surprise that many of the fictional cults being spoofed in US sitcoms of the 1970s were lent an Orientalist gloss, given the centrality of Eastern religious traditions in that decade's experimental drug and youth cultures. A distillation of this ongoing motif can be found in "Abduction" (3.16), an episode of *Barney Miller* (ABC, 1975–82) that aired eight months prior to "The De-Programming of Arnold Horshack." In one of its first scenes, a mother and father enter the 12th Precinct station, begging the police captain and his men to rescue their daughter from a religious compound masquerading as a health-food restaurant. Although, by the end of the episode, it is revealed that the Light of the East Temple and Herbarium is a legitimate business, the parents' earlier remarks about this "freak joint" and their formerly "normal" American daughter, Barbara-Lynn (a twenty-two-year-old woman who has been given "a new kind of Hindu name you can't even pronounce"), have likely colored the audience's perceptions of the long-haired cult leader, a robed man who has also been accused of selling pot and "funny mushrooms" to the restaurant patrons.

41. In "Fun with Jane and Jane" (6.17), an episode of *King of the Hill* (Fox, 1997–2010), a cult masquerading as a college sorority (the Omega House) "recruits unsuspecting young women from campus, deprives them of protein, bathrooms, and all contact with their families and friends, then ships them off to a ranch for general enslavement." These words, spoken by the perpetually paranoid conspiracy theorist Dale Gribble (voiced by Johnny Hardwick), are an accurate summary of what transpires at the Omega Ranch, where new recruits are forced to make jams and jellies against their will. Going even farther, "Marlon Joins a Cult" (5.10), an episode of the sitcom *The Wayans Bros.* (The WB, 1995–99), makes a connection between cult worship and African American slavery. Marlon Wayans, trying to prove to his family that he can be a serious actor (under his new name, Brother Ecstasy), is indoctrinated to behave like an antiquated Black servant in the Infinite Fellowship Institute, a community of comet-watchers who hand over their most valuable possessions (e.g., keys to a Lexus, a Rolex) as "sacred offerings."

42. The term "Apocrypha" is not only used as the title of this episode of *Law & Order* but is also the name of a fan-created website devoted to the series, one that published fan fiction based on storylines within the *Law & Order* universe between the years 1997 and 2007. See: http://www.podengo.com/apocrypha/archive.html.

43. In 1994, an episode of the Detroit-set sitcom *Martin* paid homage to this cult-themed storyline in *What's Happening!!* Titled "In Search of . . . Martin" (3.01), it shows disc jockey Martin Payne (Martin Lawrence) adopting the name Shaquille Sunflower once he joins a cult (the Golden Palace) and, as a "lost soul," begins communing with a rock that is the size of Rerun's head of lettuce.

44. Quoted in Laycock, "Where Do They Get These Ideas?" 89.

45. A popular, endlessly repeated chant heard on American television during the 1970s was the "Kool-Aid Song," which included the lyrics "Kool-Aid, Kool-Aid, Tastes Great! We Want Kool-Aid,

Can't Wait!" These lyrics, part of the advertising landscape of popular culture at the time of the Jonestown tragedy, took on grim resonances in its aftermath, forcing parent company Kraft Foods to initiate new commercial ad campaigns so as to distance the drink from the specter of death.

46. Although the number of cult references in narrative fiction programs dwindled during the early 1980s, a few theatrically released feature films from that period did delve into the subject. Examples include *Ticket to Heaven* (1981) and *Split Image* (1982), two motion pictures that have both been cited as influences on the writers of "The Blank Stare" episode of *Strangers with Candy*. http://www.jerriblank.com/swcep209.html#mytop.

47. In addition to these militaristic, male-focalized programs of the 1980s, the first season of the daytime soap opera *Santa Barbara* (NBC, 1984–93) featured a running storyline concerning a cult.

48. Of the four major destructive cults to gain notoriety during the 1990s, the Aum Shinrikyo ("Supreme Truth") group has probably received the least attention, with only passing references to it in a few narrative programs. However, an entire episode of the documentary series *Zero Hour*, entitled "Terror in Tokyo," details the events that led up to the 1995 Sarin gas attack staged by some of the members of this Japanese group.

49. The list of televised news reports and talk show episodes concerning Waco alone is long enough to constitute a substantial subgenre under the larger cultic umbrella. Examples include a two-part *Maury Povich Show* episode ("Answers in the Ashes"), a Biography Channel installment on David Koresh, a tenth-anniversary special aired on *Primetime Live* ("The Children of Waco"), two episodes of *Turning Point* ("The Untold Story of Waco" and "The Truth about Waco"), a CourtTV program ("Mugshots: David Koresh"), and a *Frontline* special ("Waco: The Inside Story") which, despite its title, includes only one interview with a Davidian inside the compound, foregrounding instead the roles played by "outside" players, like the FBI negotiators. These are in addition to the many made-for-TV movies, miniseries, and feature-length documentaries dealing either explicitly or implicitly with the Branch Davidians, including *In the Line of Duty: Ambush at Waco* (1993), *Waco: The Rules of Engagement* (1997), *Standoff* (1997), and *Waco* (Paramount Network, 2018). Most of these productions encourage the public to uncritically accept "the narrative promoted by law enforcement agencies—that the Branch Davidians immolated themselves as an act of suicide." Laycock, "Where Do They Get These Ideas?" 81.

50. Laycock, 81.

51. Barbara Ehrenreich, *The Snarling Citizen* (New York: Farrar, Straus and Giroux, 2000), 44.

52. Laycock, "Where Do They Get These Ideas?" 92.

53. A cult-themed episode of *Buffy the Vampire Slayer*, "Lie to Me" (2.07), likewise puts emphasis on loneliness as a contributing factor in people's willingness to join shadowy fringe religions or social networks; in this case, "the lonely ones," a bunch of misunderstood outsiders who worship vampires together.

54. Megan Goodwin, "Unpacking the Bunker: Sex, Abuse, and Apocalypticism in *Unbreakable Kimmy Schmidt*," *Cross Currents* (June 2018): 1.

55. Flor Edwards, "I Grew Up in a Cult. Here's What *Unbreakable Kimmy Schmidt* Gets Right," *Slate* (March 10, 2015): https://slate.com/culture/2015/03/unbreakable-kimmy-schmidt-cult-a-former-cult-member-on-what-the-show-gets-right.html.

56. Edwards, "I Grew Up in a Cult." Alissa Wilkinson, a contributor to the *Washington Post*, likewise argues that *Unbreakable Kimmy Schmidt* gets cult-life and post-cult-life "right," and sees herself in the "puddle-jumping newbie New Yorker." However, Wilkinson admits that her

experiences within an unnamed "branch of fundamentalism that flourished among Christian homeschoolers" during the 1980s and 1990s (when she was allowed to read only "magazines for teenagers published by Focus on the Family" and "Amish romance novels") were not nearly as destructive as the sexual abuse that Kimmy and her fellow "mole women" endured at the hands of the Reverend Richard Wayne Gary Wayne. Alissa Wilkinson, "I, Too, Thought the World Was Coming to an End. Here's What *Kimmy Schmidt* Gets Right," *Washington Post* (March 17, 2015): https://www.washingtonpost.com/news/acts-of-faith/wp/2015/03/17/why-tina-fey-kimmy-schmidt-works/.

57. Kathryn Lindsay, "5 Harrowing Real Life Kidnapping Stories Just Like Kimmy Schmidt's," *Refinery29* (May 19, 2017): https://www.refinery29.com/en-us/2017/05/155187/real-life-kimmy-schmidt-true-story-kidnapping-cults.

58. Goodwin, "Unpacking the Bunker," 9.

59. Goodwin, 2.

60. Goodwin, 10.

61. George Ritzer, *Introduction to Sociology* (Thousand Oaks, CA: SAGE Publications, Inc., 2013), 661.

62. Goodwin, "Unpacking the Bunker," 6.

63. Laycock, "Where Do They Get These Ideas?" 85.

64. According to Robert L. Snow, an estimated twenty million Americans "have been involved in cults at some time in their lives." While readers might find this a reasonable estimation, it should be noted that the author provides no explanation as to what "involved in" means. Snow, who marshals forth evidence derived from the work of Margaret Thaler Singer ("America's foremost authority on cults"), states that "the likely number of cults in the United States today [is] about 5,000." Snow, *Deadly Cults*, 5–7.

65. Emily Edwards, *Metaphysical Media: The Occult Experience in Popular Culture* (Carbondale, IL: Southern Illinois Univ. Press, 2005), 11.

5. "Drinking the Kool-Aid" of Cult TV

1. David A. Paddick, "TV as Totem: Durkheim's Sociology and Postmodern Popular Culture," Dissertation (Lincoln Christian Seminary, 1995); Chris Gregory, *Be Seeing You . . . Decoding The Prisoner* (Luton, Bedfordshire: Univ. of Luton Press, 1997).

2. Hillary Robson, "Television and the Cult Audience: A Primer," in Stacey Abbott, ed., *The Cult TV Book* (London: I.B. Tauris, 2010), 210.

3. Jonathan Gray, *Television Entertainment* (New York: Routledge, 2008), 48.

4. Henry Jenkins, *Textual Poachers: Television Fans & Participatory Culture* (New York: Routledge, 1992); Henry Jenkins, *Convergence Culture: Where Old and New Media Collide* (New York: NYU Press, 2006); Matt Hills, *Fan Cultures* (London: Routledge, 2002); Will Brooker, *Using the Force: Creativity, Community and Star Wars Fans* (New York: Continuum, 2002).

5. Darren Devlyn, "Bell's Appealing," *Melbourne Herald Sun* (November 30, 2005): H-04.

6. Malene Arpe, "Arrest Me for Loving a Sitcom," *Toronto Star* (October 13, 2005): G-10.

7. Jennifer Armstrong, "Bell of the Fall," *Entertainment Weekly* (December 10, 2004): 36–37.

8. Rachel Chang, "Bell-issima!," *Cosmo Girl*, Vol. 10, No. 3 (May 2008).

9. Peter Rainer, "Strangers with Candy," *Christian Science Monitor*, Vol. 98, No. 155. (July 7, 2006).

10. Anon., "Zany Brains Concoct Absurdly Tart *Candy,*" *San Francisco Chronicle* (July 7, 2005): E-5.

11. Sara Gwenllian-Jones and Roberta Pearson, "Introduction," in Sara Gwenllian-Jones and Roberta Pearson, eds., *Cult Television* (Minneapolis: Univ. of Minnesota Press, 2004), ix.

12. Jeffrey Sconce, "*Star Trek*, Heaven's Gate, and Textual Transcendence," in Gwenllian-Jones and Pearson, eds., *Cult Television*, 216.

13. As Mike Duffy states, "The overall audience for *Veronica Mars* may be teensy—averaging just over 2.4 million viewers each week compared to the twenty-three million or so who tune into *Desperate Housewives* each week—but they're totally hooked. And they pay very close attention." Duffy also remarks that "lousy ratings" are a "longtime curse of imaginative, high-quality cult shows from *My So-Called Life* to *Freaks and Geeks.*" Mike Duffy, "Intelligent Life on *Mars*: UPN Hopes More Viewers Will Clue In," *Detroit Free Press* (May 6, 2005).

14. Gregory, *Be Seeing You . . . Decoding The Prisoner*, 191.

15. Xavier Mendik and Graeme Harper, "Introduction," in Xavier Mendik and Graeme Harper, eds., *Unruly Pleasures: The Cult Film and its Critics* (Guildford, Surrey: FAB Press, 2000), 7–10.

16. Robert Pearson, "Observations on Cult Television," in Stacey Abbott, ed., *The Cult TV Book* (London: I.B. Tauris, 2010), 8.

17. Janet Staiger, *Perverse Spectators: The Practices of Film Reception* (New York: NYU Press, 2000), 107.

18. Roland Barthes, *The Pleasure of the Text*, trans. R. Miller (New York: Hill & Wang, 1987).

19. Eileen R. Meehan, "'Holy Commodity Fetish, Batman!': The Political Economy of the Commercial Intertext," in Roberta Pearson and William Uricchio, eds., *The Many Lives of the Batman* (New York: Routledge, 1991), 47–65.

20. Jenkins, *Convergence Culture*, 147.

21. Susan Purdie, "Secular Definitions of 'Ritual': The *Rocky Horror* Phenomenon," in Shimon Levy, ed., *Theatre and Holy Script* (Portland: Sussex Academic Press, 1999), 177.

22. Gregory, *Be Seeing You . . . Decoding The Prisoner*, 198.

23. Mark Jancovich, "Cult Fictions: Cult Movies, Subcultural Capital, and the Production of Cultural Distinctions," *Cultural Studies*, Vol. 16, No. 2 (2002): 308.

24. Antonio Lopes Lagarto, the creator of an online companion to *Strangers with Candy*, proudly refers to himself and other fans of the series as "Candy Asses" (http://www.jerriblank.com /swc.html#mytop). In the case of *Veronica Mars* fandom, a subset of followers labeled themselves "Cloud Watchers" in the months leading to the show's cancellation—a spiritualist expression associated with heavenly (textual) transcendence and wish fulfillment (despite the fact that their campaign to ensure the program's continuation ultimately failed). Tonya R. Cochran, "Neptune (Non-)Consensual: The Risky Business of Television Fandom, Falling in Love, and Playing the Victim," in Rhonda Wilcox and Sue Turnbull, eds., *Investigating Veronica Mars: Essays on the Teen Detective Series* (Jefferson, NC: McFarland, 2011), 179.

25. Sconce, "*Star Trek*, Heaven's Gate, and Textual Transcendence," 202.

26. Sconce, 202.

27. Sconce, 216.

28. An almost identical concern is voiced by an FBI agent in "Nine Wives" (3.12), an episode of the TV series *Numb3rs* (CBS, 2005–10). Near the end of the story, Special Agent Don Eppes (Rob Morrow) states, "I don't want tear gas, I don't want another Waco," as he and a SWAT team stand

outside the compound of a polygamist cult (the Apostolic Saints) moments before its leader, Abner Stone (a.k.a. The Prophet) (W. Earl Brown), sets fire to the house and kills his followers.

29. Lynn S. Neal, "'They're Freaks!' The Cult Stereotype in Fictional Television Shows, 1958–2008," *Nova Religio: The Journal of Alternative and Emergent Religions*, Vol. 14, No. 3 (2011): 95.

30. Neal, "'They're Freaks!,'" 95.

31. Emily Edwards, *Metaphysical Media: The Occult Experience in Popular Culture* (Carbondale, IL: Southern Illinois Univ. Press, 2005), 11.

32. George Gerbner, Larry Gross, Michael Morgan, and Nancy Signorielli, "Living with Television: The Dynamics of the Cultivation Process," in Jennings Bryant and Dolf Zillmann, eds., *Perspectives on Media Effects* (Hillsdale, N.J.: L. Erlbaum Associates, 1986), 17–40.

33. Edwards, *Metaphysical Media*, 11.

34. Edwards, 113.

35. Megan Goodwin, "Unpacking the Bunker: Sex, Abuse, and Apocalypticism in *Unbreakable Kimmy Schmidt*," *Cross Currents* (June 2018): 2.

36. Goodwin, 3.

37. Goodwin, 3.

38. Goodwin, 2.

39. Neal, "'They're Freaks!,'" 83.

40. Kristen Kidder, "The New Normal: Breaking the Boundaries of Vigilantism in *Veronica Mars*," in Rob Thomas, ed., *Neptune Noir: Unauthorized Investigations into Veronica Mars* (Dallas: BenBella Books, 2006), 126.

41. Neal, "'They're Freaks!,'" 99.

42. John Tulloch and Manuel Alvarado, *Doctor Who: The Unfolding Text*, London: Macmillan (1983).

43. Marybeth Ayella, "'They Must Be Crazy': Some of the Difficulties in Researching 'Cults,'" *American Behavioral Scientist*, Vol. 33, No. 5 (May/June 1990): 562–77.

44. Roseanne Barr, *Roseannearchy: Dispatches from the Nut Farm* (New York: Gallery Books, 2011), 23. With regard to religion, Barr—a Jewish American comic who grew up in Salt Lake City immersed in Mormonism (owing to her family's involvement to The Church of Jesus Christ of Latter-day Saints)—speaks with some authority as someone who has seen her own faith mocked by other comedians (though she herself has called Mormons the "Nazi Amish").

6. Very Spooky Episodes

1. For information about the ancient festival of Samhain, a combined New Year's Day for the Celts as well as a Day of the Dead that vaguely anticipates some contemporary Halloween practices and iconography, see Jack Santino, "Introduction: Festivals and Death and Life," in Jack Santino, ed., *Halloween and Other Festivals of Death and Life* (Knoxville, TN: Univ. of Tennessee Press, 1994), xiv–xvi.

2. Craig Semon, "Halloween, Horror: Harmless Fun or a Step Too Far?," *Associated Press* (October 17, 2015): https://www.apnews.com/42f2a6be8aa2491c89a294156fa29002.

3. David Skal, *Death Makes a Holiday: A Cultural History of Halloween* (New York: Bloomsbury, 2002), 17.

4. Skal, 17.

5. Skal, 9.

6. Dina Khapaeva, *The Celebration of Death in Contemporary Culture* (Ann Arbor, MI: Univ. of Michigan Press, 2017), 57.

7. Joanne Morreale, *The Donna Reed Show* (Detroit: Wayne State Univ. Press, 2012), 125.

8. Morreale, 125; Janet Lee, "Subversive Sitcoms: *Roseanne* as Inspiration for Feminist Resistance," *Women's Studies*, Vol. 21, No. 1 (1992): 87–101; Sujata Moorti, "Brown Girls Who Don't Need Saving: Social Media and the Role of 'Possessive Investment' in *The Mindy Project* and *The Good Wife*," in Rachel Moseley, Helen Wheatley, and Helen Wood, eds., *Television for Women: New Directions* (New York: Routledge, 2017), 101.

9. Bonnie J. Dow, *Prime-Time Feminism: Television, Media Culture, and the Women's Movement Since 1970* (Philadelphia: Univ. of Pennsylvania Press, 1996), 99–100.

10. Nicholas Rogers, *Halloween: From Pagan Ritual to Party Night* (New York: Oxford Univ. Press, 2002), 165, 172.

11. Rogers, 9.

12. Rogers, 163–64.

13. Rogers, 172.

14. Samira Kawash, *Candy: A Century of Panic and Pleasure* (New York: Farrar, Straus and Giroux, 2013), 9.

15. Kawash, 272.

16. Bartholomew and Reumschuessel, *American Intolerance: Our Dark History of Demonizing Immigrants* (Amherst, NY: Prometheus Books, 2018), 25.

17. Set in the early-to-mid 1970s, the Netflix comedy *F is for Family* (2015–present) features an episode ("F is for Halloween" [1.04]) that plays on the paranoia concerning candy-tampering and other holiday-associated threats to children's safety. At one point, Frank (voiced by series co-creator Bill Burr), the foul-mouthed protagonist and father of three children, shakes his fist at a group of young trick-or-treaters who—in one fell swoop—have taken all of the candy he had left out on the porch, and as the "stupid, goddamned kids" flee the scene he yells, "I hope somebody puts a razor blade in your apple!"

18. Kawash, *Candy*, 273.

19. Bartholomew and Reumschuessel, *American Intolerance*, 25.

20. Bartholomew and Reumschuessel, 25.

21. Kawash, *Candy*, 274.

22. Skal, *Death Makes a Holiday*, 54.

23. Moorti, "Brown Girls Who Don't Need Saving," 93.

24. Sarah Honeyman, *Consuming Agency in Fairy Tales, Childlore, and Folkliterature* (New York: Routledge, 2010), 84.

25. Anon., "I've Been Waiting for a Great Pumpkin and He Never Seems to Show Up," *The Moth Chase* (2012): https://themothchase.wordpress.com/2012/10/30/ive-been-waiting-for-a-great-pumpkin-and-he-never-seems-to-show-up/.

26. This idea of cultural mixing through costumed mashups is similarly spotlighted in the "Halloween" episode of another single-camera comedy, *New Girl* (Fox, 2011–18). Aired on the same network and night (October 30, 2012) as the aforementioned installment of *The Mindy Project*, the *New Girl* episode begins with Jess, the show's free-spirited main character, returning home from her work at a haunted house. Still dressed in her costume, she looks schlubby and undead, "like a zombie Woody Allen," according to her roommate Schmidt. Mimicking his imitation of the

Jewish American filmmaker, Jess responds with her own hybridized concoction, saying "Zombie Cristina Barcelona." Such comments, which might seem of little significance (as tossed-off lines and cheesy puns on popular culture), underline Halloween TV's intertextual playfulness, which is made more explicit—brought to the literal surface—by way of a narrative conceit unique to "very spooky episodes": namely, the role-playing and dress-up that the holiday not only sanctions but also encourages.

27. Joy Press, *Stealing the Show: How Women Are Revolutionizing Television* (New York: Atria, 2018), 160.

28. Moorti, "Brown Girls Who Don't Need Saving," 101.

29. Moorti, 101; Kathleen K. Rowe, *The Unruly Woman: Gender and the Genres of Laughter* (Austin: Univ. of Texas Press, 1995), 50–92.

30. Moorti, "Brown Girls Who Don't Need Saving," 93.

31. Rogers, *Halloween*, 9.

32. Sharron J. Lennon, Zhiying Zheng, and Aziz Fatnassi, "Women's Revealing Halloween Costumes: Other-Objectification and Sexualization," *Fashion and Textiles*, Vol. 3, No. 21 (2016): 1–19.

33. Lisa Morton, *The Halloween Encyclopedia* (Jefferson, NC: McFarland & Company, Inc., 2011), 85.

7. "Three-Headed Monster"

1. Lesley Goldberg, "*Roseanne* Canceled at ABC Following Racist Tweet," *Hollywood Reporter* (May 28, 2018): https://www.hollywoodreporter.com/live-feed/roseanne-canceled-at-abc-racist-tweet-1115412.

2. Jonathan Berr, "Is ABC's Monster Hit *Roseanne* Scaring Away Liberal Viewers?" *Forbes* (April 14, 2018): https://www.forbes.com/sites/jonathanberr/2018/04/14/is-abcs-monster-hit-roseanne-scaring-away-liberal-viewers/#50ec1991750f.

3. In the words of William Douglass, working-class characters—husbands in particular—are commonly portrayed as "inept, immature, stupid, lacking in good sense, and emotional," in contrast to "their middle-class counterparts." This otherizing of low-wage male workers (epitomized by slump-shouldered, beer-bellied protagonists in such primetime cartoons as *The Flintstones* [ABC, 1960–66] and *The Simpsons* [Fox, 1989–present]) is distinct from the way in which their working-class wives are typically depicted ("as relatively intelligent, rational, and responsible" women who nevertheless lack the power or monetary means to escape their fate as domestic "servants"). See William Douglass, "Subversion of the American Television Family," in Jennings Bryant and J. Alison Bryant, eds., *Television and the American Family* (Mahway, NJ: Lawrence Erlbaum Associates, 2001), 229–46. For a different, non-TV-specific take on widespread cultural attitudes toward working-class women, see Ruth Sidel, "The Enemy Within: The Demonization of Poor Women," *Journal of Sociology and Social Welfare*, Vol. 27, No. 1 (March 2000): 73–84.

4. Richard Butsch, "Six Decades of Social Class in American Sitcoms," in Nicole Cloarec, David Haigron, and Delphine Letort, eds., *Social Class on British and American Screens: Essays on Cinema and Television* (Jefferson, NC: McFarland & Company, Inc., 2016), 27.

5. Melissa Williams, "'Excuse the Mess, But We Live Here': Roseanne Barr's Stardom and the Politics of Class," in Kylo-Patrick R. Hart, ed., *Film and Television Stardom* (Newcastle upon Tyne: Cambridge Scholars Publishing, 2008), 191–92.

6. Diana Elizabeth Kendall, *Framing Class: Media Representations of Wealth and Poverty in America* (Lanham, MD: Rowman & Littlefield, 2005) 157.

7. Williams, "'Excuse the Mess, But We Live Here,'" 192; Susan McLeland, "*Roseanne*, Reality, and Domestic Comedy," in Mary M. Dalton and Laura R. Linder, eds., *The Sitcom Reader: America Re-viewed, Still Skewed* [second edition] (Albany, NY: SUNY Press, 2016), 168.

8. Tison Pugh, *The Queer Fantasies of the American Family Sitcom* (New Brunswick, NJ: Rutgers Univ. Press, 2018), 124.

9. Saniya Lee Ghanoui, "Mediated Bodies: The Construction of a Wife, Mother, and the Female Body in Television Sitcoms," *Proceedings of the New York State Communication Association*, Vol. 2012, No. 5 (2013): 14; http://docs.rwu.edu/nyscaproceedings/vol2012/iss1/5.

10. Lynn Spigel, *Make Room for TV: Television and the Family Ideal in Postwar America* (Chicago: Univ. of Chicago Press, 1992), 47.

11. Pugh, *The Queer Fantasies of the American Family Sitcom*, 125.

12. Pugh, 125.

13. Lynne Joyrich, "Epistemology of the Console," in Glyn Davis and Gary Needham, eds., *Queer TV: Theories, Histories, Politics* (New York: Routledge, 2009), 20.

14. Joyrich, 38.

15. Joyrich, 20.

16. Originally airing on October 31, 1995, "Halloween: The Final Chapter" would be followed by Season Nine's equally scattershot "Satan, Darling" (9.07), broadcast one year later.

17. The short-lived sitcom *In-Laws* (NBC, 2002–3) demonstrates suburban dwellers' tendency to let the holiday's built-in competitiveness (to out-scare or out-decorate one's neighbors) get the best of them. In the episode "Halloween: Resurrection," an already combative Italian American family informs its most recent member—the young Jewish-American man who has married into it—that past years' celebrations have nearly brought about the ruin of their neighborhood, owing to the destructive vandalism that sometimes creeps into the proceedings. Regardless, the Pellets (led by the tellingly named patriarch Victor) succumb to the pressure of competing against their neighbors once more, installing a giant crypt on their front lawn that, despite costing a fortune, might be "the difference between [them] winning and losing."

18. Taylor Nygaard and Jorie Lagerwey, *Horrible White People* (New York: NYU Press, 2020).

19. Nygaard and Lagerwey, 7.

20. Julie Bettie, "Class Dismissed? *Roseanne* and the Changing Face of Working-Class Iconography," *Social Text*, No. 45 (Winter, 1995): 135.

21. *Roseanne*'s final episode famously pulled one last "prank" on its audience by revealing that the ninth season—and many of the events leading up to it—was a "lie," only to upend that claim with yet another revelation at the beginning of its 2018 relaunch.

22. Tyler Curry, "There's a Reason Why Queer Folks Love Halloween So Much," *The Advocate* (October 30, 2019): https://www.advocate.com/exclusives/2019/10/30/theres-reason-why-queer-folks-love-halloween-so-much.

23. Curry, "Queer Folks."

24. For example, the pre-credits scene in Season Four's "Trick Me Up, Trick Me Down" shows an undead version of Dan tricking his neighbor into believing that he is the latest victim of his homicidal wife, who appears to have stabbed him in the stomach with a knife. As his guts spill out from the bloody wound onto the kitchen floor, the woman, shocked beyond belief, rushes toward the front door, gasping, "That was a horrible, horrible, *horrible* thing to do!"

25. Dina Khapaeva, *The Celebration of Death in Contemporary Culture* (Ann Arbor, MI: Univ. of Michigan Press, 2017), 56.

26. Williams, "'Excuse the Mess, But We Live Here,'" 193; Bettie, "Class Dismissed?" 130, 133; Michael Grabowski, "Resignation and Positive Thinking in the Working-Class Family Sitcom," *Atlantic Journal of Communication*, Vol. 22, No. 2 (2014): 127.

27. Lauren Michele Jackson, *White Negroes: When Cornrows Were in Vogue and Other Thoughts on Cultural Appropriation* (Boston: Beacon Press, 2019), 2.

28. Jackson, 2.

29. The creators of a few recently produced sitcoms, including *Scrubs* (NBC, 2001–10) and *30 Rock* (NBC, 2006–11), have asked network and cable TV executives to remove episodes featuring scenes of white actors in blackface from their programming schedules, a move that has been supported by many creative personnel in the industry (including the actors who appeared in those episodes) but also mocked by naysayers as a symptom of contemporary "cancel culture."

30. Billy Nilles, "A TV Wasteland: When Beloved Stars' Bad Behavior Ruins Their Classic Comedies Forever," *E Online* (June 1, 2018): https://www.eonline.com/news/940458/a-tv-wasteland -when-beloved-stars-bad-behavior-ruins-their-classic-comedies-forever.

31. See, for instance, Gary Abernathy's *Washington Post* article "Roseanne Barr's Tweet Was Horrible, with Sad Consequences" (May 29, 2018).

32. Anon., "'A Monster in the White House': Why Donald Trump is a Wild Card for Wary Wall Street," *Financial Post* (November 9, 2016): https://financialpost.com/investing/why-donald -trump-is-an-absolute-wild-card-for-wall-street.

33. Jeff Wise, "Michael Cohen on How 'Monster' Trump Will Undermine Biden," *New York* (December 3, 2020): https://nymag.com/intelligencer/2020/12/michael-cohen-on-how-monster -trump-will-undermine-biden.html.

34. Jennifer Finney Boylan, "Trump, the Monster Who Feeds on Fear," *New York Times* (November 28, 2018): https://www.nytimes.com/2018/11/28/opinion/trump-the-monster-who-feeds-on -fear.html.

35. Boylan, "Trump."

36. Nilles, "A TV Wasteland."

8. "Ugly Americans"

1. Dina Khapaeva, *The Celebration of Death in Contemporary Culture* (Ann Arbor, MI: Univ. of Michigan Press, 2017), 14, 47.

2. Khapaeva, 186.

3. Khapaeva, 56.

4. Jack Santino, "Introduction: Festivals and Death and Life," in Jack Santino, ed., *Halloween and Other Festivals of Death and Life* (Knoxville, TN: Univ. of Tennessee Press, 1994).

5. Richard Kearny, *Strangers, Gods, and Monsters: Interpreting Otherness* (New York: Routledge, 2003), 230.

6. Tina Marie Boyer, "The Anatomy of a Monster: The Case of Slender Man," *Preternature: Critical and Historical Studies on the Preternatural*, Vol. 2, No. 2 (2013): 250.

7. Kearny, *Strangers, Gods, and Monsters*, 230.

8. Jeremy G. Butler, *Television: Critical Methods and Applications* (New York: Routledge, 2012), 57.

9. A. Bowdoin Van Riper, "Spy Versus Reality: *Get Smart*, Satire, and Absurdity," in Laura Westengard and Aaron Barlow, eds., *The 25 Sitcoms That Changed Television* (Santa Barbara, CA: Praeger, 2018), 54–67.

10. Lorna Jowett and Stacey Abbott, *TV Horror: Investigating the Darker Side of the Small Screen* (London: I.B. Tauris & Co., Ltd., 2013), 24.

11. Stephen Tropiano, *The Prime Time Closet: A History of Gays and Lesbians on TV* (New York: Applause Theatre & Cinema Books, 2002), 185.

12. Barrett Holmes Pitner, "Viewpoint: US Must Confront Its Original Sin to Move Forward," BBC.com (June 3, 2020): https://www.bbc.com/news/world-us-canada-52912238.

13. Pitner, "US Must Confront Its Original Sin."

14. Anon., "NAACP Commends ABC for Cancellation of *Roseanne*," *NAACP* (May 29, 2018): https://www.naacp.org/latest/naacp-commends-abc-cancellation-roseanne/.

15. W. Scott Poole, *Monsters in America: Our Historical Obsession with the Hideous and Haunting* (Waco, TX: Baylor Univ. Press, 2011): xvi–xvii.

16. Poole, xvi–xvii

17. Stephen T. Asma, *On Monsters: An Unnatural History of Our Worst Fears* (Oxford: Oxford Univ. Press, 2009), 233.

18. Poole, *Monsters in America*, xvi.

19. Walter Metz, *Gilligan's Island* (Detroit: Wayne State Univ. Press, 2012), 32.

20. Erika Lee, *The Making of Asian America: A History* (New York: Simon & Schuster, 2015), 285.

21. Lee, 286.

22. M. Keith Booker, *Drawn to Television: Prime-time Animation from "The Flintstones" to "Family Guy"* (Westport, CT: Praeger, 2006), 32–33.

23. Elizabeth Young, *Black Frankenstein: The Making of an American Metaphor* (New York: NYU Press, 2008).

24. Young, 5.

25. Susan E. Lederer, *Frankenstein: Penetrating the Secrets of Nature* (New Brunswick, NJ: Rutgers Univ. Press, 2002), 35. See also Angela Smith, *Hideous Progeny: Disability, Eugenics, and Classic Horror Cinema* (New York: Columbia Univ. Press, 2011), 66.

26. Young, *Black Frankenstein*, 4.

27. Robin R. Means Coleman, *Horror Noire: Blacks in American Horror Films from the 1890s to Present* (New York: Routledge, 2011), 24.

28. As Joshua David Bellin states, "The racist portrait of the African American male as 'a monstrous beast, crazed with lust' for the white woman . . . had, of course, a long and ignominious pedigree." In his study of monsters as social constructs, the author gestures toward "statistics on the nearly three thousand African Americans lynched between 1889 and 1933," pointing out that "though fewer than one-quarter were directly accused of raping or attempting to rape a white woman, rumors of rape were almost always circulated to vindicate, if not any particular act, then the more general need for lynching as a means of keeping the savage sexuality of the black 'buck' in check." Joshua David Bellin, *Framing Monsters: Fantasy Film and Social Alienation* (Carbondale, IL: Southern Illinois Univ. Press, 2005), 27.

29. Coleman, *Horror Noire*, 27.

30. Mark Voger, *Monster Mash: The Creepy, Kooky Monster Craze in America, 1957–1972* (Raleigh, NC: TwoMorrows Publishing, 2015).

31. Voger, 23.

32. Helen Wheatley, *Gothic Television* (Manchester: Manchester Univ. Press, 2006), 129.

33. In keeping with this theme of transgression, darker thanatological subject matter also emerges in this and its rival network's monster comedy, *The Addams Family*; including talk of suicide in "Uncle Fester's Toupee" (1.31), an episode from the first season of the latter program. *The Addams Family* furthermore includes verbal references to domestic abuse, in "The Winning of Morticia Addams" (1.34) and "Gomez, the People's Choice" (2.05) that would have been inappropriate if spoken about in the Anderson or Cleaver households.

34. Significantly, "Munsters on the Move" was broadcast in the spring of 1965, just a few months before civil unrest occurred in Los Angeles. Referred to as the Watts Rebellion (or Uprising) and framed by newscasters at that time as a "riot" and a "revolt," this insurrectionary moment in modern American history, which took place in a largely working-class African American neighborhood of LA between August 11 to 16, 1965, retroactively imbues this episode about folks standing their ground in the face of the city's redevelopment efforts with deeper sociopolitical meaning.

35. This plot element in the pilot episode of *The Addams Family* would be echoed in Season Two's "Morticia, the Writer" (2.08). When Pugsley and Wednesday complain about their school's required readings, including "terrible literature" about "wicked" goblins and witches, Morticia sets about penning stories that will not "poison" children's minds, including her first book, *Cinderella, the Teenaged Delinquent*. Realizing that he had a hand in spurring his wife to take such action (leading her to become so successful a writer that she is asked by her publisher to go on book tour and leave parenting duties to her husband), Gomez exclaims, Gadzooks, I may have created a Frankenstein!"

36. Michel Foucault, *Abnormal: Lectures at the Collège de France, 1974–1975* (New York: Picador, 2003), 55–56.

37. Kris King "*Ugly Americans*, Season One," *Slate* (April 9, 2010): https://www.slantmagazine.com/tv/ugly-americans-season-one/.

Beyond Bad and Evil

1. Christine Tibbles McBurney, "Writing *One Day at a Time*: Reflections on a Life Inside the Tube," in Laura Westengard and Aaron Barlow, eds., *The 25 Sitcoms that Changed Television: Turning Points in American Culture* (Santa Barbara, CA: ABC-CLIO, 2018), 114.

2. Wheatley, *Gothic Television*, 129.

3. Jason Mittell, *Television and American Culture* (New York: Oxford Univ. Press, 2010), 319.

4. Charles Pinkney, *From Slaveships to Scholarships: The Plight of the African-American Athlete* (Bloomington, IN: AuthorHouse, 2017), 11.

5. Greta Bjornson, "Herman Munster's Speech Praised on Twitter as 'Words of Wisdom,'" *Decider* (June 4, 2020): https://decider.com/2020/06/04/herman-munster-equality-speech/.

6. Hank Steuver, "How Herman Munster Can Be So Right about Racism and Still Be a Little Wrong," *Washington Post* (June 4, 2020).

7. Jack O'Keefe, "Some Relationships Can't Survive Trump's Administration on *One Mississippi*," *Bustle* (September 8, 2017): https://www.bustle.com/p/remy-vickys-breakup-on-one-mississippi-shows-how-the-aftermath-of-the-2016-election-can-bring-relationship-problems-to-the-forefront-2301794.

8. Laura Bradley, "*The Good Place* Isn't Just Funny: It's Necessary," *Vanity Fair* (September 27, 2018): https://www.vanityfair.com/hollywood/2018/09/the-good-place-season-3-premiere-review.

9. Dylan Matthews, "How *The Good Place* Taught Moral Philosophy to Its Characters—and Its Creators," *Vox* (January 30, 2020): https://www.vox.com/future-perfect/2019/9/26/20874217/the -good-place-series-finale-season-4-moral-philosophy.

10. Maliya V. Ellis and Woojin Lim, "Asking Philosopher T. M. Scanlon 'What We Owe to Each Other,'" *Fifteen Minutes* (October 10, 2019): https://www.thecrimson.com/article/2019/10/10 /scanlon-and-the-good-place/.

11. Jeremy Egner, "Michael Schur on *The Good Place*, Ted Danson and Kantian Ethics," *New York Times* (January 18, 2017): https://www.nytimes.com/2017/01/18/arts/television/michael-schur -on-the-good-place-ted-danson-and-kantian-ethics.html.

12. Aletha C. Huston, Diana Zuckerman, Halford Fairchild, Brian L. Wilcox, and Ed Donnerstein, *Big World, Small Screen: The Role of Television in American Society* (Lincoln, NE: Univ. of Nebraska Press, 1992), 4–5.

13. David Marc, *Comic Visions: Television Comedy and American Culture* (Malden, MA: Blackwell Publishers, Inc., 1989); Darrell Hamamoto, *Nervous Laughter: Television Situation Comedy and Liberal Democratic Ideology* (New York: Praeger Publishers, 1989); Joanne Morreale, ed., *Critiquing the Sitcom: A Reader* (Syracuse, NY: Syracuse Univ. Press, 2003).

14. Michael V. Tueth, *Laughter in the Living Room: Television Comedy and the American Home Audience* (New York: Peter Lang Publishing, Inc., 2005); Doyle Greene, *Politics and the American Television Comedy: A Critical Survey from I Love Lucy Through South Park* (Jefferson, NC: McFarland & Co., Inc., 2008); Christina von Hodenberg, *Television's Moment: Sitcom Audiences and the Sixties Cultural Revolution* (New York: Berghahn Books, 2015); Rosie White, *Television Comedy and Femininity: Queering Gender* (London: I.B. Tauris, 2018); Alice Leppert, *TV Family Values: Gender, Domestic Labor, and 1980s Sitcoms* (New Brunswick, NJ: Rutgers Univ. Press, 2019).

15. Mary Ann Watson, *Defining Visions: Television and the American Experience in the 20th Century* (Malden, MA: Blackwell Publishing, 2008), 265–66.

16. Erik Adams, "*The Good Place*, Annotated: 'Pandemonium,'" *AV Club* (January 25, 2019): https://tv.avclub.com/the-good-place-annotated-pandemonium-1832069778; David Canfield, "Why *The Good Place* is NBC's Meta Successor to *Community*," *Entertainment Weekly* (October 20, 2017): https://ew.com/tv/2017/10/20/the-good-place-community-nbc/.

17. Jack Katz, *How Emotions Work* (Chicago: Univ. of Chicago Press, 1999), 87.

18. Katz, 141.

19. Erik Kohn, "*It's Always Sunny in Philadelphia* Delivered One of Its Wildest Episodes with Season 11's 'Being Frank,'" *IndieWire* (February 17, 2016): https://www.indiewire.com/2016/02/its -always-sunny-in-philadelphia-delivered-one-of-its-wildest-episodes-with-season-11s-being-frank -21995/.

20. Kohn, "*It's Always Sunny in Philadelphia.*"

21. Dennis Perkins, "Getting Inside Frank's Head Makes for a Funny, Tragic *It's Always Sunny*," *AV Club* (February 20, 2016): https://tv.avclub.com/getting-inside-frank-s-head-makes-for -a-funny-tragic-i-1798186608.

22. Adam Henschke, "Frank Reynolds, Role Model," in Roger Hunt and Robert Arp, eds., *"It's Always Sunny" and Philosophy: The Gang Gets Analyzed* (Chicago: Open Court, 2015), 91.

Bibliography

Abernathy, Gary. "Roseanne Barr's Tweet Was Horrible, with Sad Consequences." *Washington Post*, May 29, 2018. https://www.washingtonpost.com/blogs/post-partisan/wp/2018/05/29/roseanne-barrs-tweet-was-horrible-with-sad-consequences/.

Acham, Christine. *Revolution Televised: Prime Time and the Struggle for Black Power.* Minneapolis: Univ. of Minnesota Press, 2004.

Adams, Erik. "*The Good Place*, Annotated: 'Pandemonium.'" *AV Club*, January 25, 2019. https://tv.avclub.com/the-good-place-annotated-pandemonium-1832069778.

Aletta, Elvira G. "7 Reasons Charlie Sheen May Hate Alcoholics Anonymous." *PsychCentral*, July 8, 2018. https://psychcentral.com/blog/7-reasons-charlie-sheen-may-hate-alcoholics-anonymous/.

Ames, Genevieve, and Carol Cunradi. "Alcohol Use and Preventing Alcohol-Related Problems Among Young Adults in the Military." *Alcohol Research & Health* 28, no. 4 (2004): 252–57.

Anon. "Alcoholism Held Illness Rising Out of Problems." *Los Angeles Times*, October 24, 1947.

Anon. "Opinion." *New York Times*, November 14, 1987.

Anon. "Leno Calls Telecast on *Cheers* 'a Mistake.'" *Los Angeles Times*, May 28, 1993. https://www.latimes.com/archives/la-xpm-1993-05-28-ca-40740-story.html.

Anon. "Zany Brains Concoct Absurdly Tart *Candy*." *San Francisco Chronicle*, July 7, 2005.

Anon. "I've Been Waiting for a Great Pumpkin and He Never Seems to Show Up." *The Moth Chase*, 2012. https://themothchase.wordpress.com/2012/10/30/ive-been-waiting-for-a-great-pumpkin-and-he-never-seems-to-show-up/.

Anon. "'A Monster in the White House': Why Donald Trump is a Wild Card for Wary Wall Street." *Financial Post*, November 9, 2016. https://financialpost.com/investing/why-donald-trump-is-an-absolute-wild-card-for-wall-street.

Anon. "NAACP Commends ABC for Cancellation of *Roseanne*." NAACP, May 29, 2018. https://www.naacp.org/latest/naacp-commends-abc-cancellation-roseanne/.

Apthorp, Stephen P. *Alcohol and Substance Abuse: A Handbook for Clergy and Congregations.* Lincoln, NE: iUniverse, 2003.

Armstrong, Jennifer. "Bell of the Fall." *Entertainment Weekly*, December 10, 2004.

Arnold, Gordon. *The Afterlife of America's War in Vietnam: Changing Visions in Politics and on Screen.* Jefferson, NC: McFarland, 2006.

Arpe, Malene. "Arrest Me for Loving a Sitcom." *Toronto Star*, October 13, 2005.

Asma, Stephen T. *On Monsters: An Unnatural History of Our Worst Fears*. Oxford: Oxford Univ. Press, 2009.

Austerlitz, Saul. *Sitcom: A History in 24 Episodes from "I Love Lucy" to "Community."* Chicago: Chicago Review Press, 2014.

Ayella, Marybeth. "'They Must Be Crazy': Some of the Difficulties in Researching 'Cults.'" *American Behavioral Scientist* 33, no. 5 (May/June, 1990): 562–77.

Bainbridge, William S. *The Sociology of Religious Movements*. London: Routledge, 1997.

Barr, Roseanne. *Roseannearchy: Dispatches from the Nut Farm*. New York: Gallery Books, 2011.

Barrett, David V. *Sects, "Cults" and Alternative Religions: A World Survey and Sourcebook*. London: Blandford, 1996.

Barthes, Roland. *The Pleasure of the Text*. Trans. R. Miller. New York: Hill & Wang, 1987.

Bartholomew, Robert, and Anja Reumschuessel. *American Intolerance: Our Dark History of Demonizing Immigrants*. Amherst, NY: Prometheus Books, 2018.

Batchelor, Edward A. "I Was Cured of TV." *Coronet* 37, (February 1955): 38–40.

Beach, Bob. "Authority in Storytelling: Comedy Central's *Drunk History*, Intoxication, and the Historian's Craft." *Points*, December 11, 2018. https://pointsadhs.com/2018/12/11/authority-in-storytelling-comedy-centrals-drunk-history-intoxication-and-the-historians-craft/.

Bellin, Joshua David. *Framing Monsters: Fantasy Film and Social Alienation*. Carbondale, IL: Southern Illinois Univ. Press, 2005.

Béra, Matthieu. "Émile Durkheim: A Biography by Marcel Fournier." *Sociologica* 7, no. 3 (2013): 1–9.

Berr, Jonathan. "Is ABC's Monster Hit *Roseanne* Scaring Away Liberal Viewers?" *Forbes*, April 14, 2018. https://www.forbes.com/sites/jonathanberr/2018/04/14/is-abcs-monster-hit-roseanne-scaring-away-liberal-viewers/#50ec1991750f.

de Bertodano, Helena. "Dick Van Dyke: 'I'd Go to Work with Terrible Hangovers.'" *Telegraph*, January 7, 2003. https://www.telegraph.co.uk/culture/film/film-news/9779018/Dick-Van-Dyke-Id-go-to-work-with-terrible-hangovers.-Which-if-youre-dancing-is-hard.html.

Bethell, Ben. "Cagney and Lacey." In *Cop Shows: A Critical History of Police Dramas on Television*, edited by Roger Sabin, 99–106. Jefferson, NC: McFarland & Company, Inc, 2015.

Bettie, Julie. "Class Dismissed? *Roseanne* and the Changing Face of Working-Class Iconography." *Social Text* 45, (Winter 1995): 125–49.

Billig, Michael. *Laughter and Ridicule: Towards a Social Critique of Humour*. Thousand Oaks, CA: SAGE Publications, Inc, 2005.

Bjornson, Greta. "Herman Munster's Speech Praised on Twitter as 'Words of Wisdom.'" *Decider*, June 4, 2020. https://decider.com/2020/06/04/herman-munster-equality-speech/.

Booker, M. Keith. *Drawn to Television: Prime-time Animation from "The Flintstones" to "Family Guy."* Westport, CT: Praeger, 2006.

Boyer, Tina Marie. "The Anatomy of a Monster: The Case of Slender Man." *Preternature: Critical and Historical Studies on the Preternatural* 2, no. 2 (2013): 240–61.

Boylan, Jennifer Finney. "Trump, the Monster Who Feeds on Fear." *New York Times*, November 28, 2018. https://www.nytimes.com/2018/11/28/opinion/trump-the-monster-who-feeds-on-fear.html.

Bradley, Laura. "*The Good Place* Isn't Just Funny: It's Necessary." *Vanity Fair*, September 27, 2018. https://www.vanityfair.com/hollywood/2018/09/the-good-place-season-3-premiere-review.

Bray, Robert, Mary Ellen Marsden, John F. Mazzuchi, and Roger W. Hartman. "Prevention in the Military." In *Prevention and Societal Impact of Drug and Alcohol Abuse*, edited by Robert T. Ammerman, Peggy J. Ott, and Ralph E. Tarter, 345–67. Mahwah, NJ: Lawrence Erlbaum Associates, 1999.

Breed, Warren, and James R. De Foe. "Drinking and Smoking on Television, 1950–1982." *Journal of Public Health Policy* 5, no. 2 (June 1984): 257–70.

Brooker, Will. *Using the Force: Creativity, Community and Star Wars Fans*. New York: Continuum, 2002.

Bugliosi, Vincent, with Curt Gentry. *Helter Skelter: The True Story of the Manson Murders*. New York: W.W. Norton & Company, Inc, 1974.

Butler, Jeremy G. *Television: Critical Methods and Applications*. New York: Routledge, 2012.

Butsch, Richard. *The Citizen Audience: Crowds, Publics, and Individuals*. New York: Routledge, 2008.

———. "Six Decades of Social Class in American Sitcoms." In *Social Class on British and American Screens: Essays on Cinema and Television*, edited by Nicole Cloarec, David Haigron, and Delphine Letort, 18–33. Jefferson, NC: McFarland & Company, Inc., 2016.

———. "Boob Tubes, Fans, and Addicts." In *Communication in History: Stone Age Symbols to Social Media*, edited by Peter Urquhart and Paul Heyer, 283–88. New York: Routledge, 2019.

Caesar, Sid. *Caesar's Hours: My Life in Comedy, With Love and Laughter*. New York: PublicAffairs, 2003.

Cafiso, Jenny, Michael S. Goodstadt, Warren Garlington, and Margaret A. Sheppard. "Television Portrayal of Alcohol and Other Beverages." *Journal of Studies on Alcohol* 43, no. 11 (1982): 1232–43.

Caldwell, John T. *Televisuality: Style, Crisis, and Authority in American Television*. New Brunswick, NJ: Rutgers Univ. Press, 2020.

Cambria, Catie, Richard Drew, and Danielle Robinson. "*Mad Men*: Bad Behavior All Around." *The Atlantic*, August 23, 2010. https://www.theatlantic.com/entertainment/archive/2010/08/mad-men-bad-behavior-all-around/61889/.

Canfield, David. "Why *The Good Place* is NBC's Meta Successor to *Community*." *Entertainment Weekly*, October 20, 2017. https://ew.com/tv/2017/10/20/the-good-place-community-nbc/.

Carroll, Noël. *Humour: A Very Short Introduction.* Oxford: Oxford Univ. Press, 2014.

Castoriadis, Cornelius. *The Imaginary Institution of Society.* Trans. Kathleen Blamey. Cambridge, MA: The MIT Press, 1975.

Chaney, Jen. "Why Is Everyone Projectile Vomiting on TV?," *Vulture,* March 29, 2017. https://www.vulture.com/2017/03/projectile-vomit-why-is-everyone-on-tv-throwing -up.html.

———. "*Wild Wild Country* May Be the Craziest Series You Watch All Year." *Vulture,* March 16, 2018. https://www.vulture.com/2018/03/wild-wild-country-review.html.

Chang, Rachel. "Bell-issima!" *Cosmo Girl* 10, no. 3 (May 2008).

Cheever, Susan. *My Name Is Bill: Bill Wilson—His Life and the Creation of Alcoholics Anonymous.* New York: Washington Square Press, 2015.

Chidester, David. *Authentic Fakes: Religion and American Popular Culture.* Berkeley, CA: Univ. of California Press, 2005.

Clayton, Alex. "Why Comedy Is at Home on Television." In *Television Aesthetics and Style,* edited by Jason Jacobs and Steven Peacock, 79–92. New York: Bloomsbury, 2013.

Cochran, Tonya R. "Neptune (Non-)Consensual: The Risky Business of Television Fandom, Falling in Love, and Playing the Victim." In *Investigating "Veronica Mars": Essays on the Teen Detective Series,* edited by Rhonda Wilcox and Sue Turnbull, 167–88. Jefferson, NC: McFarland, 2011.

Cohen, Ted. *Jokes: Philosophical Thoughts on Joking Matters.* Chicago: Univ. of Chicago Press, 2001.

Crawley, Melissa. *The American Television Critic: A History.* Jefferson, NC: McFarland & Company, Inc, 2017.

Critchley, Simon. *On Humour.* London: Routledge, 2002.

Curry, Tyler. "There's a Reason Why Queer Folks Love Halloween So Much." *The Advocate,* October 30, 2019. https://www.advocate.com/exclusives/2019/10/30/theres-reason -why-queer-folks-love-halloween-so-much.

Curtin, Michael, and Jane Shattuc. *The American Television Industry.* London: Palgrave Macmillan, 2009.

Curtis, Wayne. "The Lost Art of Acting Drunk." *The Daily Beast,* September 24, 2018. https://www.thedailybeast.com/the-lost-art-of-acting-drunk.

Dant, Tim. *Television and the Moral Imaginary: Society Through the Small Screen.* London: Palgrave Macmillan, 2012.

Darowski, Joseph J., and Kate Darowski. *"Cheers": A Cultural History.* Lanham, MD: Rowman & Littlefield, 2019.

Dasgupta, Amitava. *The Science of Drinking: How Alcohol Affects Your Body and Mind.* Lanham, MD: Rowman & Littlefield, 2011.

Dawson, Lorne L. *Comprehending Cults: The Sociology of New Religious Movements.* Oxford: Oxford Univ. Press, 2006.

Denzin, Norman K. *The Alcoholic Society: Addiction & Recovery of the Self.* New York: Routledge, 2017.

Devlyn, Darren. "Bell's Appealing." *Melbourne Herald Sun,* November 30, 2005.

Diffrient, David Scott. *M*A*S*H*. Detroit: Wayne State Univ. Press, 2008.

Diffrient, David Scott, and Hye Seung Chung. "TV Hybridity: Genre Mixing and Narrative Complexity in *M*A*S*H*." *Quarterly Review of Film and Video* 29, no. 4 (2012): 285–302.

Dillon, Jane, and James T. Richardson. "The 'Cult' Concept: A Politics of Representation Analysis." *Syzygy: The Journal of Alternative Religion and Culture* 3, no. 3/4 (1994): 185–97.

Dodes, Lance, and Zachary Dodes. *The Sober Truth: Debunking the Bad Science Behind 12-Step Programs and the Rehab Industry*. Boston: Deacon Press, 2014.

Douglass, William. "Subversion of the American Television Family." In *Television and the American Family*, edited by Jennings Bryant and J. Alison Bryant, 229–46. Mahway, NJ: Lawrence Erlbaum Associates, 2001.

Dow, Bonnie J. *Prime-Time Feminism: Television, Media Culture, and the Women's Movement Since 1970*. Philadelphia: Univ. of Pennsylvania Press, 1996.

Duffy, Mike. "Intelligent Life on *Mars*: UPN Hopes More Viewers Will Clue In." *Detroit Free Press*, May 6, 2005.

Durkheim, Émile. *The Division of Labor in Society*. Trans. W. D. Halls. New York: Free Press, 2014.

Edwards, Emily. *Metaphysical Media: The Occult Experience in Popular Culture*. Carbondale, IL: Southern Illinois Univ. Press, 2005.

Edwards, Flor. "I Grew Up in a Cult. Here's What *Unbreakable Kimmy Schmidt* Gets Right." *Slate*, March 10, 2015. https://slate.com/culture/2015/03/unbreakable-kimmy-schmidt-cult-a-former-cult-member-on-what-the-show-gets-right.html.

Egner, Jeremy. "Michael Schur on *The Good Place*, Ted Danson and Kantian Ethics." *New York Times*, January 18, 2017. https://www.nytimes.com/2017/01/18/arts/television/michael-schur-on-the-good-place-ted-danson-and-kantian-ethics.html.

Ehrenreich, Barbara. *The Snarling Citizen*. New York: Farrar, Straus and Giroux, 2000.

Elkins, Evan. "Excessive Stand-Up, the Culture Wars, and '90s TV." In *Taboo Comedy: Television and Controversial Humour*, edited by Chiara Bucaria and Luca Barra, 139–54. London: Palgrave Macmillan, 2016.

Ellis, Maliya V., and Woojin Lim. "Asking Philosopher T. M. Scanlon 'What We Owe to Each Other.'" *Fifteen Minutes*, October 10, 2019. https://www.thecrimson.com/article/2019/10/10/scanlon-and-the-good-place/.

Everitt, David. *King of the Half Hour: Nat Hiken and the Golden Age of TV Comedy*. Syracuse, NY: Syracuse Univ. Press, 2001.

Fearn-Banks, Kathleen, and Anne Burford-Johnson. *Historical Dictionary of African American Television*. Lanham, MD: Rowman & Littlefield, 2014.

Flynn, Kathleen Anne. "Performing Sobriety: Story and Celebration in Alcoholics Anonymous." Ph.D. Dissertation. Northwestern Univ., 1994.

Foster, Claire Rudy. "What #MeToo Looks Like When You're in Recovery." *The Establishment*, April 10, 2018. https://theestablishment.co/what-metoo-looks-like-when-youre-in-recovery-64c0ade43411-2/index.html.

Foucault, Michel. *Abnormal: Lectures at the Collège de France, 1974–1975.* New York: Picador, 2003.

Galanter, Marc. *Cults: Faith, Healing, and Coercion.* Oxford: Oxford Univ. Press, 1999.

———. *What is Alcoholics Anonymous?* Oxford: Oxford Univ. Press, 2016.

Garlington, Warren K. "Drinking on Television; a Preliminary Study with Emphasis on Method." *Journal of Studies on Alcohol* 38, no. 11 (1977): 2199–2205.

Gately, Iain. *Drink: A Cultural History of Alcohol.* New York: Gotham Books, 2008.

Genzlinger, Neil. "Realism Splashing a Screen Near You." *New York Times,* March 8, 2014.

Gerbner, George, Larry Gross, Michael Morgan, and Nancy Signorielli. "Living with Television: The Dynamics of the Cultivation Process." In *Perspectives on Media Effects,* edited by Jennings Bryant and Dolf Zillmann, 17–40. Hillsdale, NJ: L. Erlbaum Associates, 1986.

Ghanoui, Saniya Lee. "Mediated Bodies: The Construction of a Wife, Mother, and the Female Body in Television Sitcoms." *Proceedings of the New York State Communication Association* 2012, no. 5 (2013). http://docs.rwu.edu/nyscaproceedings/vol2012/iss1/5.

Gimbel, Steven. *Isn't that Clever: A Philosophical Account of Humor and Comedy.* New York: Routledge, 2018.

Glaser, Gabrielle. *Her Best-Kept Secret: Why Women Drink—And How They Can Regain Control.* New York: Simon & Schuster, Inc, 2014.

Glasgow, Rupert D. V. *Madness, Masks, and Laughter: An Essay on Comedy.* Cranbury, NJ: Associated Univ. Presses, 1995.

Goodwin, Megan. "Unpacking the Bunker: Sex, Abuse, and Apocalypticism in *Unbreakable Kimmy Schmidt.*" *Cross Currents,* June 2018.

Goldberg, Lesley. "*Roseanne* Canceled at ABC Following Racist Tweet." *Hollywood Reporter,* May 28, 2018. https://www.hollywoodreporter.com/live-feed/roseanne-canceled-at-abc-racist-tweet-1115412.

Goldman, Marion S. "Controversy, Cultural Influence, and the Osho/Rajneesh Movement." In *Controversial New Religions,* edited by James R. Lewis and Jesper Aa. Petersen 176–94. Oxford: Oxford Univ. Press, 2014.

Grabowski, Michael. "Resignation and Positive Thinking in the Working-Class Family Sitcom." *Atlantic Journal of Communication* 22, no. 2 (2014): 124–37.

Gray, Jonathan. *Television Entertainment.* New York: Routledge, 2008.

Greene, Doyle. *Politics and the American Television Comedy: A Critical Survey from "I Love Lucy" Through "South Park."* Jefferson, NC: McFarland & Company, Inc, 2008.

Gregory, Chris. *Be Seeing You . . . Decoding The Prisoner.* Luton, Bedfordshire: Univ. of Luton Press, 1997.

Grow, Doug. "Drunks Who Once Got Laughs Get Convictions." *Minneapolis Star Tribune,* August 21, 1990.

Guida, Matthew. "10 Worst Things That Homer Simpson Has Done." *ScreenRant,* July 8, 2019. https://screenrant.com/worst-things-homer-simpson-done/.

Gunn, John, and Pamela J. Taylor. *Forensic Psychiatry: Clinical, Legal and Ethical Issues.* Boca Raton, FL: CRC Press, 2014.

Gwenllian-Jones, Sara, and Roberta Pearson. "Introduction." In *Cult Television*, edited Sara Gwenllian-Jones and Roberta Pearson, ix–xx. Minneapolis: Univ. of Minnesota Press, 2004.

Habermas, Jürgen. *Between Facts and Norms: Contributions to a Discourse Theory of Law and Democracy.* Trans. William Rehg. Cambridge, MA: MIT Press, 1996.

Hamamoto, Darrell. *Nervous Laughter: Television Situation Comedy and Liberal Democratic Ideology.* New York: Praeger Publishers, 1989.

Henry, Matthew A. *"The Simpsons," Satire, and American Culture.* New York: Palgrave Macmillan, 2012.

Henschke, Adam. "Frank Reynolds, Role Model." In *"It's Always Sunny" and Philosophy: The Gang Gets Analyzed*, edited by Roger Hunt and Robert Arp, 91–102. Chicago: Open Court, 2015.

Hills, Matt, and Henry Jenkins. "Intensities Interview with Henry Jenkins." *Intensities: The Journal of Cult Media* 2, 2001. http://intensities.org/Essays/Jenkins.pdf.

Hills, Matt. *Fan Cultures.* London: Routledge, 2002.

Hofstede, David. *5000 Episodes and No Commercials: The Ultimate Guide to TV Shows on DVD.* New York: Back Stage Books, 2006.

Honeyman, Sarah. *Consuming Agency in Fairy Tales, Childlore, and Folkliterature.* New York: Routledge, 2010.

Horton, Andrew. *Ernie Kovacs & Early TV Comedy.* Austin: Univ. of Texas Press, 2010.

Horvath, Cary W. "Measuring Television Addiction." *Journal of Broadcasting & Electronic Media* 48, no. 3 (2004): 378–98.

Hunter, James Davison. *Culture Wars: The Struggle to Define America.* New York: Basic Books, 1991.

Huston, Aletha C., Diana Zuckerman, Halford Fairchild, Brian L. Wilcox, Ed Donnerstein. *Big World, Small Screen: The Role of Television in American Society.* Lincoln, NE: Univ. of Nebraska Press, 1992.

Jackson, Lauren Michele. *White Negroes: When Cornrows Were in Vogue and Other Thoughts on Cultural Appropriation.* Boston: Beacon Press, 2019.

Jancovich, Mark. "Cult Fictions: Cult Movies, Subcultural Capital, and the Production of Cultural Distinctions." *Cultural Studies* 16, no. 2 (2002): 306–22.

Jenkins, Henry. *Textual Poachers: Television Fans & Participatory Culture.* New York: Routledge, 1992.

———. *Convergence Culture: Where Old and New Media Collide.* New York: NYU Press, 2006.

Jensen, George H. *Storytelling in Alcoholics Anonymous: A Rhetorical Analysis.* Carbondale, IL: Southern Illinois Univ. Press, 2000.

Jowett, Lorna, and Stacey Abbott. *TV Horror: Investigating the Darker Side of the Small Screen.* London: I.B. Tauris & Co., Ltd, 2013.

Joyrich, Lynne. "Epistemology of the Console." In *Queer TV: Theories, Histories, Politics*, edited by Glyn Davis and Gary Needham, 15–47. New York, NY: Routledge, 2009.

Karavitis, John V. "In a Mirror Is Our Image." In *"The Twilight Zone" and Philosophy: A Dangerous Dimension to Visit*, edited by Heather L. Rivera and Alexander E. Hooke, 55–66. Chicago: Open Court Publishing Company, 2018.

Kassell, Michael B. "*M*A*S*H*." In *The Guide to United States Popular Culture*, edited by Ray B. Browne and Pat Browne, 520–21. Madison: Univ. of Wisconsin Press, 2001.

Katz, Jack. *How Emotions Work*. Chicago: Univ. of Chicago Press, 1999.

Kawash, Samira. *Candy: A Century of Panic and Pleasure*. New York: Farrar, Straus and Giroux, 2013.

Kearny, Richard. *Strangers, Gods, and Monsters: Interpreting Otherness*. New York: Routledge, 2003.

Kelly, Richard Michael. *The Andy Griffith Show*. Winston-Salem, NC: John F. Blair, Publisher, 1981.

Kendall, Diana Elizabeth. *Framing Class: Media Representations of Wealth and Poverty in America*. Lanham, MD: Rowman & Littlefield, 2005.

Khapaeva, Dina. *The Celebration of Death in Contemporary Culture*. Ann Arbor, MI: Univ. of Michigan Press, 2017.

Kich, Martin. "*The Honeymooners*: American Dreaming Scaled Down to the Small Screen." In *The 25 Sitcoms that Changed Television: Turning Points in American Culture*, edited by Laura Westengard and Aaron Barlow, 15–27. Santa Barbara, CA: ABC-CLIO, 2018.

Kidder, Kristen. "The New Normal: Breaking the Boundaries of Vigilantism in *Veronica Mars*." In *Neptune Noir: Unauthorized Investigations into "Veronica Mars*," edited by Rob Thomas, 124–33. Dallas: BenBella Books, 2006.

Kimmel, Lisa. "Media Violence: Different Times Call for Different Measures." *University of Miami Law Review* 10, no. 3 (2014): 687–714.

King, Kris. "*Ugly Americans*, Season One." *Slate*, April 9, 2010. https://www.slantmagazine.com/tv/ugly-americans-season-one/.

Kirkpatrick, Graeme. *Computer Games and the Social Imaginary*. Cambridge: Polity Press, 2013.

Klaver, Elizabeth. *Performing Television: Contemporary Drama and the Media Culture*. Bowling Green, OH: Bowling Green State Univ. Popular Press, 2000.

Kohn, Erik. "*It's Always Sunny in Philadelphia* Delivered One of Its Wildest Episodes with Season 11's 'Being Frank.'" *IndieWire*, February 17, 2016. https://www.indiewire.com/2016/02/its-always-sunny-in-philadelphia-delivered-one-of-its-wildest-episodes-with-season-11s-being-frank-21995/.

Komarovsky, Mirra. *Blue-Collar Marriage*. New Haven, CT: Yale Univ. Press, 1964.

Kreps, Sarah. "Flying Under the Radar: A Study of Public Attitudes Towards Unmanned Aerial Vehicles." *Research and Politics* 1, no. 1 (2014): 1–7.

Kubey, Robert, and Mihaly Csikszentmihalyi. "Television Addiction is No Mere Metaphor." *Scientific American* 286, no. 2 (2002): 74–80.

Kutulas, Judy. "Liberated Women and New Sensitive Men: Reconstructing Gender in 1970s Workplace Comedies." In *The Sitcom Reader, Second Edition: America Reviewed, Still Skewed*, edited by Mary M. Dalton and Laura R. Linder, 121–32. Albany, NY: SUNY Press, 2016.

Kuzmarov, Jeremy. *The Myth of the Addicted Army: Vietnam and the Modern War on Drugs*. Amherst, MA: Univ. of Massachusetts Press, 2009.

Laberge, Yves. "Representations of Drinking and Temperance in Film." In *Alcohol and Temperance in Modern History: An International Encyclopedia*, Vol. 1, edited by Jack S. Blocker, Jr., David M. Fahey, and Ian R. Tyrrell, 234–40. Santa Barbara, CA: ABC-CLIO, Inc., 2003.

Lair, Meredith H. *Armed with Abundance: Consumerism and Soldiering in the Vietnam War*. Chapel Hill, NC: Univ. of North Carolina Press, 2011.

Lake, Dianne, and Deborah Herman. *Member of the Family: My Story of Charles Manson, Life Inside His Cult, and the Darkness That Ended the Sixties*. New York: William Morrow, 2017.

Lalich, Janja. *Bounded Choice: True Believers and Charismatic Cults*. Berkeley, CA: Univ. of California Press, 2004.

Langone, Michael D. "Cults: Questions & Answers." *Cultic Studies*, June 7, 2002. www .csj.org/studyindex/studycult/cultqa.htm.

Laycock, Joseph. "Where Do They Get These Ideas? Changing Ideas of Cults in the Mirror of Popular Culture." *Journal of the American Academy of Religion* 81, no. 1 (March 2013): 80–106.

Lederer, Susan E. *Frankenstein: Penetrating the Secrets of Nature*. New Brunswick, NJ: Rutgers Univ. Press, 2002.

Lee, Erika. *The Making of Asian America: A History*. New York: Simon & Schuster, 2015.

Lee, Janet. "Subversive Sitcoms: *Roseanne* as Inspiration for Feminist Resistance." *Women's Studies* 21, no. 1 (1992): 87–101.

Leigh, Barbara C. "A Thing So Fallen, and So Vile: Images of Drinking and Sexuality in Women." *Contemporary Drug Problems* 22, no. 3 (Fall 1995): 415–34.

Lennon, Sharron J., Zhiying Zheng, and Aziz Fatnassi. "Women's Revealing Halloween Costumes: Other-Objectification and Sexualization." *Fashion and Textiles* 3, no. 21 (2016): 1–19.

Leppert, Alice. *TV Family Values: Gender, Domestic Labor, and 1980s Sitcoms*. New Brunswick, NJ: Rutgers Univ. Press, 2019.

Lindsay, Kathryn. "5 Harrowing Real Life Kidnapping Stories Just Like Kimmy Schmidt's." *Refinery29*, May 19, 2017. https://www.refinery29.com/en-us/2017/05/155187/real-life -kimmy-schmidt-true-story-kidnapping-cults.

Lisanti, Thomas. *Hollywood Surf and Beach Movies: The First Wave, 1959–1969*. Jefferson, NC: McFarland & Company, Inc, 2005.

Lloyd, Robert. "Disjointed' on High Road." *Los Angeles Times*, August 24, 2017.

MacAndrew, Craig, and Robert Edgerton. *Drunken Comportment: A Social Explanation*. Clinton Corners, NY: Eliot Werner Publications Inc, 1969.

Mansfield, Nick. *Soldiers as Workers: Class, Employment, Conflict and the Nineteenth-Century Military.* Liverpool: Liverpool Univ. Press, 2016.

Marc, David. *Comic Visions: Television Comedy and American Culture.* Malden, MA: Blackwell Publishers, Inc, 1989.

Martin, Brett. *Difficult Men: Behind the Scenes of a Creative Revolution: From "The Sopranos" and "The Wire" to "Mad Men" and "Breaking Bad."* New York: Penguin Books, 2014.

Mast, Gerald. *The Comic Mind: Comedy and the Movies.* Second Edition. Chicago: Univ. of Chicago Press, 1979.

Matthews, Dylan. "How *The Good Place* Taught Moral Philosophy to Its Characters—and Its Creators." *Vox,* January 30, 2020. https://www.vox.com/future-perfect/2019/9/26/20874217/the-good-place-series-finale-season-4-moral-philosophy.

McBurney, Christine Tibbles. "Writing *One Day at a Time*: Reflections on a Life Inside the Tube." In *The 25 Sitcoms that Changed Television: Turning Points in American Culture,* edited by Laura Westengard and Aaron Barlow, 108–17. Santa Barbara, CA: ABC-CLIO, 2018.

McClellan, Michelle L. *Lady Lushes: Gender, Alcoholism, and Medicine in Modern America.* New Brunswick, NJ: Rutgers Univ. Press, 2017.

McGuiness, Kristen. "The 13th Step: People Who Prey on Newcomers." *The Fix,* April 15, 2011. https://www.thefix.com/content/13th-step.

McGowan, Todd. *Only a Joke Can Save Us: A Theory of Comedy.* Evanston, IL: Northwestern Univ. Press, 2017.

McKee, Gabriel. *The Gospel According to Science Fiction: From "The Twilight Zone" to "The Final Frontier."* Louisville: Westminster John Knox Press, 2007.

McLeland, Susan. "*Roseanne*, Reality, and Domestic Comedy." In *The Sitcom Reader: America Re-viewed, Still Skewed,* edited by Mary M. Dalton and Laura R. Linder, 165–76. Albany, NY: SUNY Press, 2016.

Means Coleman, Robin R. *Horror Noire: Blacks in American Horror Films from the 1890s to Present.* New York: Routledge, 2011.

Meehan, Eileen R. "'Holy Commodity Fetish, Batman!': The Political Economy of the Commercial Intertext." In *The Many Lives of the Batman,* edited by Roberta Pearson and William Uricchio, 47–65. New York: Routledge, 1991.

Meier, Kenneth J. *The Politics of Sin: Drugs, Alcohol and Public Policy.* London: Routledge, 2016.

Mendik, Xavier, and Graeme Harper. "Introduction." In *Unruly Pleasures: The Cult Film and its Critics,* edited by Xavier Mendik and Graeme Harper. Guildford, Surrey: FAB Press, 2000.

Meslow, Scott. "The History of Alcoholism on TV: From Comedy to Empathy." *The Atlantic,* March 20, 2012. http://www.theatlantic.com/entertainment/archive/2012/03/the-history-of-alcoholism-on-tv-from-comedy-to-empathy/254750/.

Metz, Walter. *Gilligan's Island.* Detroit: Wayne State Univ. Press, 2012.

Miles, Jr., John A. "Laughing at the Bible: Jonah as Parody." *The Jewish Quarterly Review* 65, no. 3 (January 1975): 168–81.

Miller, Joe. *US of AA: How the Twelve Steps Hijacked the Science of Alcoholism*. Chicago: Chicago Review Press Inc, 2019.

Minow, Newton N. "Television and the Public Interest." Address to the National Association of Broadcasters, Washington, D.C. 1961.

Mittell, Jason. *Television and American Culture*. New York: Oxford Univ. Press, 2010.

Moorti, Sujata. "Brown Girls Who Don't Need Saving: Social Media and the Role of 'Possessive Investment' in *The Mindy Project* and *The Good Wife*." In *Television for Women: New Directions*, edited by Rachel Moseley, Helen Wheatley, and Helen Wood, 90–109. New York: Routledge, 2017.

Morreale, Joanne. *The Donna Reed Show*. Detroit: Wayne State Univ. Press, 2012.

———. *The Dick Van Dyke Show*. Detroit: Wayne State Univ. Press, 2015.

Morreall, John. *Comic Relief: A Comprehensive Philosophy of Humor*. Chichester, West Sussex: Wiley-Blackwell, 2009.

Morton, Lisa. *The Halloween Encyclopedia*. Jefferson, NC: McFarland & Company, Inc, 2011.

Mosbaugh, Erin. "Infographic: How Much Does Don Draper Drink in One Day?" *First We Feast*, March 18, 2015. https://firstwefeast.com/eat/2015/03/don-draper-is-an-alcoholic-infographic#:~:text=According%20to%20Detox.net%2C%20the,164%20drinks%20in%20a%20season.

Mundey, Lisa M. "'Bilko's Bombers': Anti-Militarism in the Era of the 'New Look.'" In *American Militarism on the Small Screen*, edited by Anna Froula and Stacy Takacs, 17–29. London: Routledge, 2016.

Murphy, Chris. *The Violence Inside Us: A Brief History of an Ongoing American Tragedy*. New York: Random House, 2020.

Murray, Jim. "Only Way to Drink." *Los Angeles Times*, June 2, 1972.

Nachman, Gerald. *Seriously Funny: The Rebel Comedians of the 1950s and 1960s*. New York: Pantheon Books, 2003.

Neal, Lynn S. "'They're Freaks!' The Cult Stereotype in Fictional Television Shows, 1958–2008." *Nova Religio: The Journal of Alternative and Emergent Religions* 14, no. 3 (2011): 81–107.

Nelson, James B. *Thirst: God and the Alcoholic Experience*. Louisville: Westminster John Knox Press, 2004.

Nero, Dom. "Everything About *Barry* Is Strange." *Esquire*, May 7, 2018. https://www.esquire.com/entertainment/tv/a20090096/barry-hbo-bill-hader-review/.

Nichols, Bill. *Blurred Boundaries: Questions of Meaning in Contemporary Culture*. Bloomington, IN: Indiana Univ. Press, 1994.

Nichols-Pethick, Jonathan. *TV Cops: The Contemporary American Television Police Drama*. New York: Routledge, 2012.

Nilles, Billy. "A TV Wasteland: When Beloved Stars' Bad Behavior Ruins Their Classic Comedies Forever." *E Online*, June 1, 2018. https://www.eonline.com/news/940458/a-tv-wasteland-when-beloved-stars-bad-behavior-ruins-their-classic-comedies-forever.

Normand, Jacques, and Richard O. Lempert. *Under the Influence?: Drugs and the American Work Force.* Washington, DC: National Academies Press, 1994.

Nygaard, Taylor, and Jorie Lagerwey. *Horrible White People.* New York: NYU Press, 2020.

O'Brien, Daniel. *Robert Altman: Hollywood Survivor.* New York: The Continuum Publishing Company, 1995.

O'Keefe, Jack. "Some Relationships Can't Survive Trump's Administration on *One Mississippi.*" *Bustle,* September 8, 2017. https://www.bustle.com/p/remy-vickys-breakup-on-one-mississippi-shows-how-the-aftermath-of-the-2016-election-can-bring-rela tionship-problems-to-the-forefront-2301794.

Ouzounian, Richard. "John Larroquette: This is a Dark Ride." *Toronto Star,* April 1, 2011. https://www.thestar.com/entertainment/2011/04/01/john_larroquette_this_is_a_dark _ride.html.

Paddick, David A. "TV as Totem: Durkheim's Sociology and Postmodern Popular Culture." Dissertation. Lincoln Christian Seminary, 1995.

Pash, Melinda L. *In the Shadow of the Greatest Generation: The Americans Who Fought the Korean War.* New York: NYU Press, 2012.

Pearson, Robert. "Observations on Cult Television." In *The Cult TV Book,* edited by Stacey Abbott, 7–18. London: I.B. Tauris, 2010.

Perkins, Dennis. "Getting Inside Frank's Head Makes for a Funny, Tragic *It's Always Sunny.*" *AV Club,* February 20, 2016. https://tv.avclub.com/getting-inside-frank-s-head -makes-for-a-funny-tragic-i-1798186608.

———. "*The Good Place* Walks, Finally, Right into the Good Place." *AV Club,* January 23, 2020. https://tv.avclub.com/the-good-place-walks-finally-right-into-the-good-plac -1841179535.

Pickering-Iazzi, Robin. *The Mafia in Italian Lives and Literature: Life Sentences and Their Geographies.* Toronto: Univ. of Toronto Press, 2015.

Pinkney, Charles. *From Slaveships to Scholarships: The Plight of the African-American Athlete.* Bloomington, IN: AuthorHouse, 2017.

Pollner, Melvin, and Jill Stein. "Doubled Over in Laughter: Humor and the Construction of Selves in Alcoholics Anonymous." In *Institutional Selves: Troubled Identities in a Postmodern World* edited by Jaber F. Gubrium and James A. Holstein, 46–64. Oxford: Oxford Univ. Press, 2001.

Poole, W. Scott. *Monsters in America: Our Historical Obsession with the Hideous and Haunting.* Waco, TX: Baylor Univ. Press, 2011.

Pratt, David. "Television." In *The SAGE Encyclopedia of Alcohol: Social, Cultural, and Historical Perspectives,* edited by Scott Martin, 1240–43. Thousand Oaks, CA: SAGE Publications, 2015.

Press, Andrea L. "Women Watching Television: Issues of Class, Gender, and Mass Media Reception." In *Transmission: Toward a Post-Television Culture,* edited by Peter d'Agostino and David Tafler, 53–90. Thousand Oaks, CA: Sage Publications, Inc., 1995.

Press, Joy. *Stealing the Show: How Women Are Revolutionizing Television.* New York: Atria, 2018.

Pugh, Tison. *The Queer Fantasies of the American Family Sitcom*. New Brunswick, NJ: Rutgers Univ. Press, 2018.

Purdie, Susan. "Secular Definitions of 'Ritual': The *Rocky Horror* Phenomenon." In *Theatre and Holy Script*, edited by Shimon Levy, 171–90. Portland: Sussex Academic Press, 1999.

Rainer, Peter. "Strangers with Candy." *Christian Science Monitor* 98, no. 155 (July 7, 2006).

Rall, Ted. "Trash TV: Insightful and In Touch with America." *The Baltimore Sun*, April 9, 1996.

Rich, Frank. "A Funny Man's Sad Story." *New York Times*, October 24, 1982.

Ritzer, George. *Introduction to Sociology*. Thousand Oaks, CA: SAGE Publications, Inc, 2013.

Robson, Hillary. "Television and the Cult Audience: A Primer." *The Cult TV Book*, edited by Stacey Abbott, 209–20. London: I.B. Tauris, 2010.

Rogers, Nicholas. *Halloween: From Pagan Ritual to Party Night*. New York: Oxford Univ. Press, 2002.

Ron, James, Howard Lavine, and Shannon Golden. "No, Americans Don't Support Airstrikes That Kill Civilians, Even When They Target Terrorists." *Washington Post*, May 6, 2019. https://www.washingtonpost.com/politics/2019/05/06/no-americans-dont-support-airstrikes-that-kill-civilians-even-when-they-target-terrorists/.

Ross, Rick. "Watch Out for Tell-Tale Signs." *The Guardian*, May 27, 2009. https://www.theguardian.com/commentisfree/belief/2009/may/27/cults-definition-religion.

Rowe, Kathleen K. *The Unruly Woman: Gender and the Genres of Laughter*. Austin: Univ. of Texas Press, 1995.

Rubin, Steven. *"Twilight Zone" Encyclopedia*. Chicago: Chicago Review Press, 2018.

Ruddick, Susan M. *Young and Homeless in Hollywood: Mapping the Social Imaginary*. New York: Routledge, 1996.

Russell, Dale W., and Cristel A. Russell. "Embedded Alcohol Messages in Television Series: The Interactive Effect of Warnings and Audience Connectedness on Viewers' Alcohol Beliefs." *Journal of Studies on Alcohol and Drugs* 69, no. 3 (2008): 459–67.

Ryan, Patrick. "TV Comedies Get Real About Addiction, Recovery." *USA Today*, March 10. https://www.usatoday.com/story/life/tv/2016/03/10/addiction-depression-tv-mom-cbs-love-flaked-netflix/81508984/.

Saenz, Michael. "China Beach." In *Encyclopedia of Television*, edited by Horace Newcomb, 515. London: Routledge, 2013.

Sandvoss, Cornel. *Fans: The Mirror of Consumption*. Cambridge: Polity Press, 2005.

Santino, Jack. "Introduction: Festivals and Death and Life." In *Halloween and Other Festivals of Death and Life*, edited by Jack Santino, xi–xxvii. Knoxville, TN: Univ. of Tennessee Press, 1994.

Scepanski, Philip. "Addiction, Abjection, and Humor: Craig Ferguson's Confessional Stand-up." In *The Dark Side of Stand-Up Comedy*, edited by Patrice A. Oppliger and Eric Shouse, 89–107. London: Palgrave Macmillan, 2020.

Schroeder, Audra. "The Warped Tour: Tim and Eric Perfect the Anti-Joke." *The Austin Chronicle*, April 25, 2008. https://www.austinchronicle.com/screens/2008-04-25/616136/.

Schumach, Murray. "Judge Rejects Charges of 'Brainwashing' Against Hare Krishna Aides." *New York Times*, March 18, 1977.

Sconce, Jeffrey. "*Tim and Eric's Awesome Show, Great Job!*: Metacomedy." In *How to Watch Television*, edited by Ethan Thompson and Jason Mittell, 74–83. New York: NYU Press, 2013.

———. "*Star Trek*, Heaven's Gate, and Textual Transcendence." In *Cult Television*, edited by Gwenllian-Jones and Pearson, 199–222. Minneapolis: Univ. of Minnesota Press, 2004.

Sedita, Scott. *The Eight Characters of Comedy: Guide to Sitcom Acting and Writing*. Los Angeles: Atides Publishing, 2006.

Segal, Erich. *The Death of Comedy*. Cambridge, MA: Harvard Univ. Press, 2001.

Semon, Craig. "Halloween, Horror: Harmless Fun or a Step Too Far?" *Associated Press*, October 17, 2015. https://www.apnews.com/42f2a6be8aa2491c89a294156fa29002.

Sepinwall, Alan, and Matt Zoller Seitz. *TV (The Book): Two Experts Pick the Greatest American Shows of All Time*. New York: Grand Central Publishing, 2016.

Sheehan, Steven T. "To the Moon! Working-Class Masculinity in *The Honeymooners*." In *The Sitcom Reader: America Re-viewed, Still Skewed*, edited by Mary M. Dalton and Laura R, 43–54. Linder. Albany, NY: SUNY Press, 2016.

Shepherd, Glen R. "Alcoholism Can Be Cured." *The Washington Post*, February 4, 1952.

Sherwood, John Darrell. *Officers in Flight Suits: The Story of American Air Force Fighter Pilots*. New York: NYU Press, 1998.

Sidel, Ruth. "The Enemy Within: The Demonization of Poor Women." *Journal of Sociology and Social Welfare* 27, no. 1 (March 2000): 73–84.

Singer, Dorothy G. "Alcohol, Television, and Teenagers." *Pediatrics* 76, no. 4 (1985): 668–674.

Skal, David. *Death Makes a Holiday: A Cultural History of Halloween*. New York: Bloomsbury, 2002.

Skeggs, Beverley, Leslie Moran, Paul Tyrer, and Jon Binnie. "*Queer as Folk*: Producing the Real of Urban Space." *Urban Studies* 41, no. 9 (August 1, 2004): 1839–56.

Smith, Angela. *Hideous Progeny: Disability, Eugenics, and Classic Horror Cinema*. New York: Columbia Univ. Press, 2011.

Smith, Cecil. "Susskind Won't Gamble with Sponsors' Millions." *Los Angeles Times*, September 13, 1959.

———. "Drunk Act Lands Series for Brooks." *Los Angeles Times*, September 20, 1972.

Shanley, J. P. "TV: Fun with *Sergeants*: Mac Hyman's Novel Adapted on ABC." *New York Times*, March 18, 1955.

Snierson, Dan. "See Owen Wilson as a Cult leader in *Documentary Now*'s Parody of *Wild Wild Country*." *Entertainment Weekly*, December 21, 2018. https://ew.com/tv/2018/12/21/owen-wilson-cult-leader-documentary-now-wild-wild-country/.

Snow, Robert L. *Deadly Cults: The Crimes of True Believers*. Westport, CT: Praeger, 2003.

Spigel, Lynn. *Make Room for TV: Television and the Family Ideal in Postwar America*. Chicago: Univ. of Chicago Press, 1992.

———. "Seducing the Innocent: Childhood and Television in Postwar America." In *The Children's Culture Reader*, edited by Henry Jenkins, 110–35. New York: NYU Press, 1989.

Staiger, Janet. *Perverse Spectators: The Practices of Film Reception*. New York: NYU Press, 2000.

Stark, Rodney, and William Sims Bainbridge. "Of Churches, Sects, and Cults: Preliminary Concepts for a Theory of Religious Movements." *Journal for the Scientific Study of Religion* 18, no. 2 (1979): 117–31.

Steger, Manfred B. *The Rise of the Global Imaginary: Political Ideologies from the French Revolution to the Global War on Terror*. Oxford: Oxford Univ. Press, 2008.

Sterritt, David. *The Honeymooners*. Detroit: Wayne State Univ. Press, 2009.

Steuver, Hank. "How Herman Munster Can Be So Right about Racism and Still Be a Little Wrong." *Washington Post*, June 4, 2020. https://www.washingtonpost.com /entertainment/tv/how-herman-munster-can-be-so-right-about-racism-and-still-be-a -little-bit-wrong/2020/06/04/fc17fe6e-a6aa-11ea-b473-04905b1af82b_story.html.

Swinson, Brock. 2016. "Mel Brooks on Screenwriting." *Creative Screenwriting*, January 14, 2016. https://creativescreenwriting.com/mel-brooks-on-screenwriting/.

Taylor, Charles. *Modern Social Imaginaries*. Durham, NC: Duke Univ. Press, 2004.

Thompson, Robert J. *Adventures on Prime Time: The Television Programs of Stephen J. Cannell*. West Port, CT: Praeger, 1990.

———. *Television's Second Golden Age: From "Hill Street Blues" to "ER."* Syracuse, NY: Syracuse Univ. Press, 1996.

Tolman, Albert H. "Shakespeare Studies: Part IV. Drunkenness in Shakespeare." *Modern Language Notes* 34, no. 2 (February 1919): 82–88.

Trivigno, Franco V. "Plato on Laughter and Moral Harm." In *Laughter, Humor, and Comedy in Ancient Philosophy*, edited by Pierre Destrée and Franco V. Trivigno, 13–34. Oxford: Oxford Univ. Press, 2019.

Tropiano, Stephen. *The Prime Time Closet: A History of Gays and Lesbians on TV*. New York: Applause Theatre & Cinema Books, 2002.

Tueth, Michael V. "Breaking and Entering: Transgressive Comedy on Television." In *The Sitcom Reader: America Viewed and Skewed*, edited by Mary M. Dalton and Laura R. Linder, 25–34. Albany, NY: SUNY Press, 2005.

———. *Laughter in the Living Room: Television Comedy and the American Home Audience*. New York: Peter Lang, 2005.

Tulloch, John, and Manuel Alvarado. *"Doctor Who": The Unfolding Text*. London: Macmillan, 1983.

Van Riper, Bowdoin. *"Baa Baa Black Sheep* and the Last Stand of the WWII Drama." In *American Militarism on the Small Screen*, edited by Anna Froula and Stacy Takacs, 77–92. New York: Routledge, 2016.

Van Riper, A. Bowdoin. "Spy Versus Reality: *Get Smart*, Satire, and Absurdity." In *The 25 Sitcoms That Changed Television*, edited by Laura Westengard and Aaron Barlow, 54–67. Santa Barbara, CA: Praeger, 2018.

Virilio, Paul. *The Paul Virilio Reader*. New York: Columbia Univ. Press, 2004.

Voger, Mark. *Monster Mash: The Creepy, Kooky Monster Craze in America, 1957–1972*. Raleigh, NC: TwoMorrows Publishing, 2015.

von Hodenberg, Christina. *Television's Moment: Sitcom Audiences and the Sixties Cultural Revolution*. New York: Berghahn Books, 2015.

Waldron, Vince. *The Official "Dick Van Dyke Show" Book: The Definitive History and Ultimate Viewer's Guide to Television's Most Enduring Comedy*. New York: Applause, 2001.

Wallack, Lawrence, Warren Breed, and John Cruz. "Alcohol on Prime-Time Television." *Journal of Studies on Alcohol* 48, no. 1 (1987): 33–38.

Wallack, Lawrence, Joel W. Grube, Patricia A. Madden, and Warren Breed. "Portrayals of Alcohol on Prime-Time Television." *Journal of Studies on Alcohol* 51, no. 5 (1990): 428–37.

Watson, Mary Ann. *Defining Visions: Television and the American Experience in the 20th Century*. Malden, MA: Blackwell Publishing, 2008.

Weinstein, Steve. "*Night Court's* Prosecutor Confesses to a Serious Side." *Los Angeles Times*, October 25, 1988.

Westheider, James. *Fighting in Vietnam: The Experiences of the U.S. Soldier*. Mechanicsburg, PA: Stackpole Books, 2011.

Wheatley, Helen. *Gothic Television*. Manchester: Manchester Univ. Press, 2006.

White, Rosie. *Television Comedy and Femininity: Queering Gender*. London: I. B. Tauris, 2018.

White, William L. *Slaying the Dragon: The History of Addiction Treatment and Recovery in America*. Second Edition. Bloomington, IL: Chestnut Health Systems, 2014.

Wilcox, Danny M. *Alcoholic Thinking: Language, Culture, and Belief in Alcoholics Anonymous*. Westport, CT: Praeger, 1998.

Wilkinson, Alissa. "I, Too, Thought the World Was Coming to an End. Here's What *Kimmy Schmidt* Gets Right." *Washington Post*, March 17, 2015. https://www.washingtonpost.com/news/acts-of-faith/wp/2015/03/17/why-tina-fey-kimmy-schmidt-works/.

Williams, Melissa. "'Excuse the Mess, But We Live Here': Roseanne Barr's Stardom and the Politics of Class." In *Film and Television Stardom*, edited by Kylo-Patrick R. Hart, 180–204. Newcastle upon Tyne: Cambridge Scholars Publishing, 2008.

Wise, Jeff. "Michael Cohen on How 'Monster' Trump Will Undermine Biden." *New York*, December 3, 2020. https://nymag.com/intelligencer/2020/12/michael-cohen-on-how-monster-trump-will-undermine-biden.html.

Wittebols, James H. *Watching "M*A*S*H," Watching America: A Social History of the 1972–1983 Television Series*. Jefferson, NC: McFarland, 1998.

Young, Elizabeth. *Black Frankenstein: The Making of an American Metaphor*. New York: NYU Press, 2008.

Index

Figures are indicated by italicized page numbers.

David Scott Diffrient is Professor of Film and Media Studies in the Department of Communication Studies and former William E. Morgan Endowed Chair of Liberal Arts at Colorado State University. His articles and chapters have been published in several journals and edited collections about film and television topics. He is the coeditor of *Screwball Television: Critical Perspectives on "Gilmore Girls"* (Syracuse University Press, 2010) and the author or coauthor of four books: *M*A*S*H* (Wayne State University Press, 2008), *Omnibus Films: Theorizing Transauthorial Cinema* (Edinburgh University Press, 2014), *Movie Migrations: Transnational Genre Flows and South Korean Cinema* (Rutgers University Press, 2015), and *Movie Minorities: Transnational Rights Advocacy and South Korean Cinema* (Rutgers University Press, 2021).

CPSIA information can be obtained
at www.ICGtesting.com
Printed in the USA
LVHW072226201222
735676LV00020B/1647